Fiscal Underpinnings for Sustainable Development in China

Ehtisham Ahmad · Meili Niu
Kezhou Xiao

Editors

Fiscal Underpinnings for Sustainable Development in China

Rebalancing in Guangdong

 Springer

Editors
Ehtisham Ahmad
University of Bonn
Bonn
Germany

and

London School of Economics
London
UK

and

Pao Yu-Kong Professor
Zhejiang University
Hangzhou
China

Meili Niu
Center for Chinese Public Administration
    Research
Sun Yat-Sen University
Guangzhou, Guangdong
China

Kezhou Xiao
Department of Economics
London School of Economics
London
UK

ISBN 978-981-10-6285-8   ISBN 978-981-10-6286-5   (eBook)
https://doi.org/10.1007/978-981-10-6286-5

Library of Congress Control Number: 2017955263

Printed on acid-free paper

This Springer imprint is published by Springer Nature
The registered company is Springer Nature Singapore Pte Ltd.
The registered company address is: 152 Beach Road, #21-01/04 Gateway East, Singapore 189721, Singapore

Foreword I

The world is urbanizing at an extraordinary pace. In nowhere is this more important than in China where the process has been moving rapidly over the last few decades and will continue to do so. We already see the difficult consequences, in terms of congestion, pollution, and urban sprawl of some of the earlier decisions, explicit or implicit, around the growth of towns and cities. If the lock-in, in terms of long-lasting infrastructure, of still further difficulties is to be avoided, strong development and urban planning decisions have to be taken now. The prize, if this goes well, is attractive cities where people can move, breathe, and be productive. If it goes badly, standards of living in cities will be deeply compromised.

Many of China's problems, and this is true of many cities around the world, are in large measure associated with limitations in public finance. City and regional governments need the right tax and incentive instruments in an efficient and equitable way and one which can be delivered with administrative effectiveness and transparency. Thus, for example, an examination of the way changes can be levied on property and congestion, revenue streams from public facilities, the opportunities for finance from markets, and so on are all of the highest importance. It is the great strength of this book that it provides such an analysis.

At the same time as looking forward to the future of China's cities and their role in sustainable development, we must recognize how far China has come and China's growing leadership in the world around sustainable development, innovation, trade, finance, connectivity, and so on. President Xi Jinping's speech at Davos at the World Economic Forum in January 2017 was of great significance in articulating China's vision and leadership.

China has come so far so fast that many people are unaware of how much progress it has made, from investing in renewable energy to tackling air pollution. It still faces significant adjustment challenges, particularly around reducing coal consumption, but it is displaying the commitment and creativity needed to tackle this urgent and complex challenge. China has recognized not only the grave risks of unmanaged climate change, to which it is very vulnerable, but also the great attractions of an alternative path for growth which is cleaner, more efficient, innovative, and dynamic.

At home, its most recent 5-year development plan reflected profound changes to its economic strategy that incorporate sustainable development. On the global stage, Beijing's support was indispensable to the success of the Paris climate negotiations and it is moving quickly to implement its pledges under the resulting agreement. By acting decisively now both domestically and abroad, China will reap the early benefits of the low-carbon economy. China is well placed to catalyze action on five fronts.

First, China's cities, which is home to more than 750 m people, are already at the forefront of the government's climate priorities. It is acting fast to address the deadly smog that is making headlines: poor air quality is killing more than 1.6 m Chinese each year. It is designing better cities, investing in new public transport and improving energy efficiency. This new urban agenda could dramatically raise the quality of life while reducing air pollution and emissions.

Second, China is leaving the rest of the world behind on clean energy. It is home to five of the top six solar panel manufacturers and five of the top 10 wind turbine makers. In 2016, it invested $88bn in renewable energy, the highest in the world. It is building capacity at an astonishing speed, installing on average more than one new wind turbine every hour. There is now compelling evidence that China's coal consumption peaked in 2014. In the future, it should make sure that coal is not given priority over renewables on the grid. Over the long term, new coal plants simply do not make sense for it in terms of public health, the environment, or the economy.

Third, Beijing is set to implement the world's largest emissions trading system later this year. It will expand its seven pilot carbon trading systems to the national level. If the price levels are high enough, it will create strong incentives worldwide.

Fourth, China is exploring new, innovative financial vehicles to finance the low-carbon transition. Its emerging green bonds market could deliver about $230bn for renewable energy investment in the next 5 years. Those parts of the financial sector that are not explicitly green are also making changes. The People's Bank of China has proposed mandatory disclosure of climate-related financial risks as part of reforms to make its banking system sustainable.

Fifth, China's foreign investment could play a big role in tipping the balance toward a greener global economy. In 2016, it spent a record $32bn on renewable projects abroad, made up of 11 new foreign investment deals worth more than $1bn each. It is also rethinking its approach to international coal finance.

What China does at home will continue to be of vital importance to the world, both as a very large country and as a leader. China's future is critical to the world's future. China's future will in large measure be shaped by its cities. And the organization of urban and regional finance is crucial to the future of its cities. That is why this book is so important.

Prof. Lord Nicholas Stern
IG Patel Chair
London School of Economics
London, UK

Foreword II

The School of Government, Sun Yat-Sen University and the Asia Research Center of the London School of Economics held a conference in Guangzhou on January 9–10, 2015, to examine the Sustainable Development Agenda in China—with special reference to the province of Guangdong. The generation of information and appropriate incentive structures require the joint consideration of taxes and social policies at different levels of government together with more appropriate institutional arrangements.

We invited staff of the International Agencies to participate—largely with a view to providing a context for the Chinese reforms and acting as Chairs and Discussants. However, the volume focuses only on presentations that directly address the Chinese or Guangdong context.

We also invited senior academics—including Prof. Giorgio Brosio (Emeritus Professor, University of Turin and former President of the Italian Public Economics Society–SIEP) and Prof. Massimo Bordignon (Catholic University, Milan, then President of SIEP, and now a member of the EC Fiscal Council). Both have collaborated with co-organizer, Prof. Ahmad, in examining similar issues in Europe, and Prof. Brosio coedited with Prof. Ahmad the Handbook of Multilevel Finance that is of clear relevance to the issues and problems in emerging market economies, including China.

Dr. Ying Qian (Director, Asian Development Bank) explained some of the interlinkages and ADB's support to the Government of China in area related to expenditure and revenue assignments, transfer design, and management of subnational liabilities as part of the new growth strategy. The rebalancing toward new green urban centers is designed to achieve a more ecologically sustainable growth path, together with redistribution toward lagging regions. Dr. Joy Kim (UNEP) explained some work being done by the UN agencies to examine the general equilibrium consequences of "green growth" in a number of countries, suggesting that this might be a useful path to follow in developing options for the Chinese context.

We are grateful to Dr. Sanjeev Gupta, Deputy Director of the IMF's Fiscal Affairs Department for his commentary and stressing the need to place macroeconomic decisions in a medium-term framework.

Given the buildup of local debt and liabilities highlighted by the China National Audit Office, and the likelihood of an increase in repayment pressures in the next couple of years, the framework for the measurement and management of liabilities takes on an increasing importance. Dr. Lili Liu (Lead Economist, World Bank) presented some international examples of measurement of subnational debt. Mrs. Ter-Minassian (former Director of the IMF's Fiscal Affairs Department) presented alternative approaches used around the world to manage subnational liabilities. Drawing on the literature, she drew some lessons for China: (1) administrative controls do not work well, and it is also unrealistic to prohibit borrowing or rely only on market discipline; and (2) borrowing should be allowed subject to tight fiscal rules with limits related to debt service capacity, existence of own-source revenues, and comprehensive accounting standards including PPPs and SOEs.

Professor Bordignon (Milan, drawing on the volume on the Crisis in Europe, edited by Ahmad, Bordignon, and Brosio) focused on the problems with fiscal rules in Europe that led to a sense of false security among national and EC policymakers. Indeed, he argued that Europe represents examples of how **not** to establish fiscal rules. For China, he argued for tight monitoring, based on standardized flows of information on not only current expenditures but also investments, including PPPs and SOEs. He urged caution concerning new financial and hedging instruments. Moreover, hard budget constraints are needed and this requires own-source revenues at appropriate levels of government. Three subnational levels in China will be difficult enough to manage, and attempts to rationalize levels of government in the EU have been particularly difficult to achieve (recent papers by Profs. Ahmad and Brosio).

The volume contains a paper written for the G24 Group of Countries and the Global Green Growth Institute for the Sustainable Development Summit held in Addis (Ahmad, Bhattacharya, Vinella, and Xiao) earlier in the year, which draws extensively on the Chinese context of financing investment, including PPPs.

The volume is divided into two parts—the first pertaining to issues relating to China. Although he was unable to attend the conference, Prof. Liu Shangxi, President of the Chinese Academy of Fiscal Sciences, Ministry of Finance, presented a very relevant paper summarizing a general approach to risk management in the Chinese context that is extremely relevant to our topic of rebalancing inclusive and sustainable growth. As discussed more extensively in the Introduction, the second part pertains particularly to Guangdong.

In sum, the volume presents a timely discussion of the key policy debates regarding policy reforms in China, drawing on the specific insights from Guangdong Province. This should be relevant for other Chinese provinces and regions, as well as for Emerging Market countries in general especially in the context of the Belt and Road Initiative. We hope to develop some of these research themes in the future, both with Chinese scholars as well as our counterparts in leading universities and International Agencies.

Prof. Jun Ma
Vice President
Sun Yat-Sen University
Guangzhou, China

Contents

Introduction

The Context

Guangdong has been at the forefront of economic reforms in China since the start of the Responsibility System in the late 1970s. Its successes and challenges reflect those in China. The need for rebalancing toward a more inclusive and sustainable path is also critical in Guangdong as it is in China. Strengthening the fiscal underpinnings and the next stages of tax reforms are critical drivers for generating the requisite structural changes. This volume focuses on issues related to the rebalancing strategy, new clean cities as "hubs", liability management, and involving the private sector, including through PPPs, in Chinese context, with specific examples from Guangdong. Within province spatial and interpersonal inequalities, congestion and pollution in the Pearl River Delta (Guangzhou–Shenzhen is already the largest conurbation in the world, exceeding Tokyo) are a microcosm of the patters seen in China as a whole. We see the Guangdong story as providing very useful options that might be useful for policymakers in Beijing and in other parts of China.

This volume is divided into two parts: (1) Sustainable Growth—Chinese context; and (2) Perspectives from Guangdong.

Sustainable Growth: The Chinese Context

The issue of fiscal underpinnings of sustainable development has been on the agenda for the UN Commission on Sustainable Development. The applicability of the general framework and global issues to the Chinese context, however, needs to be linked to the special institutional and incentive considerations in China. This is highlighted in the chapter by Ahmad. It illustrates the theme that structural reforms lead to tax reforms lead to structural reforms (Ahmad et al. 2013). Second, contrary to the general perception in Western countries about the centralized nature of the Chinese state, the highly decentralized structure of spending together with relatively incomplete information generates risks associated with local government behavior that cannot be addressed purely by diktat.

Modern instruments for taxation and financial management are essential, even in a governance structure based on administrative progression and promotions via governing Party's internal reviews. Both the generation of information and appropriate incentive structures require the joint consideration of taxes and social policies at different levels of government together with compatible institutional arrangements.

The historic fiscal reform in 1993/4 had played an important role in consolidating the reforms initiated in Guangdong for China by Deng Xiaoping in the late 1970s. As emphasized by the 5th Plenum in November 2015, further tax reforms are needed in order to stimulate and support further structural change. To further future fiscal and tax reforms, the central theme of this volume is to understand and analyze the information generating process, the incentive structure in multilevel fiscal relationships, and governance mechanisms in the current Chinese context.

While the completion of value-added tax (VAT) reforms in 2015 was needed in order to ensure the competitive position of the Chinese economy and reducing the cost of doing business, a provincial replacement of the business tax, e.g., by a "piggy-back" on the personal income tax, is needed to ensure accountability (even in a Chinese-administrative model) and sustainable access to credit.

The full VAT reforms also generate full information that would help prevent rent-seeking and tax avoidance for the corporate and personal income taxes. The expansion of the personal income tax base would clearly be important to address the issue of growing interpersonal inequalities. Spatial issues would be addressed through a full implementation of the equalization framework that is already in place in China, together with an active public investment strategy designed to provide the basis for "sustainable" green hubs in the interior consistent with the commitments made by China to reduce emissions and pollution. The expansion (beyond wage incomes) of the personal income tax to capture the fastest growing tax base would also provide more revenues to the provinces and permit a rationalization of the social security system—with a budget-financed basic pension, and a contributory system for firms and workers with lower rates and uniform criteria across the country. This would facilitate the labor mobility that is needed for the rebalancing in China.

Ahmad also argues the case for a Marshallian-type property tax at the third tier of government, linked to the delivery of public services. This would avoid the difficulties that have been observed in the US-style property tax experiments in Shanghai based on ownership and valuation—both problematic in the Chinese context. A simple property tax based on occupancy and spending needs, as is now also implemented in the United Kingdom, is also important in the effective provision of public services and access to credit.

Subnational own-source taxes are also an essential ingredient to fully implement the recent changes in the budget law that permit the issuance of local government bonds. Additional fiscal reforms include the full implementation of

GFSM2001/2014 framework at all levels of government and being able to follow the cash. Together, these are important in a better calibration of "risk" and holding local officials accountable—and in line with President Xi's emphasis on "honest and clean governance."

Land sales, which generate revenue under the direct control of local governments, have been one of the most important financing channels for subnational governments. Wang, Wu, and Ye's paper on "Land Use Reforms: Towards Sustainable development in China" maps the evolution and impact of land-usage system on resource allocation and local finance. They argue that the land-use system has functioned as a relative stable tenure system for household and enterprises, while becoming the main source of revenue for local finances. However, there is not much land left to sell in the congested metropolitan cities along the Eastern seaboard. In addition, the system generates predatory and corrupt behaviors. The limited land-based assets heighten the risks associated with the liabilities generated at the local level.

The issues of risk management in the Chinese context are addressed in a comprehensive manner in the chapter by Liu Shangxi and Li Chengwei: "Evaluation of Public Service Based on Public Risk". After providing an analytical framework on fiscal and public risks, Liu and Li provide an evaluation of Chinese public services through the lens of public risk management. A balance between public revenue generation and public good provision is needed in order to ensure minimization of public risks.

The gap between revenue and spending responsibilities for local governments generated distorted behaviors and incentives for subnational governments. Local governments were barred from borrowing directly from financial markets, but until recently, used local government financing vehicles (UDICs) and other state-own companies that were permitted to borrow. This was a form of "golden rule", since the expectation was that the companies would borrow for investment purposes. However, since the local governments controlled the companies, there was incomplete information about the sources and uses of the funds; it was not clear that the funds were being used primarily for productive investments. With the budgetary pressures telescoping down to lower levels of government, as spending continues to be decentralized, and the major revenue sources largely centralized, effectively unconstrained access to credit was too much of a temptation for the local governments. The budget law was changed in 2015 to permit local governments to issue bonds. While this is a sensible policy instrument for the longer term, effective own-source revenues are needed in order to underpin the credibility of the measure.

Ahmad and Xiaorong Zhang in their paper "Towards Monitoring and Managing Subnational liabilities in China: Lessons from the Balance Sheet for County K" connect the monitoring of local liabilities to institutional and governance aspects of fiscal reform. Even in a relatively advanced county in one of the country's more advanced provinces, the balance sheets are incomplete and do not pick up liabilities of SOES, utilities, and arrears. With valuable information from policy experimentation in County K conducted by People's Bank of China (PoB), the paper highlights the challenges and difficulties of the ongoing accounting reform, and the shift from cash to an accrual-based system and its implication for County K. They argue for a speedy and comprehensive application at the subnational level of the IMF's GFSM2001/14 standard adopted by China over 15 years ago at the central level.

A full and timely recording and reporting of liabilities in the balance sheets is needed for transparency and tightened responsibility as increasingly required by the Central Government, especially in the drive to ensure accountable and honest local administrations. Note that detailed performance indicators applied to local officials are meaningless if the officials are able to finance the "targeted spending" through increasing "hidden" liabilities that are borne several years after the event probably by the Central Government.

Farber and Wang provide a comparison between China and Germany. Despite the many differences in levels of development and income, there are useful parallels between the two major countries, which could be examined to the benefit of both. In Germany, as in China, there are overlapping spending competences between levels of government. German Länder, like Chinese provinces, lack own-source revenues —or the ability to raise or lower tax rates on specified tax bases. As in China, pre-1993, the German Bund (Center) lacks tax administration powers. And incomplete information on subnational liabilities make it problematic to impose fiscal rules. Most of these design failures were imposed on Germany after the Second World War and are seen as a problem—however, it has been extremely hard to address—despite a coalition Government of both major parties during 2004–2007 that tried to fix them. In order to disguise the failed attempt to fix the underlying problems, the then Government adopted a "debt break" that will prevent the Länder from borrowing from 2019. Färber and Wang's conclusion is that the liabilities will be telescoped down to the municipal level and to enterprises owned by them, and the fiscal rule will likely fail, with potentially disastrous impacts on public investment (see also Milbradt 2016—former Prime Minister of Saxony and Vice Chair of the German Fiscal Council—and had prohibited his state from operating PPPs, as there was no effective manner to manage them). There is a direct parallel to the zero-borrowing requirement imposed on local governments in China in 1994. Borrowing gets telescoped to the lowest levels of government, or agencies that are not visible (as pointed out by Ahmad and Xiaorong Zhang).

The Chinese government, much like the SDG agenda for sustainable growth, puts great store in using private financing to augment public funds to finance public investments. This has the objective to utilize private sector management expertise, that may be better than that available to the public sector. This also permits, in principle, risk-sharing to the benefit of both the private sector and the state. And budget constraints, especially at the local level, are eased. However, local governments are typically interested in PPPs largely to circumvent resource constraints and the tightening of access to credit. Ahmad, Bhattacharya, Vinella, and Xiao: "Involving the Private Sector and PPP in Financing Public Investments: Opportunities and Challenges" address the importance of accurate information and contractual design for PPP projects in ensuring the success of the implementation throughout all stages of the contract. A review of case studies on sectoral and country level, initially carried out for the G24 as background to the SDG summit in Addis in July 2015, shows that Information asymmetry, commitment problems, and enforcement problems could all result in deviation of PPP contracts from intended policy objectives. Nonetheless, properly designed and managed, PPPs carry a potential to significantly enhance financing and private sector risk-sharing for public investment. However, a precondition is that the PPPs should be recorded in the balance sheets of the appropriate level of government, with requisite provisioning.

Rebalancing in Guangdong

Guangdong Province provides a microcosm of the patterns seen at the national level in China. Xiao's paper on "Managing Subnational Liability for Sustainable Development: Using Guangdong Province as an Example" shows that there is increasing concentration of income in Guangdong, as in China. Moreover, there is an increasing and unevenly distributed liability burden telescoped to the local levels. Financial strains at the township level result in debt accumulations, with implications for social stability. Digging deeper down the layers of government, the heterogeneous fiscal inequality and liability is worrisome across municipalities in Guangdong. The unevenness in liability burden and repayment ability require a careful microanalysis of the heterogeneous impact of any fiscal reform.

This will also require a regulatory and own-source revenue framework for township economic management and stronger ability to meet local investments while managing local debts in sustainable manner.

Options for rebalancing within Guangdong are provided in Luo and Zhu's contribution on "Hub-periphery development pattern and inclusive growth: case study of Guangdong province". The paper examines the patterns of migration and its implication for the success of a "double transfer" program to support Guangdong's growth and development in an inclusive and sustainable manner.

Guangzhou's BRT system has been taken as a prototype for similar arrangements to reduce reliance on automobile transport and reduce congestion and pollution in many large metropolitan areas. Yuan, from the Guangzhou local government, provides a vivid example of citizen and beneficiary involvement in auditing the "supposedly successful" infrastructural Guangzhou BRT project, "Looking at Local Fiscal Sustainability through BRT Auditing Evaluation". Congestion around BRT terminuses leads to long waiting times, and the architecture of the BRT system is seen to add to bottlenecks. Dedicated bus lanes are possibly much cheaper, and the overall preference is for light rail or underground systems. This illustrative experience shows how the general public could act in a supervisory role to correct issues of information asymmetry.

This view is complemented by a project-level perspective by Niu, who analyzes PPP projects *Datianshan* Project focused on Guangzhou's waste management from the catering industry. This very useful example illustrates the problems associated with pricing policies and incentives, as well as the potential buildup of liabilities associated with such projects. The contractor was guaranteed a certain/price/quantity of operations, and this led to poor effort. Poor contract management, inconsistent public commitment, and supervision led to considerable environmental risks as the plants were not effectively managed.

In short, the contributors to this volume approached the central theme of local government financing from different angles, stressing different aspects of information generation, incentive structure, and governance mechanisms in varying degrees. The following section builds on these contributions to tease out policy implications for current policy reforms and directions for further research.

Policy Implications and Future Research

The rebalancing toward new green urban centers is part of China's strategy to achieve a more ecologically sustainable growth path, together with redistribution towards lagging regions. This is relevant for discouraging polluting activities and congestion along the coastal metropolitan areas, and also to finance the local infrastructure and services needed for new hubs within Guangdong, and China in general.

Many Western models of governance are based on the implicit assumption of interjurisdictional competition using the electoral process a disciplinary mechanism. However, difficulties arise without accurate and standardized information, or asymmetric information that permits "hiding liabilities", to pass the buck to the central government or future administrations, if not generations. This has been seen recently during the crisis in Europe (Ahmad, Bordignon and Brosio, 2016). The need for such information is even greater when public officials are mostly appointed as in the Chinese case. The evaluation of fiscal transmission mechanism in the Chinese context should be empirically evaluated and monitored. Further studies should look into magnification and amplification mechanisms for the transmission of fiscal risks and how to monitor and evaluate different counterbalancing policies and reforms.

As the VAT has replaced the local business tax, there is a need for new tax handles for provinces. There is a significant role for an appropriately designed personal income tax (PIT) to tap the most rapidly growing base of revenues in China, and also address growing interpersonal and spatial inequalities. While the PIT should continue to be administered by SAT, along with the VAT, there is scope for designating a certain number of percentage points for the provinces to set their "rates" within an overall limit for the tax. This is critical to anchor responsible access to credit, and also to generate local information on nonwage income needed to expand the base. The PIT would also be an instrument to keep local officials honest, as part of a feedback mechanism for accountability.

A local "community charge" or simple property tax based on occupancy and size of property and linked to service delivery could be a useful mechanism for "own-revenues" at the municipal level. A US-style property tax would be difficult to implement in China. This is because of "fuzzy property rights" and difficulty in establishing valuations given imperfect market information. This is a major area for further research.

The Chinese governance model can be strengthened through an increasing participation by citizens in the choice and design of investment options. This is seen in the case of the Guangzhou BRT.

There is extensive work being done to move towards accrual accounting, in line with the IMF's Government Financial Statistics (GFSM 2014) standards, as well as on the relevance of the US GASB and IPSAS standards in the Chinese context. However, these standards are not yet applied fully in China. While there is a need for uniformity of standards and treatment of assets and liabilities, a basic problem is that financing vehicles for state-owned enterprises are not on the balance sheets of local governments. Local governments often establish enterprises to shift assets or liabilities. New accounting and reporting standards have been finalized, including also the information system requirements for greater transparency, but these will take time to implement. In the meantime, it should be possible to use financing information as a proxy for the determination of the magnitude of liabilities in different localities. This is also identified as an area for further research.

Given the buildup of local debt and liabilities, highlighted by the China National Audit Office, and the likelihood of an increase in repayment pressures in the next couple of years, the framework for the measurement and management of liabilities takes on an increasing importance.

The issue of developing local bond markets for deepening the financial system, as permitted by the new budget law, is an important element in China's capital market development and the efficient availability of finance for investment. However, the full operation of this feature will depend on the linkages of local debt with own-source revenues to assure markets that these liabilities will be repaid. It is also an important element for the central government in establishing local hard budget constraints and ensuring that the liabilities do not end up on the doorstep of the Ministry of Finance.

The liabilities generated by PPPs should be recorded in local balance sheets with appropriate provisioning in local budgets—in order to avoid "kicking the debt can down the road." The use of PPPs should be carefully monitored and evaluated to avoid gameplay between the private and public sectors.

Focusing on appropriate levels of "responsible" government turn on which levels should have the power to impose, say a piggy-backed tax such as the PIT, or a community charge/property tax. It is hard enough to expand beyond three. However, achieving this will not be easy—although perhaps it is easier in China than in Europe. For instance, the complex reforms carried out in China in 1993/1994 that effectively created a central tax administration by a judicious use of taxes and transfer to offset gainers and losers could usefully be a model for the needed reforms in Germany.

Finally, the issue of sustainable investment for hubs, both domestic and in neighboring countries, could usefully be examined in the context of the Belt and Road Initiative. This has the potential to open up the Western regions and also provide better and safer linkages with trading partners, potentially increasing the production possibility frontiers and growth potential in all associated countries. However, some of the preconditions, as outlined in this volume, would need to be developed in further policy-related research.

References

Ahmad, E., James R., Stern, N. (2013). Structural change leads to tax reforms leads to structural change. *China Development Forum March 2013*.

Ahmad, E., Bordignon, M., & Brosio, G. (Eds.). (2016). *MultiLevel finance and the euro crisis*, Edward Elgar.

Milbradt, G. (2016). History of the constitutional debt limits in Germany and the new debt break: Experiences and critique. In E. Ahmad, M. Bordignon, & G. Brosio (Eds.), *op cit.*

Part I
Managing Risks: Chinese Perspectives Within an International Norm

Chapter 1
Rebalancing, Taxation and Governance: Fiscal Policies for Sustainable Growth

Ehtisham Ahmad

Abstract The Fiscal Responsibility System (FRS) relied on incentives to unleash an investment and growth potential that has transformed China since the early 1980s. However, the structural changes led to a fiscal crisis by the early 1990s, and the 1993/4 fiscal reforms were intended to create modern instruments and institutions for national taxation and redistribution. These were needed to consolidate the FRS. We argue that both additional tax reforms particularly at the local level, as well as strengthened oversight on the sources and uses of funds at all levels, are needed with the administrative progression model used in China, to ensure accountable governance, and sustainable and inclusive growth in the future

1.1 Introduction

The primary focus of public policy in China in recent decades has been on sustainable growth to ensure full employment. The reforms underpinning the Responsibility System initiated by Deng Xiao Ping in the late 1970s, led to increasing reliance on the private initiative in coastal provinces, like Guangdong. There was also an increasing devolution of decision-making power on spending and investment decisions to local officials. The Responsibility system led to a reduction

This paper is based on a conference at Sun Yat-Sen University (SYSU) in 2014 and seminars presented by the author during 2015 at Zhejiang University, as well as SYSU. Helpful comments from Xubei Luo, Meili Niu, Nick Stern, Kezhou Xiao and Zhikai Wang and seminar participants are gratefully acknowledged. The usual disclaimer applies.

E. Ahmad (✉)
Development Research Center, University of Bonn, Bonn, Germany
e-mail: seuahmad@gmail.com; s.e.ahmad@lse.ac.uk

E. Ahmad
London School of Economics, London, England

E. Ahmad
Pao Yu-Kong Professor, Zhejiang University, Hangzhou, China

© Springer Nature Singapore Pte Ltd. 2018
E. Ahmad et al. (eds.), *Fiscal Underpinnings for Sustainable Development in China*,
https://doi.org/10.1007/978-981-10-6286-5_1

in tax rates on enterprises to leave more potentially investable resources in the hands of firms. However, this led to a reduction in the overall revenues generated, generating pressures at the local level that were transmitted up to the center.

Prior to 1993/4, a critical constraint was that the fiscal institutions had been largely centered around local governments, including for raising revenues and actual spending, even though policy was largely determined by the center. The central government did not have a tax administration capable of managing modern taxes and relied on locally administered taxes with upward revenue-sharing. Such an institutional arrangement was common in the middle ages in China and Central and South Asia. The upward-sharing arrangement worked with officials appointed by and loyal to the Center with more or less success over the centuries. However, with the responsibility reforms, the shrinking total resource pie meant that there was insufficient financing for local spending, and reduced incentives to share upwards with the central government.

A major tax-cum-transfer was needed by the early 1990s, in order to (i) reverse the decline in the general government tax/GDP ratio, (ii) create modern tax instruments and administration, and (iii) lay the foundations for rapid growth (see Ahmad 2008). The tax-transfer nexus was particularly important to garner the support from the provinces for the reform that entailed ceding tax administration authority to the center (for the first time since the middle ages). This permitted the operation of economy-wide taxes, like the VAT, while at the same time avoiding losses for individual local governments as a result of the reforms.

The origin-based (downward) revenue-sharing mechanism implemented from 1994, ensured buy-in from the well-off provinces that stood to gain from additional revenues generated. An equalization system preserved the interests of the poorer provinces with more limited tax bases and higher costs of provision of public services. The most innovative measure, given the limited domestic connectivity in China at that time, was a "revenue-returned" transfer that greatly helped in preserving and encouraging the growth of the coastal "hubs" for rapid export-led growth. The fiscal measures, very strongly supported the overall strategy with great success—and largely maintained full employment, facilitating major rural-to-urban and interior to coastal migrations, with one of the largest reductions in poverty in the world within a decade.

The consequences of the success of the strategy have led to new challenges, including considerable imbalances between coastal and interior provinces and the appearance of significant interpersonal inequalities. Further, the growth of mega-cities along the coast has led to increasing congestion and pollution, putting living standards under stress.

In China, from antiquity, several levels of administration were needed in order to act as cross-checks on information flows and on governance. Further the administrative progression governance structure precludes Salmon-type yardstick competition (formalized by Besley and Case (1995) and many political economy models—see Lockwood (2015). While there have been attempts to impute political cycles to the spending patterns in China, these are based on the very imperfect data that cannot distinguish between local own-spending and mandated spending directed by the central government (see Pi-Han Tsai 2016). We therefore argue in this paper that the models and standards used to evaluate intergovernmental fiscal relations in market economies have to be adapted to the Chinese context. However, some of the international standards that are used to monitor spending and liabilities in the are not only relevant in China, but may need to be strengthened. In order to prevent misappropriation of resources by local officials, much tighter information is needed on the sources and flows of funds and buildup of liabilities than might be required in Western-style yardstick competition models.

Section 1.2 provides the background to the evolution of China's governance framework and focuses on the resulting economic performance to date. With one of the most decentralized spending systems in the world, given the size and complexity of China, the system of appointed officials with overlapping responsibilities worked well over the centuries, with upward revenue sharing, provided the officials remained honest. However, the grim five decades or so preceding the establishment of the Peoples' Republic also show that the system can lead to conflict and turmoil if not managed effectively. Some critical elements of this model includes: (1) rigorous selection process of the officials; and (2) arms' length evaluation criteria, with full information or independent verifiable feed-back mechanisms, to prevent extortion and unfair treatment of the masses, as well as rent-seeking behavior by the local officials. The model is evolving, as the Chinese economy has undergone a period of extraordinary structural change, especially since the 1980s, relying increasingly on local incentives and initiatives with the Responsibility System. The current emphasis to ensure that increasing public resources are not misappropriated by local officials is critical in ensuring that the administrative progression governance structure continues to function efficiently. The key elements of this are taxes to affect incentives, and full information on the sources and uses of public funds.

As pointed out in Ahmad et al. (2013), tax reforms were needed to consolidate the growth and rapid development that came about as a result of the Responsibility System, that additional tax reforms are needed for the next stages of the structural reforms. Indeed, in this paper we argue that tax reforms are necessary to provide the right incentives, but not sufficient, especially if there is uncontrolled access to credit.

The Chinese government established in 1993/4, a package of reinforcing measures including the establishment of a central tax administration (SAT) that administered a national VAT with "downward" revenue-sharing, and a concomitant equalization system. The VAT was of the "investment type" that did not provide credits for taxation on capital goods, and the business tax largely on services was left in the hands of local administrations. While these measures added to the cost of doing business, these were all that were politically or administratively feasible at the time, and have been addressed gradually since then, as described in Sect. 1.3.

Measures were also needed to strengthen information flows and governance to ensure that the incentive structures actually work. Since the late 1990s, there has been a progressive improvement in public financial management instruments, such as treasury single accounts and the use of international standards for budget classification and accounting and tracking public spending, particularly at the central and provincial levels. While significant and possibly better than in some other G20 countries, this process, is far from complete, especially at the lower levels of government where most of the spending transactions take place—see Ahmad and Zhang (2018, Chap. 4).

This evolution of policies and institutions since 1993 has implications for the governance model. The first relates to the overall incentives facing local officials, and whether the risks and opportunities of their actions can be linked to their relevant jurisdictions or whether these are likely to spread to higher levels, particularly to the central government (see Liu Shangxi and Li Chengwei, this volume). This is critical in establishing hard budget constraints and ring-fencing liabilities, and in addressing the new challenges of rebalancing of the economy and generating sustainable and equitable growth.

Full information on sources and uses of public funds and possible risks associated with public policy are critical in the effective operation of the administrative progression model. These measure are integral to establishing clean governance, that has come to the center of public policy making under the current administration.

Both own-source taxes and improved governance are critical in establishing proper incentives for local officials, also to prevent the buildup of liabilities and rent-seeking behavior. Indeed, ad hoc measures such as the issuance of bonds at the provincial level, while desirable in themselves, may not function as expected, whether the focus is on China or Germany (see Färber and Wang 2018). Indeed, if municipal bonds are implemented before ensuring ability to service debt, there is likely to be a loss of reputation for an essential instrument that will be needed in due course.

We argue that a combination of national infrastructure policies with local connectivity and improved public services is critical in generating incentives for sustainable local "hubs." One of the objectives of the One Belt One Road (OBOR) initiative is to develop lagging regions and ensure sustainable growth especially in the Western and interior regions of China. While the nationally financed physical infrastructure is a necessary condition, we argue that a package of measures, including subnational taxes and transfers and improved local services in less well-endowed areas, is needed. This is to better access credit for sustainable investment, and make full use of opportunities for utilizing the new connectivity, in order to achieve the productive rebalancing and a more equal distribution of opportunity throughout China.

Section 1.4 focuses on additional tax reforms that are needed in order to generate incentives for further structural change (following Ahmad et al. 2013). The VAT for business tax reform completed in May 2016, was designed to reduce the cost of doing business and maintain the competitive advantages in an increasingly difficult external environment. However, the removal of the last tax handle under the control of the local governments makes them entirely dependent on transfers and shared revenues—with no room to raise additional resources in case of need, for example, to pay for any debts incurred by them. This reduces the "accountability" of local officials for decisions that they take, particularly in relation to investments and liabilities incurred.

In Sect. 1.5 we outline some of the changes and governance and institutions that need to be accelerated or completed in order for an orderly financing of the new "sustainable hubs." As seen elsewhere in this volume (Luo and Zhu 2018; Xiao 2018), the experience of Guangdong provides a very useful example of the sorts of measures needed for the rebalancing agenda—both within provinces and within China. The wider realization of substantially expanding production possibility frontiers depends both on new technologies that will be greatly influenced by the tax reforms as well as the investment in connectivity infrastructure implied by the OBOR.

1.2 Governance and Structural Change in Context

1.2.1 Historical Antecedents

Over the centuries, China has been governed though a system of local officials appointed by and responsible to the central government in Beijing. The fiscal system was one of upward revenue-sharing. When the officials were honest and governed responsibly, and without resorting to extortions, the country remained strong and prosperous, and able to withstand natural disasters and exogenous shocks. However, with the size of the country, and limitations flows of information and on connectivity (despite the old silk route), there were periods when governance weakened, and corruption and rent-seeking made the country more vulnerable to shocks—setting in motion the cyclical periods of prosperity and hardship throughout Chinese history (see Zhang 2015). A complex institutional arrangement evolved over time that cannot be described as purely autocratic, as in many of the successor states of the Former Soviet Union.

The cyclical governance pattern was evident during the 20th Century—the first half was one of the most turbulent in Chinese history. Stability was restored with the establishment of the Peoples Republic in 1950, and the traditional governance model has been used, with some interesting variations since then. The fundamental tradeoff has been that very tight central control reduces incentives to invest, against a greater degree of autonomy that can generate rapid growth. But a very decentralized alternative, with poorly developed institutions of fiscal management—with weak or absent national taxes and administration, as well as weak budget allocation and management/monitoring systems—risks the loss of macroeconomic control, as well as generation of spatial and interpersonal inequalities. The system also generates a potential for irresponsible investments and potential for rent-seeking. There has been considerable emphasis by President Xi's Administration in addressing the rent seeking behavior by officials at all levels, and we see this as a critical element in the efficient functioning of the administrative hierarchy model.

1.2.2 The Responsibility System

The Responsibility System was designed in the late 1970s to allow a greater role for production incentives in generating growth and employment generation, to better unleash the investment and growth potential, or "animal spirits" that are critical in structural transformation. This was achieved by reducing the effective tax on profits, while maintaining the governance system of appointed local administrators. It had a significant impact on growth and unleashing the latent productive capabilities of the Chinese economy.

While there was a positive impact on producers, the declining overall revenue generation had a negative impact on local finances—with the total tax/GDP ratio falling from 25% at the start of the reforms to around 10% by 1992/3 (see Chart 1.1). This initiated a "game-play" between local officials and the central government. Consequently, the central government *share of total revenues* also fell precipitously, despite various attempts to incentivize local officials (Gao Qiang, 1995). The central share, which had been around 55% of total revenues at the start of the Responsibility Reform, fell to well under 30% by 1993 (see Chart 1.1). The implication was that, although nominally responsible to the central government, local officials focused on local welfare and interests—especially since promotion prospects depended on local growth performance. The expansion of local public activities along with private investments, despite "grey property rights", led to significant growth opportunities. However, the consequence was that there was a reduced incentive at the local levels to share revenue upwards.

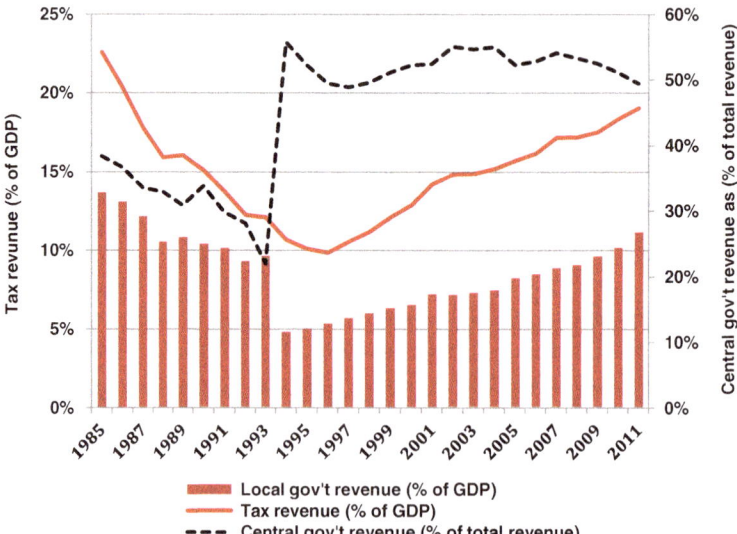

Chart 1.1 Evolution of tax/GDP ratios and central-local shares. *Source* Ahmad, Rydge and Stern, China Development Forum 2013. See also Green and Stern, 2016

By 1992/3, the plummeting tax/GDP ratio, as well as the decline in the share of revenues going to the center, meant that the central government's ability to maintain macroeconomic stability, ensure redistribution, or meet the fundamental responsibilities of a nation state were seriously compromised. The constraints on resources led to highlighting the tensions that typically exist in a large multilevel country between those responsible for service delivery and investments at the lower levels and those at more senior levels of government—even if the latter may have been responsible for the appointments of local officials.

We see that the policy options and responses relevant to the Chinese context are different from those based on electoral competition models at the subnational level —e.g., based on the US experience. The Chinese government focused on taxes and transfers as a means to strengthen central coordination and redistribution functions. At a second stage, it became clear that it had to turn attention to budget institutions and processes to develop information flows, with a view improving governance and developmental outcomes. As we shall argue in the final part of the paper, both areas need to be strengthened further to achieve sustainable structural change.

1.2.3 Structural and Tax Reforms Since 1993/4

The twin objectives of the 1993/4 reforms were to restore macroeconomic balances and ensure continued and sustained growth. In order to maintain the center's ability to conduct macroeconomic policy and redistribution, as well as a consistent public investment strategy, it became necessary to address the critical domestic resource mobilization shortcomings by the early 1990s. A central tax administration—the State Administration of Taxation (SAT) was established, and a "package" of policy reforms was introduced by 1994. The key elements were to establish a VAT on goods, accompanied by a system of revenue-sharing and equalization transfers designed to prevent a negative impact on provinces and give them incentives to operate efficiently. However, the VAT was of the investment-type that did not provide credits for taxes on capital purchases.[1]

The objective was to restore macroeconomic balances as well as to improve the business climate. However, the measures reintroduced a degree of recentralization for the central government.

The reform worked well in restoring revenues for general government, with the central government's share increasing to just over half within a very short period, ensuring financing for redistribution and investment (Ahmad et al. 2002). The shared revenues and "revenue-returns" permitted the development of coastal hubs, such as in the Pearl River Delta, and provided connectivity for a successful

---

[1]This was dictated both by administrative constraints and revenue concerns and while it created an additional cost for exporters, lower Chinese wage levels more than compensated for the disadvantage. This lacuna was addressed in the move towards crediting of input taxation on investments, or the shift from an investment type to a consumption-type VAT, in the reforms of 2006.

export-led growth strategy. However, the coastal hubs, attracting migrants from the interior, have become mega-metropolises with attendant problems of congestion and pollution. And both inter-regional and inter-personal inequalities have widened significantly.

Given the severity of the macroeconomic constraints in the early 1990s, and the fact that "incentives" to persuade local governments to increase the central government share of revenues had largely failed, the Chinese government in the early 1990s decided to introduce a central tax administration and national tax policy powers for the first time in history. This institutional transformation was to have far-reaching effects, as we described below. However, this reform was not just imposed from the center, as might have been the case in a purely autocratic institutional arrangement. The very careful balancing of gainers and losers as a result of the reform was a masterly illustration of the new "positive" approaches to institutional change in a multilevel economy (see Ahmad and Brosio 2015, for a review).[2] This approach could provide lessons for more "market-based" countries in the OECD that rely on "yardstick" competition, at least in principle, or in emerging market countries facing the need for structural change.

The key measures adopted by the Chinese government in 1993/4 were designed to persuade local governments to cede tax collection powers to the center. The State Administration of Taxation (SAT) was designed to manage wide area tax instruments, such as the VAT. This was not done by diktat, but involved an admirable consultation process that generated a "package" of tax administration and policy reforms designed to minimize losses and share benefits across rich and poor provinces alike. The key elements of the "package" included the following:

- Prevention of losses among local governments by a "hold harmless" clause— this guaranteed all provinces 1993 levels of revenues in absolute terms in perpetuity;
- Providing a share of the (increasing) revenues from the VAT with the provinces that generated the value added—these were mainly the richer ones;
- Introducing a modern "equalization framework"—this enabled all provinces to provide similar levels of services at similar levels of effort. The version adopted in China was based on the Australian model, but with simpler factors,[i] and provided a "buy-in" from the poorer provinces; and
- Through a most innovative measure, the "package" provided for a revenue-returned policy to provide additional funds to the better-connected provinces, but on a gradually decreasing basis. This measure was criticized by some international agencies at the time as generating regional inequalities. However, this measure was critical in providing for a concentration of resources in existing "production hubs", largely along the coast, making use of the

---

[2]For a review of the positive theories of multilevel finance that address gainers and losers of alternative institutional and policy arrangements in relation to various interest groups, and associated policy implications, see Ahmad and Brosio (2015). Handbook of Multilevel Finance.

existing connectivity in the short run to generate investment, exports and employment opportunities.

The 1993/4 reforms took into account incentive effects, not just on local governments, but also on firms. As described in Xu Shanda and Ma Lin (1995), one of the main objectives of the introduction of the VAT was to remove cascading from the indirect tax system so as to make Chinese manufacturing more competitive. This was to be achieved eventually by a "wide base and simple rates" (Xu Shanda and Ma Lin 1995, p. 144).

Similarly, rationalizing and reducing rates of the Enterprise Income Tax was critical in removing distortions facing firms (Shi Yao Bin 1995), and in particular separating profits from tax payments in SOEs. The 1994 reforms reduced the EIT rate from 55% to 33%; and this was further reduced to 25% in the aftermath of the 2008 crisis, and applied uniformly across types of enterprises—regardless of ownership (foreign, central or local).

It is useful to note that the prevailing perspective in the literature in the early 1990s, was for a very US-centric "normative" approach (much favoured by the international agencies and recommended in other transition economies at the time). The normative policy prescription is to first address spending assignments and then the revenue assignments and financing arrangements.

The Chinese policy makers took a contrary, albeit very pragmatic approach, which was endorsed by the IMF (see Ahmad et al. 1995). Given the absence of appropriate revenue handles, and adequate tax administration, it made little sense for the Chinese Central Government to assume additional direct spending responsibilities. And the dissolution of the USSR was a timely reminder that the central government had to be able to play an effective macroeconomic coordination role, as well as ensuring minimum standards and redistribution, with full employment. Thus tax reform at the time was designed to consolidate the structural reforms that had been underway since the start of the Responsibility System reforms from the early 1980s (Ahmad, Rydge and Stern 1993). The focus on the revenue side was also a precursor of the "positive approaches" that were popularized in the literature almost a decade later (Ahmad and Brosio 2015).[3]

This "package" approach between taxes and transfers/spending policies has been very influential, including in other G20 countries, such as Mexico, underlying the fiscal reforms in 2007 and 2013.

1.2.4 Effects of the Measures Adopted

The success of the reforms was spectacular (see Chart 1.1), with an improvement in the overall tax/GDP ratio as well as the central government's share. Double-digit growth was maintained for over two decades, and with the freeing up of the

---

[3]See also Ahmad and Brosio (2015) for more recent developments in the positive literature.

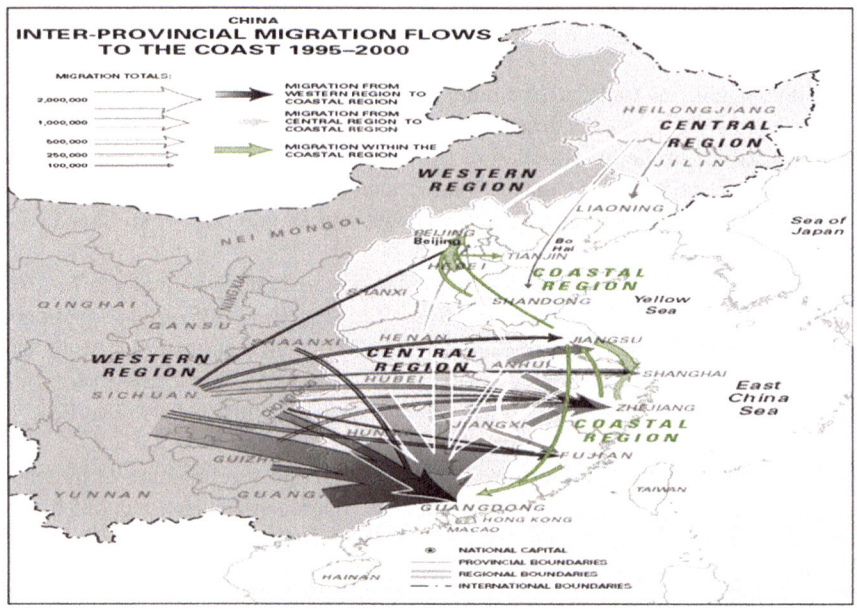

Chart 1.2 Growing reliance on coastal "hubs"

labour-market with more than 150 million migrating to the coastal hubs (see Chart 1.2) and more than 700 million people were taken out of poverty.

However, there were a number of drawbacks. The VAT was applied only to manufacturing, largely because of administrative constraints (recall that the SAT had just been created), and because of the need to leave at least some tax handles in the hands of local governments (the local business tax mainly on services was one of the main instruments available. Further, the VAT was of "investment type"—i.e., that VAT on capital purchases could not be offset against VAT on sales. This again was to meet the revenue targets of the government and was simpler to administer with the nascent SAT. Almost 15 years later, in the aftermath of the 2008 global economic crisis, in order to reduce the cost of doing business and protect Chinese competitiveness, the investment-type VAT was converted to a consumption type VAT, with VAT on capital purchases permitted to be offset against VAT on sales.

Moreover, given origin-based revenue-sharing arrangements this imposed differential burdens on different governments, falling more heavily on the predominantly industrial provinces. This made it more difficult to push through the integration of the business tax with the VAT, especially since the same provinces were likely to face revenue losses.

With the growing competitive pressures heightened by the economic crisis in the recent past, many trading partners including in the EU and Latin America have moved to reduce the cost of doing business by shifting from payroll and other taxes (that cannot be refunded on exports) to a "reformed" VAT. This, in particular, integrates the taxation of services, an increasingly important base of production in

China, with the main tax on goods. In other words, the VAT now fully removes the tax element in the price of exports. In this regard, China has had to speed up the VAT for business tax reform that was initiated over five years ago on a pilot basis, for specific sectors. However, the sector-by-sector approach led to protracted discussions with the local governments and line agencies, generating complex industry-specific arrangements. China undertook the full replacement of the business tax by the VAT in May 2016, accompanied by transfers to ensure that no province would lose revenues as a result of the reform.

Widening personal income and regional disparities pose problems for the long term sustainability of the Chinese development strategy. As pointed out in IMF (2016), the increase in the Chinese level of inequality has been particularly high—rising from around 0.4 in 1992 to around 0.52 in 2013 (see Chart 1.3). This is now at levels in the market-based emerging economies in Latin America, such as Chile, that have relied on the service sector to generate "rebalancing" opportunities. Given the implicit social contract in China, high levels of inequality are likely to be less sustainable than in Chile, although the absence of adequate employment opportunities have begun to pose problems in Chile.

A major consequence of the success of the coastal hub phenomenon in China (as in Chile) is the high level of pollution and congestion in the metropolitan areas, e.g., Beijing, Guangzhou-Shenzhen, Hangzhou-Shanghai corridor. The congestion makes it costlier to do business. And rising pollution levels seriously degrade the quality of life. Beijing's fine particle air pollution level remains well above acceptable health standards despite constant high-level political attention that has led to some improvement in recent years (see e.g., Chart 1.4).

Thus, the solution to the problems of success in the coastal growth strategy is to move production inland, closer to population concentrations and sources of raw materials, through the creation of smaller inland urban "hubs" that are less dependent on fossil fuels for transportation needs and where the choice of techniques adequately reflects social costs and benefits.

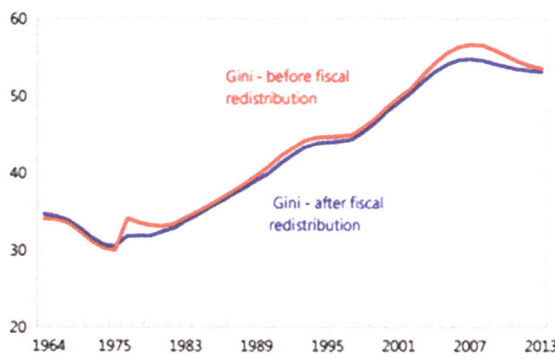

Chart 1.3 Changes in interpersonal inequalities in China. *Source* IMF (2016)

Chart 1.4 Beijing PM 2.5 Index (fine particle air pollution). *Source* IMF (2016)

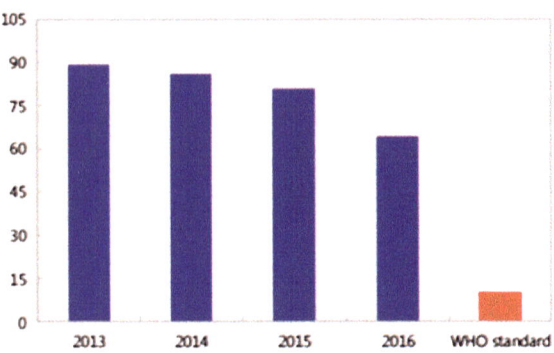

1.3 Tax Reforms for Structural Change

1.3.1 Improving Competitiveness and Accountability: VAT for Business Tax

With a fully integrated VAT to replace the local business tax, it is clear that the cost of doing business will be reduced, especially since the focus of structural reforms emphasizes the development of the service sector. A VAT on a complete base should also generate full information on value added (wages and profits) and would be critical in providing a crosscheck to reduce evasion and avoidance in the income taxes. This was a key element in the structural fiscal reforms implemented in Mexico in 2013 Ahmad (2017). Additional VAT revenues could also compensate for reductions in the payroll tax that adds to the cost of doing business, and more efficiently finance social benefits.

Following the 1993/4 reforms, the business tax was the last major source of revenues in the hands of provinces, and generates significant revenues in the more advanced coastal provinces like Guangdong, and is even more important in relative terms in the middle-income provinces. However, it meant that the VAT chain was incomplete with loss of information on the production process. Also, the Business Tax generates cascading and adds to the cost of doing business in China. Replacing the Business Tax by a VAT, while improving overall effiiency would generate losses, especially in the middle income provinces (see Chart 1.5, and Ahmad et al. 2004; and Lou Jiwei and Shulin Wang 2008).

In China the replacement of the business tax by the VAT has been dictated by the structural reform agenda. Given the rising wages in China and greater inter-national competition, it has become important to reduce the competitive burden on enterprises, especially vis à vis imports and for removing taxation from exports. The main services (such as transport, construction, banking and insurance) form a critical part of most productive activities.

Experimentation of the replacement of the business tax by the VAT for selected services was initiated in Shanghai in 2012. It was followed in other metropolitan

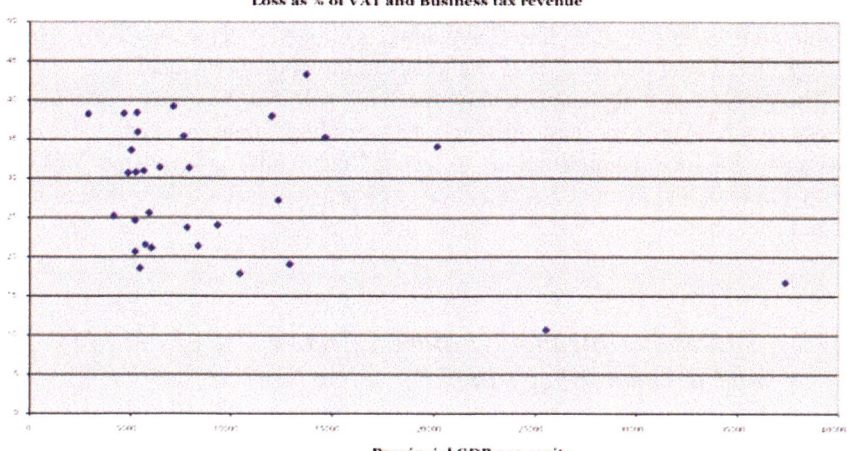

Chart 1.5 Final stage of the VAT reform—provincial losses. *Source* Ahmad et al. (2004); Ahmad (2008)

areas for selected services including telecommunications, transport and construction. However, the service-by-service approach has proved to be difficult, as it generates gainers and losers, including among State service suppliers. The response has been to "negotiate" VAT rates with the sectors. But the sector-by-sector approach to the VAT makes it complicated and loses the simplicity needed for the tax to be an efficient generator of revenues as well as information.

The VAT for business tax reforms will generate a complex set of gains and losses among local governments, as seen in Chart 1.2. In general, central revenues will increase (depending on the rate applied, and the rate of the business tax replaced) but provincial revenues will decline. Although the relative losses in the middle-income provinces are large relative to overall revenues, the absolute losses in provinces like Guangdong, will be very large and likely greater than the losses in the poorer provinces.

The equalization system cannot be used to compensate for the loss of the business tax, even though it will need to be recalibrated as a result of the choice of replacement provincial tax. There are two main considerations. If the equalization system fully compensates well to do provinces, Guangdong say will likely require a larger absolute amount of transfers than the poorer interior provinces. Consequently, full compensation for Guangdong will likely violate the equalization principle. However, less than full compensation for Guangdong will exacerbate budgetary problems in the province, especially at the lower levels (see Lin and Xu, in this volume).

The Chinese government correctly decided to complete the VAT for business tax in one go in May 2016. This was facilitated by an adjustment in the origin-based sharing ratios, as well as a lump-sum transfer to compensate provinces for any losses incurred. From Chart 1.5 it is clear that a complex set of transfers will be involved with higher amounts going to the middle-income provinces. Yet the absolute losses in provinces like Guangdong, will be very large and likely require greater "lump-sum transfers" than the losses in the poorer provinces.

The problem with the compensation mechanism is that the transfers are seldom "lump-sum." Typically, they operate as "gap-filling" transfers and add to the incentives for local administrations to "game" the central government. This certainly does not add to greater accountability or generate incentives to shift to more sustainable "hubs".

1.3.2 Addressing Inequality: More Effective Use of the PIT and a Local "Piggy-Back"

Increasing inequality has emerged as a major problem in China. The typical instrument to address inter-personal inequality is the personal income tax (PIT). However, the Chinese PIT is not equipped to perform this role. This is because it is largely a tax based on withholding from wages—and may exacerbate inequalities: by taxing middle income groups more heavily than the richest groups. The richest people of course benefit from asset-based income—both physical (property related) as well as from financial instruments, including capital gains and dividends.

The Chinese PIT is shared on an origin-basis with local governments. However, this does not constitute an "own-source" revenue as the recipient government is neither able to influence the rate or the base. The shared tax is effectively like a transfer, and is typically discounted by ratings agencies in examining the strength of the jurisdiction in financing its liabilities, including local bond issues.

A piggy-back tax could be set above the central rate for the PIT, or below in order to avoid an increase in the overall tax burden. Further, setting of a local rate within a band established by the National People's Congress would incentivize local governments to expand the relevant bases, e.g., by providing information to the SAT on the major untapped assets (e.g., luxury homes and expensive cars). This may permit a *reduction* in the total rate available to a local government as the base is expanded, while additional revenues might be generated if there is an increase in the high value-added activity levels. More importantly, this feature becomes a critical element determining the eligibility of a local government in access to credit given relevant own-sourced revenues (Chart 1.6).

It is clear that the coastal provinces would benefit from the "piggy back" on the income tax arrangements more than the interior provinces. Consequently, it would be necessary to recalibrate the equalization framework. In order not to create disincentives for provincial governments, the equalization system would have to be based on estimates of standard bases across the country, and not actual revenues collected in any region. This would also make the equalization system introduced in 1994 work more efficiently—as it is based on the principle of providing all relevant governments the capability to provide similar levels of service at similar levels of

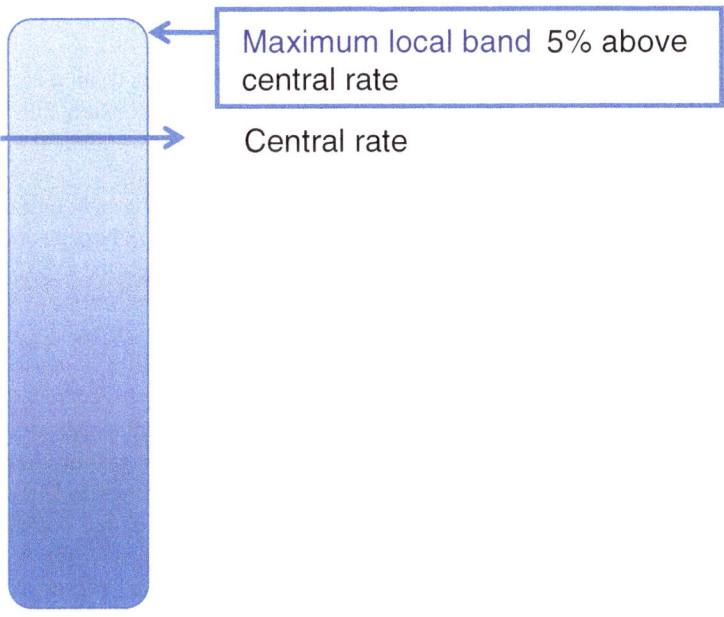

Chart 1.6 Provincial Piggy-back bands on the PIT

tax effort. Operating on the spending part of the equation in isolation, as is largely the case at present in China, does not provide full incentives for efficient operations at the sub-national level (see Ahmad and Brosio 2006).

1.3.3 Congestion and Environmental Damage and a Carbon Tax

Given the emphasis being placed by the Chinese government on climate change and structural reforms, a proposal is to develop **a** carbon tax, including an excise on petroleum products (see Ahmad et al. 2013). As with the PIT, a piggy-back rate with a "band" (e.g., up to 5% points) legislated by the NPC on a central base, would give an incentive to local governments to aggressively pursue the taxation of emissions, while avoiding the risk of a race to the bottom and ineffective implementation of the tax.

A carbon tax simply introduces a wedge above the international price of carbon-based products, such as coal, petroleum and natural gas, both to reduce consumption and encourage more efficient and sustainable alternatives. The difficulty is that carbon taxes fall on intermediates and would affect the price element of other goods. Thus it is important to evaluate "effective taxes", and consequently the effects on producers and consumers as well. Some of the additional revenues should be earmarked towards R&D for new technologies, and support for industrial restructuring in the rust-belt in China.

It is desirable to maintain a uniform base for the carbon tax, if not a central tax. This would help to avoid a race to the bottom and also address externalities across local governments. A piggy-back arrangement for local governments would be possible, as in the income tax case.

In theory, the revenues generated by a system of cap-and-trade can replicate those generated by a carbon tax. The popularity of cap-and-trade is largely due to the difficulty, rather impossibility, of passing any new tax through the US Congress. Nonetheless, a carbon tax may be more transparent and therefore more likely to generate the production and consumption responses that are needed for reducing emissions and ensuring structural change. The experience with cap-and-trade systems in Europe has been mixed at best. Yet most European countries maintain high excises on petroleum products—mimicking a carbon tax that generates a great deal of revenue and has contributed, with other measures such as congestion charges and restrictions on emissions, to improvements in the air quality of cities such as London.

In China, there has been experimentation with seven regional cap-and-trade exchanges, but the revenues generated appear to have been meager. In due course, as the regional exchanges are integrated with the proposed national exchange and the cap-and-trade system begins to operate more effectively, there should be a possibility of discontinuing some of the measures described above—such as the quantitative restrictions on emissions. But in the medium term, a tax on petroleum products (or a carbon tax) and a cap-and-trade system are likely to continue in tandem.

A range of taxes is possible in relation to polluting motor vehicles—these would be both environmentally friendly as well as strongly redistributive. For instance, both purchase tax and annual registration fee could be made a function of engine size, hence corresponding to the likely emissions generated. Hybrid or electric vehicles could be exempted or subject to lower rates. The vehicle taxes could be determined and collected by third tier governments that have to deal with the consequences of the vehicle pollution. The larger metropolitan areas, e.g., Shanghai and Beijing, may also want to consider congestion charges, as practiced in London, or rationing by license plate numbers, as in Singapore.

Natural resource taxes are common as part of an array of instruments that also include production excises or a carbon tax, royalties, production-sharing arrangements, as well as standard VAT and corporate income taxes. A proper assessment would include all the taxes, which may have different components or objectives. As with the case of the VAT and excises described above, different objectives come into play vis à vis the taxation of natural resources that would require different instruments. The use of the VAT in the natural resource sector is taking on greater relevance as both private firms and SOEs may have incentives to cheat and hide transactions. Thus, the full VAT chain is taking on a great importance, even in the natural resource sector. The Chinese practice of requiring the VAT on capital purchases to be offset against the VAT on sales of petroleum products is an example that should be more widely adopted in countries that have suffered from diversion of resources from natural resource, such as Nigeria.

It may be appropriate to design a specific local resource tax that is based on the quantities extracted. This has the advantage that it would provide resources in proportion to the environmental damage inflicted by the extraction. And it would not be subject to the vagaries of international prices. However, as resources are depleted, the responsibility for restructuring or retraining would fall to the higher levels, which would also have access to the ad valorem revenues needed for stabilization in the medium-term. As suggested in the Third Plenum directive, there should be a review and rationalization of all the charges associated with environmental purposes in China, together with the evaluation and introduction of a carbon tax.

The issue of depleted mineral reserves and affected enterprises and cities is an increasingly important issue for China. Clearly resources have to be generated to finance the restructuring of industries and retraining of affected workers—this is receiving considerable attention at the present time as the restructuring is being implemented.

A number of "environmental taxes" are appropriate for the city/municipal level —ranging from vehicle registration and annual use permits, together with congestion charges. There could also be local excises on the exploitation and transmission of natural resources, e.g., on pipelines that could defray the costs of the environmental damage. Similarly, there could be taxes on the discharge of polluted water, or fees for the water treatment facilities. There are thus a range of taxes and fees and charges for environmental purposes that could be assigned to different levels of government.

1.3.4 Municipal/Community Charges for Local Benefits

Traditional US-style property taxes levied on ownership of property based on established records and up-to-date valuations typically perform poorly in emerging market economies, including in the more advanced Latin American countries. There are a number of reasons for this, as surveyed in Ahmad et al. (2015), including ownership titles and the difficulty in establishing a proper cadaster as well as valuation. Moreover, the tax is very visible and generates a lot of opposition. Finally, there are opportunities for rent-seeking when the tax is administered locally, especially when rates are set at higher levels (as in Mexico). Local officials are not then accountable and often do "deals" with friends and relatives.

Many of these problems are not confined to emerging markets, and the issue of valuation was one of the reasons that the UK abandoned the property tax system under Margaret Thatcher—although the poll-tax that replaced it was even more unpopular and regressive.

A "beneficial tax" linked to the delivery of local public services is a possible alternative to a property tax, as described in Ahmad et al. (2015), is an idea developed by Alfred Marshall that links the tax or charge to be paid to the benefits that are provided at the local level. These could include water supply and electricity transmission, sewage and sanitation, transport and connectivity.

The "beneficial tax" or "community charge" could operate on a system of bands, linked e.g., to the size and location of the property and the number of inhabitants— this is the logic of the system now in operation in the UK. The bands are linked to the cost and quantities of services consumed, and are linked to the number of inhabitants and not necessarily ownership. This mechanism gets around both the cadaster and valuation difficulties that are legendary in emerging market countries with "fuzzy" property rights.

The community charge would also get around the issue of local resistance, and would generate accountability on the part of local officials if they do not deliver the services that the community effectively pays for. The discipline of "yardstick competition" operates in countries with local elections. And in bureaucratic progression models, the promotion criteria could be linked to the satisfaction of local inhabitants with the quality of services provided. The big advantage of this system of community-based charges is that it can be put in place relatively quickly, without the need for a top-heavy bureaucratic apparatus, or the need for a cadaster and tracking of property prices.

While a judicious choice of bands could reflect the variations in property valuations in metropolitan areas, equity considerations could be enhanced by a stamp duty on sales above a particular valuation. This is also the practice in the UK—and relate particularly to high-priced London properties.

The community charge is an effective "own-source" revenue and would qualify as the basis for an orderly access to credit or borrowing. This, in turn, would be reflected in the quality of public services provided.

It should be possible to begin a pilot project in, for instance, a city like Guangzhou or Shenzhen. These cities would generate much of the community charge in Guangdong, and there would be a need to establish a within-province equalization framework that would not disadvantage the poorest municipalities that may have relatively poor services or lower value bands.

1.4 Governance Changes

China was too large and diverse a country to be managed efficiently by diktat, especially in the presence of poor information available to the center on subnational operations on both revenue-generation, which was in the hands of provinces, as well as public spending. The evolution continues, especially as institutions and information generation are modernized, representing one of the most significant structural transformations in modern times. However, the process needs to be further strengthened in order to provide the right incentives at the sub-national level for a sustainable rebalancing and better utilization of the investment opportunities for lagging regions, across provinces inherent in the Belt and Road Initiative, as well as within provinces such as Guangdong.

1.4.1 Budget Institutions and Governance

Although the 1993/4 reforms constituted a significant "recentralization" on the revenue-side (Ahmad et al. 2002), spending continued to be increasingly decentralized. This was financed by limited and decreasing revenue handles assigned to the local governments, but also by equalization (untied) as well as earmarked transfers. As with the reluctance to share upwards a declining revenue pool in the 1980s, it became quickly evident to the central government that it was largely futile to impose conditions on local spending if the categories for spending were vaguely defined, or if there was poor information on the actual spending as well as the flow of funds.

With the realization that there would be limited influence over local governments without full information on the allocation and use of resources and the flow of cash, a fundamental reform of the budget institutions and processes was initiated in the late 1990s. China became one of the first major countries to adopt the IMF Government Financial Statistical Manual 2001 (GFSM2001, recently revised to 2014). The main advantage of the GFSM2001/14 format is the generation of standardized fiscal data consistent with the System of National Accounts (SNA). The links with the SNA are critical in verifying and ensuring consistency of the data with the real sector. And without standardized and consistent data, it is hard to prevent local governments from "playing games."

The absence of standardized information across levels of government has been identified as a contributing factor in the on-going crisis in Europe (see Ahmad et al. 2016). In particular, it facilitated the generation of liabilities at the local level that were hidden as arrears (e.g., in the Portuguese region of Madeira), or implicit liabilities associated with Public-Private Partnerships (PPPs)[ii] and only surfaced with the pressure on the banking system as a result of the crisis. In many cases, e.g., in Spain, quasi-private activities associated with local governments—e.g., building apartments and holiday resorts—that were not counted as debt either at the central or local levels, also very quickly became public liabilities as a result of the crisis, leading to a sharp rise in the total general government debt. The ability to "hide" local liabilities or pass them on to other jurisdictions vitiates many of the perceived advantages of the electoral competition models.

Although China does better than the European countries in that it has adopted the GFSM2001/14 standards, given the complexity of the measures, and the time it takes to record and value assets and liabilities in the balance sheet, the government decided to focus initially on the cash basis. This standard is being rolled out to lower levels of government. Consequently, the provisions on accruals and the establishment of the full balance sheets are not yet implemented, especially at the local levels, and consequently for general government (see Ahmad and Xiaorong Zhang 2018, Chap. 4).

1.4.2   Number of Levels of Government

Multiple levels of government were useful as a mechanism of information generation and control in a medieval institutional context. This was also the case in Europe, and has been one of the main constraints in the modernization of state functions, say in Italy (see Ambrosanio et al. 2016), and has been the focus of the rationalization attempts that were given a fillip by the current economic crisis. The main reasons for this reform are that the overlapping functions make it difficult to assign responsibilities and reduce costs, and also accountability is made more diffuse since it is harder to assign meaningful "own-source" revenues to more than three levels. A final point is that modern budget management and information generation systems become unwieldy at multiple levels, and difficult to implement say with the full GFSM2014 framework. Indeed, the existence of modern Government Financial Management Information Systems (FMIS) that can generate accurate and timely information on government operations at all levels makes the multiple levels of administration redundant.

In the European case, it has been observed that there is a tendency for liabilities to be telescoped down to the lower levels. These governments tend to have weaker financial information management systems, so that the liabilities are easier to disguise. Moreover, the ability of lower levels to manage PPPs efficiently is considerably reduced, accentuating the information asymmetries that exist anyway between the private parties and the lower levels of government or their entities involved. Similar considerations will apply in China (see Färber and Zhang 2018, for a comparison between the Chinese and German cases).

1.4.3   Managing Sub-National Risks and Liabilities

The Chinese budget law revised in the early 1990s did not permit local governments to borrow directly. However, in order to encourage investment, a 1992 provision allowed sub-national borrowing through locally-owned or managed investment companies (UDICs). Implicitly, this was designed to encourage investment, and would have corresponded to the "golden rule" of borrowing for investment only if the local companies had performed as anticipated. However, in the absence of full information on borrowing and the buildup of liabilities, it has not been possible for the central government to ensure that funds raised ostensibly for "productive" capital spending were not utilized for less productive current spending of local governments, or by local enterprises—including for keeping on the right side of local officials.

The estimate of local government debt for June 2013, at around 31% of GDP, by the Audit Bureau was not large in relation to the reserves held by the central government. However, the liabilities appear to have been growing fastest at the county and township level that have very limited tax handles to be able to service the debt, much of which is relatively short-term. Consequently, many local governments would likely have difficulty in servicing their debt in the medium-term. In order to address the issue, some international agencies recommended the issuance of US-style local government bonds. And this indeed would be a component of a fully-fledged system of local government financing and tax reforms. The Budget Law was revised in 2015 to permit local governments to issue bonds, including for existing liabilities. However, unlike US States and local governments, Chinese local administrations do not have access to own-revenue handles[iii] in the sense that rates could be raised on a specified base (or band, see below). Consequently, it is not surprising that the response from banks and financial institutions to the local government bond issue was not particularly enthusiastic.

Indeed, the option for the central government to assume some of the local debt may be the only solution in the short-run, as announced in March 2016, especially in relation to the counter-cyclical spending on behalf of the central government that was needed after the start of the 2008 crisis. However, this may generate disincentives that would need to be addressed through the creation of an own-source revenue-generation mechanism for each level of responsible government. And as mentioned above, responsible levels may relate to only the provincial level, and county/townships.

1.4.4 Next Stage of Governance and Fiscal Reforms for Sustainable Growth

Both short term stabilization measures, and structural changes for sustained development, pose challenges for China and need to be coordinated. Indeed, rebalancing is proposed to move production away from the congested and polluted coastal metropolitan areas towards smaller cities in the interior and opening up lagging regions, as well as enhancing connectivity with neighboring regions through the Belt and Road initiative. This provides opportunities to both meet the short-term adjustment needs, as well as the longer-term structural changes to ensure cleaner growth, and sustained employment in China, together with reduced spatial and interpersonal inequalities.

This ambitious restructuring agenda will require that incentives for the private sector and local governments are properly aligned to prevent wasteful spending, including on non-productive construction projects, but focus on "new sustainable hubs" with improved service delivery and improved governance. Consequently, it is useful to examine the role to be played by both tax policy, as well as more effective spending and generation of information on budget processes. As we shall see, the incentive effects for firms and households are closely linked to those for local governments/officials.

The evolution of the Chinese governance model over the past 25 years has illustrated the importance of a balance between incentives and sanctions that keep local officials honest. As in the medieval systems in South Asia and Europe, trusted officials were assigned regions, although multiple layers and overlapping responsibilities ensured some oversight in distant capitals. The creation of a modern tax administration in the hands of the central government, to administer the most modern of tax instruments, was a true revolution, and has changed the dynamics of intergovernmental fiscal relations in China, although as noted above, the policy agenda is far from complete.

The difficulty in assigning meaningful own-tax handles and spending responsibilities, has led to a three-layer structure that many countries are trying to achieve. Consequently, if the present 5+ layers administrative structure is maintained, two of the layers could become "deconcentrated" organs for say the provinces (prefectures); and counties/townships (village bodies).

The same three-tier arrangement would simplify spending assignments, including a needed recentralization of social security responsibilities, and the maintenance of minimum standards, to the central level as in most advanced countries. This reassignment would considerably reduce the spending pressures, including of unfunded mandates, at the lower levels of administration, and it would also become easier to hold officials accountable for the performance of assigned tasks, particularly effective service delivery and adhering to potential subnational fiscal responsibility legislation. The current aggregate growth targets are much too broad, create significant disincentives and open up the possibility of diversion of resources and rent-seeking.

Of course, there is not much point in establishing detailed performance targets for local appointed officials if these cannot be monitored on a timely basis. It is also not sufficient just to track outcomes. Consider the case of two identical local governments. Government A manages to achieve all the performance targets, but at the cost of pushing liabilities to other jurisdictions or to the future (e.g., through opaque PPP contracts), so that the true costs of provision are not clearly delineated. Government B manages its finances prudently, and does not incur debts. It may have a lower level of absolute performance, but the services are delivered more efficiently than in A. A simple performance based system would reward officials in A, and reduce the incentives for B to manage spending efficiently.

The same criticism applies to models of "yardstick competition" based on electoral evaluations of outcomes in neighboring jurisdictions. As pointed out in Ahmad et al. (2016), the overlapping responsibilities in many European countries, together with considerable "game-play" at the sub-national level, resulted in passing on liabilities to other jurisdictions (typically in the end to the central government, although the initial response is to move the liabilities downwards where they might be less visible). Consequently, the electoral process ceases to perform the discipline that the yardstick or electoral competition models suggest. Weak information flows remove the advantage that the electoral models are assumed to have over appointed officials. In general, however, the governance based on appointed officials is likely to involve the need for considerable detail and accuracy of information flows on budgetary transactions and outcomes.

1.4.4.1 Fiscal Institutions and Governance with Modern Instruments

Fiscal institutions in China have evolved with changing technology, and with greater emphasis on managing information flows in both tax administration and budget management. The tax administration innovations, particularly the SAT's Golden Tax Project in the 1990s, that enabled VAT invoices to be matched electronically, has become the standard being replicated from Mexico to Portugal in recent years. The technological developments open up possibilities to streamline and tighten the governance possibilities that were just not available through the centuries, and had led to an overlapping and complex structure of governments in order to establish appropriate checks and balances.

As seen above, the tax design and assignments affect incentives and costs facing producers and consumers, but also local government officials—even if they are nominally appointed by the center. In particular, both the resources available to local governments, and a proper evaluation of their effectiveness in meeting public service delivery requirements are critical in ensuring good local governance.

In the context of budget systems, while China has made good progress with the GFSM2001 framework in the early years of the 21st Century in China (Brazil is only just beginning this reform at the subnational level), significant work is needed to generate full information on liabilities within local balance sheets for the benefit of markets and investors (Ahmad and Xiaorong Zhang 2018, Chap. 4). The process will become more complicated with the emphasis on PPPs (Ahmad, Bhattacharya, Vinella and Xiao, this volume, and Ahmad et al. 2017). While the involvement of the private sector is an important step in financing public investments, this has to be managed carefully.

Treasury systems in China were modernized at the same time as the introduction of the GFSM2001 framework, with the establishment of a nested system of Treasury Single Accounts for the Central and Provincial governments. Again, this is a critical reform made feasible by the use of modern banking and clearing mechanisms, as well as (eventually) electronic payments and receipts. This way, all cash flows in the economy can be tracked, minimizing the possibilities for diversion of funds.

With the full GFSM2001/14, as well as a Treasury Single Account, a central government should be able to establish more detailed targets for local officials, and be able to monitor outcomes on a real time basis. In principle this also applies to arrears, and the build-up of liabilities. With the full balance sheets, it should be possible to ensure compliance by local governments of (potential) fiscal responsibility targets in their jurisdictions, as well as monitoring of the effectiveness of service delivery. Although China had moved towards the GFSM2001 format almost ten years ago, together with a system of TSAs, local operations are mainly managed on a cash basis, and liabilities are not recorded effectively in the budget and treasury systems, or in local balance sheets. As argued in Ahmad and Xiaorong Zhang (this volume), recording full information on liabilities in the local level balance sheets, while desirable, will take many years to become fully operational.

1.4.4.2   Financing Productive Subnational Investments and Management of Liabilities

As mentioned above, although local governments were unable to borrow directly, they were able to establish companies that could do so. In the absence of information on the sources and uses of the funds, and the full extent of liabilities, it had become very difficult to ensure that the resources were being used effectively. Issues are complicated in borrowing from shadow banks, arrears, as well as potential losses of local SOEs.

It is more difficult to manage future liabilities generated through PPPs. These have been very problematic in Europe (Ahmad et al. 2016). There is an incentive for local governments to use PPPs to "kick the can down the road"—as part of "game-play" with the center. Also, as there is asymmetric information between the private party and the government, or between different levels of government, that could lead to renegotiation of terms and higher incidence of liabilities than contracted. IPSAS Rule 32 requires that the buildup of PPP liabilities should be reflected in the local government balance sheet with appropriate provisioning—this is very hard to achieve in the short-run.

Without the full information consistent with GFSM2001/14 and IPSAS standards (and this will take time to generate) it is not evident that the local governments or their companies would be able to service the debt without having to pass it on to Beijing. Clearly the Central Government has the capability to handle local debt easily, but it would create a moral hazard and weaken the budget constraints if it were to do so on a regular basis.

The revision of the Chinese budget law in 2015 now permits local governments to issue bonds. This is a welcome and needed step, and needs to be part of the financing arsenal of local governments. However, the measure in itself is unlikely to be sufficient to generate a solution to local government indebtedness in China without the development of own-source revenues at the provincial and municipal levels.

Two components are critical for local bond markets. The most important is that local governments should have own-source revenues against which their ability to pay can be judged by the bond-holders and markets. Consequently, the ability to contract debt at the local level and pass on the liabilities to higher levels of government reduces the incentives either to utilize own-sources of revenues or manage spending efficiently. The second is that there should be full information available on the nature and magnitude of the liabilities concerned.

1.5   Conclusions

The Chinese governance model is evolving with the advent of modern institutions and information flows. Additional progress on tax reforms to reduce the costs of doing business and lead to more sustainable investment decisions is dependent on new revenue assignments at all levels of government. This reform needs to be coordinated with rationalization of numbers of tiers, clarity in spending assignments, as well as the institutions and information generation capabilities of modern tax and budget systems. In this manner, the appointed officials can be held accountable for more effective service delivery and maintaining fiscal responsibility together with sensible complementary investments needed to make sustainable "rebalancing" a reality and make full use of Belt and Road connectivity.

While rebalancing involves generating new activities in the interior provinces, the within-province differentials are significant enough to warrant a similar consideration as at the national level in China. For instance, as argued elsewhere in this volume, restructuring of activities outside the Pearl-River Delta, but within the province of Guangdong, also provides a microcosm of the fiscal reforms and investments needed at the national level in China. This related both to the connectivity within China and with neighboring countries under the One Belt One Road initiative, as well as local linkages to connect "lagging" regions to the new "hubs". Thus, the fiscal institutions and policy options that could be used in Guangdong may be examples for the rest of the country.

Notes

i. There has been a move over the past decade to simplify the Australian equalization system—this was to enhance transparency and in a significant manner moved the advanced Australian model closer to the design chosen by China a decade earlier.

ii. For a recent review of PPPs and incentive issues at multiple levels of government, see Ahmad, Bhattacharya, Vinella and Xiao, this volume, and Ahmad et al. 2017.

iii. Shared revenues do not strictly correspond to own-source revenues, as the local governments have no control over rates or bases. In the sense of effects on incentives, they are more like transfers.

References

Ahmad, E. (2008). Tax reforms and the sequencing of intergovernmental reforms in China: Preconditions for a Xiaokang society. In Lou Jiwei and Shulin Wang (Eds.).

Ahmad, E., & Brosio, G. (Eds.). (2006). *Handbook of Fiscal federalism.* Edward Elgar.

Ahmad, E., & Brosio, G. (Eds.). (2015). *Handbook of multilevel finance.* Edward Elgar.

Ahmad, E., Qiang, G., & Tanzi, V. (1995). *Reforming China's public finances.* International Monetary Fund.

Ahmad, E., Keping, L., & Richardson, T. (2002). Recentralization in China? In E. Ahmad & V. Tanzi (Eds.).

Ahmad, E., Lockwood, B., & Singh, R. (2004). Financial consequences of the Chinese VAT reform. *International VAT Monitor* May/June, 181–186.

Ahmad, E., Rydge, J., & Stern, N. (2013). Structural change leads to tax reforms leads to structural change. China Development Forum March 2013.

Ahmad, E., Bhattacharya, A., Vinella, A., & Xiao, K. (2015). Involving the private sector and PPPs in financing public investments. G24-GGGI infrastructure working paper 5 (this volume).

Ahmad, E., & Brosio, G., & Pöschl, C. (2015). Local property taxation and benefits in developing countries: Overcoming political resistance. In Ahmad and Brosio, op cit.

Ahmad, E., Bordignon, M., & Brosio, G. (2016). *Multilevel finance and the Euro crisis*. Edward Elgar.

Ahmad, E. (2017). Political economy of tax reforms for the SDGs. G24 Background Paper, Washington.

Ahmad, E., Vinella, A., & Xiao, K. (2017). Contracting arrangements and PPPs for sustainable development. G24 background paper.

Ahmad, E., & Zhang, X. (2018). Towards Monitoring and Managing Subnational Liabilities in China: Lessons from the Balance Sheet for County K. *Fiscal Underpinnings for Sustainable Development in China.*

Ambrosanio, F., Balduzzi, P., & Bordignon, M. (2016). Economic crisis and fiscal federalism in Italy. In Ahmad, Bordignon and Brosio (Eds.), *op cit.*

Besley, T., & Case, A. (1995). Incumbent behavior, vote-seeking, tax-setting and yardstick competition. *American Economic Review, 85*(1), 25–45.

Färber, G., & Zhang, Z. (2018). Subnational public debt in china and germany: A Comparative Perspective. *Fiscal Underpinnings for Sustainable Development in China.*

Green, F., & Stern, N. (2016). A new development model for China: Growth, urbanization and environment at crossroads, China Development Forum.

IMF. (2016). China: Article IV Consultation.

Lockwood, B. (2015). Political economy of decentralization In Ahmad and Brosio (2015).

Lou, J., & Wang, S. (2008). *Fiscal reforms in China*. Oxford University Press.

Luo, X., & Zhu, N. (2018). Hub-periphery development pattern and inclusive growth: Case study of guangdong province. *Fiscal Underpinnings for Sustainable Development in China.*

Qiang, G. (1995). Problems in Chinese intragovernmental fiscal relations, tax-sharing system and future reforms. In Ahmad, Gao and Tanzi, *op cit.*

Tsai, P. H. (2016). Fiscal incentives and political budget cycles in China. *International Tax and Public Finance.*

Xiao, K. (2018). Managing subnational liability for sustainable development: A case study of guangdong province. *Fiscal Underpinnings for Sustainable Development in China.*

Xu, S., & Ma, L. (1995). Reform and the market economy and tax in China. In Ahmad, Gao and Tanzi, op cit.

Yao Bin, S. (1995). Unifying the Enterprise Income Tax and reforming profit distribution between Government and State Owned Enterprises. In Ahmad, Gao and Tanzi.

Zhang, J. (2015). Government Finances and Public Interests: Perspectives on State Building. *Journal of Chinese Governance.*

Chapter 2
Land Use Reforms: Towards Sustainable Development in China

Wen Wang, Alfred M. Wu and Fangzhi Ye

Abstract This article explores the nature of China's land-use rights system, its evolution and impact on resource allocation and local governments' public finances. In recent decades, the public ownership of land has not hindered the development of a thriving market economy. Since the inception of the economic reform, land-use rights, a new institution, have been introduced to address the rigidness and ineffectiveness of land ownership in China. The current land-use rights system (LURS) has provided enterprises and individuals with a largely stable land tenure system while permitting local governments to leverage land finance for infrastructure investment. Nevertheless, rampant corruption and predatory behaviors by local governments are associated with land transactions, which pose a threat to social stability at the grassroots level. The Chinese experience sheds fresh light on the development of a sound land administration system in developing countries.

2.1 Introduction

China's rapid urbanization has impressed the world. Urbanization in China and high-tech development in the United States have been cited by Joseph E. Stiglitz, the former chief economist at the World Bank, as the two most crucial forces shaping the development of the 21st century. After being an agrarian economy for several centuries, China has become an urbanized economy with the size of its

W. Wang (✉)
School of Public Affairs and Administration, Rutgers University-Newark, Newark, NJ, USA
e-mail: wenwang@gmail.com

A. M. Wu
Lee Kuan Yew School of Public Policy, National University of Singapore, Singapore, Singapore
e-mail: wumuluan@gmail.com

F. Ye
School of Economics, Zhejiang University, Hangzhou, People's Republic of China
e-mail: yefangzhi@hotmail.com

© Springer Nature Singapore Pte Ltd. 2018
E. Ahmad et al. (eds.), *Fiscal Underpinnings for Sustainable Development in China*,
https://doi.org/10.1007/978-981-10-6286-5_2

urban population surpassing its rural population in 2011. Behind this, China's land policy has contributed substantially to urbanization. Without land reform in China, urbanization would have been less effective in transforming its economy (Ye and Wu 2014).

Land matters greatly in local public finance. Local governments around the world often have a wide array of assets on their balance sheets, among which land assets are frequently the most valuable (Peterson 2006, 2009). In a city where the government has great control over land, the sale or lease of publicly owned land to the private sector can raise a substantial amount of money for public projects (Wong 1991; Ping 2006). Moreover, using land as collateral for borrowing or as public contributions in public-private partnership (PPP) programs to construct subways, airports or other large public capital projects are commonly adopted approaches for monetizing land assets around the world.

In the development trajectory of Western countries, tapping land values by selling or leasing land ownership or land-use rights had been a large part of the investment strategy for financing urban infrastructure during the 20th century, or even earlier, at a time when urban populations grew fast (Peterson 2009). Over the past several decades, in many developing countries where it is hard to receive large long-term loans for urban infrastructure, the revenue generated by land sales or land leases seems to be a good way to fund infrastructure development (Sagalyn 1992).

For local governments, resorting to land sales or land leases for fiscal revenue has both merits and demerits. "[L]ocal governments often have more flexibility in managing their assets than they do in adjusting tax rates, introducing new taxes, increasing user fees or borrowing funds for investment—all of which may require higher-level governmental approval or be prohibited altogether by the intergovernmental fiscal framework" (Peterson and Annez 2007, p. 284). "When land finance substitutes for borrowing, it reduces the risk surrounding future debt repayment capacity and the need to generate future revenue streams to meet future debt service" (Peterson and Kaganova 2010, p. 7).

From the perspective of intergovernmental fiscal relations, well-disposed land assets and the use of land proceeds in local capital budgets without incurring debt or requiring intergovernmental grants would win applause from higher-level governments and the general public as well. Nevertheless, dependence on land sales or land leases for revenue generation may create a variety of problems and potential risks. It poses a great threat to financial stability and sustainability at the local level. With a strong incentive to obtain increased land revenue through shoring up the land market, local governments may boost a property bubble. If the bubble bursts, it will in turn jeopardize local governments financially.

The experiences of both developed and developing countries reveal that the sale and lease of publicly owned land assets have been an important financing tool for local governments around the world. Similar to their counterparts in other countries, Chinese local governments have relied heavily on land leasing revenue since the 1990s, but the magnitude of land finance in China overshadows any other country in the world. This research analyzes the development trajectory of the land system and land finance, which may reveal the underlying mechanism and impetus for changes in land finance in China. This study explores the following two research questions: First, what major reforms of the land-use rights system (LURS) have been carried out in China? Second, what are the implications of the evolution of China's land management system for China and other developing countries?

This study, mainly based on a comprehensive review and analysis of relevant documents, academic works, and historical data, aims to analyze the evolution of the land system in the People's Republic of China (PRC) after 1979. This study will focus on a discussion of the interaction between the state and the market concerning the reform of the LURS, and will identify the significant milestones and underlying forces behind the development of the LURS during the past three decades. In the first section, a review of the evolution of China's land system and the LURS reform will be presented in chronological order, followed in the second section by a discussion of the contributions and the risks brought about by the LURS reform and local government land finance activities. The last section concludes and presents policy implications.

2.2 The Evolution of China's Land System and Land Finance

The Chinese government gradually eliminated private ownership of land after the founding of the PRC in 1949. After a series of structural and institutional reforms, almost all of the rural land in the country was owned by rural collectives, and urban land by the state, when the Cultural Revolution ended in 1976. During this era, China's land system featured strict state control over land distribution, land allocation free of charge by the state, and non-transferable land-use rights (Xie et al. 2002; Zhang 1997).

When China opened its door to embrace foreign investment, land became a bottleneck for the state to attract capital. The Chinese government, modeling on Hong Kong's experience, has promoted a land tenure system with public ownership to deal with this issue (Zhang and Pearlman 2004). Under this system, the land-use rights in the urban area could be leased to non-state actors, including foreign companies, while rural land could be converted into urban land before the lease of its land-use rights to land users.

Since the first case of the paid conveyance of land use rights took place in Shenzhen (on the border with Hong Kong), Guangdong Province in 1987, the land-use rights system has experienced substantial institutional changes. In this process, market forces have been playing an increasingly important role in the institutional design of the LURS. The Chinese socialist state has also loosened its tight control over land use rights (Chan 1999; Yeh and Wu 1999).

In 1990, the paid conveyance of land use rights became legalized across the country with the approval of the National People's Congress (Tang 1989). It was not until 2002, more than one decade later, that market-oriented land transaction modes became legal requirements for the paid conveyance of land-use rights (Wang et al. 2011). In correspondence with these significant milestones, this study roughly divides the development trajectory of the LURS into three phrases: 1979–1990, 1991–2002, and 2003–present.

2.2.1   The First Stage of the LURS (1979–1990)

Economic liberalization began with the open-door policy of 1978 and resulted in a demand for land-use reform. Since 1979, foreign and overseas Chinese capital has started to flow into China, pushing the Chinese government to re-examine and deal with the land-use issue (Yeh and Wu 1996; Ho and Lin 2003). On July 1st, 1979, the People's Congress passed *The Sino-Foreign Joint Ventures Enterprises Law* (1979), which marked the start of the 'free' land-use (*wuchang shiyong*) policy. In the same year, a real estate company owned by the Shenzhen Municipal Construction Commission, a government organization, signed a contract with a Hong Kong company, in which both sides agreed that the profits of a real estate project, whose land was provided by the Shenzhen Municipal Government, were to be proportionally shared by both sides (Tang 1989). This was the first case in which land was treated as property, and a price for land-use rights was charged on the transaction between the Chinese side and a foreign investor. More importantly, this case signified that land had its price, and should not be allocated to users for free.

On July 26th, 1980, the State Council (1980), the chief administrative authority of the Chinese government, promulgated the *Tentative Regulations on Land-use for Sino-Foreign Joint Enterprises*, requiring all foreign enterprises to pay for land-use rights (Zhang 1997). This regulation marked the beginning of the paid use of urban land in China. In the following years, a number of municipalities, such as Shenzhen, Shanghai, Guangzhou, Dalian, Hangzhou, Qingdao, Chongqing, and Nanjing, promulgated their own regulations concerning how to charge fees for urban land-use by China-foreign joint enterprises. In the period of 1980–1987, the experiments with charging land-use fees were only carried out in the Pearl River Delta region, including Shenzhen, Guangzhou, and Foshan (Dowall 1993; Yeh and Wu 1995), and were mostly limited to land-use involving foreign investments. Furthermore, land leasing was still forbidden, and the land-use fee was normally set at a level lower than the true land value (Zhang 1997).

2.2.1.1   The Pilot Reform of the LURS in Shenzhen and Shanghai

The reform of the LURS was piloted in two important cities in China, namely Shenzhen—the neighboring city of Hong Kong—and Shanghai, and then spread to the whole country. This was a fundamental step to establishing the LURS in China. When the Shenzhen Special Economic Zone was founded in 1979, the Chinese policy makers, such as Deng Xiaoping, pointed out that Shenzhen would function as a role model for other cities in the country during the reform era.

Since its founding, the Shenzhen government had initiated a series of reforms in a variety of institutional and socioeconomic aspects, including urban planning, infrastructure construction, the labor market, the capital market, the information market, the foreign exchange market, and so forth. Due to the lack of a legalized open land market, land-use rights could not be traded in Shenzhen, however (Liu 2008). Even without a legal land market, land transactions frequently occurred on the black market; but these transactions could not be fully monetized to generate revenue for urban infrastructure because there wasn't a legal land market.

By the end of 1986, the Shenzhen government had spent CNY 1.35 billion in infrastructure construction, among which CNY 670 million was bank loans with a total annual debt service (i.e. interest charge) of CNY 50 million. The Shenzhen government, however, had only generated CNY 38 million in total revenue via charging land-use fees, which could not even cover the annual debt service (Liu 2008). Thus, under a great burden to finance urban infrastructure construction, the Shenzhen government attempted to explore institutional innovations to alleviate the financial burden.

In the second half of 1987, the Shenzhen government attempted to separate urban land ownership and urban land-use rights, and conveyed land-use rights from the state to industrial and commercial users in the forms of negotiations (*xieyi*), tenders (*zhaobiao*), and auctions (*paimai*). On September 9th, 1987, the Shenzhen government for the very first time (also the first time nationally) conveyed the land-use rights of a piece of land to a Shenzhen company at a price of CNY 200 (USD 24) per m^2 in the form of a negotiation. The tenure of the land-use rights was 50 years. In the following several months, the Shenzhen government conveyed the land-use rights in the forms of tenders and auctions, respectively, to industrial and commercial users. On December 29th, 1987, *Land Management Ordinance of Shenzhen Special Economic Zone* (1987) was promulgated and laid a legal foundation for the leasehold-based land-use rights system in Shenzhen, and the practice had immediately spread to other cities in the Pearl River Delta region (Zhang 1997).

Although Shenzhen's practice gained much media attention, Shanghai's practice of land-use rights conveyance followed a more rigorous procedure. First, in 1987, the Shanghai municipal government promulgated a regulation coupled with six detailed implementation directives for land-use rights conveyance. Later on, in 1988, the Shanghai municipal government asked the tenders to bid for the land. As a result, three out of six tenders were from overseas, including the United States, Japan and Hong Kong, which made the auctions competitive. In consequence, the Shanghai government collected more land conveyance fees than originally expected (Zhang 1997).

2.2.1.2   A Nationwide Implementation of the LURS

The LURS was promoted across the country after the successful pilot reforms in Shenzhen and Shanghai. A number of laws and the Constitution were made to facilitate the implementation of the LURS. In 1988, at the First Session of the Seventh People's Congress of the PRC, the paid conveyance of land-use rights (*tudi youchang zhuanrang*) was made official. Perhaps more significantly, the clause "land use right can be transacted according to the law" was added to Article 10, Section 4 of *The Constitution of the PRC* (1988) (Deng and Huang 2004). This legal amendment to *The Constitution of the PRC* was endorsed by the National People's Congress on April 12th, 1988 (Tang 1989). Furthermore, in 1988, the State Council (1988) promulgated *A Tentative Regulation of China's Land-use Tax in Cities and Towns*, which granted permission to local governments to collect land-use taxes and fees. In May 1990, the State Council permitted foreign capital to enter the real estate market in Mainland China. In June, the State Council (1990) promulgated *A Tentative Regulation for China's Urban Land Rights Conveyance and Transfer*, in which the detailed provisions for land conveyance and transfers were articulated. More importantly, this regulation laid a foundation for the establishment of a land market, where the price mechanism could play a role in the process of land-use rights conveyance and transfer. These milestone events in the late 1980s, and especially in 1990, opened up urban land markets and a new era for lawful land transactions nationwide in China (Dowall 1993).

2.2.2   The Second Stage of the LURS (1991–2002)

The years between 1991 and 2002 were a critical period for land management in China. Since the early 1990s, an urban land market has developed along with the Chinese style market economy and the legal framework of the land market has been put in place (Xie et al. 2002). Before discussing the new developments in the land-use rights system in the period 1990–2002, it is necessary to analyze the structure of China's land market and the role of actors in the development of China's land market.

2.2.2.1   The Structure of China's Land Market and the Role of Different Actors

In the existing literature, researchers prefer to divide the current land market into three sub-markets namely, the requisition of rural land (**I**), the conveyance of land-use rights (**II**), and the transfer of paid land-use rights (**III**) (Yeh and Wu 1996) (Table. 2.1).

Table 2.1 Urban land markets in China

Transaction types	Land markets	Actors	Subject of transaction	Transaction prices
I-1 Acquisition of rural land for administrative allocation	Land ownership market	Buyer: the state Seller: rural collectives User: work unit	Land ownership	Requisition fee
I-2 Acquisition of rural land for leasing	Land ownership market	Buyer: the state Seller: rural collectives User: industrial and commercial users	Land ownership	Requisition fee
II-1 Conveyance of LURs by acquisition of rural land	Market of the conveyance of LURs	Buyer: land-user Seller: the state	Land-use rights (LURs)	Land price
II-2 Conveyance of LURs by acquisition of urban land	Market of the conveyance of LURs	Buyer: land-user Seller: the state	LURs	Land price
II-3 Conveyance of LURs by marketing of administratively allocated land	Market of the conveyance of LURs	Buyer: new user Seller: the state	LURs	Payment to the state and existing user
III Transfer of paid LURs	Market of the transfer of LURs	Buyer: land-user Seller: land-user	Paid LURs	Land price

Source Adapted from Yeh and Wu (1996), p. 340

(I) The Land-ownership market: the requisition of rural land

According to Article 2 of the *Land Administration Law* (1998), rural land, whose property rights are collectively owned, could be requisitioned by the state "in the public interest," whereby villagers who lose their land would be entitled to compensation.[1] The land ownership will be converted from rural collective-owned into state-owned after the requisition of rural land. The requisition of rural land could serve for administrative allocation or lease arrangement for commercial purposes.

---

[1]Rural areas where land is state-owned are not included in the cases of requisition. Moreover, according to the Constitution of the PRC adopted on September 20th, 1954, requisition by the state would be the only way to change the rural collective land into the state-owned land.

The procedure for the requisition of rural land for allocation purposes is as follows: On behalf of the state, local governments acquire rural land from rural collectives and convert it into urban land; and then, local governments grant the use rights of the requisitioned rural land to the intended users—work units (*danwei*), such as government bodies, public schools, public hospitals, and state-owned enterprises. The holding period for land that has been requisitioned for administrative allocation is unlimited; it is a 'freehold'. This requisition procedure existed during the pre-reform era. In a requisition of rural land for leasing, the intended land-users are industrial and commercial users rather than work units.

Due to the monopoly power of the state in this process, the requisition of rural land is neither based on market price nor following market mechanisms. The compensation paid to land-lost villagers is usually lower in the first type than in the second type of requisition (Xie et al. 2002).

(**II**) Market for the conveyance of land-use rights

The major actors in the market for the conveyance of land-use rights are the state and urban land-users. As the only supplier of land-use rights in this market, the government alone conveys land-use rights to land-users. In practice, local governments represent the state in the conveyance of land-use rights and collect land conveyance fees. Specifically, the state-owned land available to the market for conveyance comes from three different sources. The first source is the rural land requisitioned from rural collectives in the aforementioned land-ownership market. The second source is the existing urban land, which is taken back by local governments from the existing urban land-users with compensation. The third source involves the commoditization of administratively allocated urban land. In this market, users hold the tenancy for a certain period of time. The longest period for land-use rights is 70 years for residential land while the period of occupation is 50 years for industrial, educational, cultural, health, sports or mixed use, and 40 years for commercial, entertainment and tourism use (Zhang 1997).

(**III**) Market for the transfer, sub-lease and mortgage of land-use rights

According to the *Land Administration Law* (1998), land-use rights purchased by industrial and commercial users may be transferred, sub-leased, and mortgaged. The main actors in this market have little to do with the government in theory; thus, it is beyond the discussion of this study. This study mainly focuses on the market for the conveyance of land-use rights from which local governments have collected a colossal amount of land conveyance fees as their own-source revenue.

2.2.2.2   The New Developments in the Land Market

From 1988 to 1992, China experienced a "rectification period" from an overheated economy to an economic downturn (Brandt and Rawski 2008). Even though there was no land boom during that time period, the scale of land transactions surpassed that in the late 1980s. Since 1992, inspired by Deng Xiaoping's Southern Tour, reasserting his Open Door policy and economic reform, and the 14th National Congress of the Chinese Communist Party in which the establishment of a socialist market economy was made a national strategy, China entered into a new epoch of fast-track economic development.

The land market, as one of the most important components in the Chinese economy, had started a round of high-speed development (Zhang 1997). In 1993, the total number of land conveyance cases reached 440,000 with a total turnover of CNY 123.1 billion (Liu 2008). Land conveyance activities expanded nationwide, from coastal to interior regions. Land conveyance fees had become critical extra-budgetary revenue for local governments (Lin 2007). By the first half of 1994, all of the provinces, municipalities, and autonomous regions in China had implemented the LURS and collected land conveyance fees.

For the sake of attracting investment to promote economic development and employment growth, local governments were eager to set up a variety of "development zones" and "economic zones." Up until the end of 1992, more than 6,000 development zones were being launched across the country, gobbling up more than 1,600,000 hectares of agricultural land (Cartier 2001). The number of land conveyance cases and the total turnover from land conveyance fees had been on the increase from 1987 to 2001, even though it dropped somewhat from 1995 to 1999 with the macroeconomic crunch (see Fig. 2.1).

Among the vast majority of land conveyance cases, to attract investment, local governments arbitrarily undervalued land prices, and even adopted the "zero-premium" strategy when conveying land-use rights to investors (Chan 1999; Cartier 2001; Tao et al. 2010). The prices and areas of land involved were not subject to the mechanism of supply and demand, but were largely maneuvered by local governments. "Negotiation", wherein local governments negotiated with the developers on land prices, was the most commonly used approach in the land conveyance transactions during that time period (Zhu 2005). Table 2.2 reveals the number and percentage of land conveyances based on negotiations in the total number of conveyances for city governments in China.

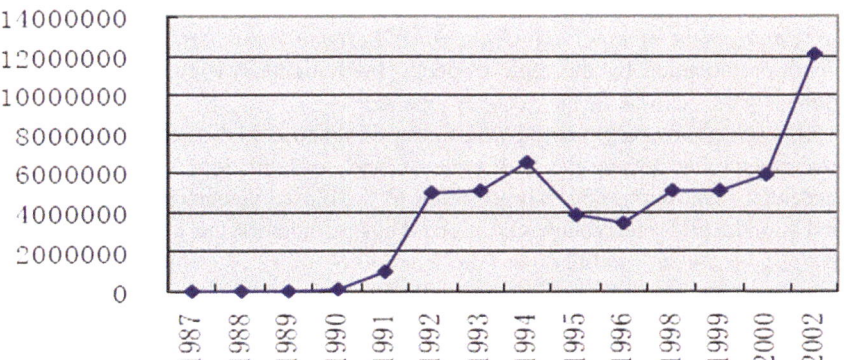

Fig. 2.1 Amount of land conveyance fees. *Unit* CNY 10,000. *Source China Land and Resource Almanac, 1987–2003*

Table 2.2 Number and percentage of land conveyance cases by negotiation for municipal governments

Year	Average number of cases	Negotiated transfer	Market-based transfer
1999	290.3	249.7 (80.0%)	50.6 (20.0%)
2000	374.5	321.1 (85.7%)	53.4 (14.3%)
2001	519.2	442.8 (85.3%)	66.4 (14.7%)
2002	597.4	472.8 (79.1%)	116.6 (20.9%)

Source See Tao et al. 2010, p. 2228

The rampant negotiation-based land transaction gave rise to various problems, including corruption, inefficient use of land, land hoarding, the engulfment of prime agricultural land, and so forth. From 1999 to 2000, there were more than 510,000 cases involving land law violations. To solve these problems, it was not until 2002 that the Ministry of Land and Resources (2002) promulgated the *Provisions for the Conveyance of State-owned Land by Tender, Auction and Open Listing* to put a stop to the commonly used negotiation-based conveyance of land-use rights. It required that "land conveyance involving commercial, tourist, and residential uses of land must be traded in the form of tenders, auctions, and open listings." Thus, the year 2002 marked another significant milestone in the development of the LURS. Since then, a market-oriented LURS has been legally established, even though in practice it has encountered strong resistance from local governments.

2.2.2.3 The Allocation of Land Conveyance Fees

The allocation of land conveyance fees among different levels of government had been bargained for since the fledging stage of the LURS in the late 1980s, and moved towards fiscal decentralization as local governments had later gained more discretion to collect and dispose land conveyance fees (Zhang 1997; Peterson and Annez 2007). Originally, according to *The Ordinance Concerning Strengthening the Management of the Paid Conveyance Revenue from State-owned Land-use Rights* promulgated by the State Council (1989) in May 1989, the central government retained 40% of land conveyance fees.

This split, however, incurred widespread indignation and discontent since local governments had to pay the high price of land consolidation, land development, residential demolition, and compensation to land-lost villagers before leasing the land to industrial and commercial users. Thus, to address the local demands, the central government modified the ratio from 40:60 to 32:68, with the central government getting the 32% (Zhang 2008). However, this minor change did not encourage local governments to lease more lands. Many local governments chose to hide the real number of land conveyance cases and the fees they collected to avoid remitting it to the central government. In 1992, the central government announced a compromise in the allocation of land conveyance fees, allowing its local agents to

Table 2.3 Price difference between land requisition and land conveyance fees

Year	Price of land requisition (P1)	Land conveyance fees (P2)	Price difference	P2/P1
1987	1.77	223.46	221.69	126.25
1988	1.84	106.98	105.14	58.14
1989	1.92	71.53	69.61	37.26
1990	2.13	32.99	30.86	15.49
1991	2.35	509.35	507	216.74
1992	2.49	385.46	382.97	154.80
1993	2.71	89.15	86.44	32.90
1994	2.99	131.44	128.45	43.96
1995	3.83	90.05	86.22	23.51
1996	4.64	102.56	97.92	22.10
1998	7.09	81.81	74.72	11.54
1999	12.03	113.31	101.28	9.42
2000	11.71	122.46	110.75	10.46
2001	10.42	143.36	132.94	13.76
2002	10.89	194.54	183.65	17.86
Average	5.25	159.90	154.64	52.95

Unit CNY 1/m^2

Source China Land and Resource Almanac and *China Statistical Yearbook*, 1987–2002

keep 95% of the land conveyance fees. When the tax-sharing reform[2] was launched by the central government in 1994, in order to mitigate local governments' fiscal budgetary deficits, the central authority allowed local governments to retain the land conveyance fees (Liu 2008; Zhang 2008). This was an important step towards the decentralized management of land finance, which greatly inspired local governments' enthusiasm to lease land for gaining extra-budgetary revenue.

With respect to the financial relationship between local governments and land-lost villagers, the latter are under an adverse situation because the compensation received by them is usually far below the land revenue collected by local governments (Yep and Fong 2009). According to the *Land Administration Law* (1998), land-lost villagers would be entitled to compensation with the highest level being 30 times of the annual average agricultural output value in the 3 years before the requisition. However, in real practice, the calculation of the "annual agricultural output value" was problematic, and the compensation was kept very low. Table 2.3 summarizes, from 1987 to 2002, the average price the government paid to villagers in land requisition and the average price collected by the government through

---

[2]The bulk of tax-based revenue is collected by the central government while local governments shoulder substantial responsibility for providing basic public services such as education and health care to the general public. On the impact of the tax-sharing system reform wherein expenditure remains decentralized while revenue has been recentralized, see Wu (2012).

leasing land to industrial and commercial users. The price difference is a true reflection of the exploitation of land-lost villagers under China's land administrative system (Ding 2007; Yep and Fong 2009).

To sum up, from 1990 to 2002, China's land market experienced a stage of fast development, during which local governments were enthusiastic about setting up various "economic zones" to attract investment. However, it caused a series of problems in land administration, in particular, the encroachment on arable land. Due to the lack of relevant laws and regulations, the vast majority of land conveyance cases relied on backdoor negotiation rather than market-oriented transaction during the entire 1990s and the early 2000s. This situation resulted in low transparency, insufficient market competition, inefficient land-use, land hoarding, and rampant corruption.

2.2.3 The Third Stage of the LURS (2003–Present)

In the third stage of the LURS, the Chinese central government aims to utilize the Chinese land tenure system to promote economic development while curtailing local governments' predatory behaviors. To address the problems of negotiation-based land conveyance and to integrate land conveyance fees into the budgetary system, the Chinese central government promulgated a series of regulations governing land conveyance activities beginning in 2002 (Zhu 2005). The market-oriented transaction approaches, the land fund (*tudi jijin*), and the land reserve center (*tudi chubei zhongxin*) are the three most important institutions established to improve the LURS and land administration. The market-oriented transaction approach plays a fundamental role in the LURS, ensuring a market-based allocation of land resources. The land fund is an institution designed to help consolidate land conveyance fees, an important category of extra-budgetary revenue, into the budget system. It means that local governments cannot hide land revenue from public scrutiny. The land reserve center has been set up for the sake of achieving sustainable utilization of land resources and avoiding intergenerational inequity (Liu 2008).

2.2.3.1 Market-Oriented Land Conveyance

The market-oriented transaction approaches are essential to the LURS, playing a fundamental role in reducing government intervention and manipulation in the land market. In 2002, the Ministry of State Land and Resources promulgated the *Regulations Concerning the Approaches of Tender, Auction and Open Listing in the Conveyance of State-owned Land*, which mandated local governments to use tender, auction or open listing as the transaction approaches for land conveyance cases involving commercial, tourist, and residential uses of land (Zhu 2005).

The procedure of tenders (*zhaobiao*) includes several steps. First, the local land administration bureau publishes a tender notice and provides relevant documents to potential bidders. Second, bidders then turn in sealed bids together with the payment of a deposit to the land administration bureau before the deadline. Third, public officials from the land administration bureau together with external experts assess and select the finalists based on certain criteria. Fourth, a land-use contract will be awarded to the successful bidder. In the meantime, all unsuccessful bidders will be informed about the result in writing (Zhang 1997).

Auctions (*paimai*), or English auctions, are usually announced publicly by local governments. During the auction, bidders offer their prices against each other. The bidder who offers the highest price obtains the land (Cai et al. 2009).

The open listing (*guapai*) method is also called a two-stage auction. Open listing is also announced in advance as local governments offer the details of the land parcel. A key difference is that an open listing has two stages. When the auction starts, the first stage takes 10 working days. During the first stage, bids are posted by the land administration bureau. If only one bidder has submitted a bid and the bid price is higher than the baseline price, that bidder is assigned the property at its bid price. In this situation, the open listing process ends, and the second stage will not start. If there is more than one bidder, the one with the highest bid price wins the bid. Similarly, the open listing process ends, and the second stage will not start. But suppose at the end of the 10 working days, there are still more than two bidders trying to update their bid prices; in that case, the second stage, which is the English auction, will start. The one who offers the highest price in the English auction will win the open listing.[3]

The promulgation of the regulations governing the establishment of tenders, auctions and open listings as a means of leasing land-use rights was a significant milestone in improving the institutional framework of the LURS in China. Nevertheless, it encountered hidden resistance from local authorities because it limited their freedom to grant land to their preferred land-users (Zhu 2005). Previously, to attract industrial investment, local governments used the strategy of "low-premium" or even "zero-premium" through negotiation. This new regulation implemented in 2002 literally prevented them from doing so. Thus, local governments initiated various approaches to circumvent this regulation.

For instance, local governments sought loopholes in the regulation, which stated that land conveyance involving "commercial, tourist, and residential use of land" must take the form of tender, auction or open listing; but whether or not this regulation should be applied to "industrial" use of land was legally ambiguous. Thus, local officials tended to tamper with the process by passing off other types of land-use as an industrial use, and leased land at unreasonably low prices (Yu 2005).

According to the statistics released by the Ministry of State Land and Resources, the number of instances of land conveyance in the form of tender, auction or open listing accounted for only 28.8% of the total number of land conveyance transactions in the first half of 2004 (Ministry of Land and Resources of PRC, 2004). For

---

[3]Cai et al. (2009) argue that the open listing approach of land transaction is more likely to be subject to corruption than tender and auction.

most cases of land conveyance involving land conversion from agricultural use to non-agricultural use, the negotiation approach was still the most frequently adopted. A report released by the National Audit Office in 2006 revealed that among the 87 investigated development zones, 60 were illegally leasing land-use rights at arbitrarily low prices. This resulted in a loss of land conveyance fees of about CNY 5.6 billion (Gu 2006).

Over the period of 2002–2007, the Ministry of State Land and Resources promulgated a series of strict regulations to further rectify the land market and to strengthen the dominant role of market forces on land conveyance activities (Zhou 2007). In 2007, market-based land conveyance finally became the major type of land conveyance activity in the land market.

2.2.3.2 Land Fund: The Budgetary Control of Land Conveyance Fees

Since its inception, the LURS has arguably favored urban areas for two reasons. First, local governments turned a large amount of agricultural land into non-agricultural land, but the land-lost villagers received extremely low compensation when compared with the price at which the local government leased the newly requisitioned land to industrial and commercial users. Second, the majority of land conveyance fees flowed into urban regions and financed urban construction rather than public expenditure in rural areas (Jiang 2006).

To change this urban-rural imbalance, in early 2004, the State Council issued a document requiring local governments to devote at least 15% of the net land conveyance fees (i.e. the gross land conveyance fees after deducting the cost of land development) to public expenditure in rural areas (Liu 2008). Moreover, Wen Jiabao, the then Chinese Premier, emphasized at different government meetings in 2006 that the revenue local governments received by leasing land requisitioned from villagers should be used for public expenditures in rural areas. However, Lin and Ho (2005) observe that "[The] Chinese socialist state is better seen as a dynamic, complex, heterogeneous, and self-conflicting institutional ensemble in and through which the forces and interests of different levels of the state are contested, negotiated, and mediated" (p. 411). As these fees were a type of extra-budgetary revenue, the local People's Congress had no power to monitor its usage under the legal budgetary framework.

In December 2006, the State Council promulgated the *Notice regarding Standardizing the Management of Revenues and Expenditures from the Transfer of State Land-use Rights*, stipulating the requirement for local governments to create land funds under the formal budgetary system. This regulation required local governments to turn over the land conveyance fees to the local treasury as one category of "funds" and spend it according to budgetary arrangements. Thereby, since 2007, local governments have integrated most of their land conveyance fees into land funds. Thus, transparency and accountability in the management and the use of land conveyance fees have improved substantially (Liu 2008). Nevertheless, it should be noted that the management of land conveyance fees is still different from budgetary revenue in China's local state. Local governments still enjoy considerable discretion over the collection and usage of land conveyance fees, with limited oversight by local People's Congresses and higher levels of government (Ye and Wang 2013).[4]

2.3 Contributions and Risks of Land Finance in China

Land conveyance fees have functioned as important revenue streams for Chinese local governments in the twin process of rapid urbanization and industrialization, in particular, contributing to capital accumulation and infrastructure construction. However, the dependence of local governments upon land conveyance fees has also resulted in some challenges and potential risks both economically and politically. In this section, this study investigates both the merits and disadvantages of land finance.

2.3.1 Contributions of China's Land-Use Rights System

China's land-use rights system contributes substantially to urbanization, industrialization, and broadly the market economy in China. Since the economic reform, the state's control over the land market has been challenged by the introduction of market-based land allocation. Economic considerations have played a more significant role than political ideology in the institutional design of land-use policies. Therefore, land finance and the land-use rights system reform have contributed to the growth of China's transition to a market economy. More importantly, since 1987, land conveyance fees have become a vital source of funding for urban infrastructure projects, greatly contributing to local infrastructure upgrades in China (Cao and Zhao 2011).

Table 2.4 presents the revenues that are generated from different sources and invested in urban infrastructure projects. According to official interpretation, the category 'Other' contains mixed revenues, including land conveyance fees, urban infrastructure fee (chengshi jichusheshi peitaofei) and the sale of state-owned assets and other fees (Wang et al. 2011). During the past ten years, land conveyance fees have grown substantially and have been the most important component of the category 'Other,' carrying much more weight than other components. Table 2.4 reveals that the amount of revenue from the category 'Other' increased from CNY 7,792 million to CNY 278,570 million, an increase of 3500%. From the same data source, Fig. 2.2 shows that the revenue from the category 'Other' had been the

---

[4]Some local governments have experimented on reviewing land fund under the budgetary framework. See Xiamen City's comprehensive budgetary review: http://www.xmrd.gov.cn/dygz/201506/t20150624_1136224.htm.

Table 2.4 Revenue for urban infrastructure by sources (1990–2007)

Year	Total	Urban construction and maintenance tax	Central grant	Local grant	Public utility surcharge	Water resource fee	Domestic loan	Foreign investment	Self-raised fund	Other
1990	21,049	6,509	1,091	1,984	2,262	279	884	247		7,792
1991	26,612	6,957	999	2,776	2,701	353	2,930	1,071		9,462
1992	39,348	7,797	1,342	5,766	3,109	425	3,226	735		16,948
1993	58,119	9,802	2,696	5,946	3,296	485	4,457	1,382		30,055
1994	67,480	11,612	2,136	5,994	4,139	471	4,133	1,833		37,163
1995	77,437	14,091	2,135	7,258	4,474	520	4,767	2,549		41,645
1996	84,764	15,781	1,037	8,626	5,559	605	9,569	5,587	11,947	26,053
1997	111,034	19,067	1,394	11,542	5,612	612	16,574	14,072	10,780	31,381
1998	143,332	21,532	6,494	15,810	6,040	637	30,696	7,384	17,694	37,044
1999	162,712	21,920	10,520	17,146	6,316	778	37,420	4,945	23,748	39,920
2000	198,893	23,729	11,507	20,813	5,415	1,006	41,470	8,471	33,322	53,160
2001	252,627	27,094	8,958	32,378	4,881	1,111	74,166	5,632	40,956	57,451
2002	315,618	31,604	7,595	39,273	4,988	1,238	87,390	6,105	60,076	77,348
2003	427,619	37,174	7,713	53,293	5,569	1,598	133,183	6,811	76,968	105,311
2004	525,760	44,629	5,264	66,577	5,903	2,069	144,555	7,418	90,020	159,325
2005	542,251	55,129	6,216	79,589	5,548	2,500	166,989	9,271	94,603	122,406
2006	354,063	56,677	5,666	107,485	7,622	2,445				174,167
2007	476,175	61,706	3,481	121,379	8,243	2,795				278,570

Unit CNY 1 million

Source *Statistical Yearbook of China's Urban Construction 2007*. Department of General Finance, Ministry of Housing, Urban and Rural Construction (2008) with reference to Wang et al. (2011), pp. 2982–2983

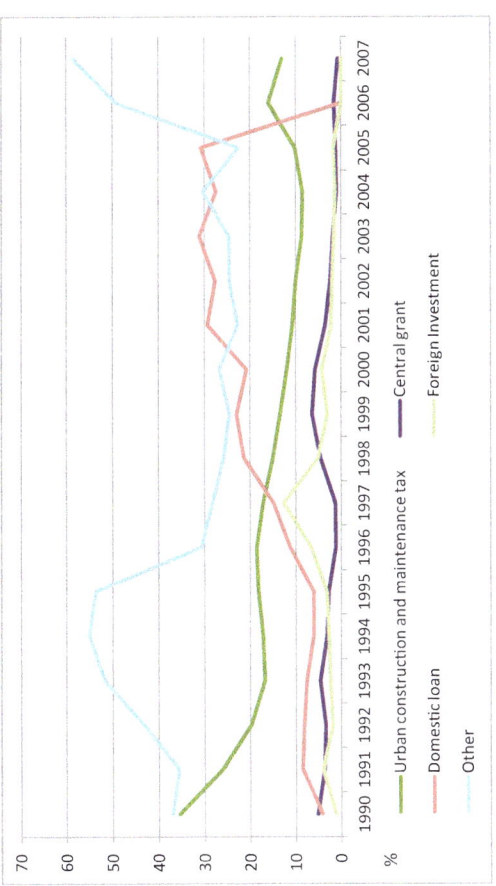

Fig. 2.2 Percentage of different resources in infrastructure financing. *Source Statistical Yearbook of China's Urban Construction 2007*, Department of General Finance, Ministry of Housing, Urban and Rural Construction (2008)

most important component among the different revenue sources, and accounted for nearly 60% of the total revenue for urban infrastructure projects. In particular, as suggested by Wang et al. (2011), for county-level governments, which more often than not have little financial capital but control a large amount of rural land, revenue generated from converting rural land to urban land has become an important source of funds for financing infrastructure.

2.3.2 Problems and Risks

2.3.2.1 Risk of Property Bubble Bursting

Although the causal relations between housing prices and land prices are not entirely clear, there is no denying the correlations between these two items (Kuang 2005; Gao and Mao 2003). During the past decade, there has been a real estate boom in China, and housing prices in urban regions, especially in the metropolitan cities (e.g. Beijing, Shanghai, Shenzhen), rose rapidly. The skyrocketing price of houses and apartments was partially attributable to the rising land prices charged by local governments. As a matter of fact, many local governments have relied on continually rising land values for financing local infrastructure. In addition, local government borrowing is often backed up by state-owned land.

In order to promote economic growth, around 8,800 investment vehicles have been set up by local governments to take up massive infrastructure projects during the past decade (Su and Zhao 2006). Due to institutional constraints on local government borrowing behavior, these vehicles, namely urban development investment corporations (UDICs), have sprung up in a relatively short period.

Using land as collateral, local governments attempt to obtain substantial bank loans for infrastructure projects. Victor Shih estimated total bank lending to UDICs had ballooned to CNY 20 trillion (about USD 3.16 trillion), or around 40% of Chin's Gross Domestic Product in 2010 (Credit Suisse 2010). If a big drop in the value of the land occurs, a series of financial crises could be triggered. Thus, land finance may be associated with the potential risk of a property bubble burst.

2.3.2.2 The Unsustainable Nature and Volatility of Land Finance

Given the fluctuation of the property market, the question remains as to whether or not cities can depend on land conveyance fees as an important funding source of infrastructure development (Wang et al. 2011). The current practice of land finance is unsustainable because land conveyance fees are basically a major, extra source of revenue for local governments. The fast pace of land conversion from agricultural to non-agricultural use has also harmed villagers' interests (Chau and Zhang 2011; Deng et al. 2006; Lichtenberg and Ding 2008; Zhu and Huang 2007).

According to the statistics of the Ministry of Land and Resources, the cultivated land area dropped from 130.0 million hectares in 1996 to 123.4 million hectares in 2003 (Lin and Ho 2003). However, some data based on remote sensing and detailed surveys suggested a much worse scenario (Lichtenberg and Ding 2008). Moreover, the land price fluctuates severely.

Land-leasing revenue will drop when the demand for public investment in infrastructure projects declines. Based on the data from *China Land and Resource Almanac* (1999–2009) and *China Data Online* (1999–2009), we calculated the ratio of total land conveyance fees to the total budgetary revenue of sub-provincial governments, in order to measure the degree to which Chinese local governments rely on land finance. The results reveal that this ratio was only 11.7% nationwide in 1999, but hit a historic high of 73.7% in 2003, and fluctuated largely within the range of 45–70% in the following years. In this respect, land finance is volatile and unstable.

In addition, a big potential risk to local finance is that the proceeds from land sales or land leases may be put to use for financing operating expenditures, which is likely to induce the dependence of local operating budgets on those proceeds. It may also aggravate the expansion of government employment as local governments have more money to pay public sector wages. This could substantially increase the volatility of the entire budget system.

2.3.2.3 Rampant Corruption and Social Unrest

The real estate sector and the land market have witnessed rampant corrupt activities. The decentralized management of land assets grants local governments the power to monopolize the planning, development and leasing of land. Government officials can make money through abusing this power. "Possessing the power to decide whether or not, how, to whom, and at what price, to lease the land, they can easily abuse that power by requesting bribes from interested individuals or institutions" (Gong 1997, p. 280). Even though the introduction of the market-based transaction approach may reduce corruption, the land market is still subject to corrupt activities due to the strong government control over the land market (Cai et al. 2009). In 2004, the *China Daily* wrote:

> China's Ministry of Lands and Resources announced new measures to crack down on corruption and inefficiency in the land sector. The new rules *forbid officials to receive personal benefits from parties under their administration.* It is estimated that in 2003, the country faced 168,000 violations of its Land Law. (Cited from Cai et al. 2009)

In June 2008, according to the National Audit Office, governments in 11 cities, including Beijing and Shanghai, misused land conveyance fees substantially. Illegal land conveyance cases are rampant in China's major cities (Jia and Liu 2012).

Land corruption and land acquisition without a sufficient compensation have been one of the major triggers of social unrest. The land-lost villagers' sense of vulnerability mainly comes from the low level of compensation they receive and the high prices at which local governments lease the requisitioned land to commercial and industrial users. In addition to the low monetary compensation, relinquishing land has fundamental implications for rural people as they rely on land for food and even welfare support. Due to the insufficient provision of basic public goods in rural areas, losing land means that villagers have few assets to cushion themselves against any shocks in their lives (Yep and Fong 2009). By 2005, due to the government requisition of rural land, around 40 to 50 million villagers in China had lost their land. According to an estimate (Wen 2012), the number of land-lost villagers has been increasing by 2 to 3 million people per year. Such a colossal army of land-lost villagers may well be a time bomb for creating social unrest.

2.4 Conclusion

China's land reforms have some implications for the rest of the world. The sale or lease of the use rights of publicly owned land to the private sector is an approach adopted by local governments in China to finance public projects. Like other reforms in China since the late 1970s, land reforms started from scratch and gradually moved toward the separation of land-use rights from ownership. The separation of land-use rights from ownership, as the defining feature of China's land reform, can be viewed as a combination of economic capitalism and ideological socialism (Zhang 1997). This move has contributed to a substantial change in the urban landscape with some potential risks still unfolding.

From the late 1980s to the present, the Chinese government has gradually promulgated laws and regulations to institutionalize the market-oriented principles involved in the land-use rights system. These laws and regulations have replaced the negotiation approach with market-based approaches (i.e. tenders, auctions and open listings) for land conveyance activities and consolidated land conveyance fees into the budgets of local governments. Land revenue has also become more transparent to the general public, and land reserve centers have been set up to provide for sustainable land-use. All of these measures place China on the right track for developing a healthy and viable land administration system, which is one crucial component of the government's goal for the establishment of a market economy.

Land finance has made a substantial contribution to infrastructure financing, and has become one of the main drivers of China's urbanization and economic growth in the reform era. It remains controversial to allow local governments to retain 100% of the land conveyance fees. On the one hand, the arrangement may aggravate the risk of a housing market bubble as local governments have an incentive to boost the market. Nevertheless, on the other hand, land finance helps a local government enhance its fiscal capacity and promote its local economy.[5]

---

[5]As noted by Chen et al. (2017), local governments even use public housing programs to promote local economy. In general, Chinese local governments work like private corporations maximizing their profits. This leads to a number of problems and risks.

However, a variety of problems and risks caused by, or associated with, land finance deserves attention. The risk of a property bubble, land-related corruption, and possible social unrest may be a big hurdle for the Chinese economy in the future. The heavy reliance on land finance by local governments drives up the demand for limited land resources, which causes concerns about the sustainability of this development approach. Future reforms need to address these challenges when local governments rely on land assets as an important source of local government financing.

References

Brandt, L., & Rawski, T. G. (2008). *China's great economic transformation*. Cambridge: Cambridge University Press.

Cai, H., Henderson, J. V., & Zhang, Q. (2009). *China's land market auctions: Evidence of corruption* (No. w15067). National Bureau of Economic Research.

Cao, C., & Zhao, Z. (2011). *Funding China's urban infrastructure: Revenue structure and financing approaches*. Center for Transportation Studies, University of Minnesota.

Cartier, C. (2001). 'Zone fever', the arable land debate, and real estate speculation: China's evolving land use regime and its geographical contradictions. *Journal of Contemporary China, 10*(28), 445–469.

Chan, N. (1999). Land-use rights in mainland China: Problems and recommendations for improvement. *Journal of Real Estate Literature, 7*(1), 53–63.

Chau, N. H., & Zhang, W. (2011). Harnessing the forces of urban expansion: The public economics of farmland development allowances. *Land Economics, 87*(3), 488–507.

Chen, J., Yao, Li., & Wang, H. (2017). Development of public housing in post-reform China. *China & World Economy, 25*(4), 60–77.

Credit Suisse. (2010). Locking horns with China's bad loans. Retrieved from https://www.credit-suisse.com/conferences/aic/2012/en/reporter/day1/china_government_debt.jsp.

Deng, F. F., & Huang, Y. (2004). Uneven land reform and urban sprawl in China: The case of Beijing. *Progress in Planning, 61*(3), 211–236.

Deng, X., Huang, J., Rozelle, S., & Uchida, E. (2006). Cultivated land conversion and potential agricultural productivity in China. *Land Use Policy, 23*(4), 372–384.

Ding, C. (2007). Policy and praxis of land acquisition in China. *Land Use Policy, 24*(1), 1–13.

Dowall, D. E. (1993). Establishing urban land markets in the People's Republic of China. *Journal of the American Planning Association, 59*(2), 182–192.

Gao, B., & Mao, F. (2003). Fangjia yu dijia guanxi de shizheng jianyan: 1999–2002 [A test for relationship between estate price and land price: 1999–2002]. *Chanye Jingji Yanjiu [Industrial Economics Research], 3*(19), 19–25.

Gong, T. (1997). Forms and characteristics of China's corruption in the 1990s: Change with continuity. *Communist and Post-Communist Studies, 30*(3), 277–288.

Gu, W. (2006). Guojia jiaqiang tudi churangjin shouzhi guanli defang caizheng xian weiji [The state strengthened the management of land conveyance fees, local public finance is exposed to crisis]. Retrieved from http://finance.people.com.cn/GB/4823563.html.

Ho, S. P., & Lin, G. C. (2003). Emerging land markets in rural and urban China: Policies and practices. *The China Quarterly, 175*(3), 681–707.

Jia, K., & Liu, W. (2012). "Tudi caizheng:" fenxi yu chulu [Land finance: Analysis and resolutions]. *Caizheng Yanjiu [Public Finance Research], 1*, 2–9.

Jiang, F. (2006). Tudi churangjin de zhengshou shiyong yu guanli [The collection and management of land conveyance fees]. *Zhongguo Tudi [China Land], 5*, 17–18.

Kuang, W. (2005). Fangjia yu dijia guanxi yanjiu: moxing ji zhongguo shuju jianyan [The relation between housing price and land price: Model and Chinese data validation]. *Caimao Jingji [Finance & Trade Economics]*, (11), 56–63.

Lichtenberg, E., & Ding, C. (2008). Assessing farmland protection policy in China. *Land Use Policy, 25*(1), 59–68.

Lin, G. C. (2007). Reproducing spaces of Chinese urbanization: New city-based and land-centered urban transformation. *Urban Studies, 44*(9), 1827–1855.

Lin, G. C., & Ho, S. P. (2003). China's land resources and land-use change: Insights from the 1996 land survey. *Land Use Policy, 20*(2), 87–107.

Lin, G. C., & Ho, S. P. (2005). The state, land system, and land development processes in contemporary China. *Annals of the Association of American Geographers, 95*(2), 411–436.

Liu, Z. (2008). *Woguo tudi churangjin zhidu de lishi bianqian yanjiu* [A study on the historical changes of China' land conveyance fee system]. Unpublished Master thesis. Party School of the Central Committee of Communist Party of China, Beijing.

Peterson, G. E. (2006). *Land Leasing and Land Sale as An Infrastructure-financing Option* (Report No. 4043). World Bank Policy Research Working Paper.

Peterson, G. E. (2009). *Unlocking land values to finance urban infrastructure*. Washington, DC: The World Bank.

Peterson, G. E., & Annez, P. C. (Eds.). (2007). *Financing cities: Fiscal responsibility and urban infrastructure in Brazil, China, India*. Poland and South Africa: SAGE Publications.

Peterson, G. E., & Kaganova, O. (2010). *Integrating land financing into subnational fiscal management* No. Policy Research Working Paper 5409. Washington DC: World Bank.

Ping, X. (2006) *Woguo tudi caizheng guimo guji [Estimation of the size of land-based revenues in China]*. Newsletter No. 56, China Centre for Economic Research, Peking University.

Sagalyn, L. B. (1992). *Public development: Using land as a capital resource*. University of Pennsylvania.

Su, M., & Zhao, Q. (2006). *The Fiscal Framework and Urban Infrastructure Finance in China*. World Bank Publications, Vol. 4051.

Tang, Y. (1989). Urban land use in China: Policy issues and options. *Land Use Policy, 6*(1), 53–63.

Tao, R., Su, F., Liu, M., & Cao, G. (2010). Land leasing and local public finance in China's regional development: Evidence from prefecture-level cities. *Urban Studies, 47*(10), 2217–2236.

Wang, D., Zhang, L., Zhang, Z., & Zhao, S. X. (2011). Urban infrastructure financing in reform-era China. *Urban Studies, 48*(14), 2975–2998.

Wen, T. (2012). *Zhongguo shidi nongmin jiang chaoguo 1 yi* [The number of land-losing villagers will exceed 100 million]. Retrieved from http://opinion.hexun.com.tw/2012-12-05/148701100.html.

Wong, C. P. (1991). Central-local relations in an era of fiscal decline: The paradox of fiscal decentralization in post-Mao China. *The China Quarterly, 128,* 691–715.

Wu, A. M. (2012). Economic miracle and upward accountability: A preliminary evaluation of Chinese style of fiscal decentralization. *Asian Review of Public Administration, 23,* 104–120.

Xie, Q., Parsa, A. G., & Redding, B. (2002). The emergence of the urban land market in China: Evolution, structure, constraints and perspectives. *Urban Studies, 39*(8), 1375–1398.

Ye, F., & Wang, W. (2013). Determinants of land finance in China: A study based on provincial-level panel data. *Australian Journal of Public Administration, 72*(3), 293–303.

Ye, L., & Wu, A. M. (2014). Urbanization, land development, and land financing: Evidence from Chinese cities. *Journal of Urban Affairs, 36*(s1), 354–368.

Yeh, A. G. O., & Wu, F. (1995). Internal structure of Chinese cities in the midst of economic reform. *Urban Geography, 16*(6), 521–554.

Yeh, A. G. O., & Wu, F. (1996). The new land development process and urban development in Chinese cities. *International Journal of Urban and Regional Research, 20*(2), 330–353.

Yeh, A. G. O., & Wu, F. (1999). The transformation of the urban planning system in China from a centrally-planned to transitional economy. *Progress in Planning, 51*(3), 167–252.

Yep, R., & Fong, C. (2009). Land conflicts, rural finance and capacity of the Chinese state. *Public Administration and Development, 29*(1), 69–78.

Yu, Z. (2005). Guoyou tudi shiyongquan zhaopaigua churang shizheng fenxi [An empirical analysis of the conveyance of state-owned land by tender, auction and open listing]. *Zhongguo Fangdichan Jinrong [China Real-Estate Finance],* (5), 33–35.

Zhang, Q. (2008). Zhongxiang caizheng jingzheng, taojia huanjia yu zhongyang-difang de tudi shouru fencheng—dui 20 shiji 80 niandai yilai tudi shouru de kaocha [Vertical fiscal competition, bargaining, and the land revenue sharing relationship between central and local governments in China]. *Zhidu Jingjixue Yanjiu [Research of Institutional Economics], 4,* 107–127.

Zhang, X. Q. (1997). Urban land reform in China. *Land Use Policy, 14*(3), 187–199.

Zhang, S., & Pearlman, K. (2004). China's land use reforms: A review of journal literature. *Journal of Planning Literature, 19*(1), 16–61.

Zhou, Y. (2007). Yetan gongye yongdi zhaopaigua [A discussion of tender and auction in the conveyance of industrial land]. *Guotu Ziyuan [Land & Resources], 68,* 30–31.

Zhu, J. (2005). A transitional institution for the emerging land market in urban China. *Urban Studies, 42*(8), 1369–1390.

Zhu, L., & Huang, J. (2007). Chengzhenghua dui gendi yingxiang de yanjiu [Urbanization and cultivated land changes in China]. *Jingji Yanjiu [Economic Research Journal], 2*(1), 137–145.

Chapter 3
Public Services Evaluation from the Perspective of Public Risk Governance

Shangxi Liu and Chengwei Li

Abstract As the foundation of state governance, the key objective of public finance is to mitigate public risk. Public finance directly helps supply public services through raising public revenues, and minimize public risk and ensure fiscal sustainability. Further, governing fiscal risk can also provide a policy tool for controlling public risk. Therefore, the interacting relationships between public risk, public service, public revenue, and fiscal risk should be studied carefully. It is of great significance to get a balance between fiscal risk and public risk. Minimizing public risk with fiscal risk under control should be the ultimate goal for state governance and a benchmark for public service provision. The factors constraining fiscal risks might change over time and need to be considered in a sustainable and long term growth context. Additionally, it is important to focus on effectiveness of public service provision, or in other words, increasing the capacity to govern public risk. Despite the fact that there is relatively limited room for China to increase fiscal risk currently, the Chinese government can also achieve its public policy target by optimizing revenue structure, improving effectiveness of public service and capacity for public service provision, reforming central-provincial and local government relations. These are the theoretic and practical foundations for deepening fiscal reform and optimizing fiscal policy. Using the analytical framework developed in this article which links public service evaluation to public risk management, we argue that the gap between public service provision and the requirement of public risks governance can be reflected in fiscal risks. These are the key reasons why countries such as Greece, Spain and Ireland suffered from sovereign debt crisis in the recent past (see Ahmad et al. in MultiLevel finance and the euro crisis. Edward Elgar, 2016). Traditional theories on the role of government and public service provisions are based on public welfare theory and

This article was prepared in Chinese, "基于公共风险治理的公共服务评估", and translated by Kezhou Xiao, London School of Economics and Political Science. Dr. Shangxi Liu (email: mofliu@126.com), President of the Chinese Academy of Fiscal Sciences (CAFS). Dr. Chengwei Li, Deputy Director at CAFS.

S. Liu (✉) · C. Li
MOF Chinese Academy of Fiscal Sciences, Beijing, China
e-mail: mofliu@126.com

E. Ahmad et al. (eds.), *Fiscal Underpinnings for Sustainable Development in China*,
https://doi.org/10.1007/978-981-10-6286-5_3

market failure theory. When analyzing market failures, traditional theories urges a role played by the government to address market failures. There may also be government failures, and there is a new "positive" literature devoted to this topic (see Ahmad and Brosio in Handbook of multilevel finance. Edward Elgar, 2015 for a review). This provides a basis for our analysis in this paper.

3.1   Public Service Evaluation: An Analytical Framework

Why do we need public services? How to determine the extent and constraints to public service provision and the level of public services at each level of government? How to fund these public services while minimizing fiscal risks to overall sustainability? To answer these questions, it is necessary to discuss the nature of public service given the need to govern public risks.

3.1.1   The Nature and Function of Public Service: Public Risk Governance

The nature of public services is determined by a view on the role of government. Adam Smith divided the role of government into three parts: the first is to protect the nation from invasion, the second is to protect citizens in the society from being hurt through judicial institutions, and the third is to provide public infrastructure.[1] Assuming free market economy is justifiable (attaining justice and efficiency), the government can only step into the realm where market fails. Therefore, Admin Smith advocates that if the activity can be provided by market, then the government should serve only as a guardian. If there is no market failure, according to Smith, the government has no economic role. The public finance literatures did not go very far from this principle proposed by Smith, only adding a few contents. One of the additions to this line of thought is welfare economics. From the point of view of maximizing social welfare, the government should intervene when the market outcome is not Pareto Optimality. This provides a normative benchmark for government intervention through which questions such as "what governments can do" and "how to allocate public spending" can be addressed. However, this line of thoughts was attacked by Buchanan[2] from the perspective of public goods theory.[3] Public goods have two defining features—nonexclusivitiy and nonrivalry—that can be provided only by the government. This extends to the role of the state. Many aspects

[1]Adam, S. 1776, The Wealth of Nations. London: J M Dent and Sons.
[2]Buchanan, Public Finance, 1991 version in Chinese.
[3]Conceptually speaking, public good provision and public service are the same. In this text, these two concepts will be used interchangeably.

of public governance including defense, law and order, environmental regulation, monetary stability, and redistribution provide a justification for government intervention. These functions are typically hard to provide by the private sector.

There are substantial differences between public and private good provision. The question then is how is the level of public good provision decided? Why is there any need for public good provision? We argue in this article that the level and process of public good provision should be decided by the level of public risks and managing these in a sustainable manner.[4] Every public good provision can be seen as a design for managing public risks. If we regard public risk as the potential to impose damage to the society, then public good provision is designed to constrain the risk. Once out of control, public risks can have detrimental impacts on the society as a whole. For example public security is a classic public good, without public security, life and property can be in danger. Environmental regulation can be seen as another example. Without proper regulation and environmental regulation, our homeland can be destroyed. From a longer perspective, the public good provisions can be used for public risk management and mitigation, now and in the future to reflect changing needs.[5] In this sense, we have provided another perspective to the role of government intervention, not necessarily linked to the pitfalls of market failure.[6]

Basic human needs include water, food, air, and health care. Security is also a basic need, including physical security and freedom from disease. To satisfy these personal needs, individuals can reach a level of comfort through personal efforts, but may not be able to because of public risks. Under these circumstances, the state should provide adequate levels of public service so as to protect against these risks. Risks and opportunities are intertwined (World Bank's World Development Report). Managing the risks right, with careful public management, generates good opportunities; otherwise crises can arise.[7] The generation of information on which

Fig. 3.1 Relationship between public risk and public service

---

[4]Public risks here refer to risks with social impact and high externality. These type of risks have three characteristics: internal correlations (highly contagious), inseparability, and exclusivity. For more information, please consult Liu Shangxi, "Public Finance under the Perspective of Public Risks". 刘尚希《公共风险视角下的公共财政》, 经济科学出版社2010年版.

[5]Liu Shangxi, "Public Finance under the Perspective of Public Risks". 刘尚希《公共风险视角下的公共财政》, 经济科学出版社2010年版.

[6]This can then explain why is it that the core of governance is public risks management and public finance is the pillar and foundations of state governance.

[7]World Bank, 2014 World Development Report: Risks and Opportunities.

level of government spends what and what are the liabilities are the critical building blocks. Thus, Fig. 3.1 shows the following logical relationship:

3.1.2   Nature and Function of Public Revenue: Financing Public Service in Order to Manage Public Risks

Public risk governance is in essence a process of managing public spending. From here we have another logical relationships: public risks equals managing public service (public spending). This entails that public service (public spending) is the consequence of public risk governance. On the one hand, the level of public spending coexists with public risks and changes along with public risks. On the other hand, public service provision (public spending) is also the tool for public risk governance. In other words, public risks are mitigated through the use of public spending. Problems and tools of solving problems come side by side. If the tools for governing risks evolve slower than that of public risks, different forms of public risks would eventually emerge. Using the metaphor for relationships between war and army, we can say that the existence of war necessitates the existence of army while the army is deployed to prevent war and pacify the situation.[8]

The process of public service provision requires financial resources to make it work. Theoretically speaking, public service provision can be supplied through social or governmental channels. In practice, most public services are provided by the government.[9] The public service provision would need government financing, but public revenues can be used for public service spending and other spending.

Public revenue comes from citizens and should be used for their welfare.[10] The normative requirement of using public revenue for the welfare of citizens clarifies the goal of public revenue to govern public risks and prevent public crises. The fact that these revenues come from citizens stipulates that the government would need to concentrate part of the general public's welfare on mitigating public risks. This further means that the choice for the level of public spending is determined by general public's perception of public risks. However, given free riding on public services, not all levels of public risks can be perceived and identified by the general public. This results in the approved level of public spending being lower than that required for public risk mitigation. This is also one of the reasons why democratic governments usually face fiscal gaps. Therefore, the government would have to

---

[8]Liu Shangxi, "Public Finance under the Perspective of Public Risks". 刘尚希《公共风险视角下的公共财政》, 经济科学出版社2010年版.

[9]Public service refers to public good provision in the broadest sense, e.g., every public service activity with the purpose of managing public risks. Conceptually this is broader than the narrow meaning of public expense in the general public good provision.

[10]The public revenue here means all revenue aimed at providing public spending, including fiscal revenue intake from debt financing because deficit financing is also a source of public revenue for managing public risks and providing public service.

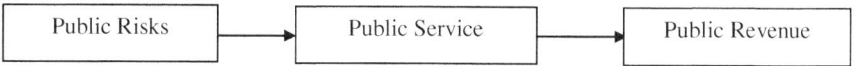

Fig. 3.2 Public risks, public service (public spending) and public revenue

evaluate public risks thoroughly, propose a reasonable level of fiscal spending for the general public and explain to the citizens the motive of such choice. From this line of thought, we can derive the following logical relationships (Fig. 3.2):

3.1.3 Nature and Function of Fiscal Risks: Policy Tools for Managing Public Risks

Governing public risks is not without costs, it would usually require financing generating fiscal risks as a natural part of the cost. The process of governing public risks through public service provision is essentially about aggregation of decentralized public risks into manageable fiscal risks, so as to avoid contagion. If fiscal risks are under control, then public resources can be used as a tool for governing public risks. From the point of view of risk governance, decentralized risks are harder to manage than centralized risk. Decentralized risks can result in systemic risks, leading crises. For example, before the 2008 financial crisis, financial derivatives in the OTC markets created highly correlated risks, resulting in enormous systemic risks and the final financial crisis spreading to multiple countries. In Greece, hidden costs associated with employment in SOEs providing public services spilled over into unsustainable fiscal risks. In Ireland and Spain, prior to 2008, fiscal risks were contained within Maastricht levels, but the buildup of private liabilities affected locally-owned banks, and again spilled over into unsustainable fiscal risks during the post-2008 economic crisis.

Financing public services by indebtedness is not without their limit, as increases in fiscal risks not only constraints the normal working of fiscal process but also creates spillover risks beyond a tipping point. This was the case for the European sovereign debt crisis[11] where increasing debt adversely affected the real economy, as countries exceeded the Maastricht debt and deficit limits. As mentioned above, in the case of Spain and Ireland, debt and deficit ratios were generally below the Maastricht tipping points, private liabilities affected the financial and banking system, and rapidly led to an explosion of public debt that became unsustainable. The sustainable level of debt or fiscal risk, however, depends on country circumstances, and some countries with high savings rates may be able to sustain relatively

---

[11]Overseas Office, Ministry of Finance. 财政部对外财经交流办公室：《从国际视角看财政风险管理作为政策工具的意义》，《外经要情与分析》，2013年第26期。.

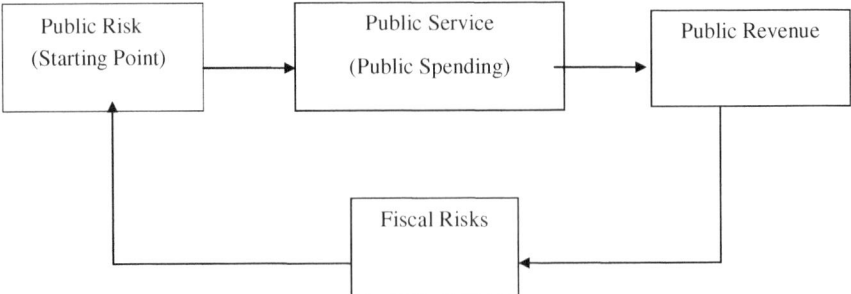

Fig. 3.3 Clockwise relationship between public risks, public goods provision (public spending), public revenue and fiscal risks

high levels of debt—although the limits of fiscal risks need to be approached with care as it is relatively easy to slip over the limits.

In the further analysis, in order to provide public service and govern public risks,fund raising is required. Minimization of public risks determines level of public service and the size of public revenues. Under the basic needs associated with the Millennium Development Goals, the broad target to finance basic services and investments was between 18–20% of GDP. But minimization of public risks is not without prior conditions; the solution would have to be placed under appropriate limits of fiscal risks. Therefore, public risks, public service provision (public spending), public revenue and fiscal risks become a closed loop in a logical circle:

From Fig. 3.3, starting from public risks, we establish a derivative relationship. The existence of public risks paves the way for the need for basic public services (public spending). To satisfy the need for public services (public spending) requires public revenues. If tax revenue stagnates the fiscal risks would increase. When this type of risks increase to a large extent the contagion effect for fiscal risks would amplify leading to large public risks, economic crisis, and exposed financial fragility. This has been exposed in the crisis in Europe, as we have stressed above.

3.1.4 Theoretical Foundation for Public Goods Evaluation: Public Risks Minimization Under Sustainable Fiscal Risks

Providing public service and governing public risks with sustainable fiscal risks is important under increasing uncertainties in present society and economy. From above logical relationships, public service is the link between public risks and fiscal risks. But both side of the relationship play different policy goals. Minimizing public risks is part of government responsibility. Sustainable fiscal risks become the ceiling for public risk minimization. In this analysis, there is a limit to which public

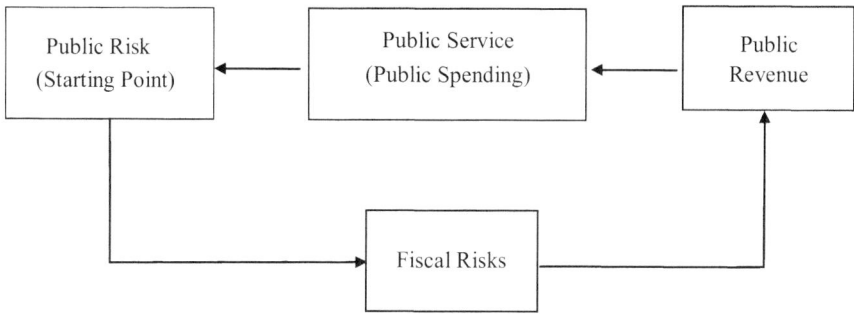

Fig. 3.4 Counter-clockwise logical relationship for public good evaluation

services can be reduced to achieve fiscal risk sustainability.[12] This is linked to public revenues and forms a clockwise logical relationship. On the other hand, the process of public service evaluation would be driven by the constraining factors. From this perspective, we have the following counter-clockwise logical relationship between public risks, public service (public spending), public revenue, and fiscal risk (See Fig. 3.4).

This counter-clockwise relationship is not derivative but represents constraining factors. Although fiscal risk is a variable that can fluctuate, the downside risks have their own limits and the fiscal deficit cannot be enlarged infinitely through debt financing. That is to say, fiscal risks generate fiscal revenue requirements. In the similar analysis, the size of fiscal revenue limits the level of public service provision (public spending), and public spending determines the level of public risk governance and its feasible reductions. The pursuit of minimization of public risks would require sustainable fiscal risks. In the end, this is a balancing between fiscal risks and public risks.

From the above discussion, in order to have a thorough evaluation of public service provision from the point of view of minimization of public risk under sustainable fiscal risks, we need to consider the following aspects:

First, can fiscal risk be controlled? Is there room for using this policy tool? Controlling fiscal risks becomes the boundary condition for minimization for public risks. Evaluating public service provision would need to first evaluate fiscal risks and ask whether there is room for using fiscal risk as a policy tool. If fiscal risk is controllable, then public service provision is not excessive. If there is room for increasing fiscal risks, then the level of public service can be further increased and public risks further minimized.

---

[12]Although fiscal risk is a constraining condition, it does not remain unchanged. Rather this boundary condition is a variable or a function. When the level of public risk changes the level of fiscal risks would need to respond to that change. For example, in the European crisis, some countries would need to tolerate higher level of fiscal deficit in face of systemic risks. In simple terms, fiscal risks provide a moving ceiling as a function of the balancing between public risks and fiscal sustainability.

Second, given a certain level of fiscal risk, can public risk reach a maximum frontier? The higher the level of public revenue, the larger the level of public services, and the lower the public risks. This also means that higher levels of fiscal risks might be generated by higher levels of fiscal deficit. A given level of fiscal risks might respond to different levels of public revenue. This is also related with the structure of public spending. If the level of debt is constant while tax revenues and public property income increase, the higher public revenue level would not increase fiscal risks. This means that given a level of fiscal risks, the level of public revenue can be maximized.

Third, does public spending effectively provide public services given financing through public revenues? And does the level and composition of spending minimize public risk? From public revenue to risk governance, we can establish a complicated link involving multiple steps. From one step to another there are logical relationships. But given steps have different levels of efficiency so that there are nonlinear relationships between them. In simple terms, public revenues determine the level of public services, and the extent of public risk governance. From the efficiency of public risk governance, this is related not only with level of public service but also the structure and quality of public services. Unreasonable levels of public service would not only fail to decrease public risks but may also increase and amplify them.

Fourth, is the fiscal relationship between central-provincial and local governments and the public resources allocation between them is adequate? To minimize public risks, we need to clarify intergovernmental relationships and assign responsibilities. This is a complex task, and depends on historical and institutional factors.

3.2 Evaluation of Chinese Public Service from the Perspective of Public Risk Governance

Following the analytical framework proposed above, we provide a preliminary evaluation of public risks and public services for China.

3.2.1 Public Risk Evaluation for China

Uncertainty lies at the root of public risk because of incentive effects, information asymmetry and imperfect institutions.[13] The combination of uncertainties from the nature, society, economy, and the international realm, alongside with the fragility of the institutions are the key factors affecting public risks. The decline in income from economic and financial crisis, unemployment and social instability disrupt the world economy. Earthquake plagued places from Haiti to Japan creating massive

---

[13]The end of Certainty. 伊利亚·普利高津:《确定性的终结》, 上海科技教育出版社, 1998年版。.

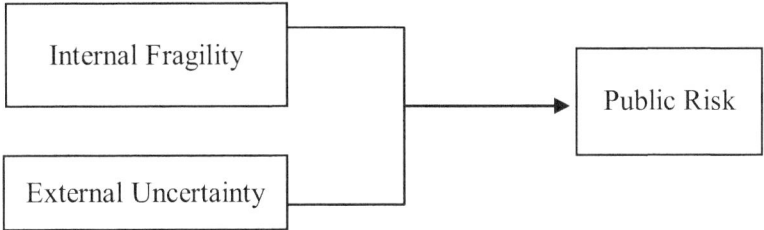

Fig. 3.5 External uncertainty and internal fragility breed public risks

economic destructions. In additions there are concerns over global warming and spread of disease (Fig. 3.5).[14]

Currently the socio-economic conditions in China have following aspects of internal fragility and public risks:

First, the vulnerability of environment resources and the sustainable development of public risk. China's existing per capita GDP is much lower than the developed countries and there should be room for improvement. Chinese has a low per capita resource availability, with one-fifth of the world's population, but per capita arable land, water, energy, minerals and others are amongst the lowest. Per capita oil use is a tenth of the world's average. To reach the current level of consumption of the United States, all the world's oil would not be enough. Both the rapid economic growth, limited capacity of the resources, and environmental concerns have become increasing constraints. China's resource and environmental vulnerability and natural disasters put sustainable development at risk.

Second, the economic vulnerability and the recent global economic recession also generate huge public risks. In the Chinese economy, the role of the government and the market are not well defined. The ability of original innovation is obviously insufficient. The adjustment costs for reform continue to increase, and the friction with international trade is more and more frequent. Factor costs continue to rise, and human resource costs continue to increase. The fragility of the economy is likely to lead to a risk of recession. For example, there is an imbalance between current investment and consumption in China, and some industries face overcapacity. If this trend is not effectively managed, China's economy will face serious risk of recession.

Third, increased inequality and social differentiation and disorder might engender the public order. China's recent development has been uneven, marked by difference between urban and rural areas, between different regions and between different social classes. The rapid economic growth with the social development seriously lagging creates problems for parents to pay for school for their children and go to hospitals when sick. The reason is that this gap is not caused by the expansion of the market society, but long term social development has been

---

[14]World Bank 2014.

constrained by misallocation of resources. The allocation of resources in the fields such as compulsory education and public health is inadequate. In addition, the gap between rich and poor is considerable. Government officials commonly take bribes; and there is a crisis of trust among ordinary people. The vulnerability of the people's livelihoods could trigger public risks of social confrontation, disorder and turmoil. The industrial structure adjustment, the social security system, the education and health systems, the income distribution system, the "agriculture, countryside and peasant" systems and other social and economic institutions are generating the social contradictions and intensified conflicts every day. Social disorder and unrest can hinder the pace of reform and development.

3.2.2 An Assessment of Fiscal Risks: Are Fiscal Risks Manageable?

We believe that China's fiscal risks are still manageable but the room for increasing fiscal risks is limited. From the point of view of the financial situation, although current fiscal situation remains healthy and the main financial indicators apparently are within manageable limits, the level of the deficit and debt has been rising rapidly, raising questions of sustainability. The changing external environment implies that the next decade of economic growth is likely to be slower, combined with the fact that China's fiscal revenue to GDP growth would decline even further. Assuming that 2017 GDP grew at an average annual rate of 7%, inflation rate rose an average of 3%, foreign trade import and export with an average annual growth rate of 8%, estimates, fiscal revenue over the next few years, with an average annual growth rate of 8.5%, fiscal revenue growth will drop to a single digit stage. While the growth rate fell sharply, the required fiscal spending increased, resulting in a widening of the fiscal deficit. In 2014, the national budget deficit reached 1.2 trillion yuan, or 2.1% of GDP. In the next few years, in the case of the decline in the growth of fiscal revenue and increase in required spending the deficit rate may exceed 3%. In addition, since 2007 local government debt grew at an average annual rate of more than 20%, in 2013 the National Audit Office announced the scale of local government debt is 1.78 trillion yuan, while some places have experienced a serious debt overhang. The above data shows that while China's overall financial risk remain controllable, but there are many uncertain factors and the policy space for increasing financial risk becomes increasingly narrow.

3.2.3 Structure of Fiscal Spending and Revenues Given the Level of Fiscal Risks

Given the level of fiscal risks, we believe that there is room to increase the level and optimize the structure of public revenues. Public revenue can be divided into taxes and income from public property, based on the ownership of the state.[15]

There is room to enhance public revenues while reducing economic efficiency loss for a given financial risk level with the manner in which public income affects economic efficiency. Thus an incomplete structure of a VAT was adopted in 1993/4, given that institutions and processes were relatively weak, and provinces needed to retain an income source-the business tax. However, this split base added to the cost of doing business—and this was no longer tenable as there is now a market-determined exchange rate and greater competition. The VAT for business tax reform was forced by the need to maintain market share, but addressing the multilevel tax agenda becomes acute to minimize fiscal risks emanating from local governments (see Ahmad, this volume). Other sources of income are from public assets—both physical and financial, as we depict in Fig. 3.6.

Income based on public property is limited, resulting in the loss of public revenue, such as business of proceeds of state-owned assets, non-operating state-owned capital gains and other resources of state-owned asset. In addition, the permission for usage rights of communication channels and other franchises belonging to state assets do not generate enough public revenue.

The income tax does not function effectively, and is narrowly focused on wage earners—making it relatively regressive, rather than the redistributive tool of the state. Both the coverage and the rate structure are problematic, particularly the taxation of non-wage incomes.

Finally, the property tax is dysfunctional and much work needs to be done to convert it into an effective revenue handle for local governments. Without adequate own-source revenues at each level of government, the financial risks are enhanced, as well as the probability that the central government may bear the consequences of local mistakes and risky investment, as has been the case in several European countries.

---

[15]Liu Shangxi, Yang Liangchu, and Li Chengwei, 2005. "Optimizing Fiscal Revenue Structure: A way to Improve Public Finance" 刘尚希、杨良初、李成威, 2005: 《优化公共收入结构:财政增收的重要途径之一》, 《杭州师范学院学报》第5期。.

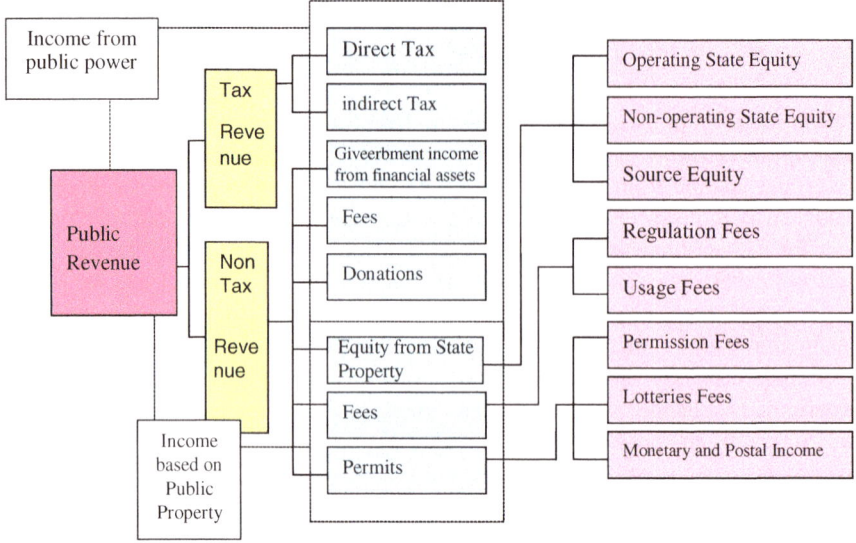

Fig. 3.6 Structure of fiscal revenue

3.2.4   An Assessment of the Efficiency of Public Risk Governance and Adequacy of Public Revenues for the Effective Governance of Public Risks

Most public revenue has been used for the effective provision of public service. But there are some inefficiencies and waste, with limited scope for governing public risks. It is useful to distinguish between efficient and inefficient public service provision. Effective public service cost refers to necessary investments required for the public organization to function. Any spending beyond this level is inefficient (Fig. 3.7).

Inefficient public service costs include: first, the cost coming from public organizations which fail to provide the required public service; second, from the public organization providing unwanted public services that do not satisfy public needs, and thus cannot meet the requirements of public risk management; and third the additional resources used beyond providing necessary public goods.[16]

In recent years, with steady public finance reform and a general increasing expenditure, the structure of expenditures has also improved, at all levels of government. However, the ratio of social and public expenditure continues to increase. In particular, the equalization of basic public services in urban and rural areas, improving the minimum livelihoods of the people, and support for scientific and

---

[16]Fu Daopeng, Li Chengwei, Internal Report, "Questions related to Public Service Costs". 参考傅道鹏、 李成威《公共行政成本相关问题研究》, 内部报告,2010年3月。.

| Inefficient Public Service Costs1: Costs incurred through failure of organization to provide service or wastes. | Inefficient Public Service Costs2: Costs incurred through invalid public good services | **Inefficient Public Service Costs 3:** Costs beyond efficient use of resources for public good provision |
| | | **Efficient Public Service Cost:** Necessary cost for efficient provision of public goods |

Fig. 3.7 Diagram for efficient and inefficient public service costs *Source* Internal Report, "Questions related to Public Service Costs". 参考傅道鹏、李成威《公共行政成本相关问题研究》, 内部报告, 2010年3月。

technological innovation and environmental protection and other aspects of spending increased significantly. This implies that public revenues largely provide effective public services. But there is also more serious waste, inefficiency and other problems. This weakens public risk governance and is mainly manifested in the following aspects:

1. *Governance of the fragile environment, leading to risks for sustainable development.* Industrialization increased the productivity, added social wealth, and promoted material civilization. But the external costs are high: the ecological environment is facing a crisis. The polluted water and gas waste, and others are increasing, leading to pollution of the environment and the ecological damage. The changes from acid rain, ozone, the climate, air quality and water pollution are the serious threat to the living environment. As industrialization and urbanization, the contradiction between food and the huge population intensified. Biotechnology, gene food, network technology and other high-tech also increased the vulnerability of human survival and economic security. In the past industrialization, the negative effects were overlooked, and caused the environmental crisis.

2. *Limited understanding of economic vulnerability and public risk.* One problem is the constant tendency for the government to substitute for the market, thus preventing market competition. Government intervenes too much at the micro level. In addition to SOE refinancing and subsidies, local governments tend to intervene in private firms, given a blurred distinction between the state and market forces. Some of the problems that should be resolved by the market self-regulation, are addressed through financial subsidies and other means, such as the widely criticized sow subsidies, and so on. Many problems need to be addressed through institutional mechanisms rather than through fiscal subsidy.

Another problem is the weakening of macro prudential policies. Over a long period of time, the macro-control has made many errors, including failure to recognize market mechanism and misunderstanding of macroeconomic controlling policies. Many local governments are concerned too much about the short-term macroeconomic regulation and controls that they think can bring immediate effects. In response to the international financial crisis, this mentality has been quite strong. In fact, the so-called "control" type macroeconomic policies generated huge costs, resulting in inefficient allocation of resources and waste, some inefficient investment projects in operation for a period of time, creating financial burden, and increasing public risk.

3. *Managing problems of livelihood. The prevention of social polarization and social imbalance as a source of public risks has not been paid enough attention.* With the increase in the degree of economic marketization and rapid economic growth, social stratification has been formed. Because of the difference between personal endowments, knowledge, opportunity and environment there is little upward mobility. For the poorest, the government needs to provide social security, education, medical training, and employment opportunities to reduce extreme poverty and inequality. This is not only moral but needed to resolve social contradictions. However, the role of the government in this regard failed to perform well with limited improvements and low level of satisfaction among ordinary citizens, despite the fact that the public spending in these areas has continued to expand. The problem of people's livelihood is a matter of starting point, and public policies should be implemented to improve the quality and ability and mobility of the members of the society. But the tendency of current welfare system is based on "rights" and "qualification", with conditionality on transfers as the basis to allocate funds, creates disincentives and poverty traps, making the problem of social mobility even worse. The fragmentation of the system along with the fragmentation of the allocation of funds creates a gap between public services between urban and rural areas. Despite large sums being spent, the outcomes are not well documented. To improve the vulnerability in livelihoods, governments at various levels would need to adjust their policies.[17]

4. *Too many inefficient and inappropriate costs leading to low efficiency of public service provision.* Special purpose funds are quite rigid and lack incentive-compatible mechanisms. In some areas, public finances are exposed to considerable risks through accounting manipulations. In addition, some public projects are vulnerable to disorder, embezzlement and waste, leading to the fragmentation of public service provision, with short sighted policies, and inefficient use of funds.

---

[17]Liu Shangxi, "Public Finance under the Perspective of Public Risks". 刘尚希《公共风险视角下的公共财政》, 经济科学出版社2010年版.

3.2.5 An Assessment of Public Service Allocation Among Inter-Governmental Relationships: Reasonable Intergovernmental Fiscal Relationships

In our view, there is a mismatch between inter-governmental fiscal relationships and public service allocation in the new era, which could adversely affect public risk governance and enlarge public risks.

The 1994 fiscal reform laid the foundation of sound inter-governmental fiscal relationships. In a historical perspective, the current inter-governmental fiscal relationships have made noticeable progress. The first is the establishment of revenue-sharing system as the core of the tax system. The 1994 decentralized tax system reshaped relations between the governments and was used to satisfy the requirement of market economy, leading to the stable inter-governmental relationships, breaking the long-term "decentralization-correction" cycle, paving the way for future administrative reforms and economic decentralization. The fiscal decentralization gives the local governments financial autonomy, improves the efficiency of the allocation of government resources, and is also conducive for the local governments to provide public services tailored to local conditions. Secondly, the fiscal reform changed the previous revenue-sharing and equalization systems, making the central government less dependable on local authorities and easier for the central government to balance different regions. Thirdly, fiscal decentralization stimulated the development of economic enthusiasm. This kind of enthusiasm under decentralized tax system forced local governments to develop the local economy, boost GDP as a means of getting promotion, and provide the conditions for local economic dynamics.

However, we should also notice the problems concerning inter-governmental fiscal relationships and public service allocation[18]:

First, the fiscal resources and administrative requirements do not match, especially in lower tier governments. The revenue assignment has not been reformed, and in particular the absence of own-source revenues is a source of considerable fiscal risk at the lower levels of government. Local governments generally imitate the financial relationship between central and local levels, decentralizing within the decentralization system. The problems are severe for poor areas so that even with better matching between fiscal resource and revenue assignments, some lower governments cannot provide adequate services generating the risk of unrest.

Second, departmentalism plagues each tier of public finance. Each tier of government cares only about its own welfare, trying to balance its own budget on the basis of its own economy. This has negative effects. Forcing a matching between fiscal revenue and expenditure assignments would pressure each layer of

---

[18]Please refer to the internal research report from Ministry of Finance, "Building Optimal Inter-Governmental Fiscal Relationships". 参考财政部财政科学研究所课题组:《建立有利于科学发展的政府间财政关系》, 内部报告, 2011年5月。.

government to focus on economic development, at the expense of environmental degradation and other distortions, making poor localities even poorer.

Third, the local government financial risk diffusion should be taken into account. Due to the mismatch between spending and revenue assignments, local governments at all levels had no choice but do everything possible to finance the gap, either through non-tax income (particularly land sales, see Wang, Wu and Ye, this volume) or debt financing. The pursuit of political achievements has been the main driver behind debt financing. Without own-source tax revenues the increase in local government debt leads to larger local fiscal risks.

Fourth, the heterogeneity of public services across different regions has been quite large. The inequality across regions is serious and has shown signs of worsening. The gap between public services in the current period reflects the gap in people's quality of lives between different areas, and in the long run this gap will become the gap of human capital across different regions, resulting in realization of public risks.

Fifth, the gap in public service provision is not conducive to public risk governance, and may even enlarge public risk. The core of the current inter-governmental fiscal relationships is to increase fiscal revenue at each tier. The basic premise of the government charge is to develop the economy as a way to broaden tax base. This incentive structure links GDP growth as a major performance indicator for the promotion of public official, generating large political-economy dynamics. This, however, is not without side effects. These effects include emphasizing quantity over quality; less emphasis on efficient energy use; emphasizing development of cities over rural places; encouraging economic development over environment protection; incentivizing production of goods over development of human beings.

3.3   Conclusion and Policy Implications

We started from the analytical framework on public and fiscal risks as a basis for the evaluation of public service provision. Using this benchmark framework, we examined the public service provision in China, and the scope for revenue generation and governance of fiscal risks.

3.3.1   Basic Conclusions

Public services function as the basis of public risk governance. Public revenue finances the provision of public services and governance of public risk. Fiscal risk limitation is policy tool of public risk governance. Evaluation of public services should be placed under the constraints of sustainable fiscal risks to reduce or eliminate public risks. Therefore, the overall assessment of public services should include the following aspects: (1) is the fiscal risk controllable? Are there any rooms for improvement? (2) Is the maximum public revenue achieved under given risk level? (3) Whether the public revenue covers reasonable public services? Are the number and types of public services meeting the requirements of public risk governance? (4) Is the allocation of public services between the different levels of government reasonable? Based on the empirical analysis of Chinese public service provision, we have the following assessments: First, we did not see any trends of convergence between the fragility of China's economic and social development and the implied public risk. Second, the overall fiscal risk is controllable, but the space to undertake further financial risk has been contracting. Third, given fiscal risk level, fiscal revenues in China have not yet reached their appropriate level, and the public revenue structure also requires further adjustments to enhance both efficiency and equity. Fourth, there is serious waste in public service provision with low efficiency and high costs. Governance of fiscal risks can pose serious problems. Fifth the inter-governmental fiscal relationships and public service allocation are not compatible with future development requirements, which are not conducive to public risk governance and are vulnerable to fiscal risk magnification.

3.3.2 Policy Implications

Public finance is the foundation and important pillar of state governance, at the core of which lies public risk governance. On the one hand, public risk can be mitigated through public service provision facilitated by an appropriate level of fiscal revenues. On the other hand, handling fiscal risks can become a policy tool for controlling public risks. At present, the vulnerability of China resources, economy and people's livelihood contains a large public risk, which shows that public service provision must be improved. From the point of view of China's current fiscal situation, there is limited space to contract further debt to control public risk. Some possibilities exist to improve the structure of public income and public services, and reforming inter-governmental fiscal relationships and public service configurations. These measures would work together to manage fiscal risk under the constraint of public risk minimization. It is essential to deepen the reform of the fiscal and taxation system, and enhance the fiscal policy.

We need to learn lessons from the Crisis in Europe by identifying and defining the public risk in social and economic terms. Researching the proper channel as how to provide appropriate public services as a way for effective governance of public risk, and controlling fiscal risks in the process of public service provision will be important topics for the future.

References

Adam, S. (1776). *The Wealth of Nations*, J.M. Dent and Sons.
Ahmad, E., Bordignon, M., & Brosio, G. (Eds.). (2016). *MultiLevel finance and the euro crisis*, Edward Elgar.
Ahmad, E., & Brosio, G. (Eds.). (2015). *Handbook of multilevel finance*, Edward Elgar.
Buchanan, J. (1968). *Public Finance in Democratic Process: Fiscal Institutions and Individual Choice*, Chapel Hill.
Liu, S. (2010). *Public Finance under the perspective of public risk* (in Chinese, processed).
Liu, S., Yang, L., & Li, C. (2005). *Optimizing fiscal revenue structure: a way to improve public finance* (in Chinese, processed).
Ministry of Finance, Government of China. (2011). *Building optimal intergovernmental fiscal relationships*, Beijing (in Chinese, processed).
World Bank. (2014). *World development report: risks and opportunities*. Washington DC.

Chapter 4
Towards Monitoring and Managing Subnational Liabilities in China: Lessons from the Balance Sheet for County K

Ehtisham Ahmad and Xiaorong Zhang

Abstract The monitoring and managing of subnational liabilities is taking on considerable importance in China. Considerable efforts have been underway to strengthen national institutions and public financial management processes and procedures—this includes the move towards a GSFM2001/14 budget system that ensures consistency of fiscal information with national accounts. In essence, this requires the development of balance sheets at different levels of government to generate full information on general government operations. We use a detailed survey from an advanced county, K, in Jiangsu Province, that has started developing a local balance sheet. This shows considerable gaps and lacunae that need to be addressed to be certain that the full magnitude of liabilities is being captured, and that appropriate measures to address these are formulated at the local level. Otherwise there is a danger that liabilities will continue to be generated in the expectation that the central government will eventually provide, despite the recent strengthening of the budget law in this regard. Without own-source revenues, no bailout sanctions are not credible, especially if the information base is incomplete.

4.1 Introduction

The Chinese economic strategy since the 1980s has been to facilitate a "responsibility system"—that has led to one of the most decentralized spending patterns in any country. However, in order to maintain macroeconomic stability, and in order

E. Ahmad (✉)
University of Bonn, Bonn, Germany
e-mail: seuahmad@gmail.com; s.e.ahmad@lse.ac.uk

E. Ahmad
London School of Economics, London, UK

E. Ahmad
Pao Yu-Kong Professor, Zhejiang University, Hangzhou, China

X. Zhang
Department of Finance, School of Management, Fudan University, Shanghai, China
e-mail: xrzhang@fudan.edu.cn

© Springer Nature Singapore Pte Ltd. 2018
E. Ahmad et al. (eds.), *Fiscal Underpinnings for Sustainable Development in China*,
https://doi.org/10.1007/978-981-10-6286-5_4

71

to reduce the cost of doing business, the tax system has been gradually centralized, particularly since 1993/4 (Ahmad et al. 2001, Ahmad, this volume). The centralization of revenues has continued with the replacement of the business tax by the VAT. Again, this was a desirable reform needed to ensure competitiveness and also to generate information on the full value-chain needed for all other taxes. However, the mismatch between own-source revenues and spending responsibilities puts pressure on local governments to finance spending through arrears or borrowing, indirectly through state-owned enterprises or special purpose vehicles. Although access to the bond market has now formally been permitted with the new budget law, and there has been considerable progress to adopt the IMF's 2001/14 framework at the higher levels, the full operation of the systems at the lower levels of government, which will involve the full recognition of arrears and intertemporal liabilities, is very much work in progress. In this paper, we examine the case of County K in establishing a balance sheet, and draw lessons for the short-to-medium term management of local liabilities with incomplete information.

As seen in the European context, incomplete information was one of the contributing factors to the crisis in the Eurozone, and also made reform adjustments more difficult (see Ahmad et al. 2016). With incomplete information "game play" by lower levels of government with higher levels and particularly the center increases the risks associated with the overall sustainability of finances at the general government level.

In this paper, we first examine some of the steps taken to tighten the flows of information across levels of government over the past two decades. In particular, the adoption of the GFSM2001 methodology over a decade ago was a step in the right direction, but the full accruals basis is still to be implemented. The completion of these initiatives (that also include electronic government financial information management systems—FMIS—and cash and treasury management and Treasury Single Accounts—TSAs) has become a matter of high priority since the counter-cyclical measures were taken to address the 2008 global slowdown.

The practice of compiling government financial reports lags behind other economic reforms in China, given the lack of reliable data, diversity in regional economic development and the cost of transition from cash basis to accrual basis in government accounting. The National Bureau of Statistics in China released an experimental version of an aggregated national balance sheet (which includes the central government balance sheet) in 1998, but no official trial is made on local or regional government (LRG) balance sheets. In 2012, an academic group from Fudan University compiled a complete Chinese national balance sheet (Ma et al. 2012), which divides the domestic economy into 6 sectors, namely (1) households, (2) non-financial corporations, (3) the central government, (4) local governments, (5) the central bank, and (6) the commercial bank. In 2013, the analysis was replicated by a group from the Chinese Academy of Social Science (CASS) (Li 2013), updated in 2015 (Li et al. 2015).

Both groups used "estimated" data in their task, rather than "compiling" primary information. For example, in Li (2013), the LRG assets are composed of operating assets (by state-owned firms), non-operating assets (by administrative institutions) and natural resource assets, all of which are estimated based on available secondary data, such as equity value in listed state-owned firms, the leverage level, and the percentage of listed state-owned firms in all state-owned firms. Local government debt is classified into 4 types by using a Fiscal Risk Matrix (Hana 1998). Direct explicit liability includes local government bonds (the amount of which can be retrieved from existing database or trading platforms), and local government foreign debt (assumed as 8% of the total national debt based on historical percentage data). Direct implicit liability is simply taken as 70% of the unfunded pension liabilities. Contingent explicit liability, defined as the local government guaranteed debt and debt of the local public sector (including public institutions and local government financing vehicles), is based on the Report on the Local Government Debt Audit Work (2011, 2013) released by the NAO (National Audit Office). Finally, contingent implicit liability is the sum of local banks NPLs (assumed 52.8% of national NPLs) and local state-owned enterprises debt less LGFV (local government financing vehicles) debt (to avoid double counting).

The work is a notable attempt to depict a whole financial picture for the Chinese general government. Data sources include Finance Yearbook of China, Accounting Yearbook of China, China Statistical Yearbook, Almanac of China's Finance and Banking, CEIC, annual reports of financial institutions and survey data from National Audit Office. The reliability of the LRG balance sheet as well as the national balance sheet, however, lies in the quality of all data sources. Specifically, if official LGFV debt and banking NPLs are underestimated, the assessment of local government debt in CASS's work is consequently also underestimated. This reflects the importance of compiling LRG balance sheet from the micro-level up. We examine a model balance sheet that has been experimented with in County K, and comment on the possibilities for strengthening the information generated.

It will take a considerable time to roll-out full balance sheets at the local level, given the assessment of County K. Indeed, the rationalization of the levels of government that are eligible to maintain public financial management (PFM) institutions, particularly FMISs and TSAs, may well be part of the solution. This would need to be linked to an assessment of whether or not the particular level should be considered responsible for the liabilities being generated. Consequently, we present a possible "early warning" mechanism that would be able to triangulate the buildup of liabilities that might not be reflected in the "incomplete balance sheets." This should provide an approximation of the potential problems that may occur with sub-national debt in specific counties or municipalities, or indeed provinces.

4.2 Some Recent Institutional and PFM Developments

China made important but low-key fiscal reforms in the late 1990s, including the Departmental Budget Reform (*bumenyusuan*, DBR), the Treasury Management Reform (*guoku jizhong zhifu*, TMR), and the Government Procurement Reform (*zhengfu caigou*, GPR)—see Lou Jiwei (2002). Thus, a significant set of reforms was instituted in the late 1990s and early 2000s period—including a modernization of the budget classification structure with the move to the IMF's Government Financial Statistics Manual GFSM 2001/14 standards, and the establishment of a nested system of Treasury Single Accounts (TSAs) to track cash flows.

However, data is missing on financial and non-financial assets, particularly at the subnational levels of government, despite the progress made with respect to general government information. This is seen from China's page in the GFS Yearbook. Work is also likely to be needed to recognize liabilities, particularly from investments including PPPs, in order to assess the need for provisioning. Again, this is particularly problematic at the sub-national level. The generation of standardized information across levels of government is crucial in laying the basis for more systematic assessments of risks and liabilities associated with different actions.

As mentioned above, work is also likely to be needed to tighten the recognition of liabilities in association with Public-Private Partnerships (PPPs). This should be in keeping with the new IPSAS 32 regulations in this regard. Consequently, if assets revert to the state at the end of a PPP contract, the liabilities need to be recorded in the relevant government's balance sheet, along with appropriate provisioning in the relevant budget.

In the medium-term, China's multilevel PFM architecture will depend crucially on decisions relating to the number of levels of effective government. This is particularly important for the sub-provincial design of PFM responsibilities, and is also closely linked with the rebalancing and development of sustainable "hubs" or new cities agenda. This will also influence the financial management and institutional infrastructure in the future, including coverage of smaller municipalities within the ambit of the new hubs. In other words, it may be neither feasible nor desirable to establish comprehensive balance sheets at the very lowest levels of government, as there is a grey area between purely public functions and the operations of SOEs that may well transcend county boundaries. There are also likely to be binding capacity constraints at this level. However, modern technologies now facilitate very detailed tracking of micro-level transactions at an intermediate level, and balance sheet accounts could be prepared by responsible levels (say at the third tier) for the lower levels of deconcentrated operations.

We also examine some possibilities of triangulation of local liabilities in the presence of incomplete information and partial balance sheets. This is an area for further work, but we discuss some of the key principles that may be helpful in this regard.

4.2.1 Sub-National PFM Issues

China's progress with respect to the sub-national public financial management (PFM) reforms is one of the best performances among developing countries and comparable to the OECD countries.[1] However, there is still much work to be done on budget coverage, and recognition of liabilities.

---

[1]Mexican PFM reforms were initiated at about the same time as in China in the late 1990s, but have still to establish the GFSM2001 standards for both the Federal and the State level

Decisions will also need to be made regarding the monitoring of inflows of funds and expenses—and whether there is to be a separate Government Financial Information Management System (FMIS) at the provincial or lower level (e.g., new hubs), that would also provide for support to the lower level administrations, or whether each responsible layer (e.g., municipalities) would operate their own FMISs. In any case, a common Chart of Accounts, consistent with the GFSM2001/14, is needed to ensure that transactions are tracked on a consistent and systematic basis across the country. The full GFSM2001/14 requires accrual accounting, and this has yet to be fully implemented (see below).

As with the tax administration, it is not necessary for all levels of government to replicate the PFM institutions and architecture (Ahmad 2015). For instance, while provinces could have their own TSAs (e.g., linked to a National TSA), it is not necessary for them to also engage in detailed asset management and cash planning. If the subnational TSAs are nested with the national TSA, then asset management function could be more efficiently carried out by the Apex TSA in the MOF in Beijing. The links with the MOF TSA could also suffice for cash management purposes. Indeed, there should be a distinct policy to minimize the opening of accounts at the subnational level, given that there is the possibility of capture and leakage. Own-revenues, shared revenues and equalization transfers would provide resources for the provincial TSAs, and clearly a provincial balance sheet would be required. As we show below, the provincial TSA could be used to provide services for municipal and county-level governments on an agency basis.

It is not necessary to create TSAs below the province level. It is perfectly feasible for third tier governments (e.g., at the city level) to open zero-balance accounts to facilitate collections of revenues and make payments. These zero-balance accounts would be linked to the provincial TSA.

It is possible to utilize the zero-balance accounts for the receipt of earmarked transfers from the center for either social or investment purposes. In any case, all the transactions would be tracked real time in the provincial TSAs. This is important with respect to the need for greater accountability for funds received from the Central government, a reiterated in the Third Plenum directive #17.

The zero-balance accounts could be linked to the provincial TSA operated by the Provincial Department of Finance. An example of the use of Zero Balance Accounts at the third tier, and the pass-through of Special Purpose Programs from the Central Government is shown in Chart 4.1 This arrangement could also be used to simplify the operations of Central Government Special Purpose Transfers—these could go directly to suppliers or third level cities with the relevant zero-balance accounts linked directly to the TSA at the Central Level, operated by the MOF. This would avoid having to channel funds through the provinces to get to lower levels of

---

governments (although requirements for standardization was required from 2014), and a system of TSAs has yet to be established at any level of government.

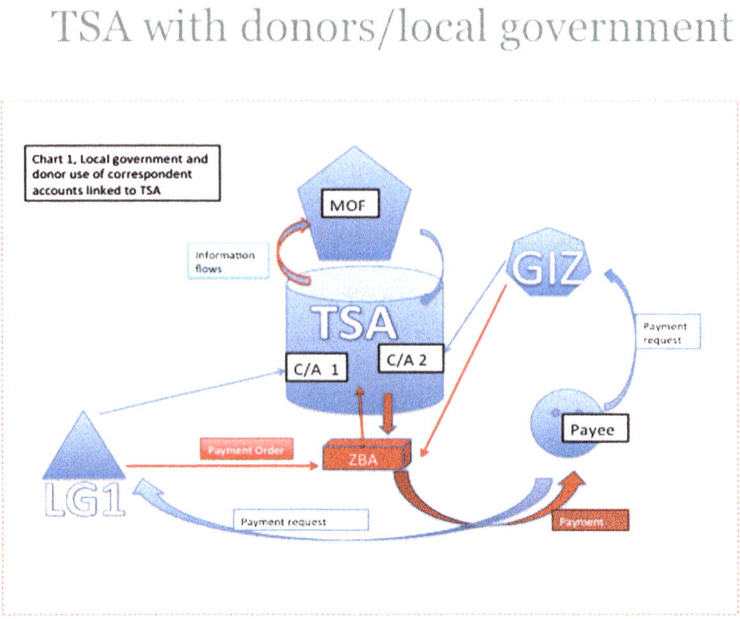

TSA with donors/local government

Chart 4.1 Sub-Provincial TSA operations. *Source* Ahmad (2015), "Institutions and Governance", in Ahmad and Brosio, *Handbook of Multilevel Finance*

government, although that would still be possible, if deemed appropriate on other grounds.

Success in all these areas is a result of complex interactions between instruments, and the failure on one, such as unconstrained access to credit or badly designed transfers can negate the positive incentive effects of the others (e.g., own-source taxes or tight budget management).

The weakening of the subnational budget constraints, especially through the indirect access to credit, and ability to keep transactions off-budget, continues to pose problems. This accentuates the unclear, overlapping or inappropriate spending responsibilities, including for minimum social standards. Despite the very impressive adoption of the standards in the GFSM 2001/14, the budget coverage and liability recognition components remain incomplete, especially at the sub-national level.

4.2.2 Local Borrowing and Management of Liabilities

In principle, borrowing for investment purposes is justified on the grounds that the investments take time and provide benefits to future generations. However, the budget law in China prevented local governments from borrowing directly.

On-lending from the Central Government was permitted under this arrangement. Also, local government financing vehicles (LGFVs)[2] or local Urban Development Investment Corporations (UDICs) were permitted to borrow in the post-1993 era, presumably to restrict borrowing for investment purposes.

The tightening of the budget and treasury systems (mandating the use of the Treasury Single Account system and injunctions on off-budget operations) may have increased incentives to rely on indirect borrowing by local governments. Weaknesses in effective monitoring meant that the LGFVs and UDICs became a convenient safety valve for local governments for all sorts of operational spending of dubious long-term value (see Qiao et al. 2012).[3]

According to Qiao et al. (2012), there were around 8800 UDICs in 2009, and presented an increasing credit risk for local governments, because of:

- Lack of transparency in accounting practices;
- Excessive leverage;
- Land based valuations;
- Dependence on short-term lending;
- Illiquid assets.

The UDICs were used for the fiscal stimulus in 2009, and contributed to the growing local indebtedness, including through bonds issued on their behalf by the central government. Information released by the PBC puts the extent of local indebtedness at around 30% of total Yuan loans. This was approximately Y14.4 trillion in 2011, or around 36% of GDP (Peoples Bank of China 2011). Evidence reported in Qiao et al. (2012) suggests that the debt is increasing in the four metropolitan municipalities—Beijing, Shanghai, Tianjin and Chongqing. For example, with Tianjin's debt to GDP burden was 50%; with a debt to revenue ratio of 457%! Extra-budgetary revenues (including revenue from land sales) were 75% of total revenues in Shanghai and 68% in Tianjin. Chongqing's general revenues only covered 50% of its general expenditures. Further, a representative sample of prefecture-level cities showed the same patterns.

The difficulty is that local governments have few incentives or resources to service the debt, or be held accountable for it. Zhejiang's[4] attempt in 2005 to set up an early warning system, as an example of provincial systems to limit the growth of sub-national debt, established limits of 10% on the debt/GDP burden; 100% on debt to revenue ratio; and 15% on the debt service ratio. However, these limits were largely ignored—including by the provincial government; and half of the city and county governments that exceeded all the criteria.[5] The State Council Document 19

---

[2]The LGFVs increased by 25% from end 2008 to over 10,000 by end 2010.

[3]See Qiao Baoyun, Qian Chen, Lezheng Liu, Shen Guo, Jiaimen Zhao, Xiangyi Meng, 2012, "Blueprint for better management of sub-national government implicit and explicit debt," Asian Development Bank.

[4]Zhejiang is one of the richest provinces in China.

[5]http://blog.caijing.com.cn/expert_article-151329-11763.

in 2010[6] prohibited guarantees or lending to non-operational projects, which provide basic services that have limited cost recovery, and thus should be brought under public budget financing. However, there is a remote likelihood of local governments taking over additional responsibilities in the absence of own-source revenues, and possible reductions in business tax revenues.

Given the large portfolio of investment in real estate, including that classified as "operational" or "quasi-operational",[7] it would be useful to subject the portfolio to stress tests for potential adverse movements in property prices and rents. As in Mexico in the 1990s, such "shocks" generated significant NPLs that eventually required a bailout from the central government, even though the debt was not guaranteed by it, or even by local governments. Tightening provisioning for banks may be sensible, but could induce a crisis especially during an economic downturn. Yet, the situation needs to be addressed in terms of the underlying structural imbalances—a key element of which is the absence of an effective system of own-revenues at the provincial and sub-provincial levels.

Shifting some of these loans to separate asset management companies and also write off some debts is a typical response in an international context. While this is sensible, the incentive problems leading to the buildup of debt cannot be solved without addressing the root causes—this will involve a set of interlocking measures to enhance local government accountability, and tighter legal and regulatory measures. This is a high priority measure needed in the short-run.

Ahmad et al. (2003) argued that the budget law should permit an asymmetric introduction of local bonds, given the differential speed with which different metropolitan areas and provinces may be able to meet the pre-conditions, particularly the establishment of own-sources of revenues. It needs to be stressed that the preconditions for formal local borrowing are quite stringent and may not be feasible for all local governments in the short to medium-term. These include measures to:

- Address intergovernmental imbalances; ensure greater clarity of responsibilities and accountability—especially through the assignment of own-source revenues to the local government level that is permitted to borrow;
- Enhance Central Government monitoring; and consolidate debt and risk management for general government in the Ministry of Finance;
- Ensure effective sub-national government financial management and administration, with greater transparency—while the GFSM2001/14 framework provides the basis, not all the provisions regarding the build-up of liabilities are being recorded for the required coverage of institutions under the framework—especially at the sub-provincial levels.

---

[6]PR China, The State Council, 2010, "Notice on Strengthening the Management of Local Financing Platforms (LFPs)".

[7]Operational is defined as being eligible for market borrowing, as they generate a cash flow that can be used to repay the bank loan; and "quasi-operational" suggests partial cost recovery but requiring a government subsidy.

- Ensure the flow of accurate and timely information on liabilities and risks, that is critical in establishing a market-based evaluation system; and
- Establish credible credit ratings for the provincial and sub-provincial governments that intend to borrow.

The key issues in establishing an effective hard budget constraint at the sub-national level to move towards local borrowing are thus, own-source revenues to be able to repay debt—and ensure credibility of any no-bailout clause; and standardized and timely information to prevent the shift of liabilities to the center or the future generations, e.g., using the GFSM2001/14 framework for general government (including state-owned undertakings at the sub-national level—and covering contingent liabilities in the future). These are summarized in Box 4.1 below.

Box 4.1 Standard and Poor's Ratings Criteria for Sub-National Government Borrowing

- **Economic growth**: outlook and degree of diversification
- **Intergovernmental fiscal relations**:
    - Expenditure responsibilities - clarity
    - Taxing powers—*control over revenue bases and rates*
    - **Equalization—system and design of transfers**
    - Borrowing regulations

- **Sub-National budget** system:
    - Medium-term budget planning framework
    - Clarity of regulations on *fiscal management, accounting and reporting*
    - Effectiveness *of cash management*
    - Independent and external audits

- **Budgetary performance, debt burden and contingent liabilities**:
    - *Sound operating balances and sustainable debt structure* and level
    - *Recognition of contingent liabilities, including from government-owned enterprises*

As mentioned above, the MOF during 2009–11, as part of the fiscal stimulus, bypassed the Budget Law and issued RMB 200 bn local bonds annually and included them in the budgets of local governments—this was increased to RMB 250 bn in 2012 and RMB 350 bn in 2013. The principal and interest would be covered by the MOF, but the final responsibility was shifted to local governments. Without own-source revenues, this does not appear to be a credible option.

In 2011, the MOF allowed the issuance of local bonds by selected local governments (partially in keeping with the Ahmad et al. 2003 recommendation).

Shanghai, Guangdong, Zhejiang and Shenzhen were chosen as the pilots. In 2013, Jiangsu and Shandong were added to the pilots (Liang 2013).[8]

The establishment of local bond markets is an important development for the more advanced local governments, especially municipalities and new cities that require considerable investments in infrastructure. This should have several advantages that will be of long-term benefit in better engaging private sector resources in the development process—these include (as emphasized in Ahmad et al. 2003):

- Helping to deepen capital markets;
- Make transparent a process that is at best semi-legal at the moment; and equally importantly,
- Free up central resources for regions that will not be able to access capital markets over the medium term.

But the preconditions remain critical. Although a local early warning system, and capability to monitor and record liabilities are clearly important, as recommended in (Liang 2013), these are not sufficient to ensure that there is a hard budget constraint, that sanctions are credible, and that there is an efficient long term management of liabilities. Indeed, the work by Qiao et al. (2012) shows that the early warning had no impact whatsoever in Zhejiang, or indeed in other large municipalities.

Hard budget constraints at the sub-national level, whether for provinces or the new cities being created, cannot work without own-source revenues as defined above (see Ambrosanio and Bordignon 2015). This is because, without the ability to raise additional revenues in case of need, a no-bailout condition cannot work. The local government, for example, can stop paying social benefits that are mandated, and the impasse continues.

In addition, macro-coordination requires that the central government should take responsibility for the global management of liabilities, including the future trajectory of accounts payable and receivable. Within an overall framework of debt sustainability for general government, including SOEs and local governments, there may be separate rules for local governments. A single numerical rule for all local governments may not work, as some jurisdictions may lack the own-source revenue base that might be available to the richer, coastal regions. Thus, the sustainable level in such cases may, perforce, have to be lower.

In other words, a single early warning system for all local governments may be misleading. For instance, Argentina copied the Maastricht rule (with the debt stock to GDP rule of 60%), but got into serious debt sustainability trouble in the early 2000s with the debt stock at 50% of GDP. A similar situation obtained in Pakistan in 2008, and despite a clear debt sustainability endorsement by the Bank and the IMF in 2012, got into trouble again in 2013, requiring yet another IMF adjustment

---

[8]See Liang 2013, "Study of Local Government Bond Market Development," Chinabond for the Asian Development Bank.

program. Thus, if even governments that fail to meet the golden rule have difficulties with counter-cyclical policies, local governments should never have this responsibility—decisions on macroeconomic policy are solidly in the central government's domain.

In establishing a risk register, as recommended in Ahmad et al. (2003), it would be important to consider both current liabilities and likely future trajectories. This is where the issue of local government balance sheets becomes critical, within a GFSM2001/14 framework (see the next section on applications to China). Stress tests are also likely to be needed, given the potential movements in asset prices that will greatly influence future risks and liabilities that have to be borne by the general government. As seen in Spain and Ireland in 2008, and Mexico in the early 1990s, *the failure to properly account for and evaluate risks (including those from the private sector that have public consequences) have major macroeconomic implications.*

Ahmad et al. (2003) suggested the following:

- The MOF would need to determine the apportionment of sub-national debt limits in aggregate among levels of government, and then its allocation among the various administrations at the second and third tier separately.
- The preconditions on full information (following the GFSM2001/14 standard for buildup of liabilities) need to be provided by all level of government, and this would require the maintenance of full balance sheets at appropriate levels.
- The MOF with the assistance of the PBC would maintain a "risk register" of sub-national liabilities and subject these to periodic stress tests.
- Macroeconomic stabilization must remain a central responsibility, although local governments would execute any required stimuli as needed.

4.3 Moving Towards Full Balance-Sheets for Local Governments in China

The absence of full information on local government operations created incentive compatibility problems after 2008, when the central government took active fiscal and monetary policies in dealing with the global financial crisis. LRGs were able to borrow from banks (directly and through local financing vehicles), piling debt during 2009 and 2010. As they are not obliged to submit formal financial reports, it is a difficult job to figure out the exact amount of total debt issued.[9] Furthermore,

---

[9]The National Audit Office in China conducted an investigation in 2011 on LRG debt at the provincial, city (or prefectural) and county level, which gave an amount of Rmb10.7 trillion. In December 2013, NAO revealed that government debt, including general government debt and contingent liabilities stemming from the borrowings of government-related entities, had amounted to Rmb19.1 trillion (US\$ 3.1 trillion) by the end of 2012. NAO also reported that government debt further rose to Rmb20.7 trillion by the end of June 2013.

most of the debt is of short or medium term duration and matures in 3–6 years. If LRGs are not able to repay the debt with their own revenues, fiscal risks become apparent; and the central government, as the guarantor and the lender of last resort, will have to absorb all the associated costs.

Perceiving the latent danger, the central government decided to enact new regulations to curb the LRGs' incentives to over-borrow without discouraging normal financing. The Chinese Ministry of Finance (MOF), therefore, launched the reform of compiling accrual-based comprehensive LRG financial reports in the end of 2010. A 100-page *Manual of Instruction*, which gives detailed explanations on how to convert current cash basis financial statements into accrual basis financial statements, was also published and distributed in that year. In the first half of 2011, the MOF selected 12 provinces as pilot LRGs in preparing the comprehensive financial reports. The list was extended to 23 in 2012, with a new version of the *Manual of Instruction* released.

In November 2013, the 3rd plenary session of the 18th CPC central committee reinforced the importance of the reform, stating "we will establish a unified national accounting system, formulate national and local balance sheets" and "...establish a cross-year budget balance mechanism, a comprehensive government financial reporting system on accrual basis, and a standardized and reasonable debt management and risk early warning mechanism for both central and local governments",[10] which conveys the signal that further firm reforms will be taken in the following years.

In 2014, the MOF required all provinces to issue comprehensive LRG financial reports, and 2015–2020 will be an experimental period, in which all LRGs, following the *Manual of Instruction 2012*, try to compile complete comprehensive financial reports, gain experience and lessons, and feed their opinions back to the MOF. The MOF, in turn, would then revise the manual further for the formal preparation and publication after 2020.

LRGs in China have long been relying on flow data (expenses and revenues) in making budgets and reporting annual fiscal status in final accounts. Stock data (government assets and liabilities, fixed assets, financial positions, etc.) are accounted at the unit level (government administration departments, public institutions and public corporations), and not disclosed in any consolidated financial statement.

LRG balance sheets in comprehensive financial reports, should present the stock quantity of assets, liabilities and net wealth explicitly at the consolidation level, disclose the term and amount of total debt obligations and the amount of liquid assets that can provide solvency in payment crises as well. It would allow the public and the central government to access the LRGs' current borrowing amount and repayment capacity, and provides financial information for municipal bonds ratings.

---

[10]In part 14 and 17 respectively. For full text of "Decision of the Central Committee of the Communist Party of China on Some Major Issues Concerning Comprehensively Deepening the Reform", see http://www.china.org.cn/china/third_plenary_session/2014-01/16/content_31212602.htm.

4.3.1 Management of Liabilities and the Balance Sheet

The Government Finance Statistics Manual (GFSM) 2001/14 issued by the IMF, presents detailed international guidelines on statistical methodologies of the government finance statistics (GFS) framework. By defining institutional units, flow and stock variables in government economic activities as well as the accounting rules with respect to the general government and the public sector, it provides a fiscal analysis framework based on the statement of operating and the balance sheet, and ensures greater accountability and fiscal transparency in GFS. Consequently, comprehensive government financial reports, complied either under IPSASB rules or GASB rules, all follow the international standards and can be compared and analyzed within the same framework.

GFSM requires using the accrual basis in the Statements of Operations and Other Economic Flows, and the Balance Sheet of the GFS framework. In contrast to the cash basis, the accrual basis is more reliable in providing financial information and helping decision-making for the government. Specifically, it is more scientific in disclosing the total amount of government debt in the balance sheet, which is crucial in analyzing fiscal sustainability. For example, if the government enters a contract in procuring a machine but no payment has yet been made, both the corresponding asset and the liability owed (in terms of accounts payable) are recorded in the book on the accrual basis, but neither is on the cash basis. More complicated examples come from the trading of financial assets. When government makes a bank loan, cash basis accounting records the cash proceeds but not the future debt repayments, thereby a fake increase in net assets. Accrual basis accounting, on the contrary, records the incurred liability in the balance sheet and discloses the full and accurate debt level.[11] See Chart 4.2 for a description of the logical framework that provides consistency with the real sector and national accounts as a cross check.

GFSM is evolving with the growing complexity of economic developments, government behavior and the sustainability of fiscal policies. The initial guidelines in *GFSM 2001* suggest all economic flows be recorded on an accrual basis, and for the first time incorporated an integrated balance sheet approach to compiling and presenting GFS. The guidelines in *GFSM 2014* have been revised to maintain consistency with other macroeconomic statistical manuals and guides (for example, *2008 SNA* and *BPM6*), in terms of coverage and reporting on public transactions, especially investment and recognition of liability.

To follow the recent practice by the public sector of many countries in financing infrastructure projects and construction, *GFSM 2014* supplemented the appendix in regard to government liabilities incurred by SPE (Special Purpose Entity). Government-related SPEs are usually established for financial convenience, involved in fiscal or quasi fiscal activities including borrowing and securitization of

---

[11]The accruals-based system needs to be supplemented by full accounting for cash. The GFSM 2014 recommends using the cash basis of recording in the *Statement of Sources and Uses of Cash*.

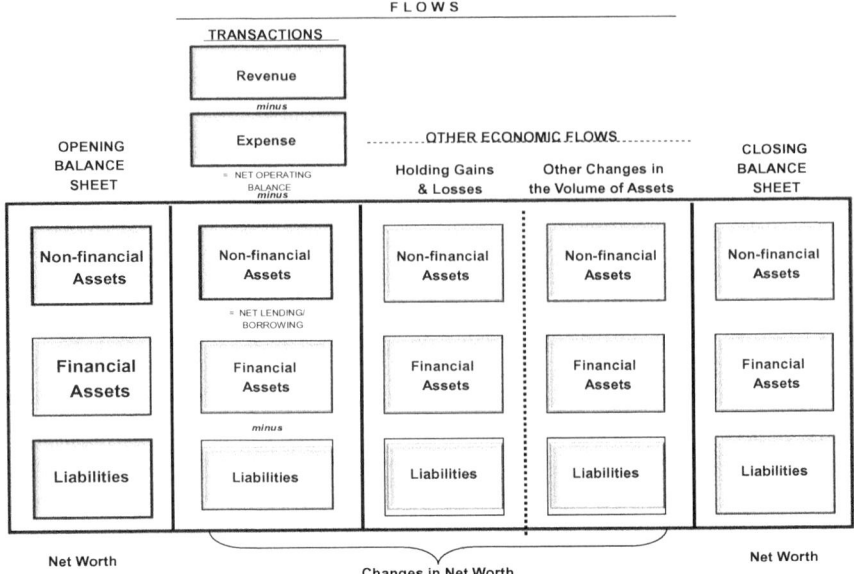

Chart 4.2 The logical structure of the GFSM framework—Importance of balance sheets

assets. As required by *GFSM 2014*, "If the SPE is part of the public sector, its debt should be part of the debt of the public sector or relevant subsector."

Cross-cutting issues such as PPPs (Public-Private Partnership) are more complicated in recognizing the government liability. PPPs are long-term contracts between a private company and the government, where the former acquires or builds an asset or set of assets (roads, bridges, water supply, etc.), operate these for a period, and then hand the asset over to the latter. PPPs assume that private management may improve efficiency in production or provision of services as well as the access to financial resources, nonetheless it brings ambiguity in recording the related assets and liabilities in either party's balance sheet. The *GFSM2014* suggests if the government is considered the economic owner of the asset(s) during the economic period, a transaction should be imputed to cover the acquisition of the asset as financial lease or a loan that equals the market value of the asset at acquisition should be imputed, but does not necessarily eliminate the agency problem: the government should meet the public goals and social obligation, while the private company looks only for economic returns. The government liabilities in PPP projects, as a consequence, may not be fully disclosed, and there is a considerable opportunity for game play as discussed in Ahmad, Bhattacharya, Vinella and Xiao (this volume). IPSAS 32 however, requires that should the asset revert to the government at the end of the contract, all liabilities must be recorded in the balance sheet of the relevant level of government with appropriate provisioning. This would close the gaps.

4.3.2 Accrual-Based Government Accounting in China

An obvious challenge in compiling LRG balance sheets (and the comprehensive financial reporting) in China comes from the difficulty in moving from the cash basis to the accrual basis.

Government accounting in China has been long focused on budget accounting that adopts the cash basis. In 1995 the MOF promulgated a new Budget Law to set up the framework of central and local government accounting, and in 1997, it further released "one guideline and three regulations,"[12] which marked the full establishment of the budgeting system. However, as the economic reform progressed and the government's role changed, the system become obsolete in providing complete information to monitor sub-national governments in delivering their mandated duty—aside from the fact that these mandates were often not very clear, and that own-source revenues are still not well defined.

Although public institutions, such as hospitals and colleges in China, began to use the accrual basis in the 1980s and 1990s, the first trial of changing the basis in budget accounting did not start until 2001, when the MOF released a supplementary regulation allowing five specific items to be recorded on an accrual basis. In 2002, in response to the issuance of *GFSM 2001* by the IMF, the MOF initiated systematic research on the base change[13] and allowed the balance between the budget and actual cash payment to be transferred to the debit item in next year, which indicates the adoption of a modified cash basis. An amendment to the Guideline on Institutional Units Accounting was then published in 2013, but did not change the accounting basis in general.

Bigger steps were taken August, 2014, and the revision of the Budget Law was filed and passed in the Standing Committee of the National People's Congress, and became effective from 2015. In this revision, provincial governments are officially allowed to issue bonds if they can justify their financially credibility, which can be reflected by the balance-sheet data. In parallel, the proposed "Reform Measure on Accrual Basis Comprehensive Government Financial Reports" was approved by the State Council in December, and the MOF required that by the end-2020 all levels of government in China should provide detailed financial reports, including their balance-sheets. The reform will be carried out in three steps. In 2015, the MOF will construct a government accounting framework and collect data on LRG debts. In 2016 and 2017, selected pilot LRGs will publish accrual-basis financial reports. Finally, governments at all levels will be required by 2020 to release the reports and accompanying financial analyses.

---

[12]They are the Regulations on Overall Budget Accounting, the Regulations on Administrative Units Accounting, the Regulations on Institutional Units Accounting, and the Guideline on Institutional Units Accounting.

[13]Xiang, Huacheng and Jiwei Lou, *"Reform of Government Budgeting in China: 1998–2003"*, Chinese Financial & Economic Publishing House, 2004.

The major task for LRGs in the experimental period lies in the conversion of cash basis financial statements in the budget accounting system into an accrual basis. Following the *Manual of Instruction* by MOF, LRG accountants should dismantle existing financial books, select and aggregate meaningful data, and fill them into the entries in the given template of the operating statement and the balance sheet. The statements are consolidated and internal lending and borrowing should be cancelled out and further adjustments made.

Complicated as the process is, it does not guarantee reliable or satisfying accrual basis financial statements, especially regarding sub-national government debt. Cash basis accounting drops much of the useful information in economic activities, so data from existing books are far from complete or accurate. Furthermore, as Chinese LRGs are deeply involved in infrastructure construction with SPVs (financing vehicles) and PPPs since 2008, the balance sheet may not be sufficient to disclose the incurred liability.

The MOF and the PBoC sent research teams in 2014 to investigate sample LRGs' progresses in preparing comprehensive government financial reports. By identifying common problems, challenges and experience, the teams contributed much insight on optimizing the reform scheme. One group took County K as an example.

4.3.3 County K's Comprehensive Financial Reports and Balance Sheets

County K is from an eastern province in China, one of the 12 pilot LRGs selected by the MOF in 2010. Located at the northern Yangzi riverside, K has a total area of 665 km^2 and a population of 0.66 million. Based on its abundant natural resources (plowed land, mineral water, fishing, coal and river sand), K has developed itself into a river port and an industrial city, specializing in machinery, auto-parts, pharmaceuticals, textiles and ship-building. From 1995, K has been listed in top 100 counties in China in terms of comprehensive economic performance. In year 2014, K's GDP reached RMB 71.2 billion, (or ¥ 104,000 per capita) and annual growth 10.2% (Table 4.1).

Following the *Manual of Instruction 2012*, K compiled the comprehensive LRG financial report for both 2012 and 2013 (see Table 4.2). The job was allocated to the local Bureau of Finance, which divides the procedures into three steps: (1) collecting financial statements from subordinate units, administration institutions, public service units and government-owned companies; (2) converting them into consolidated financial statements following the detailed instructions in the

Table 4.1 K's GDP rank in county-level cities in China

Year	Rank	Year	Rank	Year	Rank
2009	34	2011	34	2013	28
2010	86	2012	29	2014	26

Table 4.2 Balance sheet for County K in 2012 and 2013 (in million RMB)

	2012	2013		2012	2013
Assets			**Liabilities**		
Cash	5123.86	6219.24	Borrowings	6941.67	7235.02
Lendings	111.77	10.81	Interests payable	113.08	378.13
Interests receivable	40.93	119.75	Accounts payable	9285.16	18,418.51
Dividends receivable	231.36	21.55	Tax refundable	126.00	138.00
Accounts receivable	24,016.68	13,204.06	Non-tax refundable		
Tax receivable		80.47	Salaries refundable	5.69	5.82
Non-tax receivable	3.93	11.02	Government subsidies payable		
Inventory	2327.49	4522.70	Government bonds		
Of: public reserve	47.00	1.02	Of: Gov. debt due in 1 year		80.00
External investment	6600.76	11,634.94	Other liabilities	15,399.47	49.27
Of: Government investment			**Total Liabilities**	31,871.07	26,304.75
Fixed asset	8041.11	5063.86			
Of: infrastructure	4810.26	1534.59	**Net Assets**		
Projects and buildings	4529.79	3392.54	Current surplus	1822.80	652.38
Intangible assets	8319.99	6575.84	Accumulated net assets	26,064.19	27,301.88
Other assets	410.39	3402.23	**Sum of Net Assets**	27,886.99	27,954.26
Total Assets	**59,758.06**	**54,259.01**	**Liabilities and Net Assets**	59,758.06	54,259.01

manual; (3) assembling the complete comprehensive financial report. The complete report is composed of 4 parts: the financial statements (the balance sheet and the statement of operating transactions[14]), annex, government fiscal and economic description, and government fiscal management. The results, in general, give a reasonable estimation of total assets and net assets and slight decline from 2012 to 2013. However, some items show radical changes that cannot be explained by real economic activities. For example, public reserves and infrastructure decline sharply, interest payables more than triple, accounts payable more than double, and other liabilities almost disappear. In fact, as a trail, the compilation in 2012 and 2013 experiences adjustments in scope, coverage, data sources and the raw data as well.

---

[14]Cash flow statement is not required by the MOF at the present time.

4.3.3.1 Coverage of Entities

The balance-sheet provides combined assets and liabilities of all government and government-controlled or related entities, i.e., government administration departments, public institutions and public corporations (or government-owned corporations). Public corporations are classified as not-for-profit and for-profit and adopt different consolidation methods. Financing vehicles are considered as not-for-profit and adopt full consolidation.

In 2013, the Bureau of Finance in K adjusted the identity of some departments and institutions, recognized more government-owned corporations, and reclassified the not-for-profit and for-profit companies (see Table 4.3). The partial scope change led to the number changes in the balance-sheet.

4.3.3.2 Data Sources and Consolidation

All data in the balance-sheet are retrieved from the government and the subordinate units' financial statements and specialized reports. As required by the MOF, the balance sheet items are booked at historical cost; and if this is not available, replacement cost applies.

Fixed assets and depreciation. As government-owned corporations use different cost recovery methods while public institutions do not account for depreciation, the Bureau of Finance reassesses the value of all fixed assets. Accumulated depreciation is calculated linearly based on the asset type and age; for assets with unidentifiable age, it is set at 50% of the initial cost. The Bureau of Finance also verifies the numbers with data in existing statements.

Payables and receivables. They are cash payments or outlays within 1 year, and are not accounted on a cash basis. The Bureau of Finance adds up each account payable and each account receivable in the subordinate units' books to get the aggregate, and cancels out those resulting from internal transactions for consolidation. Interest payables (receivables) are calculated based on the total borrowing (deposit) and the interest rate, while dividend receivables are the realized net profit multiplied by the percentage of government equity on for-profit companies. Similarly, items that come from internal lending and borrowing and investment offset with each other.

External investments and Borrowings. External investments are defined as the equity investment on for-profit companies. The recorded amount is the

Table 4.3 Balance-sheet coverage of entities in K

	Government administration departments	Public institutions	Not-for-profit corporations	For-profit corporations
2012	49	158	24	17
2013	67	147[a]	16	43

[a]including 14 infrastructure construction companies which used to submit pubic budgets to the government

company's year-end equity multiplied by the government's share; meanwhile the net asset is augmented by the same amount. Borrowings refer to those in not-for-profit corporations and government's financing for infrastructure projects. They are recorded as fixed assets in both the government and each unit's final accounts in the cash basis budgeting system, and should not be counted twice when accrued to the government balance sheets. Internal lending and borrowing offset with each other in consolidation.

For-profit and not-for-profit and corporations enjoy different consolidation methods. For-profit public corporations are consolidated with the equity method—only the equity amount adds to the net wealth and the external investment in the LRG balance sheet. Not-for-profit public corporations, on the other hand, are fully consolidated in that each asset and liability item should be added on the corresponding item in the LRG balance sheet.

Nonetheless, assembling collected data into accrual basis consolidated balance sheet items proved to be extremely arduous. Since public institutions and corporations are not compelled to submit financial reports, the Bureau of Finance has to call for their historical accounting books, which may miss crucial information or be full of mistakes. Moreover, financial reports from most subordinate units are compiled on cash basis, so the detailed but mechanical guidelines in the *Manual of Instruction 2012* do not necessarily eliminate the inconsistency between the accounting methods. LRG accountants have to make adjustments at their own discretion, which could be crude or arbitrary and misleading.

4.3.3.3   Recognition of Asset/Liability

The process of compilation allows most of the public or government-related assets to be counted in the LRG balance sheet: libraries and parks are reported in the public institution balance sheet and consolidated in the LRG balance sheet; infrastructure such as government-run public transportation are reported in not-for-profit corporation balance sheet and then recorded in the LRG balance sheet, and so on. Some items existing in the final accounts on a cash basis are also recorded as an asset in the LRG balance sheet, for example, accumulated fund surplus in fiscal-supported programs such as education and health care.

Land. According to *GFSM 2014*, remote or inaccessible lands that government cannot exercise effective control should be excluded. Lands registered in K's Land Reserve Center, however, are developed and should be included. The ownership of these lands is attributed to government-owned real estate developing firms. As they are identified as not-for-profit companies, developed lands are presented in the LRG balance sheet through fully consolidation.

More importantly, liabilities in the LRG balance sheet include the borrowing by the government and debt in not-for-profit companies. As the total liability is explicitly disclosed, the balance sheet provides more transparency in government fiscal sustainability than flow data. Specifically, government debt in financing vehicles are disclosed in the LRG balance sheet through full consolidation.

LGFV. Local government financing vehicles (LGFVs) are entities set up by local governments to raise funds primarily for infrastructure and real estate development projects. By the end of 2013, K identified 16 LGFVs with total liability of 18.5 billion RMB, and this amount is added to the borrowing in the LRG balance sheet. Debt amount for each individual LGFV is also given in an appendix table in the comprehensive financial report. For example, the largest company X, which was established in 2004 for searching, cleaning up and exploiting lands for the local government, has a total asset of 16 billion RMB and net wealth as 9.9 billion. X issued bonds in 2010 and 2013 totaling 2.7 billion. However, it does not ensure sufficient disclosure, as discussed in next section.

4.3.3.4 Other Disclosures

Economic assets with given quantity but unknown values are not included in the LRG balance sheets. Those assets may include lands exploited but not transferred to the Land Reserve Center, natural resources (such as rivers, riverside and riverbanks) that have significant influence on local GDP and fiscal income and infrastructure that are managed by public institutions (roads in urban and rural areas). Natural resources with identified reserve amount but no clear proprietary title are not included either.[15] However, as these assets can be turned into economic assets with clear value and ownership in the future, the amounts are disclosed in the annex of the comprehensive financial report to provide more information. For example, K reports 3509 km of rivers, 52 km of riversides, 95 km of riverbanks and 1440 km of urban and rural roads in the end of 2013.

Disclosure of liabilities is more important in analyzing fiscal sustainability. While explicit borrowings are all recorded according to the *Manual of Instruction 2012,* implicit liabilities and contingent liabilities are not, which is consistent with *GFSM 2014*. However, while *GFSM 2014* recommends including net implicit obligations for social security benefits as a memorandum item to the balance sheet, K does not report unfunded superannuation accounts, local government guarantee liabilities or contingent liabilities in PPP projects in the annex, due to lack of data and valuation methods.

4.3.4 Comments on K's LRG Balance Sheet

4.3.4.1 Not Sufficiently Detailed

A direct criticism on K's LRG balance sheet is that most of the entries are too general to provide sufficient information. On the asset side, rather than

---

[15]Value of natural resources with clear proprietary title is recorded in the owner's balance sheet.

distinguishing between financial, non-financial and physical assets, it gives a detailed classification of various receivables, marking the transition from cash basis to accrual basis. However, it is the amount and term of long-term financial assets and fixed assets that may reveal more information on fiscal sustainability: in case of a debt crisis, the government can liquidate these assets to gain solvency.

On the liability side, payables have been calculated based on flow data from the budgeting system. Whereas long-term borrowings in public institutions and not-for-profit companies are presented as explicit debt in the balance sheet, the entry "other liabilities" is too comprehensive to be informative. Furthermore, disclosure in the appendix is far from complete by just reporting debts in each individual LGFV. Most LGFVs are active in investing in other companies, the debts of which, although considered as either government liability or government guaranteed by the lenders, are not recorded in the parent company's balance sheet. As a consequence, they do not finally appear in the LRG balance sheet and are not traceable until becoming problematic under adverse market conditions. For instance, in PPP projects, if the private partner quits before the contact ends, the government has to take over the asset and incur a cash outflow which is not expected when signing the contract. In fact, K's rapid expansion of government debt from 2013 to 2014 can be partially attributed to the cases that some implicit debts turned problematic and explicit.

4.3.4.2 Missing Information in the Cash Basis System

Most public institutions in K (except for 3 local hospitals) use cash basis accounting, which does not require deprecation or amortization of fixed assets. Although companies (both for-profit and not-for-profit) adopt the accrual basis rules, they are arbitrary and crude in depreciating fixed assets and have never conducted stocktaking on inventories or revaluation on non-financial assets. That may lead to the overvaluation of assets and net assets in the balance sheet.

The Bureau of Finance in K has tried to improve data accountability by requiring all subordinate units to report detailed information (amount, years used, historical cost, current depreciation and accumulated depreciation) of all tangible assets and reassessing the value with consistent depreciation rules. However, this trial is not applied to intangible assets.

4.3.4.3 Unreliable Data Sources

In the trial compilation, the Bureau of Finance in K extended the coverage of subordinate units when identifying more for-profit and not-for profit companies, which accounted for the drastic data change from 2012 to 2013 to some extent. It is expected that more accurate coverage will result in the following years.

However, problems in data sources lie in the process of gathering financial data from the subordinate units. The reported financial statements are usually prepared in simple templates with primitive entries. For example, company X, the largest LGFV in K, does not distinguish between internal debts and external debts, which leads to the inaccuracy when the Bureau of Finance offsets internal lending and borrowing to get the government debt amount. Inconsistent entries in different companies and institutions also bring much difficulty in balance sheet consolidation. Moreover, borrowings by X's subordinate companies are not reported thereby not included in the LRG balance sheet. Although, in principle each debt or loan taken by the government should be registered in a separate government office (Debt Registration Center), there still can be errors, omissions and missing of historical data.

4.3.4.4 Difficulty in Distinguishing Not-for-Profit Companies

The MOF *Manual of Instruction 2012* defines not-for-profit companies as "government-owned companies that undertake financing, construction and operating of not-for-profit projects". In general practice of the trial compilation, LGFVs are classified as in this group. However, the distinction is ambiguous: LGFVs may invest in both for-profit and not-for-profit projects, whereas for-profit companies are also involved in not-for-profit business. For example, public services such as waste water processing and trees planting in K are both undertaken by for-profit companies.

The ambiguity may distort debt disclosure in that government borrowings in not-for-profit projects taken by for-profit companies are not recorded in the LRG balance sheet. On the other hand, it also underestimates some public responsibilities already assumed by the government. For example, one specific entry "public reserves" in the LRG balance sheet template aims to report government reserves such as rice, pork, seeds, fertilizers for its obligation in handling natural disasters, stabilizing goods prices and managing agricultural productions. Unfortunately, all the reserves are held by for-profit companies; they disappear from the LRG balance sheet when the latter are consolidated with the equity method.

4.3.4.5 Suggestions to Improve the LRG Balance Sheets

The cost of compiling an accrual basis comprehensive financial report with data from a cash basis system is larger than expected. As the transition from cash basis to accrual basis cannot be made overnight, *GFSM 2014* suggests a 4-step path which is feasible for most countries. China is currently between the second step ("assembly of balance sheet information on financial assets and liabilities that would allow estimates to be made of the other economic flows as the relate to these financial instruments") and the third ("collection of a complete set of information about the stock positions of nonfinancial assets held at a given time and their valuation at current market prices".[16]

Implementation of the complete government financial report in China will take time, especially when the accounting basis has not been revised. Nonetheless, some technical improvements can be made at the current stage. For example, the MOF *Manual of Instruction* should provide a more detailed and scientific format to fully reflect the LRG's various assets and liabilities in fulfilling its obligation in public service. Implicit debt and contingent debt disclosure should be mandatory in the annex, which does not have to be the valuation of debt but the description of related transactions and the nominal amount of investment. In particular, infrastructure projects (specifically PPPs) should be separately listed in the annex to reflect the Chinese characteristic of heavy government investment. It thus provides the users (for example, bond rating agencies) information beyond balance sheet numbers. Finally, MOF can arrange training program for LRG accounts to get high quality reports.

4.4 Managing LRG Debt with Incomplete Balance-Sheet Information

It is clear from the above discussion that it will take time to develop full balance sheet information at the sub-national level in China. Even in one of the most advanced regions of China, with considerable technical sophistication and human resources, County-K does not have an adequate representation of the liabilities and their changes over time.

This means that additional efforts will be needed to track the buildup of liabilities from "below the line", or by tracking the main financing items plus operating deficits. Much of this information is available real-time with the PBoC. This method has typically been used in large countries, such as Brazil and Argentina, e.g., in the 1990s when the FMISs and balance sheets were inadequate to track the buildup of sub-national liabilities. In China, the PBoC information would need to be supplemented by information on "shadow banking" and there is now a much better understanding of the nature and effects of this type of financing (Qian 2016). Two other sources of financing would still be missing—liabilities associated with PPPs and accounts payable or arrears. If there is tight monitoring of PPPs, and recording of associated liabilities, the "below the line" methods could still be used to measure "changes in liabilities over time."

The "below the line" methods could be triangulated against the detailed information made available through the audit process—in order to get a handle on how much of the liabilities might have been captured by the financing methodology in

---

[16]Item 1.38, Page 6, *GFSM 2014*.

the past, and the same proportions used as part of an "early-warning" exercise for the build-up of liabilities.

Finally, it is important to note that the measurement of liabilities does not imply that these can be stopped easily, as this is a function of the assignments and the incentives and leverage that local governments may have in relation to the provision of basic services or missing accountability. The latter is part of a wider set of reforms to determine the appropriate levels of "accountable" government, clarity in their functions and including their potential access to own-source revenues.

References

Ahmad, E., Keping, L., & Richardson, T. (2001). Recentralization in China? *IMF Working Paper.*

Ahmad, E. (2015). Institutions and governance. In E. Ahmad and Q. Brosio, *Handbook of multilevel finance.* Edward Elgar.

Ahmad, E., Bordignon, M., & Brosio, G. (2016). *Multilevel finance and the Eurocrisis.* Edward Elgar.

Ahmad, E., Bhattacharya, A., Vinella, A., & Xiao, k., this volume.

Ahmad, E., Albino-War, M., Fedelino, A., Jacobs, D., & Gardner, J. (2003). *China: Managing sub-national fiscal risks.* IMF, Fiscak Affairs Department.

Ambrosanio, M., & Bordignon, M. (2015). *Positive and normative theories of revenue assignments.* In E. Ahmad and G. Brosio, eds.

China: "Decision of the Central Committee of the Communist Party of China on Some Major Issues Concerning Comprehensively Deepening the Reform", see http://www.china.org.cn/china/third_plenary_session/2014-01/16/content_31212602.htm.

China, Ministry of Finance, China, Regulations on Overall Budget Accounting, the Regulations on Administrative Units Accounting, the Regulations on Institutional Units Accounting, and the Guidelines on Institutional Units Accounting.

Polackova, H. (1998). Contingent liabilitie: A hidden risk for fiscal stability. *Policy Reaserch Paper WPS, 1989,* Washington.

Li, Y., et al. (2013). *Chinese national balance sheet 2013.* Beijing: Social Sciences Academic Press. (in Chinese).

Li, Y., Zhang, X., & Chang, X. (2015). *Chinese National Balance Sheet 2015: Leverage Adjustment and Risk Management.* Beijing: Social Sciences Academic Press. (in Chinese).

Liang, H. (2013). Study of local government bond market development. Chinabond for the Asian Development Bank.

Ma, J., Zhang, X., Li, Z., & Xiao, M. (2012). *A study of China's national balance sheet.* Beijing: Social Sciences Academic Press. (in Chinese).

Qian, E. (2016). The Chinese shadow banking: Structure, driving force and risk. Zhejiang University, processed.

Qiao, B., Chen, Q., & Liu, X. et al (2012). Blueprint for better management of subnational government implicit and explicit debt, Asian Development Bank.

Chapter 5
Subnational Public Debt in China and Germany: A Comparative Perspective

Gisela Färber and Zhijie Wang

Abstract Subnational public debt poses problems, including both China and Germany. In context, the total public debt amounted to 54% of GDP in China in 2012 and 74% in Germany in 2015. However, total general government debt in Japan was 274%, and 198% in Greece and 104% in USA.

5.1 Introduction

Subnational public debt poses problems, including both China and Germany. In context, the total public debt amounted to 54% of GDP in China in 2012 and 74% in Germany in 2015. However, total general government debt in Japan was 274%, and 198% in Greece and 104% in USA[1], subnational public debt significantly varies across the lower levels of government and among the governments at the same level. The total amount of subnational pubic debt is not very transparent: in China it has not been counted among the official public debt data[2] because the budget law did not permit direct borrowing until recently and much of the debt was on account of special vehicles and entities owned by local governments. In Germany, local governments in certain states illegally borrowed (so-called cash credits) against their current accounts over many years, or accumulated arrears.

In Germany the liabilities of a few Länder have been examined critically. Similarly, the high level of indebtedness at the local level in China has begun to

---

[1]See Bundesministerium der Finanzen (2016): Monatsbericht January 2016. (http://www.bundesfinanzministerium.de/Content/DE/Monatsberichte/2016/01/Inhalte/Kapitel-5-Statistiken/5-1-16-staatsschuldenquoten.html).

[2]See OECD (2015): OECD Economic Surveys China 2015, pp. 19.

G. Färber (✉)
Speyer University, Speyer, Germany
e-mail: faerber@uni-speyer.de

Z. Wang
Tianjin, China

© Springer Nature Singapore Pte Ltd. 2018
E. Ahmad et al. (eds.), *Fiscal Underpinnings for Sustainable Development in China*,
https://doi.org/10.1007/978-981-10-6286-5_5

attract strong international attention. The Chinese National Audit Office reported that local government obligations were 17.9 trillion Yuan (2.56 billion Euro or 30.44% of GDP) by the end of June 2013, which is 1.5 times as high as the debt of the central government.[3] Since January 2015, China has allowed provincial governments to issue bonds directly for the first time, but the financing dilemma has not changed for the lower levels of local government. Germany in contrast has adopted the so-called debt brake in 2009 requiring balanced budgets from 2016 for the Bund (Federal Government) and from 2020 for the States. Municipalities and counties expect increased budget pressure with declines of transfer payments when the States consolidate their budgets, and also push functions down to the level that is immune from the balanced budget rule.

The effective—legal and illegal—subnational debt is influenced by many factors. Among these are the legal rules for borrowing and repayment terms, the theoretical background applied in the specific system of fiscal federalism, and the institutional settings for supervision and sanctions. Subnational governments in both China and Germany are currently looking for ways out of their financial crisis respectively, with more sustainable financing of public expenditures. Both are facing the goals of increasing, maintaining and securing economic growth that crucially depends on efficient infrastructure investments with sustainable financing profiles. Therefore, a working concept of 'sustainable' public debt is crucial for the long term growth and economic competitiveness in both countries.

Given the very different causes, issues, risks and effects of subnational public debt, it is useful to pose how Germany is dealing with the problems associated with the "debt-break" concept, and China with the problems associated with issuance of bonds for local government debt in China. The question arises, whether the— diverging—instruments and institutional frameworks ensure a solid local fiscal policy and bring about a sustainable subnational fiscal stance in both systems, and what action is still needed and possible. We examine in Sect. 5.2, stylized facts to show the quantitative dimension of the problems. In Sect. 5.3, the different institutional and legal frameworks are discussed. The special risks and recommendations for policy actions in China and in Germany will be discussed in detail in Sect. 5.4—we suggest the German sub-national debt problems have implications for China and vice versa. The last section summarises the findings and concludes with suggestions for further research.

5.2 Stylized Facts on Subnational Public Debt in China and Germany

Subnational governments in China and in Germany refeoct different legal and institutional structures. The term "local" is defined differently in both countries which results from the fundamental divergence of a unitary country with a certain

---

[3]Chinese National Audit Office (2013): National Auditing Report on Local debt.

Level	Number	Average population
Länder (States)	16	5.063 million
Counties	323	256,000
County-free cities	117	n.a.
Inter-municipal cooperation-bodies*	1,708	n.a.
Municipalities	13,299	6,000

* Without municipal special purpose associations

Fig. 5.1 Institutional layers of the German subnational government system. * Without municipal special purpose associations. *Source* Kuhlmann, Sabine (2016)

degree of decentralization in China; and a federal state with 'administrative federalism' in Germany (Fig. 5.1).

Germany is a federal state where the Federation and the States (Länder) have both their own constitutions. Local governments are basically municipalities (cities and villages) and counties. They are dependent on the States and are the lowest levels of administration. The Constitution of the Federal Republic of Germany gives the right of 'self-administration', which includes—besides the right to decide on all tasks with immediate local concern which are not regulated by superior levels of government—the right of an adequate financial management and a certain autonomy with regard to taxes.[4] States supervise local budgets according to their respective 'state constitutions', by approving them before they become legally effective.

China, is a unitary state. According to article 30 of the Chinese Constitution, subnational (=local) governments in China are organized in a five-tiered hierarchy,[5] with each level of government reporting to the next higher level. The Budget Law requires every level of government to make its own budget and have it approved by the People's Congress at the respective level (Fig. 5.2).

5.2.1 China

Local (subnational) debt in China means the indebtedness of all five sub-national administrations, provinces, prefecture-level cities, counties, towns and villages. There are a number of different definitions of local government debt in China. A narrow explanation is the difference between the total local expenditure and the total local revenue of a local government, where total local expenditures include the

---

[4]See Henneke (2013): Gefährdung kommunaler Selbstbestimmung in Deutschland, p. 825.

[5]The two lowest levels usually are combined to the fifth and lowest level of government, so that in total the Chinese government is in total five-tiered. The actual vertical administrative reform aims at reducing the number of tiers to three: central government, provinces and counties. See Division for Public Administration and Development Management (DPADM) Department of Economic and Social Affairs (DESA) United Nations (2006): China, Public Administration County Profile, New York 2006. (http://unpan1.un.org/intradoc/groups/public/documents/un/unpan023305.pdf).

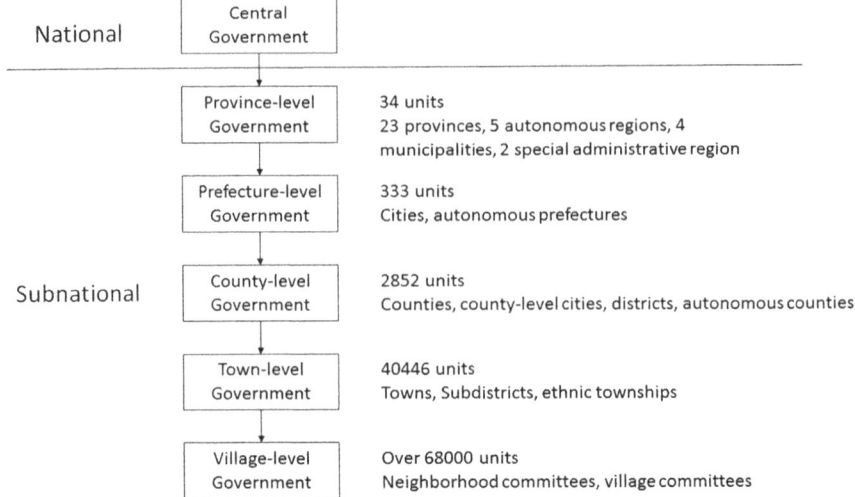

Fig. 5.2 Structure of government in China (end of 2012). *Source* China statistical yearbook 2013

budgetary, extra-budgetary and off-budget expenditures, and total local revenues include the budgetary, extra-budgetary and off-budget revenues. Government loans from businesses or banks, short-term inter-governmental loans, debts owed to construction companies or teams for public works projects constitute local government debt. However, local governments assume debt from a variety of sources. Therefore, a broader definition of local debt is including all direct or contingent, explicit or implicit debt under the local government.

The reform of the public financial management system in China initiated over 15 years ago to standardize transactions according to the GFSM 2001/14 format is not complete, especially at the lower levels (see Ahmad and Zhang, this volume). In a bid to gauge the magnitude of outstanding local debt, the central government has tried to identify all on-budget and off-budget debt. In December 2013, China's National Audit Office (NAO) released a comprehensive report of the country's local government debt. According to the NAO, China's local government debt totaled RMB 17.89 trillion at the end of June 2013, up from RMB 15.89 trillion at the end of 2012 and RMB 10.7 trillion at the end of 2010. Local governments at all levels bore the responsibility for the debt payment of RMB 10.89 trillion yuan, obligation with guarantee responsibility of RMB 2.67 billion yuan and obligation with bailout responsibility of RMB 4.34 billion yuan (Table 5.1).

At the end of 2012, total public debt amounted to 27.77 trillion RMB (44.75 billion US $, 37.28 billion Euro) or 53.47% of GDP of which central government held borrowings of 11.9 trillion RMB and local governments 15.9 trillion RMB. The latter were composed of 9.6 trillion RNB of borrowing and 6.3 trillion RMB guarantees. Until June 2013, debt with repayment responsibilities at provincial, prefectural and county levels amounted to RMB 10.58 trillion. The rate of increase

Table 5.1 Local debt in 100 million RMB

Year	Debt with repayment responsibilities	Contingent liabilities		Total
		Guarantee responsibilities	Bailout responsibilities	
2010	67,109.51	23,369.74	16,695.66	107,174.91
2012	96,281.87	24,871.29	37,705.16	158,858.32
June 2013	108,859.17	26,655.77	43,393.72	178,908.66

Source NAO (2013), author's calculations

of local debt was 14.41% in 2010, 17.36% in 2011 and 26.59% in 2012. In June 2013, the debt of local governments had increased again by 12.3% to 17.9 trillion RMB or 19.1% of GDP (10.9 trillion RNB borrowings and 7.0 trillion RNB guarantees). The prefecture level cities accounted for 40% of local debt while the share of counties increased to 28% (Table 5.2).

The data for 2014 and further estimations indicate that local debt has sharply increased since 2013 and amounted to 23–24 trillion RMB or nearly 40% of GDP.[6]

Local debt varies significantly among the provinces (aggregated levels of lower local governments). It was the highest in the four metropolitan cities with provincial status: Shanghai (more than 3500 RMB per capita), Tianjin (nearly 3500 RMB per capita), Beijing (more than 3000 RMB per capita) and Chongqing (2500 RMB per capita). However, in general poorer provinces incurred greater debt than the richer ones. On average, local debt in China amounted to about 1370 RMB per capita. And debt with repayment responsibility amounts to 61% (see Fig. 5.3).

The poorer provinces in Western and Southern China show a considerable higher indebtedness than the Metropolitan city-provinces and Eastern coastal provinces. Local debt reached more than 90% of GDP in the south-western province Guizhou, while the neighbouring Metropolitan-province Chongqing had debts of more than 60%. The lowest local debt was in the "industrial" provinces: Shandong and Guangdong amounting to around 15% of GDP. However, the within-Guangdong indebtedness is similar to the distribution within China—see Xiao, this volume (Fig. 5.4).

The NAO report provides a classification of counterparties into separate groups and sectors. The "Government" sector only covers the debt of governmental departments and not state owned enterprises, while the other entities are owned or controlled by the government are shown under the public sector. Given the prohibition of direct borrowing by local governments, urban development investment corporations (UDICs) owned by local governments were used to generate much of the local borrowing, accounting for 61.65% of total local debt. The use of UDICs was were streamlined in 2010 with considerable effect. The state-owned or holding

---

[6]See Wu (2015): An Introduction to Chinese Local Government Debt; MIT Center of Financing and Policy, October 2015. (http://cfpweb.mit.edu/wp-content/uploads/2013/08/Policy-Report-of-Chinese-Local-Government-Debt-final.pdf; download 12-2-2016).

G. Färber and Z. Wang

Table 5.2 Local debt at different levels of administration in 100 million RMB

Year	Level of administration	Debt with repayment responsibility	Contingent liabilities		Total	% of local governments (%)
			Guarantee responsibilities	Bailout responsibilities		
2010	Province level	12,699.24	11,977.11	7435.59	32,111.94	29.96
	Prefecture-level	32,460.00	7667.97	6504.09	46,632.06	43.51
	County level	21,950.27	3724.66	2755.98	28,430.91	26.52
	Total	67,109.51	23,369.74	16,695.66	107,174.9	100
June 2013	Province level	17,780.84	15,627.58	18,531.33	51,939.75	29.03
	Prefecture level	48,434.61	7424.13	17,043.70	72,902.44	40.75
	County level	39,573.60	3488.04	7357.54	50,419.18	28.18
	Town level	3070.12	116.02	461.15	3647.29	2.04
	Total	108,859.17	26,655.77	43,393.72	178,908.66	100.00

Source NAO (2013), author's calculations

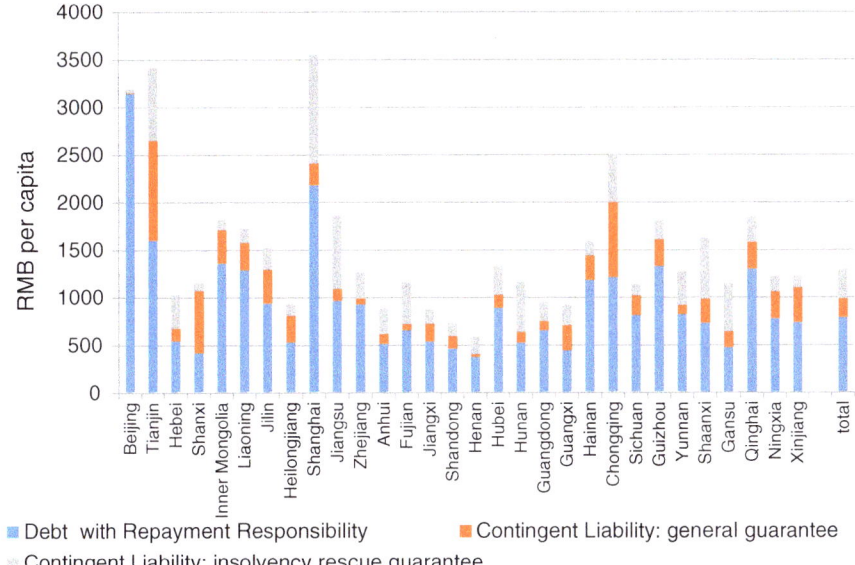

Fig. 5.3 Subnational public debt of Chinese local governments aggregated at provincial level 2012 (per capita). *Source* NAO (2013), author's calculations

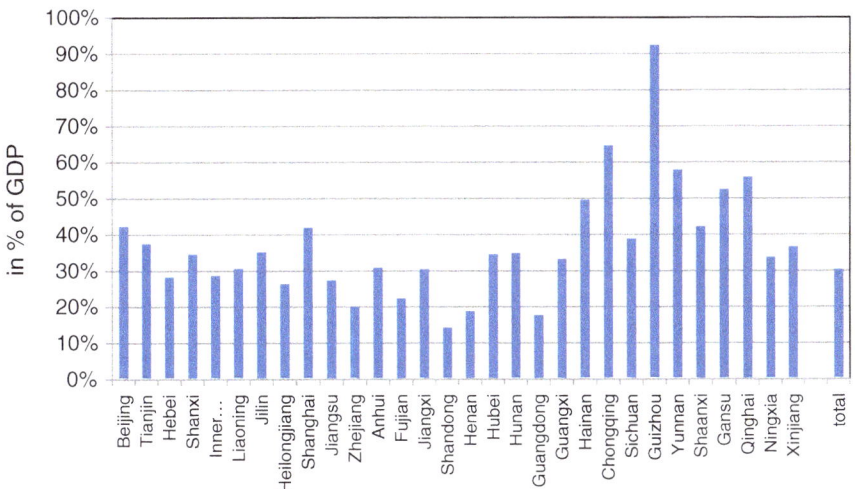

Fig. 5.4 Subnational public debt of local governments in China aggregated at provincial level end of 2012 (in % of GDP). *Source* NAO (2013), author's calculations

enterprises, with lead state-owned enterprises, generated a debt of RMB 3.14 trillion to become the third largest component of local debt (Table 5.3).

The NAO report also provides information on a breakdown of local debt by the type of creditor. Bank loans, build-transfers schemes (BOT/PPPs) and bond

Table 5.3 Local debt by expenditure areas at end June 2013 in 100 million RMB

Category	Debt with repayment responsibility	Contingent liability		Total	%
		Guarantee responsibility	Bailout responsibility		
Urban construction	37,935.1	5265.29	14,830.30	58,030.64	34.64
Land purchase and storage	16,892.7	1078.08	821.31	18,792.06	11.22
Transport facilities construction	13,943.1	13,189.00	13,795.30	40,927.37	24.43
Public housing	6851.71	1420.38	2675.74	10,947.83	6.54
Education, science, culture and public health	4878.77	752.55	4094.25	9725.57	5.81
Development of agriculture, forestry and water conservancy	4085.97	580.17	768.25	5434.39	3.24
Eco-development and environmental protection	3218.89	434.6	886.43	4539.92	2.71
Industry and energy	1227.070	805.04	260.45	2292.56	1.37
Others	1,2155.60	2110.29	2552.27	16,818.13	10.04
Total	101,189.00	25,635.40	4,0684.30	167,508.5	100.00

Source NAO (2013), author's calculations

issuance constitute the major sources of local government liability.[7] Compared with data from 2010, the proportion of bank loans fell from 79.01% in 2010 to 56.56% in 2013, showing the tendency to reduce the dependence on banks. At the same time, shadow banking and BOT and trust financing is increasing in importance—generally for (86.77% of the capital) infrastructure and public welfare projects, such as urban construction, land purchase and storage, transport, construction of subsidized housing, education, science, culture and public health, agriculture, forestry, water conservancy and eco-development.

Local governments initiate local government financing platforms (UDICs) by transferring land use rights or existing assets. UDICs are treated as state-owned enterprises in accordance to China's Company Law. Once UDICs meet the capital requirement, they could finance the rest of the needed capital from banks or raise funds from equity or bond markets. UDICs play a crucial role in promoting the economic growth and engage in the construction projects, such as local transportation, energy, water, urban infrastructure, public housing etc. As the principal financing agents, UDICs can borrow directly from debt market, including bank loans.

---

[7]See OECD (2015): OECD Economic Surveys China 2015, pp. 22.

In the late 1980s, the first UDIC was established in Shanghai to support local infrastructure development in the form of trust and investment companies. The consequence of such practice is the escalation of local government debt. In the late 1990s, the central government forced the closure of thousands of trust and investment companies. However, due to local investment demands and fiscal shortfalls the rebirth of UDICs emerged in the 2000s, which helped local governments to raise funds and to get through difficulties during the global financial crisis in 2008. According to 6576 UDICs were formed at the provincial, prefectural and even at the county level by the end of 2010. At that time, LGFP debt was around RMB 4.97 trillion.

Compared with bond issuance, financing of UDICs is more opaque and off the regular budget. In June 2010, the State Council issued a Notice regarding the Issues of Strengthening the Management of Local Government Financing Platform Firms to clean up UDICs, including detailed classification of UDIC bank loans, assessment and characterization of their risks, and caps set on their operations. NAO (2013) shows that the number of UDICs increased to 7170 by the end of June 2013. UDICs have now been severely curtailed.

5.2.2 Germany

Government 'funded' debt in Germany reached 2048.3 billion Euro on December 31, 2014. German municipalities account for less than 7% of the total debt, compared to the Länder (30%) and the Bund (63%). The debt of social insurance funds is of minor importance because these operate on a pay-as-you-go basis, and any overspending always has to be financed by an increase in contribution rates.

The share of municipal debt has dropped from 12 to 7% of the total since 1990. While the debts of the Länder have increased by a factor of 3.7 and debt of the Bund by a factor of 4.2 since German unification, the local debts have only roughly doubled in nominal terms. More than three quarters of total public debt was generated after the German unification in 1990. The economic and financial crisis led to a sharp increase of public debt during 2008–2010. Since then, Germany underwent a remarkable process of consolidation. While the Federation operates a balanced budget, state and local governments have reduced their deficits and many of them all over Germany have been able to retire some debt. The ratio of public debt to GDP which had exceeded 80% in 2009/10, declined not only for total public sector, but for each level of government.

'Funded' debts in Germany include credits and loans from capital market with repayment obligations. They cover 96% of total public debt (without guarantees). Guarantees, obligations resulting from leasing operations and others, and liabilities of accounts payable do officially not count as public debt, but are economically equal, and therefore included into the statistical reports on an information basis since 2012 (see Table 5.4). Debts at other public institutions and levels of government are of minor importance.

Table 5.4 Public debt in Germany on December 31st, 2014 in million Euro

2014	Bund	Länder	Local governments	Social Insurances	General government
Capital market	1,289,542	619,477	139,436	559	2,049,014
• Cash credits	19,936	7583	48,031	0	75,549
• Funded debt	1,269,607	611.894	91,405	559	1,973,465
Debt at public institutions	9010	32,837	7657	8550	58,054
• Cash credits	1463	2629	2306	8269	14,667
• Funded debt	7.547	30,209	5350	280	43,387
Liabilities of accounts payable	3966	2287	3527	17,248	27.028
Leasing operations etc.	205	926	899	62	2092
Guarantees	463,608	108,393	29,263	29	601,292
Total	1,766,331	763,920	180,782	26,448	2,737,481
Total without guarantees	1,302,724	655,527	151,519	26,419	2,136,189

Source Federal Statistical Office

A specific problem is related to the so-called cash credits. They are typically used to cover temporary underfunding of (current) public expenditures, e.g., as a result of shortfalls of tax revenues during the fiscal year and should be redeemed in the short term. As they represent current account deficits, they are typically an aspect of local budget approval, even if they are netted to zero at the end of the year. Cash credits are of critical importance only for local budgets as they amount to more than 50% of local debt.

The Chinese local debt definition excludes the debt of state and municipal owned enterprises from public debt statistics, although in fact and/or legally the governments are liable for the debts of their enterprises.[8] Official statistics only exclude 'extra-budgetary spending'—e.g., universities—which have independent budgets (Fig. 5.5).

Subnational public debt is highly variable across the states. In Germany, the city states have collected higher public debt than other states. The highest indebted state is Bremen, where the funded debt per capita is almost 30,000 Euro. Cash credits, debt at public institutions and guarantees amount to more than 6000 Euro per inhabitant. The lowest debt burden is in Bavaria and Saxony (Milbradt 2016—the PM of Saxony did not permit the operation of PPPs in the state to ensure accountability for local debt). While the funded debt of the Free State of Bavaria was 1900 Euro per inhabitant, that of Saxony decreased to 775 Euro. Guarantees are also important and reached 11,400 Euro per capita in Hamburg—a city State.

---

[8]The degree and the conditions of liability diverge according to the legal status of the enterprises, but in fact the governmental guarantees debt service and redemptions.

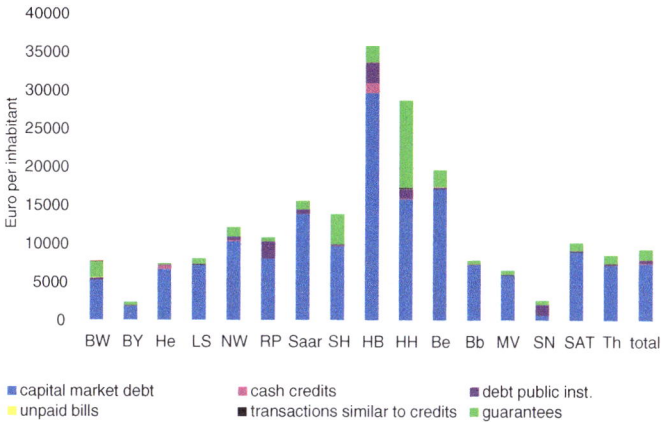

Fig. 5.5 Public debt of German Länder 2014 in Euro per capita. *Source* Federal Statistical Office

Local governments have on average only 1125 Euro funded debt per capita, ranging from 536 Euro in Brandenburg to 2050 Euro per capita in Hessen. Communities in Hessen also use guarantees extensively, amounting to 800 Euros per capita. The most important divergences are related to cash credits. Municipalities in four States generated considerable current account deficits, that were not paid off in the budget cycle, as required, and accumulated over almost 20 years. Cash credits are highest in Saarland and considerably exceed the total borrowing for investment purposes. Problems with 'chronic', in principle illegal, cash credits, also exist in Rhineland-Palatinate, Northrhine-Westfalia and Hessen, and to a minor degree in Saxony-Anhalt, Lower Saxony and Mecklenburg-Pomerania. In all other States, only a few municipalities suffer from high cash credits which cannot be redeemed by regular revenues (Fig. 5.6).

A substantive comparison of the indebtedness of the States is only valid if the debt of state and local levels of government are included because city states are 'unitary' under their constitutions and have not established an independent level of local governments. Among the other states, Saarland has accumulated the highest debt per capita. Figure 5.7 documents the different structure of state and local debt per inhabitant on December 31st, 2014 in the Länder. In addition to credit market debt and cash loans, the municipalities have relatively low levels of budgetary debt, unpaid bills and credit-related transactions. However, guarantees are quantitatively significant, In Hessen and Baden-Württemberg reaching a significantly above-average value of around 996 and 2720 Euro per inhabitant. Saarland, Rhineland-Palatinate, North Rhine-Westphalia and Hessen, with comparatively high state debt, may have a longer-term problem with the municipal cash loans due to the magnitude of borrowing.

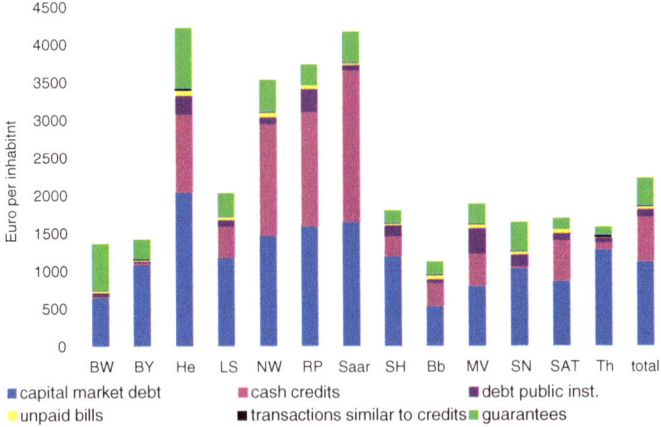

Fig. 5.6 Debt of local governments in Germany at the end of 2014 in Euro per capita. *Source* Federal Statistical Office, authors' calculations

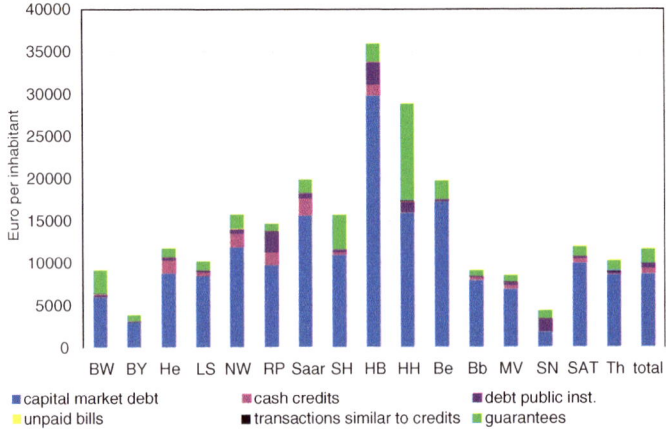

Fig. 5.7 Debt of state and local governments in Germany, end-2014. *Source* Federal Statistical Office, authors' calculations

In Germany, there is no information available regarding the type of investment projects financed by borrowing, because since 1970 all net borrowings are to part of financing spending. The Federation and the States prefer obligations, bonds and direct loans from banks and insurance.[9] Local governments rely on their saving banks, owned by them.

---

[9]See Deutsche Bundesbank (2016): Monatsbericht 1/2016, p. 64*.

5.2.3 *Comparison*

In Germany, central government public debt is the most significant. The magnitude of state and local government debt is relatively small, but several show jurisdictions face severe budgetary deficits. Public debt has been growing slower than GDP, not only at the federal level, but also at the state and the local level. However, the divergence among the Länder and among the municipalities not only all over Germany, but also within the respective States is high and needs political measures in order to maintain the uniformity of living conditions as required in Art. 72 of the Federal Constitution. Guarantees are not counted among pubic debt in the narrower sense, but constitute an important instrument of economic policy at all levels of government. They often replace direct funding through subsidies, but reflect risks of future payments.

The statistical documentation on public debt has been improved during the recent years. It includes now unpaid bills, as far as they are reflected in the accounting systems.[10] Implicit debt, like the future pension payments for civil servants, are not counted as public debt although they are not fully funded and represent the biggest item of future payment obligations in addition to official public debt. In addition, however, there are many ways and types of hidden public debt, mainly by shifting transactions to government owned enterprises or creating public-private partnerships just for the purposes of circumventing budget limits and financing investment expenditures.[11] All these hidden transactions are equivalent to borrowing, in so far as they establish future payment obligations on public budgets and burden future generations of tax-payers. But in contrast to public debt, they are not documented in any budget or official statistics, and are even not declared to the elected members of Parliament, who have the right of legislation in all budgetary affairs.

In China, local governments have accumulated more debt than central government. In China borrowings with future repayment obligations and also guarantees contribute to public debt. Local debts, and particularly those with repayment obligations, are growing across all levels of local government faster than

---

[10]New public management procedures have decentralized budgetary competences to the operating departments. In many cities, the Finance Departments do not know how many bills have arrived at the operational units, which organize their 'own' payment of invoices. Therefore, the volume of hidden debt by through arrears is not known with any certainty.

[11]See Federal Ministry of Economic Affairs and Energy (2015): Increasing Investment in Germany, Report of the Expert Commission on Behalf of the Federal Minister of Economic Affairs and Energy, Sigmar Gabriel. (http://www.bmwi.de/BMWi/Redaktion/PDF/I/investitionskongress-report-gesamtbericht-englisch,property=pdf,bereich=bmwi2012,sprache=de,rwb=true.pdf; download 18.2.2016).

GDP. However, local debt magnitudes in China are not reported annually. There is considerable debate in China concerning the magnitude and consequences of local debt.[12]

Following the financial crisis in 2008–10 in order to stabilize economic growth, there was counter-cyclical borrowing requirements mandated by the central government to the lower tiers. Other components of local debt, particularly those formally connected with UDICs and the local SOEs are much less clear and the terms and conditions under which the borrowing was undertaken remain something of a challenge to disentangle (see Ahmad and Zhang, this volume).

Another difference between China and Germany is that in China borrowing is often connected directly with public investment projects to be financed; while in Germany debt adds to the financing for all public expenditures, including investments.

5.3 The Legal Base of Subnational Public Debt in China and Germany

In all countries, public debt is governed by specific laws and regulations. These depend on whether the public sector institutions can become bankrupt, or whether this is legally excluded. In the first case, the capital market undertakes important component of control. In the second case, the regulation needs to be stricter and has to cover cases in case the governments cannot finance or repay the loans[13] without excessive burdens on future generations. Rules are needed for bail-outs in order to avoid disincentive effects.

5.3.1 China

China is characterized by a combination of centralized policy making with and decentralized decision-making.[14] In the early 1980s, the responsibility system concentrated resources in the hands of local governments. With the tax reform in 1994, there was a centralization of tax administration together with the introduction of national tax instruments such as the VAT. Although there was revenue-sharing,

---

[12]See Li, Yang, Xiaojing Zhang, Xin Chang, Duoduo Tang, and Cheng Li. 2012a. "China's Sovereign Balance Sheet and its Risk Assessment (I)." Economic Research Journal (Chinese) 47 (6), pp. 4–19; and Li, Yang, Xiaojing Zhang, Xin Chang, Duoduo Tang, and Cheng Li. 2012b. "China's Sovereign Balance Sheet and its Risk Assessment (II)." Economic Research Journal (Chinese) 47 (7), pp. 4–21.

[13]Jia et al. (2010): The risks and outways for local debt in China.

[14]Shen (2009): Vertical Management in the background of authority decentralization: model and suggestion.

local governments did not have control over tax rates or bases—a situation that also exists in Germany.

As spending continued to be decentralized (Xiao, this volume), local government budgets became precarious, especially at the lower county and town levels, which are essentially dependent on transfer payments from higher levels for 61.7% of budgetary resources in 2012.[15] The county and town governments are exposed to a high level of uncertainty, and also subject to suasion from higher levels.

Under article 28 of the 1995 budget law, local governments were forbidden to borrow directly.[16] Since the local governments had no sufficient revenue to finance public services and infrastructure, they resorted to local state-owned companies, which borrowed money on the capital market in order to finance the infrastructure projects of local governments. The new budget law permitted the provinces to directly issue bonds for the first time from January 1st, 2015.[17] in order to provide an orderly access to credit and restructuring of local debt. However, the prefectural, county and town governments were not allowed to borrow. In the absence of own-source revenues, there was limited appetite among investors to purchase the bonds.

Until May 22nd, 2015 five provinces published bond issuance plans. A large portion of these bonds were to be used to reduce the old debts. Given the creditworthiness of local governments absent own-source revenues, the banks were not eager to subscribe to the bonds. Jiangsu province postponed its planned bond issuance on April 23rd, 2015 when they could not agree on an emission price with the banks. However, with some suasion on the banks, on May 18th, 2015 Jiangsu Province successfully carried out a bond issuance of 52.2 billion RMB.

---

[15]Chinese National Audit Office (2012): National Auditing Report on financial sources of 54 cities.

[16]Article 28 of China's Budget Law, which was promulgated in 1994, stipulates (1) that "the local budgets at various levels shall be compiled according to the principles of keeping expenditures within the limits of revenues and maintaining a balance between revenues and expenditures, and shall not contain deficit" and (2) that "the local governments may not issue local government bonds, except as otherwise prescribed by laws or the State Council". Article No. 19 (2010) of the State Council stipulates (1) LGFPs with delinquent accounts, or debts that were formed by way of direct borrowing or debt guaranteed by a third-party guarantor will be under review, (2) LGFPs should stop financing public projects which rely on fiscal revenue to pay off any debts incurred, (3) local governments are prohibited from providing any guarantees.

[17]Article 35 of revised Budget Law (2014) stipulates, provincial governments are allowed to issue bonds within a quota set by the State Council, which should be approved by the NPC or its standing committee. Capital raised through bond issuance is purposed for public service-related expenditure and not for operational spending. No. 43 (2014) of the State Council includes seven areas: establishing a transparent budget system; improving the government budget system; moving from an annual budget system to a multiyear budget balance system; improving the fiscal transfer system; strengthening budget execution management; strengthening local government debt management system; and regulating tax concession policies. Yet the key lacuna that affects the credibility of local governments in meeting future debt obligations.

Table 5.5 Legal rules on local debt in recent years

1994	Budget law
2010	Notice of the State Council on Issues concerning Strengthening the Management of Local Government Financing Platform Companies (No. 19 [2010] of the State Council)
2012	Notice of the Ministry of Finance, the National Development and Reform Commission, the People's Bank of China and the China Banking Regulatory Commission on Suppressing Local Governments' Illegal Financing Activities (No. 463 [2012] of the Ministry of Finance)
June 2014	The Central Reform Leadership Team reviewed Overall Plan on Deepening the Reform of Fiscal and Tax System, which outlines the roadmap to fiscal reform including local debt management in the coming years
August 2014	Amendments to Budget Law
October 2014	Notice of the State Council on Strengthening the Management of Local Government Debt (No.43 [2014] of the State Council)

Source Author

The limit to the credit financing of provincial governments was set by the central government to 16 trillion RMB in September 2015.[18] The provincial government decides the amount of the bond, which is then approved by the People's Congress. The upper limit of bond financing is thus different from province to province. The 2014revision to the Budget law represents a big attempt to establish a modern fiscal system although some of the intergovernmental preconditions still need to be established. A list of changes in the legal framework pertaining to local government debt in China is shown in Table 5.5.

5.3.2   Germany

The legal rules for subnational public debt follow the logic of the federal constitution and differ for state and local level. The independent States regulate the limits of public debt in their constitutions but follow the rules of the Basic Law (Federal Constitution). Local debt is regulated by the Länder in their constitutions and in their specific local "constitutions" which are laws containing all important prescriptions for municipalities and counties. European regulations, particularly the so-called Maastricht criteria and the Fiscal Compact, which was established for Euro countries during the Euro crisis in 2011, provide a framework for national debt limits and are effective for the public sector in total. The Fiscal Compact has

---

[18]See Zheng (2016): Debt ceiling will check borrowing. (http://topic.chinadaily.com.cn/index/cache/collection/cbsweb/source/China+Daily/title/16+trillion+yuan+debt+ceiling+set?aid=21742972).

established a borrowing limit of 0.5% of GDP and is based on the changes to the German constitutional rules following the economic crisis.

In 1969/70, Germany had passed a fundamental financial and budgetary reform adopting the principle of Keynesian deficit spending for a more stable economic development.[19] The previously divided current and capital budgets were unified into unique budgets for Bund and Länder. Borrowing which until then was only permitted for the capital account and for specific investment projects, under a "golden rule" was restricted to *planned gross* investment expenditures and could exceed this barrier only for macroeconomic stabilization. The instruments of anti-cyclical fiscal policy were established in the famous 'Stabilitäts- und Wachstums-Gesetz' (law for stability and growth) in 1967.

During 2004–7, there was an attempt to address many of the imbalances in the German Federal system, including overlapping responsibilities, inappropriate revenue assignments (the Länder do not have own-tax raising powers but manage tax administration—almost the case as in China) and an opaque transfer system. The proposed reforms largely failed, although a Swiss-style "debt break" was adopted as a compromise. As highlighted in Milbradt (2016), the big difference between the Swiss cantons and the German Länder is that the cantons have own-tax raising powers whereas the Länder do not. However, in 2009, the Federation and the Länder agreed on a constitutional change to adopt the so-called debt-brake requiring (almost) balanced budgets from 2020. Exceptions are established for recessions and natural catastrophes; these borrowings need to be redeemed within a medium-term perspective. The States—except Northrhine-Westfalia—have meanwhile adopted these rules into their constitutions and have passed specific implementation laws. Five States with relatively high public debt (Bremen, Saarland, Schleswig-Holstein, Berlin and Saxony-Anhalt) receive transfer payments in order to achieve the balanced budget until 2020.[20]

The regulations for local debt are unchanged and not directly affected by the national 'debt brake'. Local tax sources ensure a steady fulfillment of local task such as their shares of the personal income tax and the VAT. According to the legally prescribed framework municipalities can decide the rates of taxes assigned to them, the amount of many fees and the use of their revenues in the municipal budget. For municipal fundraising, taxes, transfers and special charges such as fees take priority over loan financing. Borrowing is only permitted if all other resources cannot cover the expenditures, and is expressively dedicated to finance investment expenditures. The supervisory authorities of the Länder have the task to monitor local budgets, among them whether borrowing budget deficits can be redeemed and serviced within a five year period (mid-term financial planning period). This permits the financing of investments, including depreciation.

---

[19]See Kommission für die Finanzreform (1966): Gutachten über die Finanzreform in der Bundesrepublik Deutschland.

[20]See Gesetz zur Gewährung von Konsolidierungshilfen (Konsolidierungshilfengesetz - KonsHilfG) August 10th 2009 (BGBl. I S. 2702, 2705).

With the debt brake enshrined in Art. 109 and 115 BL in 2009, the Federal Government can only incur loans amounting to a maximum of 0.35% of GDP for financing the budget from 2016 onwards. However, the structural total borrowing ban applies to the Länder from 2020. While the debt brake does not include the indebtedness of municipalities, but indirectly affects them as transfers from the Länder would be curtailed. Moreover, there will be a downward pressure on spending from the states, and likely pressures on local debt as investments at the state level would be curtailed.

The consolidation of debt in municipalities with chronic unbalanced current accounts have been unsuccessful in many cases. Therefore, such Länder established structural adjustment programs for highly indebted municipalities.[21] The objectives and forms of assistance differ in detail. What they have in common is the objective a long-term budgetary consolidation is achieved and improving the financial capacity of the municipalities. The fear is that the debt-break without own-source revenues at the state level will have catastrophic implications for subnational investments (Milbradt 2016; Spahn 2016).

5.4 Economic Challenges and Lessons to Be Learnt

China and Germany both have attempted to address subnational borrowing recently at the state/provincial level, albeit in different ways. China has permitted the issuance of bonds at the provincial level within limits, whereas Germany has introduced a balanced budget rule for the Länder, moving towards the situation that used to operate in China. What both countries have in common is the absence of effective own-source revenue handles at the state/provincial level. These raise questions about the incentive compatibility and credibility of the reform measures in both cases, given major imbalances in the structure of intergovernmental fiscal relations.

---

[21]See Weber and Beck (2013): Kommunale Entschuldungsprogramme der Bundesländer. Specifically Kommunaler Entschuldungsfonds in Rheinland-Pfalz (see Rätz (2011): kommunale Entschuldungsfonds Rheinland-Pfalz), Stärkungspakt in NRW (see Gesetz zur Unterstützung der kommunalen Haushaltskonsolidierung im Rahmen des Stärkungspakts Stadtfinanzen (Stärkungspaktgesetz) December 9th 2011 (GV. NRW. 2011 S. 662), Kommunaler Schutzschirm in Hessen (see der Finanzen (2014): Wege aus der Verschuldungsfalle. Der Kommunale Schutzschirm in Hessen—Zwischenbilanz zu einem Erfolgsmodell), STARK II in Sachsen-Anhalt (see Investitionsbank Sachsen-Anhalt: Sachsen-Anhalt STARK II (http://www.ib-sachsen-anhalt. de/oeffentliche-kunden/investieren-ausgleichen/sachsen-anhalt-stark-ii.html   24.02.2016), Zukunftsvertrag in Niedersachsen (see Niedersächsisches Gesetz über den Finanzausgleich (NFAG) September 14th 2007 (Nds. GVBl. 2007, 466) § 14 a Zins- und Tilgungshilfen zur Zukunftssicherung von Kommunen), Konsolidierungsfonds in Schleswig-Holstein, Kommunaler Konsolidierungsfonds in Mecklenburg-Vorpommern, Kommunaler Entlastungsfonds in Saarland (Gesetz über das Sondervermögen "Kommunaler Entlastungsfonds" October 13th 2015 (Amtsbl. I S. 852).

The spending pressures, and absence of own-source taxes generate incentives for provincial/state political decision-makers to cover costs by "hidden" borrowing. This is often through public enterprises and public-private partnerships (PPPs) which are able to borrow for investment purposes (financial leasing, federal highways, economic projects, reconstruction of public buildings, etc.). While the data may not be reflected in the official statistics, in fact tax-payers continue to carry the financial risks.

Therefore, in both countries the recent data on subnational public debt are incomplete:

- The NAO data for local debt in China is incomplete. According to the China Balance Sheet 2013 released by the Chinese Academy of Social Sciences (CASS), China's total local debt amounted to RMB 19.94 trillion at the end of 2012.[22] Yet it is clear that even in the most advanced local governments, the balance sheet data are either questionable or incomplete (see Ahmad and Zhang, this volume).

- In Germany, PPP liabilities are not recorded in government balance-sheets. With borrowing restrictions imposed by the new 'debt brake' and the need of major expenditures for maintaining and modernizing public infrastructure generate incentives to establish new PPPs just for funding and generating new loans with relatively high interest rates.[23] Local governments require their own enterprises to assist in the reconstruction and new building of schools and other public institutions, by raising credits to finance the public expenditures.[24]

The lack of transparency generates the risk that capital markets may overestimate the true dimension of future payment obligations and start speculating against the governments—as was the case during the Euro debt crisis (see Ahmad et al. 2016). However, there are other problems related with poorly quantified subnational public debt. These include the effectiveness of comprehensive debt limits; and the political economy of preventing bail-outs; and the need for risk management in national and/ or international capital markets.

---

[22]See China Balance Sheet 2013 released by the Chinese Academy of Social Sciences (CASS).

[23]See Federal Ministry of Economic Affairs and Energy (2015): Increasing Investment in Germany, Report of the Expert Commission on Behalf of the Federal Minister of Economic Affairs and Energy, Sigmar Gabriel. (http://www.bmwi.de/BMWi/Redaktion/PDF/I/investitionskongress-report-gesamtbericht-englisch,property=pdf,bereich=bmwi2012,sprache=de,rwb=true.pdf; download 18.2.2016).

[24]See e.g. N.N. (2014): Geisel plant Firma für Schul-Investitionen. (http://www.rp-online.de/nrw/staedte/duesseldorf/thomas-geisel-plant-firma-fuer-schul-investitionen-in-duesseldorf-aid-1.4402099).

5.4.1 Debt Limits, Sustainability and Preventing Bail-Outs

Public debt regulations must include valid and controllable debt limits which are accepted by the public on the one hand and rules for cases of bail-out situations on the other hand in order to prevent them from the origin or prevent damages for the whole public sector and/or the economy.

In China, central government respectively the National People's Congress have set a debt limit for the provinces to 16 trillion RMB for local debt with repayment obligations. Guarantees are not included into that cap. For the first time, individual provincial debt limits were established: "According to Lou Jiwei, the minister of finance, the NPC's decision makes clear that local debts can never exceed 100% of a local economy's wealth-generating capability-as measured by their fiscal revenue."[25] A risk warning system is set up for those provinces of which the accumulated debt range between 80 and 120% of the fiscal revenues; the actual cap would cover about 86% of local debt in the end of 2015.[26] While the majority of the provinces are below the limits, some of them exceed the cap: "In fact Guizhou, a poor province in southern China, has a debt ratio of 207.73% of fiscal revenues, with total outstanding debt nearing Rmb1tn. Ningxia and Shaanxi are around 111%, whilst Zhejiang and Hubei are at risk of breaching the 100% threshold."[27] It is interesting that the poorest and the richest provinces have the highest cumulative debt stocks in China. This reflects the poor resource base of the poorer provinces (but with a hint of directed lending), and for the richer provinces, reflects the importance of credit in establishing the infrastructure that led to high incomes. But presumably the banks and financial institutions are happy to lend to Zhejiang and Shanghai. In Germany, the infrastructure gaps reflect more of the post-unification East-West divide, rather than the rich-poor split seen in China.

What about over-indebted provinces that cannot pay back their loans? Since there are no own-source revenues, the provinces cannot be expected to raise additional levies to ensure repayments—this is a key element in sub-national debt sustainability. Attempts to ring fence capital projects, such as the UDIC approach in the past in China, or the separate capital budgets in Germany, both examples of the golden rule, break down as (1) current spending, such as for operations and maintenance, and ancillary social spending, are needed to make capital investments work productively (Ahmad and Viscarra 2016); (2) public-sector pricing for social purposes, such as schools, may be set at levels that do not permit the investment generating returns for investors, although the social cost-benefit may be positive; (3) with incomplete information, it becomes impossible to ring fence the projects and prevent borrowing for "other uses" by local governments—as was the case in

---

[25]N.N. (2016): 16 trillion yuan debt ceiling set. (http://en.people.cn/n/2015/0831/c90000-8943582. html; download 18.2.2016).

[26]Ibid.

[27]N.N. (2015b): Local government debt out of control in China. (https://chiecon.wordpress.com/2015/12/08/local-government-debt-out-of-control-in-china/; download 18.2.2016).

both China and in Germany; (4) limits on borrowing at the intermediate level—whether zero as now in Germany, or positive as now in China, still generate incentives to push down spending and borrowing to lower levels that are not constrained, as in Germany (Spahn 2016), or where the spending and borrowing might be harder to verify (as in China); and (5) declines in asset values will have reverberations that will affect the financial system and are beyond the capabilities of local government to be able to handle, as was the case in many EU countries during the crisis (Ahmad et al. 2016). Consequently, it may be expected that central government will intervene before a crisis will happen. But this generates incentives for both complacency and to hide local debt problems.

Germany has constitutional limits of public debt according the above described 'debt brake' for Bund and Länder. The cases of bail-out are regulated in detail, but several judgements of the Federal Constitutional Court have confirmed the principle of mutual solidarity between the levels of federal and state government and among the States.[28] Emergency assistance in the case of 'extreme budgetary emergencies' of a Land and must be offered if all other means of consolidation are not available. Bremen and the Saarland received billions of Euros from 1994–2004. Berlin failed to obtain assistance in 2005[29] because the Court was not convinced that all other measures had been taken to reduce debt, and indeed Berlin has generated budgetary surpluses and redeemed the volume of public debt as it is a city-state and has access to own-revenues. The 2009 constitutional reform has established a supervision of state budgets by the Council of Stability.[30]

A 1931 law prevents local insolvency. Local property, needed for the provision of constitutional mandated local goods and services, cannot be impounded. It is unclear until today whether the States are liable for excessive debts of their municipalities and local governments. State governments carefully try to prevent highly indebted communities going the State Constitutional Courts in order to transfer a share of their local debt to the State, and often use specific purpose grants (Bedarfszuweisungen) to reduce the pressure in these local budgets. In recent years, experts report that particularly small communities had problems to renew their loans from private banks; here state-owned banks offered new credits. This breaches any "no-bailout" criterion for hard budget constraints and opens up a tendency for bargaining in relation to sub-national debt.

---

[28]See the following decisions of the German Constitutional Court: BVerfGE 72, p. 330; BVerfGE 86, p. 148; BVerfGE 101, p. 158; BVerfGE 116, p. 327.

[29]See BVerfG, Urteil des Zweiten Senats vom 19. Oktober 2006 - 2 BvF 3/03 - Rn. (1-256), (http://www.bverfg.de/e/fs20061019_2bvf000303.html 24.02.2016).

[30]See the details in Kemmler (2009): Schuldenbremse und Benchmarking im Bundesstaat, p. 552.

5.4.2   Risk Management and the Capital Market

The budgetary risks if public debt is too high can create turbulence in the capital markets. These risks are common, as seen recently in the EU countries during the crisis (Ahmad et al. 2016). One of the main risks, compounded with weak recording and monitoring of liabilities (Ahmad 2016) is that public liabilities can accumulate unnoticed in the balance sheets of banks and financial institutions, hidden by often unrealistic valuations of asset prices, particularly property.

For the financing of China's local government debt, the liquidity risk is considerable, reflected in the maturity mismatch of liabilities on the local governments' balance sheets and their low asset incomes. In general, UDICs that contracted the hidden local debt for local governments have been borrowing short-term funds, which is reflected in the fact that over 60% of local debt matured by the end of 2015, and another 19% will mature between 2016 and 2017. However, it will take considerably longer for infrastructure projects to start generating enough cash flow to repay these loans. As a strict mechanism would be undertaken to regulate new debts, shorter maturity of new debts will have rising financing costs. Severe maturity mismatch will exacerbate the liquidity risk and the vulnerability the short term, creating new challenges to the operation and regulation of local debt. Central government reacted here in 2015 by changing the maturity of local debt into longer term products,[31] by the issuance of bonds that state banks were instructed to hold—transferring some of the risks to the formal state-owned banking sector. The dangers of this approach, even in cases where the jurisdictions are wealthy and not running deficits, and even more in poorer jurisdictions with limited resource bases, is clearly seen in the recent Spanish example—where even the IMF gave it a clean bill of health as late as 2008. As in Spain and Ireland in 2008 onwards and with Mexican financing of road projects in the 1990s (with no state guarantees), private liabilities especially with PPPs run the risk of quickly becoming public through the impact on the banking sector.

An important share of local debt in China is held by the so-called shadow banks. The term shadow banking refers to banks that operate outside the formal banking system and is defined as the system of credit intermediation that involves entities and activities outside of the regular banking system in a broad sense. There are many risks associated with shadow banking systems, since they are not regulated financial institutions. The most significant risk stems from the leverage that they are able to operate by not holding as much in reserves as traditional banks.

Compared with US shadow banks, China's shadow banks are low leveraged and dominated in local currency. The risk of China's shadow banking market is not with its size but with its opaque nature and insufficient regulatory control. Besides, shadow banking has strong ties to traditional banks. Banks can lend funds to trust companies, who can then finance the local infrastructure projects. The fast-growing

---

[31]See N.N. (2015a): China's local government debt—Defusing a bomb. (http://www.economist. com/blogs/freeexchange/2015/03/china-s-local-government-debt; download 18.2.2016).

shadow banking system poses significant risks to the country's economy and financial sector.

The major risk of hidden subnational debt in China is connected with the deficient supervision, in particular the off-budget activities and the control of shadow banking. Hidden subnational public debt could potentially risk triggering a wider-range crisis with spillover effects. The existing financing system leaves subnational governments vulnerable to revenue-sharing changes by the central government or land price decreases. Along the administrative chain, it will weaken both the local and higher level authorities. Local governments could "shift leverage," i.e., local debts could be transferred to the central government. Along the financial chain, shadow banks are always strongly related to traditional banks, the financing source of a shadow bank is still mostly a bank. A default in shadow banks will increase the total risk exposure of the banking system. Along the social chain, although the authority forbids trusts from raising financing from the public at large, some restructured debt or derivatives debt from trust company are bought by the residents. Now a trust default is not likely to happen in the context of current strict control, there is still a hidden social harm and political crises, which could affect social stability (see Liu and Li 2016, this volume). The risks increase with the slowing down of economic growth rates.

Germany has a developed financial market and one of best ratings of government sector in Europe. European debt crisis and the policy of the European Central Bank have caused interest rates of less than 1% for government debt. Local government with high cash loans have often transformed the maturity of these short-term borrowings into mid-term debt. They insurance against increasing interest rates at the time of refinancing the credit, a bit more than 1%. They pay therefore in total interest rates slightly above 2% for their accumulated current account deficits. Capital markets have trusted the repayment ability even for highly indebted local governments. Several Ruhr region cities were able to float a loan amounting to several hundreds of million Euro in 2015 at very decent rates.[32] Actually there is no expectation that ECB could change its market flooding policy within a short perspective.

However, in a mid or long run, all subnational governments bear considerable budgetary risks from their high debt. Will the homogenous rating of all German governments continue despite the tremendous differences of public debt of states and local governments? Will all states succeed in balancing their budgets by 2020? What will be the reactions of the capital markets if they fail? Will the highly indebted local governments succeed in balancing their accrual accounts and maintain positive equity capital? Will the debt-relief programs for local governments which cost several hundred million Euro lead to the reduction of the—in principal –illegal cash loans? Although actually local governments have no

---

[32]See Press release of Helaba February 19th 2015a: https://www.helaba.de/de/DieHelaba/Presse/PresseInformationen/2015/20150219-NRW-Staedteanleihe2.html; Press release of Helaba June 10th 2015b: https://www.helaba.de/de/DieHelaba/Presse/PresseInformationen/2015/20150610-NRW-Staedteanleihe3.html.

problems finding adequate offers for loans and other credits from privately owned financial institutions, will the public-owned banks be able to pitch in when European financial markets regulations becomes tighter?

5.5 Summary and Conclusions

China and Germany differ only at the first view with concern to subnational public debt. It is remarkable that China has started to legalize borrowing at the provincial level while Germany requires balanced budgets at the state level from 2020. It is noteworthy that the debt brake at the intermediate level was needed to reinforce fiscal prudence in Germany, given the absence of own-source revenues at this level a positive limit was seen as infeasible. As agued by Spahn (2016) even this may not work, given the impact that it will have on investment and growth in the long run, and the incentives to push down the liabilities to municipalities with more complex instruments like PPPs, so that they are harder to identify and control.

At the prefectural, county and city level in China public debt continues to be illegal. German local governments (cities, villages and counties) carry forward the traditional rules and limits for local debt permitting borrowing for investment financing as long as the communities are able to service interest payments and the mature redemptions. The regulations in both countries obviously counter-balance each other. Particularly the requirement of balanced budgets and the formal ban of borrowing stand in opposition to the 'golden rule' of investment finance according to which the costs of the long lasting infrastructure should be transferred to the benefitting taxpayers' generations. Both countries obviously lack a true theory of sustainability and a practice of transparent borrowing transactions which clearly identify the risks for future tax-payers.

The most important problem in both countries obviously is that subnational governments do not respect the regulations and interdictions of public debt. Official data although improved and enlarged in the recent years do not provide a true picture of public debt. There are numerous loopholes in both countries containing forms of debt or de facto-debt which are not counted in the debt statistics. The ban on borrowing or debt limits which conflict with the specific political rationality of the governmental decision-makers seems to generate an intensive creativity to evade the officially stipulated subnational debt.

Doubts arise about the role of the respective supervising senior levels of government. In China as in Germany, the supervisory institutions did not intervene in the past to stop "unwarranted" borrowings. Further questions arise whether the sanctions—if any credibly exist—are suitable to prevent undesirable behaviour and "cheating" at the lower levels, especially if there is a tradeoff with central objectives at the local level—e.g., for basic education, health care or santiation. For Germany, at least there is—with regard to the fact that only local governments in some states have chronic current account deficits—a discussion whether the legal regulations are effective or need to be changed. Another hypothesis focusses on the observation that the critical increase local cash loans is a result of being tolerated by the States, after and because the latter had cut back local transfers. Clearly, further questions about the adequate assignment of tax revenues at the subnational levels of government and the role of earmarked and equalization transfers for 'healthy' state/provincial and local finance need to be assessed in both Germany and China.

China and Germany have changed the rules for subnational public debt recently. The 'debt brake' will start to be effective for the Länder from 2020. Chinese provinces are permitted to borrow from January 2015. Resulting real changes may be observable only in some years and depend on better data. The expected (fundamental?) transformations in borrowing behaviour will probably take place under further changes of the framework of fiscal federalism in both countries. For China, the "State Council Opinion 2015/71 on Reforming and Improving the Central-Local Fiscal Transfer System aims at addressing the mismatch by making the fiscal transfer system more transparent and increasing the share of general transfers so that sub-central governments can allocate funds more efficiently."[33] Far reaching reforms of local taxes are needed in order to relieve the dependence of local governments from land transfer income.

In Germany, the state equalization scheme will be reformed from 2020 too. Actual negotiations show some marginal changes which in total transfers lead to a bigger share of total national tax revenues to the states and probably to the local level too. Deeper changes might result from the enormous immigration of refugees and asylum seekers, which will burden the states and local budgets probably for years, but may also ease the demographic constraints faced by Germany's ageing profile at the macro-level. There are national benefits but local costs. The fiscal "rescue schemes" to balance the local current accounts after years of deficits could generate severe local disincentives and the consolidation efforts could be stopped.[34] Confidentially, many politicians expect that the 'debt brake' will not 'survive' until 2020. Consequently, a really reliable, practicable and controllable concept of sustainable public debt is needed, along with the rationalization of spending and revenue authorities and incentives at the subnational level. The German experience has enormous relevance for China.

---

[33]OECD (2015): OECD Economic Surveys China 2015, pp. 22.

[34]See Schlüter (2016): NRW: „Sanierungspläne sind Makulatur", in: Der Neue Kämmerer v 4.2.2016.   (http://www.derneuekaemmerer.de/nachrichten/haushalt/nrw-sanierungsplaene-sind-makulatur-30831/?utm_source=CleverReach+GmbH+&utm_medium=email&utm_campaign=04-02-2016+DNK+Newsletter+%28KW+05%2F2016%29&utm_content=Mailing_9867724; download 15.2.2016).

References

Ahmad, E. (2016). Political economy of information generation and financial management for subnational governments: Some lessons from international experience. In E. Ahmad, M. Bordignon & G. Brosio (Eds.), *op cit.*

Ahmad, E., Bordignon, M., & Brosio, G. (2016). *Multilevel finance and the eurocrisis.* Edward Elgar.

Ahmad, E., & Viscarra, H. (2016). Public investment for sustainable development in Chile. In *Building on the national investment system.* Inter-American development Bank, Discussion Paper No. IPD-FP-469.

Ahmad, E., & Zhang, X. (2016). This volume, *Towards monitoring and managing subnational liabilities in China: Lessons from the balance sheet for county K.*

Bundesministerium der Finanzen. (2016). Monatsbericht January 2016 (http://www.bundesfinanzministerium.de/Content/DE/Monatsberichte/2016/01/Inhalte/Kapitel-5-Statistiken/5-1-16-staatsschuldenquoten.html).

Chinese Academy of Social Sciences (CASS). (2013). China Balance Sheet 2013, Beijing.

Chinese National Audit Office. (2012). National Auditing Report on financial sources of 54 cities, (2012)26#.

Chinese National Audit Office. (2013). *National Auditing Report on Local debt,* (2013)32#.

Deutsche Bundesbank. (2016). Monatsbericht 1/2016.

Division for Public Administration and Development Management (DPADM) Department of Economic and Social Affairs (DESA) United Nations. (2006). China, Public Administration County Profile, New York 2006 (http://unpan1.un.org/intradoc/groups/public/documents/un/unpan023305.pdf).

Federal Ministry of Economic Affairs and Energy. (2015). *Increasing Investment in Germany,* Report of the Expert Commission on Behalf of the Federal Ministry of Economic Affairs and Energy, Sigmar Gabriel, Berlin 2015 (http://www.bmwi.de/BMWi/Redaktion/PDF/I/investitionskongress-report-gesamtbericht-englisch,property=pdf,bereich=bmwi2012,sprache=de,rwb=true.pdf; download 18.2.2016).

Helaba. (2015a). Press release of Helaba February 19th 2015 (https://www.helaba.de/de/DieHelaba/Presse/PresseInformationen/2015/20150219-NRW-Staedteanleihe2.html).

Helaba. (2015b). Press release of Helaba June 10th 2015 (https://www.helaba.de/de/DieHelaba/Presse/PresseInformationen/2015/20150610-NRW-Staedteanleihe3.html).

Henneke, H. G. (2013). Gefährdungen kommunaler Selbstbestimmung in Deutschland. *Die öffentliche Verwaltung,* Heft 21 November 2013, 825–834.

Hessisches Ministerium der Finanzen. (2014). *Wege aus der Verschuldungsfalle. Der Kommunale Schutzschirm in Hessen—Zwischenbilanz zu einem Erfolgsmodell,* Wiesbaden.

Investitionsbank Sachsen-Anhalt: Sachsen-Anhalt STARK II (http://www.ib-sachsen-anhalt.de/oeffentliche-kunden/investieren-ausgleichen/sachsen-anhalt-stark-ii.html 24.02.2016).

Jia, K., Liu, W., Zhang, L., Shi, Y., & Sun, J. (2010). The risks and outways for local debt in China. *Economic Research.*

Kemmler, I. (2009). Schuldenbremse und Benchmarking im Bundesstaat - Neuregelung aufgrund der Arbeit der Föderalismuskommission II. *Die öffentliche Verwaltung,* 62(14/2009), 549–557.

Kommission für die Finanzreform. (1966). *Gutachten über die Finanzreform in der Bundesrepublik Deutschland,* 2 ed. Stuttgart.

Kuhlmann, S. (2016). Local governments in Germany: Key features and current reforms. In: Y. Wang & G. Färber (Eds.) *Comparative studies on vertical administrative reforms in China and Germany, Speyerer Forschungsberichte 285, Deutsches Forschungsinstitut für öffentliche Verwaltung Speyer.*

Liu, S., & Li, C. (2016). Evaluating public services and revenues in relation to public risk management (this volume).

Milbradt, G. (2016). History of the constitutional debt limits in Germany and the new debt break: Experiences and critique. In E. Ahmad, M. Bordignon, & G. Brosio (Eds.).

Niedersachsen: Niedersächsisches Gesetz über den Finanzausgleich (NFAG), September 14th 2007 (Nds. GVBl. 2007, pp. 466).

N.N. (2014, July 22). Geisel plant Firma für Schul-Investitionen. *Rheinische Post* (http://www.rp-online. de/nrw/staedte/duesseldorf/thomas-geisel-plant-firma-fuer-schul-investitionen-in-duesseldorf-aid-1. 4402099).

N.N. (2015a, March 11). China's local government debt—Defusing a bomb. *The Economist* (http:// www.economist.com/blogs/freeexchange/2015/03/china-s-local-government-debt; download 18. 2.2016).

N.N. (2015b). Local government debt out of control in China (https://chiecon.wordpress.com/ 2015/12/08/local-government-debt-out-of-control-in-china/; download 18.2.2016).

N.N. (2016, August 31). 16 trillion yuan debt ceiling set. *People's Daily* (http://en.people.cn/n/ 2015/0831/c90000-8943582.html; download 18.2.2016).

Nordrhein-Westfalen: Gesetz zur Unterstützung der kommunalen Haushaltskonsolidierung im Rahmen des Stärkungspakts Stadtfinanzen (Stärkungspaktgesetz) December 9th 2011 (GV. NRW. 2011 S. 662).

OECD. (2015). OECD Economic Surveys China 2015, Paris.

Rätz, T. (2011). Der kommunale Entschuldungsfonds Rheinland-Pfalz (KEF-RP)—Ein Überblick mit ausgewählten Fragen und Antworten. In *Gemeinde und Stadt: Beilage*, 5, (pp. 2–24).

Saarland: Gesetz über das Sondervermögen Kommunaler Entlastungsfonds October 13th 2015 (Amtsbl. I S. 852).

Schleswig-Holstein: Gesetz zur Konsolidierung kommunaler Haushalte (Kommunalhaushaltskonsolidierungsgesetz) vom 30. Dezember 2011 (http://www.gesetze-rechtsprechung.sh.juris.de/jportal/portal/t/2dzn/page/bsshoprod.psml;jsessionid=24B680B8107787-F9AAAC23CD198ABB6A.jp44?pid=Dokumentanzeige&showdoccase=1&js_peid=Trefferliste-&fromdoctodoc=yes&doc.id=jlr-KommHKonsGSHrahmen&doc.part=X&doc.price=0. 0#focuspoint).

Schlüter, K. (2016, February 4). NRW:Sanierungspläne sind Makulatur. *Der Neue Kämmerer v* (http://www.derneuekaemmerer.de/nachrichten/haushalt/nrw-sanierungsplaene-sind-makulatur-30831/?utm_source=CleverReach+GmbH+&utm_medium=email&utm_campaign=04-02-2016 +DNK+Newsletter+%28KW+05%2F2016%29&utm_content=Mailing_9867724; download 15. 2.2016).

Shen, R. (2009). Vertical management in the background of authority decentralization: Model and suggestion. In *China Public Management* (09).

Spahn, P. B. (2016). Multilevel finance and the euro crisis: The German experience. In E. Ahmad, M. Bordignon & G. Brosio, *op cit.*

Weber, D., & Beck, S. (2013). Kommunale Entschuldungsprogramme der Bundesländer. In *Public Governance: Zeitschrift für öffentliches Management*, Winter 2013, (pp. 12–15).

Wu, X. (2015). An Introduction to Chinese Local Government Debt. MIT Center of Financing and Policy, October 2015 (http://cfpweb.mit.edu/wp-content/uploads/2013/08/Policy-Report-of-Chinese-Local-Government-Debt-final.pdf; download 12-2-2016).

Xiao, K. (2016). Managing subnational liability for sustainable development: The Guangdong Province case (this volume).

Mecklenburg-Vorpommern: Richtlinie für die Gewährung von Zuweisungen zum Ausgleich eines jahresbezogenen negativen Saldos der laufenden Ein- und Auszahlungen in der Finanzrechnung (Fehlbetragszuweisungsrichtlinie—FBZRL M-V) (http://www.landesrecht-mv.de/jportal/portal/page/bsmvprod.psml?doc).

Zheng, Y. (2016, September 8). Debt ceiling will check borrowing. *China Daily* (http://topic. chinadaily.com.cn/index/cache/collection/cbsweb/source/China+Daily/title/16+trillion+yuan+debt +ceiling+set?aid=21742972).

Chapter 6
Involving the Private Sector and PPPs in Financing Public Investments: Some Opportunities and Challenges

Ehtisham Ahmad, Amar Bhattacharya, Annalisa Vinella and Kezhou Xiao

Abstract Given the paucity of public resources, it is important to consider relying on the private sector for financing public investments and infrastructure. There are considerable expectations concerning Public–Private-Partnerships (PPPs) in supplementing public resources, but also risk sharing with the public sector. However, these contracts are subject to abuse, given asymmetric information, and game-play across levels of government that lead to the risks being borne by the central government or subsequent administrations. Specialized agencies can play a useful role in supporting subnational governments with the complex contracting arrangements needed for PPPs. We see that strengthened Public Financial Management is needed, to track the build-up of liabilities at the subnational level, and also own-source revenues to ensure accountability. Uncertainty, including with climate change, may require different arrangements—and the options are addressed in a subsequent

An earlier version of this paper was prepared at the request of the G24 group of countries (Ahmad et al. 2015) and this paper has been prepared with the permission of the G24.

E. Ahmad (✉)
University of Bonn, Bonn, Germany
e-mail: seuahmad@gmail.com; s.e.ahmad@lse.ac.uk

E. Ahmad
London School of Economics, London, UK

E. Ahmad
Pao Yu-Kong Professor, Zhejiang University, Hangzhou, China

A. Bhattacharya
Brookings Institution, Washington, USA
e-mail: abhattacharya@brookings.edu

A. Vinella
University of Bari, Bari, Italy
e-mail: annalisa.vinella@uniba.it

K. Xiao
London School of Economics, Houghton, UK
e-mail: K.Xiao@lse.ac.uk

© Springer Nature Singapore Pte Ltd. 2018
E. Ahmad et al. (eds.), *Fiscal Underpinnings for Sustainable Development in China*,
https://doi.org/10.1007/978-981-10-6286-5_6

123

paper Ahmad, Vinella and Xiao (2017), but the risk-sharing aspects of PPPs may be relevant in many cases.

Given that public investment requirements far exceed available resources in most developing countries, there is a need to both channel public resources wisely and also best leverage the opportunities to utilize both national and international sources of private or institutional finance. A range of instruments is possible, involving combinations of public and private management and financing arrangements (see Ahmad 2014, 2017).

Some investments are likely to be predominantly public, especially where there are externalities in the provision of a balanced and inclusive basis for sustainable growth (e.g., education, regional infrastructure and O&M). These are also needed to facilitate the involvement by domestic private investors and FDI. Worldwide there is a growing trend towards the involvement of the private sector in the financing of infrastructure and in the provision of public services.

Private sector involvement takes diverse organizational forms and arrangements. These range from privatization to deregulation, outsourcing, and government downsizing (see Armstrong and Sappington 2006).

An increasingly popular mechanism in which the private and public interests come together is associated with Public Private Partnerships (PPPs), to finance and manage infrastructure projects across Europe, the US, Canada, and in several developing countries. In this paper, we focus both on the form that the investment takes, e.g., PPPs, as well as the sources of financing. **A fundamental issue is the sharing of risk in the presence of information asymmetries.**

It is also clear that the risks facing private investors are particularly high during the development or construction phase. This relates not just to the costs involved, and the subsequent pricing that may be constrained by the state, but also future revenue streams in relation to the usage and demand have yet to be tested. Once the project has been completed and has become operational, it becomes somewhat easier to securitize the potential revenue streams and involve the private sector in the management of the undertaking. However, in spite of there being some evidence that the success or failure of a project is more sensitive to construction risks than operation risks,[1] a fully general classification cannot be made, as the exact kinds of risks are likely to be highly sector- and project-specific.

In this paper we stress that the issue of accurate information on the generation of sub-national liabilities is of critical importance both to generate adequate signals for investment but also for the macroeconomic management. This is especially the case in a multi-level country, and is typically ignored at some peril, as seen in the Mexican crisis exacerbated by the debts for the highway

---

[1]Gatti (2014) reports that, according to a study conducted by Moody's in 2010, infrastructure projects in the construction phase tend to default earlier, to recover more slowly, and to emerge later from bankruptcy, as compared to infrastructure projects in the operation phase.

projects that had been contracted without Federal Government guarantees. We also discuss the specific case of sub-national liabilities that have appeared in China, and point to the measures that might be needed to ensure that these do not degenerate into macroeconomic difficulties, while at the same time, remaining a sustainable mechanism for financing sustainable investments.

In some cases, macro-problems arise due to the failures of PPP contracts, and the ample room for game-play, that leads on the one hand to inefficient investments, and to the other, to a build-up of liabilities that go unheeded until there is a crisis. Following the recent economic crisis, the International Public Sector Accounting Standards (IPSAS) accounting rules for PPPs were tightened to ensure a better recognition of liabilities. Key issues relate to who owns the asset and beneficiary interests at the end of the contract. The sectoral dimensions are important, as are the public finance implications—including the recognition of liabilities, provisioning and generating public finances to cover the public component. Special issues arise in multi-level countries, both regarding the aggregate build-up of liabilities and their sustainability, as well as the credibility of contracts and incentives to renege.

In Sect. 6.1 we describe some general trends in involving the private sector in public projects. Section 6.2 focuses on PPPs and asymmetric information. We draw some policy conclusions in Sect. 6.3.

6.1 Involving the Private Sector—Some Trends

6.1.1 What Do the Data Show?

Global trends for PPPs—relating to both the total amount of investment and the number of projects (see Fig. 6.1) come from the Private-Participation in Infrastructure Project Database jointly produced by the Infrastructure Policy Unit of the World Bank's Sustainable Development Network, and the Public–Private Infrastructure Advisory Facility (PPIAF).[2] The figures present aggregate values from both sectoral and regional data. From 1991 to 2012, the overall trend for the investment in PPP projects was increasing, although a trough was reached around 2002. There was a 5.8% increase in the total nominal amount of investment commitments in year 2012, compared with 2011.[3] The number of PPP projects, on the other hand, has oscillated between 200 and 400 projects per year since 1993. In 2012, there was a 13% decline in the number of PPP projects worldwide. Overall, this means that the average size of investment commitments is increased in 2012. In

---

[2]See http://ppi.worldbank.org/index.aspx.

[3]*Infrastructure Policy Unit 2012 Global PPI Data Update* at http://ppi.worldbank.org/features/August-2013/PPI%202012%20Globa%20Update%20Note%20Final.pdf.

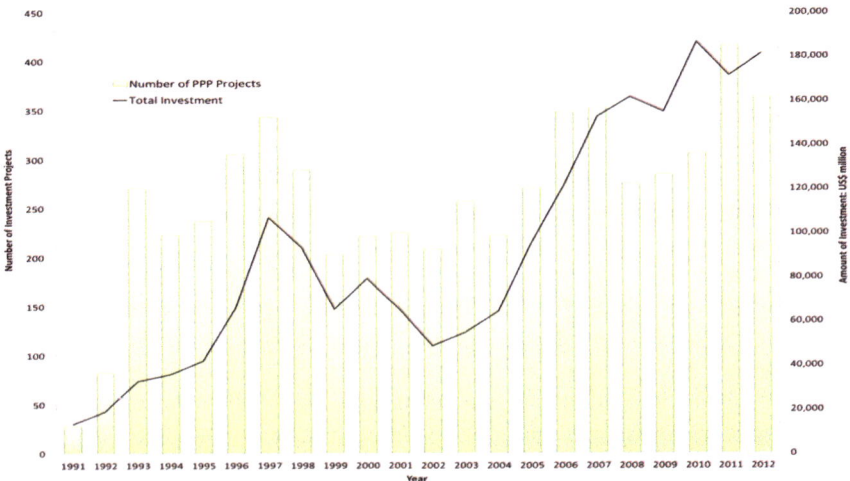

Fig. 6.1 Global Trends for PPP Projects from 1991 to 2012. *Source* World Bank and PPIAF, PPI Project Database

particular, Brazil and India accounted for about 55% of all PPP commitments across the developing countries in 2012.[4]

6.1.1.1 Sector Trends

Figure 6.2 presents the total investments by sector.

The energy sector attracted the largest amount of investments in 2012 with about $76.8 and 244 projects. From 1990 to 2012, there were 111 countries with energy PPPs and 2653 projects reaching financial closure.[5] The most important segment was renewable energy, growing at an annual average of 21% since 2007, doubling between 2007 and 2012.[6] Latin America and the Caribbean (LAC) was the region with the largest investment share (36%). In terms of the format of private participation, Greenfield projects accounted for 68% of the total investment and

---

[4]For detailed report, see (World Bank *Infrastructure Policy Unit* 2012) *Global PPI Data Update.*

[5]Financial closure in the PPI Project Database varies among types of private participation. For greenfield projects and concessions, financial closure is defined as the existence of a legally binding commitment of equity holders or debt financiers to provide or mobilize funding for the project. The funding must account for a significant part of the project cost, securing the construction of the facility. For management and lease contracts, a contract authorizing the commencement of management or lease service must exist. For divestitures, the equity holders must have a legally binding commitment to acquire the assets of the facility. The Database includes only projects that have reached financial closure. Source: http://ppi.worldbank.org/resources/ppi_faq. aspx.

[6]See sector report: http://ppi.worldbank.org/features/December-2013/Energy-Note-2013.pdf.

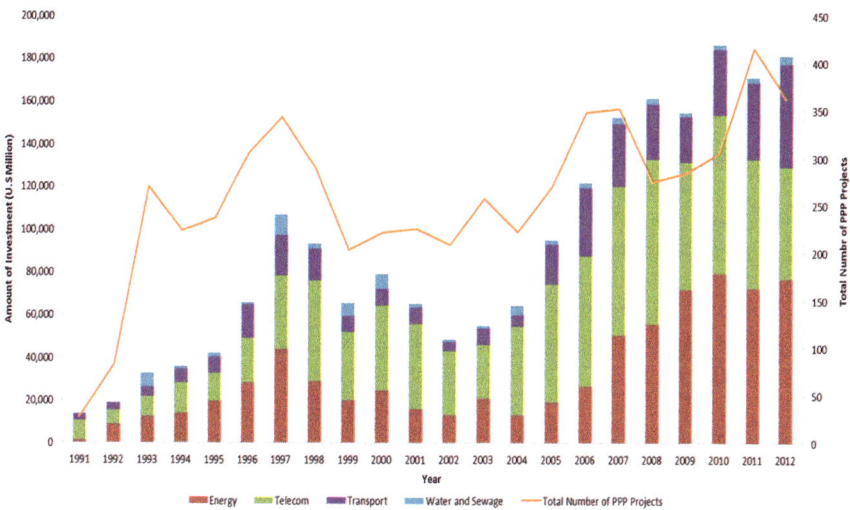

Fig. 6.2 Sectoral Composition of Investments. *Source* World Bank and PPIAF, PPI Project Database

75% of total number of projects. 126 projects were cancelled, or under stress, about 5% of the total investment between 1990 and 2012.

The telecom sector was the second largest sector for PPPs in 2012 with investments of $52.4 billion (15% lower than the $60.2 billion in 2011). In terms of investments, this is the smallest value since 2005. The number of PPP projects reaching financial closure is only four, the smallest number since the availability of the time series. Among different segments, 60% of the investments went into stand-alone mobile operators.[7] Similar with the energy sector, the telecom sector used predominantly greenfield type of projects, which accounts for 61% of the investment and 75% of the total number of projects. LAC was the most active region with 37% of the total investment in telecom PPPs. The number of projects cancelled or under stress was around 3% of the total investment representing 60 cases between 1990 and 2012.

Investments in the transport sector have been increasing over recent years, totaling $46.2 billion in 2012 with 83 projects, mainly in Brazil and India, which accounted for 78% of the investments in 2012. The investments in this sector grew about 25% between 2002 and 2012.[8] Unlike the telecom and the energy sectors, concessions were the predominant form of partnership accounting for 59% of the investments and projects. Latin America and the Caribbean is the most active region, with 42% of total investments. The number of projects cancelled or under

---

[7]See http://ppi.worldbank.org/features/December-2013/Telecom-Note-2013.pdf.

[8]See: http://ppi.worldbank.org/features/December-2013/Transport-Note-2013.pdf.

stress was around 6% of the total investment representing 78 cases between 1990 and 2012.

The water and sewage sector had the smallest investment with US$4 billion in 32 projects reaching financial closing in 2012. Despite its small relative size, the total investments and number of projects rose noticeably over the past decade. In 2012, the two countries with the greatest number of water and sewerage projects were Brazil (11 projects) and China (14 projects).[9] The predominant form of partnership was concession accounting for 62% of total investment and 41% of the overall projects. The projects in this sector were heavily concentrated in East Asia and Pacific with 44% of the total investment. The number of projects cancelled or under stress were around 30% of the total investment representing 63 cases between 1990 and 2012.

6.1.1.2 Regional Trends

The regional decomposition of PPP investment from 1992 to 2012 is shown in Fig. 6.3. **The East Asia and Pacific region grew by 19%** in 2011, reaching $17.2 billion in 2012. In 2012, most of the investment in this region came from the energy sector ($8.9 billion), followed by the telecom sector ($4.3 billion), the transport sector ($3.5 billion), and the water and sewage sector ($355 hundred million). China had the most projects (33 in total) in 2012 and Malaysia attracted the largest investment ($5.1 billion). Greenfield projects accounted for 68% of the projects and 66% of the total investment. The number of projects cancelled or under stress in this region was around 10% of the total investment representing 86 cases from 1990 to 2012.[10]

With the economic crisis, the PPP investment in Europe and Central Asia, declined about 48% in 2011 to $22.5 billion.[11] Despite this sharp drop, the region still accounted for 12% of global PPP investment. In 2012, Ukraine was the most active country with 16 energy projects and commitments of $520 million. The most common partnership in this region was the Greenfield project, covering about 56% of the total investment and 45% of the total projects. The telecom sector captured about 54% of the total investment between 1990 and 2012 and the number of projects cancelled or under stress in this region was around 2% of the total investment representing 36 cases.

The Latin America and Caribbean region saw a sharp investment increase from $56.9 billion in 2011 to $87.0 billion in 2012, although the number of PPP projects declined from 95 in 2011 to 78 in 2012. In total, this region accounted for 48% of global investment, the largest global share for a particular region in the past two decades. Between 1990 and 2012, the telecom sector attracted about 42% of the

---

[9]See: http://ppi.worldbank.org/features/December-2013/Water-Note-2013.pdf.

[10]See: http://ppi.worldbank.org/features/December-2013/2012-EAP-Regional-Note-Final.pdf.

[11]See: http://ppi.worldbank.org/features/December-2013/2012-ECA-Regional-Note-Final.pdf.

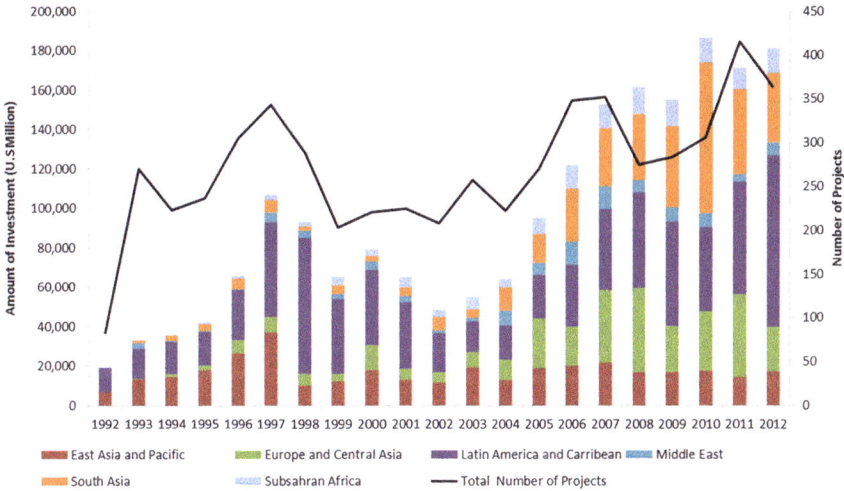

Fig. 6.3 Regional Decomposition of Investment. *Source* Asian Development Bank (2013).

total investment. Like the previous two regions, the greenfield project is the most common type with 41% of total investment and 52% of total projects. The number of projects that were cancelled or under stress in this region was around 7% of the total investment representing 135 cases.[12]

In the Middle East and North Africa region, PPPs investments increased rapidly from $3.9 billion to $6.7 billion U.S dollars, although there was a corresponding increase with doubling of number of project closures. However, the investments in this region in 2012 comprised only 4% of the global investment, about 0.4% of the regional GDP.[13] The telecom sector dominated, increasing 64% from 1990 to 2012. The common type of partnership is greenfield, as in other parts of the world. The number of projects cancelled or under stress in this region was around 1% of the total investment totaling 7 cases.[14]

South Asia experienced a 20% decline in PPP project investment in 2012, down from $43.1 billion in 2011 to 35.1 billion. The number of the projects reaching financial closures remained stable from 123 in 2011 to 128 in 2012. Despite the significant drop in total investments, South Asia was one of the most active regions in the world. India attracted the most regional investments ($31.2 billion) with 106 projects in 2012. In total, private investment comprised 1.5% of the regional investment. A majority of the projects in Bangladesh and Pakistan had their PPPs backed by payment guarantees from the central government and credit

---

[12]See http://ppi.worldbank.org/features/December-2013/2012-LAC-Regional-Note-Final.pdf.

[13]See http://ppi.worldbank.org/features/December-2013/2012-MNA-Regional-Note-Final.pdf.

[14]See http://ppi.worldbank.org/features/December-2013/2012-MNA-Regional-Note-Final.pdf.

support from Asian Development Bank.[15] Between 1990 and 2012, the number of projects cancelled or under stress in this region was around 2% of the total investment (12 cases).

In Sub-Saharan Africa, PPP investments grew about 16% to $12.8 billion in 2012, reaching 7% of the global investment. Between 1990 and 2012, 471 projects reached financial closure. The telecom sector accounted for 77% of the investments. As in the other part of the world, Greenfield projects are the most common form of contracts. The number of projects cancelled or under stress in this region over the period of 1990 and 2012 was around 5% of the total investment (50 cases).[16]

6.1.1.3   Uneven Recognition of Liabilities Within and Across Countries

The generation of standardized information is likely to be a critical factor in generating the "building blocks" for informed decision making, especially when it comes to involving the private sector (both cross-border as well as of national origin) and removing the scope for game play between governments and private contractors, as well as between levels of government. Of course, generating accountable governance is a more complex problem, involving as it does appropriate assignments, as well as institutional arrangements that provide the incentives to manage liabilities efficiently and not pass them on (see for example, Ahmad 2013).

The IMF's revised standards in the Government Financial Statistics Manual (GFSM) provide a comprehensive measure for the coverage and reporting on public transactions, **especially including investments and recognition of liabilities** (IMF 2001). This is fully consistent with the System of National Accounts; hence the linkages between the financial flows and the real sector become clear. The full operation of the GFSM is difficult in many cases, involving as it does a shift towards accruals, and some complexity in both budget frameworks and the ability to track the flows through systems of Government Financial Information Management Systems (GFMISs) and concomitant management of cash flows through a unique Treasury Single Account (TSA) or nested TSAs (as might be needed in large multilevel countries such as China).

The absence of standardized information within and across countries, e.g., in the EU, makes it harder for the private investors to judge the risks involved in particular countries. While this leads to the possibility of being able to "game the system", especially if the down-side risks are likely to be covered by higher levels of government, it may result in inefficient decisions—such as overbuilding of tourist facilities in Spain or Portugal.

---

[15]See http://ppi.worldbank.org/features/December-2013/2012-SAR-Regional-Note-Final.pdf.

[16]Please consult regional report: http://ppi.worldbank.org/features/December-2013/2012-AFR-Regional-Note-Final.pdf.

In some Federal countries, particularly Canada, subnational governments do not comply with national standards of reporting, given the high degree of autonomy of the provinces.[17] This was also the case in Brazil, until the economic crisis in the 1990s required the use of common standards for the operation of the Fiscal Responsibility Legislation. While a step in the right direction, the Brazilian standards do not comply with the GFSM standards on the recognition of liabilities. In Germany too, the Länder have disparate systems, and the 2010 Debt Break legislation hopes to persuade them to conform to common standards and balanced budgets within a ten-year period.

Improvements in IT systems and GFMIS technology now permit relatively easy and inexpensive web-based solutions that facilitate a central repository of data with decentralized accounting and operating systems. This is clearly work in progress including through a community of practice that involves a network of countries and international agencies, and could be supported by technical assistance from a new multilateral bank, or the existing agencies.

In Russia, the effort to introduce a new Treasury System, involving both GFMIS and TSAs, facilitated the introduction of GFSM2001 standards in a comprehensive manner. The shift from legacy systems is not simple, especially when it comes to assets and liabilities.

The Chinese case is also of interest. A decision in the early 2000s was taken to move to the GFSM framework as well as to create TSAs in the Provinces as well as the Center. However, Chinese provinces are larger than many countries around the world, and the issues relating to the full implementation of the GFSM framework at the sub-provincial level still remain to be designed and implemented. This reform has to go in parallel with the reform of the budget law that prohibits direct borrowing by provinces from the private sector, but allows state owned companies (UDICs) to borrow for investments (see Ahmad and Wang 2013; National Audit Report 2011; National Audit Office 2013). Given that the PPPs were creating liabilities that were hard to manage at the local levels, after an initial spurt, the PPPs were reigned in (see Fig. 6.4). Similarly, the indirect borrowing by UDICs expanded considerably, but was reigned in in the recent past. Thus, while China has made considerable progress with the GFSM framework, full implementation to cover all the potential investment-based liabilities still remains to be addressed, and would be among the preconditions along with clarity of responsibilities and local own-source revenues, to ensure the orderly access to credit needed for a more balanced development strategy. Indeed, making better use of the efficiencies generated by private management with PPPs could be better utilized in China, provided the supporting framework to recognize and manage local liabilities is also strengthened. The new budget law enunciated in 2014 permits local governments to issue general purpose and special bonds, subject to oversight and overall limits to

---

[17]Municipalities, however, are subjected to strict control by provinces, but there are no national standards, which make it difficult to report to the GFS Yearbook on general government operations.

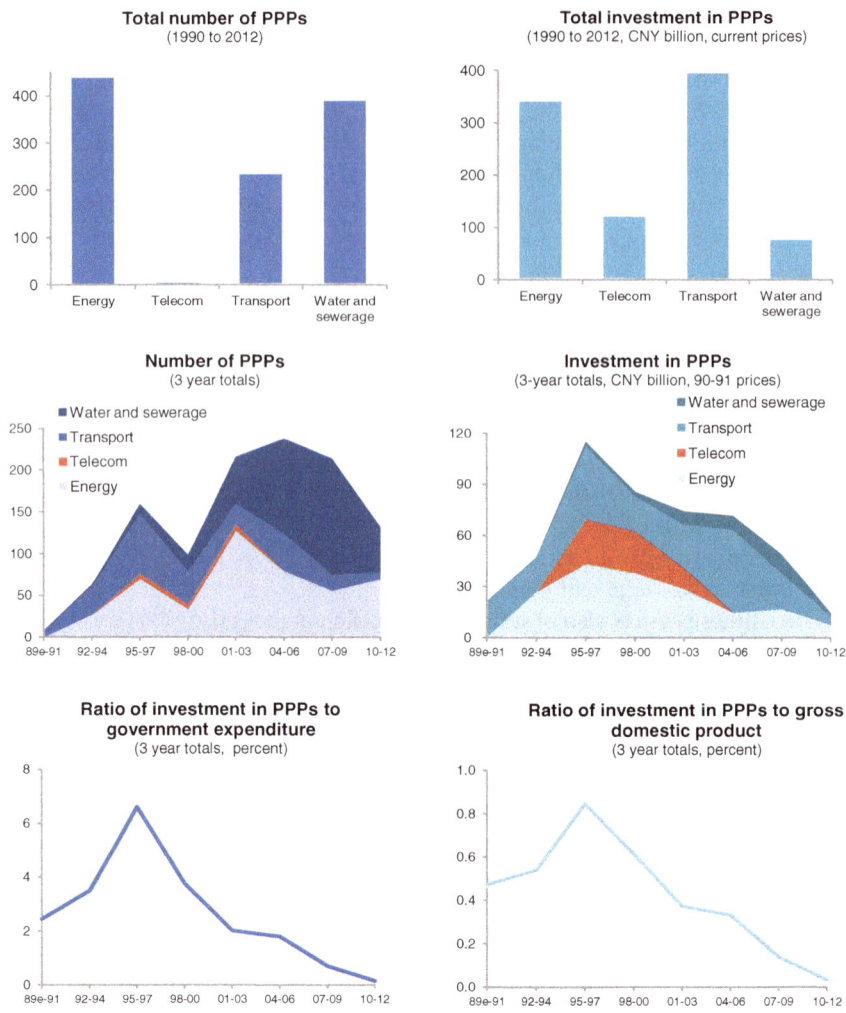

Fig. 6.4 A Snapshot of PRC's Infrastructure PPPs. *Notes* The data show the number of PPP projects and the value of the investment committed to by the project. Data for 1989 are estimated as the average of 1990 and 1991. Constant prices estimates use the gross domestic product deflator. The data show PPPs that involve a private partner, where state-owned enterprises or their subsidiaries that remain majority owned by government entities are not considered private sponsors

be coordinated by the central government (State Council Communiqué, September 26, 2014).

6.1.2 An Approach to Managing Risks While Encouraging Investments

Despite the promises and opportunities associated with PPPs, there are clearly some challenges. The difficulties arise because of the sharing of risks that are complicated by asymmetries in information. The first set of issues relate to the ability of the private partner to mask the costs of the projects and the effort extended. Thus, there are incentives for the private party to renege on contracts, and at the minimum to hide effort and costs of provision. These issues are examined in Sect. 6.2, where we take a sectoral perspective to examine the possibilities to hide information and renege on commitments.

A second set of difficulties concerns the overall public finances at different levels of government—particularly the government's ability to manage current and future liabilities. As the bulk of the investments are likely to involve sub-national governments, that tend to have limited own-sources of revenue, there is a tendency to "kick the can down the road" or to upper levels of government.

Clearly, from an investor's perspective, the credibility and sustainability of government finances is a critical element in taking sound investment decisions. Given that an increasingly large share of investments is being undertaken at the sub-national level, the generation of accurate and timely information on general government liabilities (that include all levels of government and public enterprises) becomes a critical element in an assessment of investment sustainability, especially where cross border investments might be involved. These issues are discussed in Sect. 6.3.

In general, the absence of standardized and timely information on the buildup of liabilities is likely to have two distinct effects. **In periods of boom, this is likely to lead to "irrational exuberance",** and to the generation of inadequate and unsustainable investments. The problems are likely to be magnified at the sub-national level, especially when there are no effective own-sources of revenue or incentives to ensure that the liabilities will not be passed on to the center, Brussels or to future generations.

The obverse is also likely to be a greater problem in developing countries— as investible capital fears to tread in areas where the enabling environment is problematic. Thus, even though there is no standardized information on sub-national operations in Canada, the expectation is that since they have own-source revenues, and the Federal Government is not likely to intervene, that the local governments will "behave well." This would clearly not be the case if there were no effective hard budget constraint, as may be the case at the sub-national level in most developing countries, e.g., including China.

Indeed, the "risk management" framework needs to be flexible enough to accommodate excess private liabilities that are translated into public liabilities —e.g., as seen in the US sub-prime crisis, or the excess building in Ireland and Spain (both countries that had been praised by the IMF for fiscal prudence prior to the 2008 economic crisis). In Europe, it is likely that the presence of a supranational tier blinded markets to the risks involved in specific countries (especially in Southern Europe, from Portugal and Spain to Greece). It is not enough to "assume" that there are hard budget constraints and that markets will adequately assess and discount the risks involved in specific investments. Consequently, the empty buildings in Spain are reminiscent of the Asian crisis of the late 1990s, and the earlier difficulties in Latin America.

6.2 PPPs and Information Asymmetries

A PPP, for the sake of brevity, consists of a long-term contractual arrangement between a governmental body (whether an agency at the central level or a local authority) and a private firm. Under this arrangement, the firm is delegated the delivery of some services, including provision of the associated infrastructure. This includes several tasks, namely financing the investment as well as building, managing, and maintaining the infrastructure that is necessary to provide the services. The firm takes the responsibility for accomplishing all these tasks. PPPs are aimed, on the one hand, at using private capital, together with (or in lieu of) public funds, for the realization of public projects. The fact that the private sector does not spontaneously provide the services suggests the need for public interventions of some sort, and this typically has a financial obligation that may not be realized immediately. Thus, the temptation to think of PPPs as kicking the fiscal can down the road is likely to be short-sighted and problematic.

A key feature of PPPs is the potential for generating more efficient project outcomes. Often, private investment is needed to utilize more efficient management practices than is generally possible in the public sector. Indeed, the greater efficiency in management can provide a benchmark for the improvements in the management of sectors that might have to remain largely in the public sector. Initially utilized in transportation, energy and water sectors, PPPs are currently employed in a significantly larger variety of projects. These include, *inter alia*, prisons, waste management, schools, hospitals, leisure facilities, and housing.

Despite the widespread utilization of PPPs, the evidence to date on their performance is mixed. In the UK, private finance initiative (PFI) projects have started yielding cost savings, relative to traditional procurement arrangements. However, PPPs have failed to deliver the expected benefits, e.g., in specialized IT projects. This suggests that reliance on PPPs is not equally desirable in all sectors and, in particular, that PPPs are not particularly suitable for sectors that evolve very rapidly (Iossa and Martimort 2008). The French experience in the water sector is also not especially positive, and water prices have been found to be higher under

PPP arrangements than under traditional procurement arrangements (Saussier 2006). A particular difficulty in most PPPs is that contracts are renegotiated before reaching their agreed termination date. Renegotiation phenomena are pervasive, especially (though not exclusively) in less developed countries. In Latin American and Caribbean countries a large number of projects were abandoned due to the private (or public) partners' inability to abide by contractual obligations (see, among others, Guasch 2004, and Iossa and Martimort 2008).

Given the evidence, it is now clear that structuring PPPs properly and ensuring that they deliver agreed benefits, is a complex and far from obvious task. Much of the difficulty arises due to asymmetries in information that make it easy to renege on contracts. Ensuring effective risk sharing, including the provision of public resources as agreed within the requisite timeframe is critical in making PPPs work effectively. We will also posit the need for third party arbiters in ensuring that contracts are honoured. In order to accomplish this task, it is first necessary to understand the main features of PPPs as well as the incentives that partners display in PPP arrangements. One can, thus, discuss ways in which the different incentive issues can be tackled, and identify instruments to ensure the effective delivery of services.

6.2.1 Key Features of PPPs

As mentioned above, a PPP is a long-term contractual arrangement between a governmental body and a private firm, under which the former delegates to the latter the delivery of some services. Under a PPP arrangement, the firm is made responsible for financing the investment as well as for building, managing, and maintaining the infrastructure that is used to provide the services. When a PPP is created, the whole project is delegated to the private firm through a global contract. This combines the financial aspects of the investment together with the conditions under which the infrastructure is to be built, managed, and maintained. Moreover, this contract allows for the firm and the investors to be compensated over a long period. This is likely to have budgetary consequences, over the life of the project.

The engagement of the private sector does not mean that there is no role for the public sector. Quite the opposite, governments and more generally, public institutions should ensure that social obligations are met. This requires both effective sectoral reforms as well as adequate public financial management. For successful PPPs it is important to recognize that the public and the private sectors each have certain advantages, relative to the other, in performing specific tasks. The government can contribute to a PPP in several ways. First, it can provide capital for its share of the investment (through tax revenues), transfer assets, make guarantees, or provide in-kind contributions that ease the functioning of the partnership. The government also provides social responsibility, environmental awareness, local knowledge, and an ability to mobilize political support. In its turn, the private sector provides expertise in commerce, management, operations, and innovation to run the business efficiently. The private partner is often required to invest in the project, although this may depend upon the specific contractual agreement (see, for instance, Asian Development Bank 2008). In fact, transferring responsibility to the private sector for mobilizing finance for infrastructure investment is one of the major differences between PPPs and conventional procurement (The World Bank 2012).

PPPs have several specific objectives. First, they are meant to **improve the quality and the performance of public services** to the benefit of users/consumers. Second, they are supposed to reduce or, at least, to **ease the time-profile of the tax-payers' burden**. Third, they should help the public authorities, which are responsible for delivery of the services, to **optimize the realization and quality of those services**. These objectives are pursued, in turn, by two main means. First, the public partner takes advantage of the **financial resources and the technical expertise of the private sector**. Second, the **risks associated with the project are allocated between partners so that each partner bears those that it can handle more efficiently**.

Despite some common features of PPPs, they are not approached everywhere in the same way. Some countries choose to concentrate PPPs in certain sectors. This can reflect priorities for investment or for improvement in service performance, or the willingness to prioritize **sectors** in which PPPs are expected to be most successful. Other countries, conversely, identify sectors (or services within sectors) for which reliance on PPPs is ruled out. These are sometimes called *core* services, *i.e.*, services that should be provided exclusively by the government and, hence, should not be delegated to the private sector through a PPP. Nonetheless, definitions of core services can vary across countries, mirroring local preferences and perceptions (The World Bank 2012).

6.2.2 A Sectoral Investigation

PPPs potentially provide flexible tools for decision makers to promote efficient infrastructure and/or service delivery. However, for a PPP to be successful, it must be designed with attention to the exact context within which it will be implemented. This involves tailoring the partnership to accommodate the main technical characteristics and constraints of the concerned sectors. **Developing a comprehensive and reliable investigation, thus, requires an initial sectoral analysis**.

We discuss, first, characteristics and circumstances, under which PPPs are more suitable in certain sectors than in others.[18]

Bundling. **An essential feature of a PPP is that different phases of the project are bundled in a single contractual agreement, which concerns design,**

---

[18]A rich discussion on this subject is proposed in Iossa and Antellini Russo (2008), who refer widely to the Italian PPP experience.

construction, financing, operation, and maintenance. The various firms, which will develop the project jointly, form a consortium for the Special Purpose Vehicle (SPV), which becomes the private contractual partner. Bundling the different phases of the project is useful when governmental bodies are aware of the needs that the project should address, but do not know the best way to do so. Because of this, they rely on the private sector for the design and the realization of the whole project. The contract should be designed to provide the private sector appropriate incentives to find innovative solutions and to effectively employ their technical and managerial expertise. The risks of the project must be allocated efficiently. For instance, the private partner must bear risks associated with the design, construction, and timely delivery, which it can control. If the rewards match the risks, the private partner will have incentives to complete the infrastructure and to start providing the service within the stipulated termination date and budget.

Positive externalities between phases of the project. **When the risks are allocated efficiently between the partners, the very fact of bundling the phases of the project may lead to efficiency gains if positive externalities (synergies) are present between the design/construction activities and the management/maintenance activities.** For instance, this is the case when the quality of the infrastructure, which typically affects the quality of the service, decreases the costs of management and maintenance. As bundling induces the private partner to account for the impact that the quality of the infrastructure has on the costs of management and maintenance, it helps mitigate under-investment problems, which arise whenever some quality aspects cannot be specified in contracts, but can be curbed by the private partner in order to contain the costs. We can thus say that, in general, bundling can lead to significant efficiency gains, and, hence, is desirable if building an infrastructure of a sufficient quality reduces the costs of management and maintenance. This is the case with *hospitals*. The quality of both the infrastructure and the medical equipment has an important positive effect on the performance. It is also the case in *transportation*. Both the costs of maintenance and the user benefits are strictly linked to the quality of the transport infrastructure. *Prisons* are another good example. Improvements in the infrastructure design allow for significant reductions in management costs.

Contractual length. **The presence of externalities between construction and operation is a reason for which PPP arrangements must have a long duration.** This is a core aspect that determines how carefully the private partner will account for the effects that the construction investment will have on the costs of management and maintenance. If the duration is too short, the private partner will not have the incentive to internalize those effects and consequently under-invests. On the other hand, it may not be a good idea to lengthen the duration excessively. There are two possible reasons for this. First, the prolonged absence of any competitive pressure may lead the private partner to become inefficient. Second, when the users' preferences evolve quickly over time, the contractual terms tend to become rapidly obsolete. This may require renegotiation of the contract. Therefore, PPP arrangements may not be suitable in the sectors in which the users' preferences evolve quickly. Difficulties of this kind have been experienced with the *information technology* services in the UK.

Absence of positive externalities between phases of the project. **Bundling is of little use—or not useful at all—when there are limited positive externalities—** or are completely absent for instance between construction and operation. This is the case, for instance, with the so-called *soft services*, such as, meal preparation and distribution, cleaning, laundry, maintenance of buildings and technological services, parking, etc. In the UK, these services, initially embodied in PPP arrangements, are currently regulated under independent contracts. Very often, these contracts are relatively short-term with the aim of encouraging participation by a larger number of firms. Lastly, negative externalities may arise between phases of the project, e.g., when building an infrastructure of high quality leads to an increase in the costs of management and maintenance even if generating larger social benefits. A good example is found in the *security dimensions of the plants*. It is, then, advisable not to induce the private partner to internalize the externalities because that would exacerbate the problem of under-investment in quality/security. Unbundling may, thus, be optimal.

We shall now look more closely at PPP arrangements in the provision of three services of general interest, namely transport, energy, and telecommunications. Without the ambition of being exhaustive, we shall focus on a few aspects, which seem to be especially important in those sectors.

6.2.3   Transport

6.2.3.1   European PPP Trends

Over the past two decades, the European public transport sector has experienced a substantial institutional evolution. First, reliance on contracting has become widespread over all transport modes. This has led to transfer more risk to private operators. Second, competitive tendering practices have progressively replaced direct awarding of contractual rights. Lastly, many municipal operators have been privatised. The utilization of PPPs for the realization of transport projects is a substantial part of this trend (Iossa and Martimort 2009). The Isle of Skye Bridge, which connects the Isle of Sky to the mainland was the first European transport project realized in 1992, under the UK PFI (Private Finance Initiative) approach (Grout 1997). Since then, PPPs have become widespread in urban transportation projects. They have also been used for big infrastructure projects and isolated links, such as the Eurotunnel and the London Underground upgrade-and-maintain project. After becoming very popular also in France, Italy and Spain, they have been recently adopted in Eastern Europe for the realization of transport infrastructure (European Investment Bank 2004).

6.2.3.2   Non-European Developed Countries

The trend is analogous outside Europe. In the U.S., the introduction of PPPs in transportation infrastructure goes back to the 1970s, when they were used to build inner-city infrastructure. Over time, PPPs have been extended to other road projects, such as the Dulles Greenway highway in Virginia and the SR-91 and SR-125 toll roads in California (CBO 2007), although the main interstate highways are largely public. In many cases in the US, PPPs are being used as a mechanism to raise financing for infrastructure, given the political difficulties in implementing taxes or even user charges. In Australia, toll roads were first built, through PPP arrangements, during the Nineties in New South Wales (Iossa and Martimort 2009).

6.2.3.3   Developing Countries

A more and more substantial involvement of the private sector in financing and building transport infrastructures has evolved, since the 1990s, the private sector has invested US$180 billion to develop transport projects in LDCs. Furthermore, in 2006, 1000 private projects were in progress, most of them concerning roads and many others concerning railroads (Iossa and Martimort 2009).

6.2.3.4   The Main Features of Transport PPPs

We identify four main features (see also Martimort and Iossa 2009):

1. Bundling–typically including design, building, financing, and operating—are contracted out to a consortium of private firms, which takes the responsibility for the development of the entire project.
2. A significant part of the risks involved in the project is transferred onto the private partner, but are dependent on tolls.
3. The use of private capital is a crucial aspect of the partnership. User changes are often set to reward the private investors. For instance, highway users pay a toll in countries like Italy and France[19]; airlines and lessees pay, respectively, a landing fee and a rental charge to airport contractors; train operating companies, which obtain revenues from passengers, pay railway contractors for the right to access the rail infrastructure.
4. The contractual relationship typically ranges from 20 to 35 years.

---

[19]We should, however, mention that, in some countries such as the UK, highway contractors receive payments directly from the budgets, or like *shadow tolls* from the government.

6.2.4 Risks in Transport Projects

Transport projects involve both construction risks and operational risks. Construction risks are related, *inter alia*, to incorrect time estimates, unforeseen ground conditions, failure to obtain necessary services, protestor actions. Operational risks include demand risk (directly affecting revenues—e.g., in the 1990s Mexican case), interest rate and foreign exchange risks, risks associated with hydro-geological and weather conditions.

6.2.5 The Relevance of Demand Risk

Demand risk in the operation phase is especially problematic. Actually, in the majority of cases, it is cumbersome to make reliable forecasts of future traffic flows.

- **One difficulty arises when other transportation modes and facilities are available**. Then, demand can be dramatically influenced by the competition that they induce. For instance, whether a toll road project is successful or not depends on whether alternative toll-free roads are available.
- Furthermore, **both user needs and, more generally, macroeconomic conditions tend to change over time**. In order to establish the exact extent to which these risks should be transferred onto the private firm, it is necessary to assess how efficiently the firm can tackle them.
- **In transport projects, as the service is sold to end-users**, rather than to one or few off-takers (as is the case of oil and gas, for instance), **it is difficult to hedge the demand risk** that private firms cannot efficiently tackle, say, by fixing revenue levels affecting earning and cash flows. It is, thus, necessary to rely on other instruments to mitigate demand risk in PPPs. For instance, in highway development projects, the public sector can provide the private partners with guarantees on the traffic level, in the form of traffic floors or collars (Gatti 2014).
- **The firm can influence demand** for the service in two essential ways: (1) by exerting an effort to build an infrastructure of good quality, and (2) by exerting an effort to provide the service as well as it can.

In motorway projects, for instance, the benefit that users obtain depends on how safe the motorway is. This, in turn, is related both to the quality of the motorway and to how carefully it is maintained.

In railway projects, demand is heavily affected by quality dimensions, such as comfort of trains, reliability of both transport services, and on-the-train services. Some quality dimensions are observable and verifiable. As an illustration, think about train punctuality and crash rates in rail concessions; schedule reliability in bus concessions; congestion levels and mortality rates in highway concessions. These dimensions can be contracted, and in principle it is not problematic to design the contract so that the firm takes care of them. Specifically, quality targets can be stipulated in the contractual agreement, and the firm can be motivated to meet them by means of "rewards" and "punishments." This is common practice in many real-world contexts.

Data collection on verifiable quality dimensions of services of general interest, for regulatory and accountability purposes, is by now widespread. Bergantino et al. (2011) report a few examples in transportation sectors. In the U.S., the Bureau of Transportation Statistics of the Research and Innovative Technology Administration provides detailed information about departure and arrival delays for a variety of transportation modes (ranging from aviation to maritime, highway, transit, and rail). In France, the *Observatoire des retards du transport aérien* collects and publishes data on flight punctuality. In Italy, the regulated rail company is currently compelled to disclose information about arrival delays.

Things are, of course, more problematic with effort dimensions that are not verifiable. These are at the root of the *moral-hazard problems.*

In addition, there can be *adverse-selection problems*. The firm may well hold some private information, say, about the costs of the activity, from which it can take advantage in its contractual relationship with the government. When this is the case, it becomes then necessary to find contractual solutions that address the two information issues at once. Nonetheless, in some kinds of projects, such as of highway projects, the presence of adverse selection is less likely. The reason is that the marginal cost of providing the service is very small (close to zero); and the private party often faces the same demand uncertainty as the public party. Hence, moral hazard is the main concern, in these projects.

Consequences for the profitability of the project and the enforceability of the contract. **Given the difficulty in making precise demand forecasts, the firm's profits are largely uncertain before the operation phase begins**. One natural consequence is that it becomes difficult to attract private investment, especially when projects are big and private sponsors are averse to risk. For instance, so far, cross-border infrastructure has received very little attention from private financiers in Europe (EC White Paper 2006). Even if private investors do show up, they tend to behave opportunistically. This is possible because, at the time when the right to run the project is awarded, they are generally required to present traffic forecasts, which are used to define the contractual arrangements. Thus, at that stage, they have an incentive to present overoptimistic forecasts, in order to obtain the right to the activity. However, once this is acquired, it becomes clear that traffic flows are poor, in fact.

Changing demand parameters paves the way for costly renegotiation, default, or bail out. For instance, in Latin America, many contracts for highways projects were renegotiated, during the Eighties, at the private operators' initiative (Guasch 2004). In a recent motorway project, in Hungary, the traffic flow proved to be very low during the operation phase. The private operator in charge of designing, financing, building, operating, and transferring the infrastructure, earned very little revenue and stopped paying back its debt. The public partner had to intervene to take over the debt obligations and bail out the concession (European Commission 2004). The realization of the Eurotunnel experienced several cost overruns. The list of examples of failures of PPPs in transport is extensive and we report some additional cases in Sect. 6.3.2.

6.2.6 Energy

This subsection looks at the energy sector, focusing on the EU approach to PPP arrangements in this sector. It is useful, first, to understand the EU Energy Policy objectives that govern the approach.

6.2.6.1 The EU Energy Program

The main priority of the EU Energy policy is to coordinate and optimise the *network* development on a continental basis. As specified by the European Commission (2011), this means that:

  i. **Solidarity** among member States should become fully operational;
 ii. **The internal market** should be completed;
iii. **Security of supply** dictates that alternative supply/transit routes should be made available;
 iv. **Environmental concerns** require that renewables should be further developed and begin to compete with traditional generation supply.

Accordingly, the attempt is to ensure that strategic energy networks and storage facilities will be **completed** by 2020. Twelve trans-European priority corridors and areas have been identified to this end. They include electricity and gas networks as well as carbon dioxide transport infrastructures.

It has been established that the goals must be achieved by identifying specific energy infrastructure projects (through a diligent and severe selection process), which will be attached the label of "Projects of common interest." For instance, it is expected that many such projects will focus on the European transmission system; and operators will certainly need to build many more related projects than in the past.

Financial aspects and PPP arrangements. **The EU program is ambitious and calls for huge investments.** This posits difficulties at a juncture at which resources are very scarce. It is unlikely that significant public resources can be used, especially in countries, which have developed very high public debts due to counter-cyclical policies or the realization of past liabilities. Also private resources are limited, because commercial banks have drastically reduced infrastructure investments over the last years.

Thus, two main solutions are being considered:

1. **Involvement of institutional investors** (namely, pension funds, insurance companies, mutual funds, sovereign wealth funds);

2. **Issuance of project bonds.**[20]

Involving *institutional investors* **may be useful because their liabilities are long-term**. Hence, they may buy and hold investments in long-dated productive assets, acting in a counter-cyclical manner. The EU would work as a catalyst for these investors. Actually, already in October 2011, the Connecting Europe Facility (CEF) was launched to fund €50 billion of investments in the trans-European networks for energy as well as transport and digital services between 2014 and 2020. The CEF (to be fully implemented soon), is meant to use many financial instruments, as an alternative to traditional grant funding: special lending, guarantees, equity investments.

More than institutional investors, *project bonds* **are viewed as the main EU financing instrument for the trans-European networks for energy, transport, and digital services**. A pilot phase was launched in 2012. The idea is that PPPs would be created to run specific projects. However, rather than relying on bank loans, these companies would issue long-term well-rated bonds. In order to mitigate the risk, at least to some extent, the European Commission and the European Investment Bank (rather than the single States) would participate in the projects.

This strategy seems to be supported by the following logic. As the concerned projects are essentially trans-European (rather than national), they are huge, and involve risks that involve several countries at once, and capital is to be attracted from as many countries as possible. At the same time, risks are to be shared as widely as possible across countries—The private sector is still destined to be involved. **However, the PPP companies, responsible for specific projects, will share risks with the public sector with guarantees at the EU level more than at the country level. This puts greater premium on ensuring that the public finance data across countries is standardized.**

6.2.7 Information and Communication Technology

PPP/PFI solutions do not seem to be particularly appropriate for ICT projects, especially because of the fast-moving features of (and preferences for) the involved services. This inappropriateness has been stressed in the economic literature—Iossa and Martimort (2008) for example argue that "PPPs seem unsuitable for fast-moving sectors; performance failures have been widespread in PPPs for specialised IT in the UK." Iossa and Antellini Russo (2008), concur that "in sectors where users' preferences change rapidly over time, PPP arrangements are inappropriate, as the UK experience in IT projects witnesses."[21]

---

[20]A broad overview of the financial perspectives for the European energy infrastructure is found in Tagliapietra (2013).

[21]Translation from Italian by the authors.

Apparently, real-world practice is moving in the same direction. For instance, the *Public Private Partnership Policy Framework and Guidance* of the Northern Ireland Department of Finance and Personnel (Sect. 5.2.6) states that "(…) resources should not be wasted investigating PPP solutions where they are clearly not appropriate. For instance, PFI solutions are not usually considered appropriate for Information and Communication Technology (ICT) projects." This approach seems to be confirmed by the Broadband Delivery UK project, currently in progress.

Broadband Delivery UK is meant to improve the UK's broadband network, with particular emphasis on making high-speed broadband available in rural communities. Specifically, the ambition is to provide superfast broadband to at least 90% of premises in the UK, and to provide universal access to standard broadband with a speed of at least 2Mbps. This is one of the major infrastructure projects in which there is capital investment from the *public* sector, to which Infrastructure UK (IUK) provides support. The government has allocated £530 million to stimulate commercial investment to roll out high-speed broadband in rural communities. BDUK is responsible for managing the rural program, whereas local authorities and the devolved administrations are responsible for individual projects. Local authorities can run mini-competitions to select a specific supplier to deliver broadband services for a local project.

As this project is largely targeted to rural areas, it is unlikely to be very profitable, or attract private investors. Moreover, the "social" benefits of the project are a pretty good justification for the public contribution. Nonetheless, this story seems to confirm that **PPP arrangements are not regarded as an appropriate instrument for IT projects, or where social concerns place a constraint on the user charges that might make a project interesting for the private sector**. The latter may also apply with some other rural infrastructure, such as feeder roads.

6.2.8 Informational Asymmetries Between Partners

As the creation of a PPP involves **delegation of some tasks from the government to a private firm, a natural question is whether and, if so, under which circumstances this can be done at no cost**. This depends on how aligned the interests of the partners are to being with, or can be aligned in the stipulated contract.

An immediate difficulty that arises in PPPs is the presence of informational asymmetries between the government and the firm. Hence, these must be taken into account in contract design, In many situations, during the execution of the contract, the firm is (or becomes) better informed than the government about both some relevant aspects of the activity, and its own actions that can have an impact on those aspects. For instance, the government cannot observe (or, even if it does, no third party, such as a court of justice, can verify this) whether the firm exerts a specific level of effort, which is desirable from the social perspective in building the infrastructure. **Because providing effort is costly for the firm, but the degree of effort cannot be specified in contracts, a moral-hazard problem arises,** as is usual when the source of private information is "endogenous." That is, the firm has an incentive to shirk from exertion of effort during the construction phase in order to maximise returns.

In addition, the government is unlikely to observe the exact conditions under which the firm manages **the activity once the infrastructure is in place.** For instance, it may not know whether the service demand or the production cost is high or low. By contrast, the firm learns this information by the time the project is in operation. **This is the root of an adverse-selection problem, as usual when the source of private information is "exogenous."** That is, the firm has an incentive to cheat, *vis-à-vis* the government, about the conditions under which it actually operates, because this allows it to raise its profits.[22]

The two information problems are not disjoint, in general. This is due to the presence of synergies between phases of the project, which is one of the main reasons for which various tasks are bundled in a unique activity and entrusted to a single responsible firm. The effort that the firm exerts during the construction phase has an impact on the conditions that it faces during the operation phase. For instance, exerting effort may increase the likelihood of facing a high demand for the service (because the infrastructure is more reliable) or a low cost of production (because the cost is an inner characteristic of the infrastructure). This is why effort provision by the firm is desirable.[23]

From standard agency theory, we know that moral hazard is not an issue (and can be handled at no cost) as long as the firm is risk-neutral and not protected by limited liability. Nor is adverse selection an issue if contracting occurs *ex ante*, *i.e.*, when not only the government but also the firm is uncertain about the future operating conditions, as is very often the case with PPPs. Under these circumstances, the government can prevent the firm from exploiting its informational advantage and implement the efficient allocation (namely, recommend the efficient output level and give up no rent to the firm) by offering a *state-*

---

[22]Private observation by the firm of the operating costs is, perhaps, the most common root of adverse selection issues in delegation problems. However, this is not a feature of all types of projects. A word of caution is, thus, needed. For instance, according to Engel, Fischer and Galetovic (1997, 2001), private information on costs is not an issue in highways franchise contracts. The authors argue that, once the infrastructure is built, the costs of operating and maintaining highways are known to be close to zero and, hence, there is little room for firms to cheat. This is instructive. It means that, although some problems are very widespread and can thus be legitimately accounted for in a general discussion, **a more appropriate approach to PPP issues should pay attention to the different characteristics that the various sectors and activities display.** This leads us to the sectoral analysis developed in this paper.

[23]To be more precise, effort provision by the firm is desirable as long as the expected additional benefit that it induces, as compared to a situation in which no effort is exerted, exceeds the cost that providing effort entails for the firm. When effort has a probabilistic impact, the possibility of an additional benefit follows from the fact that the operating conditions are more likely to become favourable.

dependent compensation scheme. **Differentiating the compensation to the firm across states of nature is useful for incentive purposes**.

This is backed by the well known *Revelation Principle* (Gibbard 1973; Green and Laffont 1977; Dasgupta et al. 1979; Myerson 1979). According to the latter, in principal-agent relationships, there is no loss of generality for the principal (the government, in the context of our paper) in restricting attention to *direct revelation mechanisms*. "Directness" of an incentive mechanism resides in whether the agent (the firm, in the context of our paper) has no other actions to take, besides merely reporting private information to the principal (or, equivalently, picking one particular option, within a menu of contractual options, each tailored to a different possible state). In order to make such a mechanism "truthful," it is necessary to construct it in such a way that the incentive-compatibility constraints of the agent are satisfied. **This involves motivating the agent to announce the information correctly to the principal, rather than to camouflage it** (see, for instance, Laffont and Martimort 2001).

On the one hand, moral hazard requires that the firm bear some risk. The firm is not motivated to engage in costly effort unless it is inflicted a sufficiently significant penalty when a bad state is realized, while being assigned a sufficiently large reward when a good state occurs. A compensation scheme with this characteristic mirrors the need to transfer, in the words of OECD (2012), a "sufficient and appropriate" amount of risk to the firm. In long-term PPP agreements, in which not only the level of output and the compensation to the firm are contractual variables, but also the termination date is stipulated, the firm should be allowed to enjoy the benefits of its effort for a sufficiently long period of time (see, for instance, Iossa and Martimort 2008, and Danau and Vinella 2014).

Adverse selection requires that the compensation to the firm should be sufficiently higher in good states than in bad states, though not excessively higher. The former requirement discourages the firm from claiming, *vis-à-vis* the government, that the state is bad when, in fact, it is good. Conversely, the latter prevents the firm from claiming that the state is good when, in fact, it is bad.[24]

The bottom line is that, as long as no friction arises, other than the two information problems described so far, delegation to a risk-neutral private firm generates no agency costs for the government. The firm can be induced to deliver the efficient level of output, without the need to concede any information rent to it. This goal is achieved by **designing a sufficiently dispersed compensation scheme, under which the firm breaks even *ex ante*, obtaining a higher return when the operating conditions are favourable and a lower return when they are not**.[25] This conclusion might induce one to believe that, after all, it is not

---

[24]For a general presentation of *ex-ante* contracting with adverse selection, see Laffont and Martimort (2001). With specific regards to PPP projects, see Danau and Vinella (2014).

[25]Risk neutrality of the firm is not an irrelevant aspect. When the firm is risk averse, it is necessary to insure it against the possibility of facing unfavourable operating conditions and, hence, a low return from the activity. In that case, a trade-off arises between provision of incentives and provision of insurance. The power of incentives that the government can provide to the firm is

very difficult to set up a successful PPP because information issues can be handily circumvented. In fact, an important clarification is here in order.

The conclusion above is drawn under the implicit assumption that both the government and the firm fully commit to contractual obligations within the PPP arrangement. However, in practice, the partners are often unable to do so. Then, difficulties arise with the enforcement of the contract. Consequently, delegation to the private firm is more problematic and may become costly. **One should, thus, try and understand how the contract, which decentralizes the efficient allocation under full commitment, can be made self-enforcing as it is implemented**.

6.3 Limited Ability to Commit to Contractual Obligations

In the literature on contract design, **situations where the contractual parties are unable to commit to their obligations have been labelled as situations of** *limited commitment*. Estache and Wren-Lewis (2008) illustrate that this label can be used to encompass different possible situations. First, with "limited enforcement," the firm may renege on the contract during its execution, even if the government disagrees. Conversely, in a second situation, referred to as "non-commitment," the government may renege on the contract, even if this is detrimental for the firm. Then, there is also a third situation, referred to as "commitment and renegotiation," in which the parties commit to their obligations but, if they both wish so, the contract can be renegotiated at a later stage.[26]

Examples of PPP projects, in which the firm reneges on the contract during its execution and attempts to reach a more favourable deal, are pervasive worldwide, and illustrated in Sect. 6.1. In institutionally weak contexts, such as in many developing countries, the rule of law often can be circumvented. Thus, contract reneging and, possibly, renegotiation is a likely consequence. For instance in Ghana, the current monopoly enterprise for fixed telephony entered the mobile business, despite being explicitly prohibited. In Tanzania, the regulator failed to enforce regional mobile licenses and the dominant operator began to expand at the national level (Estache and Wren-Lewis 2008). A large fraction of infrastructure

---

weakened. Note, however, that not only the attitude to risk of the firm but also that of the government is relevant. With *ex-ante* contracting, a risk-averse government may want to rely on a *sell-out* contract, under which the firm makes a payment up-front in order to have the right to produce. Thus, the government obtains a fixed payoff, regardless of the state of nature. This insurance may be interesting for small local governments, for which the project represents a significant share of the budget. Outside investors may be better diversified and, hence, they may be prone to insure small governments that privatize crucial infrastructures and services for insurance reasons (see Martimort 2006).

[26]In this case, the contract is bound to be efficient *ex post*.

renegotiations in Latin America are found to occur at the initiative of the firm.[27] Though more rarely, firms renege on contracts also in advanced economies. In principle, in the latter, institutions are more solid and, hence, contracts are more easily enforced. For instance, a firm that refuses to produce can be fined heavily. Nonetheless, very often, governments prove reluctant to engage in litigation, which can be costly and time-consuming. As an illustration, in France, a progressive increase has been detected in the subsidies awarded to urban transport concessionaires (Gagnepain et al. 2013).

There are (at least) two other reasons why governments may accommodate firms' requests. **The first set relates to "electoral" concerns**. When high-profile projects, generating much media attention, are at stake, and/or projects involving critical infrastructure and services that are essential for the population, governments may be afraid of a severe backlash, if the contractual relationship with the initial partner breaks up, and the project completion is delayed until after a new agreement is achieved, starting from scratch, with another partner. In those cases, the threat of imposing sanctions on reticent firms is, in fact, not credible. Governments end up being stuck in the partnership, and keep increasing the contractual terms as appears to have happened in some cases in India.

Corruption and rent-seeking are important as well. Politicians/bureaucrats may be ready to accept bribes from firms, together with other kinds of present or future benefits (such as, the promise of career promises for friends and relatives), in exchange for a favourable revision of the contractual conditions. In infrastructure projects, corruption may also take the form of softer *ex-post* price regulation, which allows both firms (through larger profits) and officials (through rent-seeking) to benefit at consumers' expense. Focusing on this form of corruption, Martimort and Straub (2008) show that reliance on a private firm may open the door to more corruption, as compared to public provision. This occurs, when the shadow cost of public funds, to be borne by taxpayers as long as a public firm receives subsidies out of the state budget to provide the service, is low, relative to the distortion that the price raise induces, to the detriment of consumers, when a private firm is delegated the activity. This would hold even if the taxation systems are largely inefficient, if officials and bureaucrats are corrupted at various levels in the governmental hierarchy, and are biased towards and/or influenced by the private sector. In general, countries with multi-level governments are especially prone to corruption phenomena. In many cases, this reflects a weak and opaque institutional framework especially at the sub-national level, poor information on comparable local information and term limits that reduce electoral discipline. Capture and lack of transparency are far from negligible issues, as in an increasing number of

---

[27]For examples in Latin America and the Caribbean regions, see Guasch (2004) and Guasch et al. (2006), (2008).

countries, regional and local governments are responsible for a large part of the total national capital investment.[28]

While it is expected that firms will renege on contracts, in fact, it is equally plausible that the concerned governments will lack the desire or ability to commit to contractual obligations. In developing countries, governmental failure to honour contractual terms is even more serious a concern than the firm's failure. This is because, as Estache and Wren-Lewis (2008) stress, **the governments' inability to secure investors' remuneration may discourage large-scale investments, which are desperately needed in those countries, especially in utility sectors** (see also Banerjee et al. 2006). Political risk heavily challenges public-private contracting also in transition economies, such as those in Central and Eastern Europe. For instance, in Hungary, transportation projects have been delayed by the repeated changes in political attitude towards PPPs (Brench et al. 2005).

In environments characterized by limited commitment, the obvious reason under which either the firm or the government might renege on the stipulated contract is that this may allow for a higher payoff than would be attained if the contract were honoured. At the initiative of one or the other party, a new negotiation can take place and can be successful or not. If renegotiation succeeds, then the partnership continues under a new deal. Otherwise, the partnership breaks up. In that case, the project is abandoned. Alternatively, another firm may be required to bring it to completion.

Incentives to renege on the contract arise very naturally in the environments that we have been considering along our discussion. To see why, recall that, if willing to solve information problems, the government needs to design a compensation scheme under which the firm, while breaking even *ex ante*, is "rewarded" when the state of nature comes out to be favourable, and "punished" otherwise. Consequently, one possibility is that, once the true state is observed by the firm and correctly revealed to the government, the firm is unlikely to be happy if the operating conditions are actually bad because, in that case, it receives the low compensation stipulated in the contract. Another possibility is that the government is unhappy if the operating conditions are good because, in that case, it owes to the firm the high compensation that the contract prescribes. This suggests that, while offering an **incentive-compatible scheme is helpful to tackle information problems *ex ante*, this is less safe as a strategy *ex post*.** It may well cause enforcement difficulties.

---

[28]Allain-Dupré (2011) reports that, in OECD countries, sub-national governments are in charge of nearly half of total capital expenditures. The reason is that regions and municipalities are considered to "better spend," *i.e.*, to identify the most appropriate paths for promoting the territorial development and competitiveness (Charbit 2011). It is thus clear that sub-national governments play a core role in public investment. Although the general strategies are designed at the national level, the implementation and completion of investment projects and the subsequent management of the activity depend crucially on the regional and local levels. For instance, even in federal countries like Germany, local governments provide utilities and manage local infrastructure, and have a claim to state funding, up to a level that is sufficient for a correct functioning (Fink and Stratmann 2011).

Two core points are worth making. **First, the incentive issues that arise on the firm's side, because of the information advantage that it enjoys *vis-à-vis* the government, do not exhaust the list of incentive issues that potentially challenge the overall performance of PPPs**. For a proper arrangement to be set up, it is essential to take into account another important temptation—namely, to stop abiding by the obligations during the execution of the contract. Remarkably, this temptation concerns not only the firm but also the government. Therefore, for PPP arrangements to be successful, it might be (and, in general, is) necessary to find ways to incentivize *both* partners to take a virtuous behaviour.

Second, the contractual payoffs of the two partners underline how difficult it is to have the contract honoured. In fact, **whether enforcement is problematic depends on what is at stake for each of the partners** in the renegotiation process (if any). Thus incentives to renege may appear even in the absence of information concerns, which induce the government to differentiate the firm's compensation across possible states of nature.

Thus, a clear strategy is needed, together with a set of instruments to prevent the two partners from behaving opportunistically. This requires, to begin with, a full understanding of how a hypothetical renegotiation process might unfold and what each party could lose and gain as a consequence.

6.3.1   How to Secure Contract Enforcement

Finding a way to ensure that the contract is enforced even in environments in which the partners are unable to commit is an intriguing challenge. The appropriate recipe finely depends on the particular context to which it is tailored and, hence, on the issues that are to be addressed specifically.

With regard to environments that display the characteristics previously described, *i.e.*, ***ex-ante* contracting and information issues on the firm's side**, Danau and Vinella (2014) suggest a strategy to tackle enforcement problems, which rests on a **proper choice of the financial structure of the PPP project**. We now briefly describe the recommendations that are drawn from their analysis.

First, in order to induce the firm to honour the contract, it must be required to invest a sufficiently significant amount of money up-front, and it must be allowed to recover that investment "as time goes by" during the implementation period. As the firm is aware that break-up of the partnership would impede recovery of the initial investment, it will have an incentive to preserve the relationship with the government. Of course, this involves that the private partner must be wealthy enough to be able to provide as large a contribution as necessary to motivate it to honour the contract. The bottom line is that, to be admitted to participate in the partnerships, private firms must be well endowed to begin with. This should deter the speculative and likely volatile investors.

Second, the firm's own investment should be complemented with the injection of some external/debt capital, regardless of whether this is truly

necessary to complete the investment. In other words, even a very wealthy firm, which could finance the investment entirely, should be instructed to take out a loan. This may look counterintuitive. In fact, it is explained by considering that **debt finance can play a strategic role.** Danau and Vinella (2014) show how the outcome can be attained. Specifically, the government should provide guarantees for the debt of the firm. It should be stipulated, in addition, that the guarantees will operate *conditionally* on the partnership continuing under either the initial contract or a new deal. However, the magnitude of the guarantees are not necessarily equal in the two cases. The guarantees provided for the hypothetical new deal should be made large enough to eliminate any benefit that the firm and the government could obtain by renegotiating. As a result, renegotiation would not be in the partners' interests. Then, break-up of the partnership would represent the only alternative to honouring the contract that the partners would be ready to consider. As far as the firm is concerned, we know that this option is not appealing, provided that the firm is required to put enough money on the table at the outset of the project. Thus, the only remaining concern is to find a way to make the option equally unattractive for the government.

As Danau and Vinella (2014) show, **the government may be tempted to terminate the partnership when the private investment is large and, hence, there is much to** appropriate, if the relationship breaks up. The gain would include not only the firm's investment but also the external capital, which is not covered by the governmental guarantees when the PPP is terminated prematurely. Of course, the government trades off the expropriation gain against any cost that the interruption of the partnership would generate.

A cost would come naturally, for the government, in the form of a loss of reputation and/or credibility. Reasonably enough, this may follow from the government not being sufficiently authoritative to have the contract honoured by the private firm, despite the fact that the latter invested in the project up-front (Guasch et al. 2006). It may also follow from the inability of the government itself to keep promises *vis-à-vis*, *in primis*, the private financiers involved in the project and, additionally, other potential investors, customers, and voters (Irwin 2007). It is, thus, clear that, in order to incentivize the government to honour the contract, the gain must be made small, relative to the costs associated with the failure of the partnership.

This leads to the third ingredient of the Danau-Vinella recipe. **That is, the private liabilities should be contained to a sufficiently small size.** In addition to requiring that the firm not invest too much in the project, regardless of its wealth, this requires that the firm not rely on debt massively, even if it has unlimited access to the credit market. In other words, PPP projects that are to be efficiently run and should not be excessively leveraged (see Danau and Vinella 2014).

In sum, the financial structure of the project, and, in particular, the exact mix of private and public funds (*i.e.*, own funds of the firm, funds provided by external sponsors and, possibly, governmental transfers) to be used to cover the investment, becomes the instrument for boosting commitment to contractual obligations and, hence, to promote contract enforcement.

6.3.2   A Few Examples of PPP Failures

To illustrate the relevance of the various aspects discussed and the policy recommendations previously described, **we provide a few examples of PPP arrangements that failed to achieve the desired outcomes**. The list is far from exhaustive and, yet, these stories appear instructive.

The first example is interesting in that it shows how pressed governments are to bail out projects **which are especially important from a social perspective**. Consequently they have to support banks when such projects become financially distressed, and in some cases can generate significant macroeconomic problems (e.g., excess building in Spain recently and road building in Mexico in the 1990s).

The second and the third examples illustrate how vulnerable projects are to renegotiation **and default**, respectively, when they are excessively leveraged and when debt obligations are supported by unconditional governmental guarantees.[29] Especially in cases where there is limited local government accountability, or own source revenues, there can be little accountability (Ambrosanio and Bordignon 2006).

6.3.2.1   The 1990s Mexico Road Building Project

Between 1989 and 1994, Mexico embarked on an ambitious road-building program. More than fifty concessions were awarded for 5500 km of toll roads. **The concessions were highly leveraged. Debt financing for the projects was on a floating-rate basis and provided by local banks**. Many such banks were owned by sub-national governments and faced pressure to lend money to concessionaires. Since the local governments had no own source revenues, they could not compensate the concessionaires, who ceased to repay the banks. In fact, because traffic volumes came out to be lower than forecasted and interest rates rose over time, the banking system absorbed a considerable increase in liabilities.

Although there were no explicit federal government guarantees, the failure of the projects exacerbated a banking crisis. Eventually, the government needed to restructure the entire toll road program, and it bailed out the concessions, taking over twenty-five of them, and assuming US$7.7 billion in debt (Ehrhardt and Irwin 2004).

---

[29]For further examples, see, for instance, the Reference Guide on PPPs published by the World Bank in 2012.

6.3.2.2 Victoria Trams and Trains

The State Government of Victoria, in 1999, awarded five franchises (which are similar to concessions) for operation of trams and commuter rail in Melbourne, as well as regional trains in the State of Victoria. According to the government's estimation, this would lead to total savings of A$1.8 billion over the life of the contract. However, the total equity contribution from the sponsors was only A$135 million, or only 8% of the total gains.

The payment structure of the PPP relied heavily on the expected growth in patronage and reduction in costs. In fact, the growth and cost reductions were not realized. Consequently, the franchisees experienced losses. Because the project was highly leveraged and the equity at stake relatively low, the operators had little to lose in quitting the projects. For this reason, they could credibly threaten the government to walk away from the franchises rather than to endure the losses, or striving for improvements. This weakened the position of the government *vis-à-vis* the existing operators. Eventually, the government was induced to renegotiate the contractual terms with those operators (Ehrhardt and Irwin 2004).

6.3.2.3 The London Underground Project

Even in developed countries, the central government can foot the bill in case of a default at the local level, without actually having been involved in a PPP. In 2002–3, Greater London Council launched a project for maintaining and upgrading the London underground. The public sector was uncertain whether Metronet, the consortium responsible for the realization of the project, could borrow enough funds to cover the investment. To motivate the banks to lend money to Metronet, **Transport for London, a local government body, guaranteed 95% of Metronet's debt obligations**. Eventually, the consortium failed and the partnership broke up. In spite of this, the guarantee came into force because it had been provided without specifying any condition and, hence, regardless of the continuation of the partnership.

Eventually, the tab was passed to the central Department for Transport, which had to make a £1.7 billion payment to help Transport for London meet the guarantee (House of Lords 2010). The debt risk was transferred to taxpayers, who incurred a direct loss of between £170 million and £410 million (National Audit Office 2008-9).

6.3.3 Some Policy Implications

6.3.3.1 The Need for Reliable Third Parties and the Separation of Powers

For a government with a limited ability to commit to contractual obligations, it is difficult (and, perhaps, impossible) to provide credible guarantees to the firm's financiers. This opens up a more institutional perspective on the enforceability of PPP contractual arrangements and, hence, on the attainment of desirable outcomes in PPP projects.

If the partners' interests in renegotiating the contract are to be eliminated, **it is essential that the project be partially financed with external funds, and that debt finance be employed strategically**. Danau and Vinella (2014) however argue that a credible third party should be involved, which is able to pursue its commitments, under whose aegis external sponsors can be involved and receive guarantees for their credits.

One could also think of creating some ad hoc institution, which should perform the specific task of acting as an "external guarantor" in the enforcement of PPP contracts in institutional environments where the partners (and, in particular, the government) fail to commit to their contractual obligations. This possibility implicitly calls for an appropriate separation of powers and specialization of tasks at the institutional level.

One option would be the suggestion by Bhattacharya et al. (2012), who argue for the creation of a new development bank, specifically dedicated to promote infrastructure and sustainable development as well as to deliver the technical assistance capacity in the selection, management, and funding of infrastructure projects, which is particularly needed in developing countries. The existing development banks, including the World Bank and the regional development banks, are also increasing their focus and financing on the question of public investment gaps. This issue is taken up further in Sect. 6.3.

6.4 Some Policy Design Issues and Case for Multilateral Risk Mitigation

In this paper, **we have emphasized the need to involve private sector in investments to ease the national fiscal constraints and to enhance efficiency in provision of key services**. Incentive problems arise given the asymmetric information concerning risks. This is exacerbated by the limited information on projects and on buildup of liabilities at the relevant level of government (affecting credibility of government contracts). Standardized information such as using the IMF's GFSM standard is critical for recording and reporting liabilities on an accrual basis over the medium-term. The limitation of information leads to a potential for renegotiation in favor of firms, with high risk projects together with a potential for rent-seeking, even though there are likely to be sectoral variations.

The lack of credible and complete time series at the local level is a critical concern for performing cross-country fiscal analysis, affecting potential for enhanced long-term cross-border investments. Addressing these gaps requires not only a technical framework for data collection but also political-economy mechanisms through which local authorities might be willing to generate and share consistent information.

6.4.1 Tightening the Definitions of PPP Liabilities

As a result of the difficulties above, the International Accounting Standards Board (2011) has issued a new set of guidelines (IPSAS 32)[30] that force an upfront accounting for PPPs, and would significantly affect deficits and recognition of liabilities for general government—i.e., for both central and sub-central governments and related agencies. This ensures that the operator is effectively compensated for services rendered during the period of the concession period. **It requires the government or granting public agency to recognize assets and liabilities in their financial statements**, when the following are met:

- The government or granting public agency controls or regulates the services to be provided, the target beneficiaries or the price; and
- If the grantor controls through ownership, beneficial entitlement or otherwise, a significant residual interest in the asset at the end of the arrangement.

This avoids the situation where neither the public nor private partner recognizes the asset/liability at the end of the period. Of course, as has been seen in Ireland and Spain recently (and with Mexican road in the early 1990s), even if there are no explicit guarantees by the federal or state governments and there is sufficient pressure on the banking system, it is likely that the central government will assume a significant portion of the liabilities.

The implications are that

1. The **annual budgets for each level of government must be cast in a medium-term framework**; and
2. **It is essential to undertake a full and careful evaluation of assets and liabilities and associated accounting and reporting of risks with a sufficiently long time horizon** (using international standards for budgeting and tracking liabilities, such as the GFSM 2001, which also provides consistency with the System of National Accounts).

---

[30]See IASB (2011), IPSAS 32. This standard is also likely to affect the guidelines of Eurostat that are not so tightly defined.

6.4.1.1 Importance of Contract Guarantees and Technical Assistance —Role for Multilateral Agencies

Overall, the role of a new development bank or the existing multilateral banks would span measures at the national and international levels, ranging from financial and risk mitigating aspects, as well as the provision of technical advice.

- At the **national** level, the concerned bank would provide national authorities with *technical assistance*, helping them quantify their knowledge of the country-specific factors, which are relevant for the selection, development, and management of projects displaying the highest social returns. In addition, it would enhance institutional credibility, synergies and complementarities, *fostering commitments and risk mitigation* both in the relationships between public and private sectors and in the relationships between different governmental tiers, as far as multi-level governance contexts are concerned.
- At the **international** level, it would provide *financial assistance, pledging guarantees* and *sharing the best international practices for project evaluation and risk assessment*, the most suitable instruments for risk mitigation/insurance, and the most innovative finance techniques.

In Europe, initiatives of this kind have already been undertaken, some at the country level, others at the EU level, with both technical and financial purposes. At the country level, the most important example is found, perhaps, in the UK, where the creation of **Infrastructure UK (IUK)** was announced in the 2009 Pre-Budget Report. This agency is tasked with advising the government on strategic long-term infrastructure planning, prioritization, financing, and delivery across sectors, ranging from energy and waste to water, telecommunications and transport. It was established that, to pursue these objectives, IUK would bring together, under the Treasury umbrella, the program and project delivery capability of Partnerships UK (PUK), the lending capability of the Treasury Infrastructure Finance Unit (TIFU), and the policy development capability of the Treasury PPP policy team (see World Bank Institute 2012). **This rich bulk of institutional and technical expertise reflects how complex it is to ensure that only valuable infrastructure projects are undertaken and that the risks specifically involved are properly assessed and efficiently shared between the public and the private sector so that each such project is well-structured and technically and financially viable.**[31]

---

[31]In Italy, under the 2002 Stability Law, ISpa was created with the task of involving the private sector in the construction and management of important infrastructures, requiring significant long-run investments. However, being an off-budget agency, ISpa serves an important budgetary purpose as well. It can issue state-guaranteed bonds to raise capital for the new infrastructure projects, while allowing the government to comply with the European Stability and Growth Pact. See, for instance, Maskin and Tirole (2008) on the practice, often adopted by governments, to push debt finance off their own books to quasi-public agencies not consolidated in the national budgets.

At the EU level, as previously illustrated, the **European Investment Bank, under the aegis of the European Commission, has launched the CEF programme** to promote new forms of private financing, including the participation of pension/mutual funds and insurance companies, as well as the issuance of project bonds. Arguably, involving institutional funds would be even more useful in emerging economies as their financial systems are essentially bank-based, and their financial markets are still small relative to the size of their economies (Schwartz et al. 2014). Over time, the support of the development bank would stimulate those markets to grow and consolidate, paving the way for the use of more sophisticated financial instruments, such as project bonds.

References

Ahmad, E. (2014). Public finance underpinnings for infrastructure financing in developing countries. Paper for the G24.

Ahmad, E. (2017). Political economy of tax reforms for the SDGs. Paper for the G24.

Ahmad, E., & Wang, Z. (2013). *China: Emerging issues in public finance,* Asian Development Bank (processed).

Allain-Dupré, D. (2011). Multi-level governance of public investment: Lessons from the crisis. OECD Regional Development (Working Papers, 2011/05). OECD Publishing.

Ambrosanio, M., & Bordignon, M. (2006). Positive and normative thoeries of revenue assignments federations. In E. Ahmad and G. Brosio (2006), *Handbook of Fiscal Federalism.* Edward Elgar.

Armstrong, M., & Sappington, D. (2006). Regulation, competition and liberalization. *Journal of Economic Literature, 44,* 325–366.

Asian Development Bank. (2008). *Public–Private partnership handbook.*

Asian Development Bank. (2013). *New directions for Public–Private partnerships in People's Republic of China.*

Banerjee, S. G., Oetzel, J. M., & Ranganathan, R. (2006). Private provision of infrastructure in emerging markets: Do institutions matter? *Development Policy Review, 24*(2), 175–202.

Bergantino, A. S., Billette de Villemeur, E., & Vinella, A. (2011). Partial regulation in vertically differentiated industries. *Journal of Public Economic Theory, 13*(2), 255–287.

Bhattacharya, A., Romani, M., & Stern, N. (2012). *Infrastructure for development: Meeting the challenge,* Policy Paper, June 2012.

Brench, A., Beckers, T., Heinrich, M., & von Hirschhausen, C. (2005). Public-Private partnerships in New EU member countries of Central and Eastern Europe, *European Investment Bank, 10*(2).

Charbit, C. (2011). Governance of public policies in decentralized contexts: The multi-level approach, OECD Regional Development (Working Papers, 2011/04). OECD Publishing.

Danau, D., & Vinella, A. (2014). Public-private contracting under limited commitment. *Journal of Public Economic Theory,* forthcoming.

Dasgupta, P., Hammond, P., & Maskin, E. (1979). The implementation of social choice rules: Some general results on incentive compatibility. *Review of Economic Studies, 46,* 185–216.

Ehrhardt, E. & Irwin, T. (2004). Avoiding customer and taxpayer bailouts in private infrastructure projects: Policy toward leverage, risk allocation, and bankruptcy, World Bank Policy Research (Working Paper 3274).

Estache, A., & Wren-Lewis, L. (2008). Toward a theory of regulation for developing countries: Following Jean-Jacques Laffont's lead. *Journal of Economic Literature, 47*(3), 729–770.

European Commission. (2011). *A growth package for integrated European infrastructures,* COM (2011)676.

European Commission. (2006). *EC White Paper* European Commission (2004), *Resource Book on PPP Case Studies,* Directorate General Regional Policy.

European Investment Bank. (2004). *The EIB's role in Public-Private Partnerships (PPPs).*

Fink, A., & Stratmann, T. (2011). Institutionalized bailouts and fiscal policy: Consequences of soft budget constraints. *KYKLOS, 64*(3), 366–395.

Gagnepain, P., Ivaldi, M., & Martimort, D. (2013). The cost of contract renegotiation: Evidence from the local public sector, *American Economic Review, 103*(6): 2352–2383.

Gatti, S. (2014). *Private finance for infrastructure investments. Analysis and implications for a future Multilateral Development Bank,* Report prepared for the GGGI and the G24 engagement with the BRICS.

Gibbard, A. (1973). Manipulation of voting schemes: A general result. *Econometrica, 41*(4), 587–601.

Green, J., & Laffont, J. J. (1977). On the revelation of preferences for public goods. *Journal of Public Economics, 8*(1), 79–93.

Grout, P. (1997). The economics of the private finance initiative. *Oxford Review of Economic Policy, 13,* 53–66.

Guasch, J. L. (2004). *Granting and renegotiating infrastructure concessions: Doing it right,* WBI development studies, the World Bank.

Guasch, J. L., Laffont, J. J., & Straub, S. (2006). Renegotiation of concession contracts: A theoretical approach. *Review of Industrial Organization, 29,* 55–73.

Guasch, J. L., Laffont, J. J., & Straub, S. (2008). Renegotiation of concession contracts in Latin America, evidence from the water and transport sectors. *International Journal of Industrial Organization, 26*(2), 421–442.

House of Lords. (2010). *Private finance projects and off-balance sheet debt,* First Report of Session 2009–10, Volume I: Report, HL Paper 63-I.

House of Lords. (2010). *Private Finance Projects and off-balance sheet debt,* First Report of Session 2009–10, Volume II: Evidence, HL Paper 63-II.

Iossa, E., & Antellini Russo, F. (2008). Potenzialità e criticità del Partenariato Pubblico Privato in Italia. *Rivista di Politica Economica, 98*(3), 125–158.

Iossa, E., & Martimort, D. (2009). The theory of incentives applied to the transport sector. In A. de Palma, R. Lindsey, E. Quinet, & R. Vickerman (Eds.), *A handbook of transport economics.* Edward Elgar Publishing.

Iossa, E., & Martimort, D. (2008). The simple microeconomics of public-private partnerships. CEIS Research Paper Series, 6(12), number 139.

IMF. Government finance statistics manual. (2001). http://www.imf.org/external/pubs/ft/gfs/manual/index.htm. (revised in 2014).

Irwin, T. (2007). *Government guarantees. Allocating and valuing risk in privately financed infrastructure projects.* The World Bank.

Laffont, J. J., & Martimort, D. (2001). *The theory of incentives: The principal-agent model.* Princeton University Press.

Martimort, D. (2006). An agency perspective on the costs and benefits of privatization. *Journal of Regulatory Economics, 30,* 5–44.

Martimort, D., & Straub, S. (2008). Infrastructure privatization and changes in corruption patterns: The roots of public discontent. *Journal of Development Economics, 90,* 69–84.

Maskin, E., & Tirole, J. (2008). Public–private partnerships and government spending limits. *International Journal of Industrial Organization, 26,* 412–420.

Myerson, R. B. (1979). Incentive compatibility and the bargaining problem. *Econometrica, 47*(1), 61–73.

National Audit Office, *The failure of Metronet,* HC 512, 2008.09.

National Audit Report. (2011). Audit Findings on China's Local Government Debts, http://www.cnao.gov.cn/main/articleshow_ArtID_1154.htm.

National Audit Office. (2013). Audit Results of Governmental Debt of 36 Local Governments, http://www.cnao.gov.cn/main/articleshow_ArtID_1323.htm.

OECD. (2012). *From lessons to principles for the use of Public-Private Partnerships*, public governance and territorial development public management committee.

Saussier, S. (2006). Public-Private Partnerships and prices: Evidence from water distribution in France, *Review of Industrial Organization*, 29, Special Issue.

Schwartz, J. Z., Ruiz-Nunez, F., & Chelsky, J. (2014). *Closing the infrastructure finance gap: Addressing risk*. The World Bank Group.

Tagliapietra, S. (2013). Financing the European energy infrastructure of the future, *Review of environment, energy and economics*, Oct. 03, 2013—Energy.

The World Bank. (2012). *Public–Private Partnerships. Reference Guide*, Version 1.0.

World Bank *Infrastructure Policy Unit 2012 Global PPI Data Update*.

Part II
Guangdong Case and Other Local Experiences from China

Chapter 7
Managing Subnational Liability for Sustainable Development: A Case Study of Guangdong Province

Kezhou Xiao

Abstract A counter cyclical investment of nearly 400 billion RMB was launched by the Chinese government in response to 2008 financial crisis. The fiscal package created additional strains and stresses concerning subnational liabilities. The paper argues that the rapidly increasing burdens of local liability are largely the result of the confluence of political economy incentives and policy imperatives amplified by central-local relationships and unbalanced economic development. Using Guangdong province as an example, the paper documents the worrying concerns at the deficiency of own source revenues and mismatch of spending assignments and financing sources, particularly at the lower ties of governments. A short discussion of the ongoing policy experiments and reform proposals is also provided.

7.1 Introduction

Market participants and policy makers have been concerned about Chinese subnational debt after the 2008 financial crisis, when the Chinese government launched a counter cyclical investment plan of around 400 billion RMB administered through local governments. Although the costs of financing these investments were shared between the central and local governments, the adjustment plan created an uneven fiscal pressure across various subnational governments.

This paper evaluates the magnitude of local liability and financing needs, by focusing on the underlying incentive structures facing governments at different

Kezhou Xiao is a researcher affiliated with Asia Research Centre at London School of Economics of Political Science and is working on his Ph.D. in economics at London School of Economics and Political Science. The author would like to thank Prof. Niu Meili, and Prof. Ehtisham Ahmad for inspiration and ideas. This paper was prepared for a Conference on Financing Local Investments within a Sustainable Development Strategy for P.R. China held at Sun Yat-sen University, Guangzhou, China in 2015.

K. Xiao (✉)
London School of Economics and Political Science, London, UK
e-mail: spencerxiao@gmail.com; k.xiao@lse.ac.uk

© Springer Nature Singapore Pte Ltd. 2018
E. Ahmad et al. (eds.), *Fiscal Underpinnings for Sustainable Development in China*,
https://doi.org/10.1007/978-981-10-6286-5_7

levels. The potential fiscal challenges generated by rapid accumulation of local liabilities was partially created by the policy imperative in response to the recent financial crisis, and the countercyclical investment was required to address the potential economic slowdown. This aggravated existing incentives to drive economic growth through public investment linked to the economic performance criteria for political promotion at provincial levels (Li and Zhou 2005). Driven by competition between local governments, especially at the county level, (Cheung and Coase 2008), an investment drive took place with insufficient attention to long term financing costs and investment returns in many localities in China.

To further grasp the complexity of subnational liabilities, we have to take into account two important features of the fiscal landscape. The first feature relates to the regional inequality and unbalanced development across the country. Although rich local governments should have a greater capability to finance debts than poor regions, the absence of own-source tax handles meant that even the richer localities would have difficulties in servicing their debt effectively (Ahmad and Zhang, this volume)—despite the revenue-sharing and equalization systems in place. The other feature concerns with central-local relationships and the lasting implications of the 1994 fiscal reform. The core of the 1994 reform, in a nutshell, adjusted the revenue to GDP between the central and local government, centralizing revenue from latter to the former through the implementation of Value-added Tax (VAT) and the establishment of State Administration of Taxation (SAT). However, the 1994 fiscal reform was incomplete in the sense that spending assignment was not adjusted sufficiently to address the resultant mismatch between revenue and expenditure (Ahmad 2011). The incentive implication of the 1994 reform to a large extent strengthened the reliance of local governments on central transfers.

In this paper, we argue that the rapid accumulation of local liabilities is driven by the confluence of policy imperatives and political economy incentives amplified by realignment of central-local relationships in favor of former and unbalanced economic development across the country. To develop this argument, the paper starts in Sect. 7.2 by providing stylized facts using the 2013 National Audit Office report on local government debt and the 2014 Guangdong Audit Report. We wish to highlight aggregate trends at the national level, and capture variations of local liability within Guangdong province. Specifically, we will discuss Guangdong Provincial Rural Affairs Committee report on village debts, a report published in 2012. After establishing the main empirical facts, we put these figures in the context of the 1994 fiscal reform and trace the looming liability to the mismatch between subnational revenue and expenditure as a result of the fiscal reform in the following section. In Sect. 7.4, we discuss Guangdong province as a case study of several interrelated issues regarding the use of land sales, the reform of transition from business tax to value-added tax (VAT), and implementations of budgetary reforms. The key finding that the complementary fiscal reforms would **drain local revenue even further and increase fiscal risks at the local level** at least in the short run despite their importance in information collection and tax reduction for small business merits careful attention for policy design. New information on VAT reforms would be discussed. Last but not the least in Sect. 7.5, we conclude with a preliminary discussion on the revised budget law and the implications for possible reform items in Guangdong proposal.

7.2 Expanding Subnational Government Debts: National and Guangdong Context

Legally, local governments were prevented from borrowing under the pre-2015 budget law.[1] However, the subnational governments could generate investment financing through the Urban Infrastructure Development Corporations (UIDCs)[2] and using Local Government Financing Vehicles (LGFVs). Given insufficient public information on these quasi-government activities, estimations of the magnitude of debt are subject to intense debate. Some scholars argued that the size of off-budget liability is about 30% of GDP (Liu 2010). Other estimates developed an "augmented fiscal deficit and debt" index by accounting for land sells and off-budget activities and put the total size of debt at around 45% of GDP (Barnett and Zhang 2014).

By far, the most authoritative figures were provided by National Audit Office (NAO). At the end of 2013, NAO conducted a nationwide audit of local government debt, a follow-up to its 2011 report. We compare these two NAO reports (NAO 2011, 2013) and conclude with three observations. **One, there has been rapid subnational debt accumulation between the two reporting periods.** Comparing the NAO 2013 report with NAO 2011 report, the overall size of debt increased rapidly for the subnational governments from 2010 to 2013 June. Specifically, subnational government debt with repayment responsibility increased from 6,710 billion RMB to 10,886 billion RMB, a 60% increase; subnational government debt with guarantees increased from 2,337 billion RMB to 2,666 billion RMB, a 14% increase; and subnational government debt financed through subsidies increased from 1,669 billion RMB to a worrying level of 4,339 billion RMB, an increase of 150%. **Two, different layers of subnational governments face unbalanced debt pressures.** Lower tier governments are especially vulnerable to increasing liabilities, as less of the shared revenues tends to trickle down. **Third, repayment pressure was felt, especially in 2014 and 2015, and is expected to intensify given the short tenor of most of the debt.**

These pressures combined exacerbated the previously under-the-table dependence on land sales as a revenue source to service debt and finance local investment programs. Repayment pressure started to pile up in year 2014

---

[1]The new budget law (effective in January, 2015) will allow subnational government to issue debts directly, subject to central supervision. Along with amendments on local borrowing, the new budget law requires a streamlining of government revenue and expenses by including general budget, government managed funds, state-owned enterprise balance sheet, and social security.

[2]The development of infrastructure bond market is a relatively new phenomenon. See Yuanfan Zhou, "City Construction Investment Bond—Chinese Municipal Bond", 周沉帆, "城投债-中国式市政债券" for an introduction.

and 2014, accounting for 21.89% and 17.05% repayment duties respectively. Even the NAO 2013 report noted that until end of year 2012, 11 provincial governments, 316 municipality governments, and 1396 county governments explicitly promised to pay back their debts using current revenue streams from land sale proceeds amounting to 3,487 billion RMB, about 37.23% of the explicit debt. Given unsustainable housing booms and bubbles, municipalities without strong inflows of immigrants and economic prospects (mostly cities in the northeast and inlands) would have a difficulty banking on future land sales revenues. This type of demand risks and asset pricing risks associated with housing market would expose fiscal fragility even more to a varieties of localities.

The Guangdong Auditing Office, under the guidance of NAO, conducted its own debt audit at the beginning of 2014.[3] The report (GAO 2014) showed that at the end of June, 2013, explicit government debt, contingent debt with guaranteed responsibility, contingent debt with aiding responsibility (subsidies) are 693.1 billion RMB, 102.1 billion RMB, and 221.3 billion RMB, respectively. Most of the debts were concentrated at the municipality and county level, consistent with National Audit report. The majority of these debts were in the form of bank loans and the top three indebted institutions were local financing vehicles, government organizations, and public service units. Unlike pressures for national debt service, the future repayment peak (about 30% of the total debt) for Guangdong province will mostly arrive after 2018, which would provide some fiscal flexibility for subnational governments to respond. Overall, the debt ratio for explicit debt lies at 54.41% and maximum possible ratio would reach to 59.41%, according to GAO 2014 report. The rate for overdue payments among explicit government debt, contingent debt with guaranteed responsibility, contingent debt with aiding responsibility (subsidies) are 1.9%, 3.39%, and 1.55% respectively. Figure 7.1 shows the magnitude of local liability and growth rate of debts across provinces. Among provinces with debt audits, Guangdong province exhibited a relatively low debt growth rate and average debt magnitude (as percentage of revenue indicator[4]) despite second largest debt level in absolute terms.

A detail analysis of the Guangdong Audit Report provides several worrying concerns in terms of local distribution and sectoral distribution of liabilities.[5] **One, the debt burden was unevenly distributed across municipalities and county governments**. At the end of 2012, 19 municipality and 63 county level governments guaranteed repayment of 167 billion RMB based on future land sales, accounted for 26.99% of the total explicit debt. The explicit government debts were heavily

---

[3]A report of Guangdong Local Government Debt Auditing can be found at http://news.southcn.com/g/2014-01/23/content_90965741.htm.

[4]In GAO 2014, the denominator of the ratio is denoted by general revenue capacity, 综合财力, a measure of provincial revenue. Using the figure in the report and compare against Statistical Yearbook from each province, we could deduce that this measure of general revenue capacity measures the revenue of each province after central transfers. If we exclude central transfers from the calculation in denominators the total estimates of liabilities would be much higher for most of the provinces.

[5]See summary of GAO report.

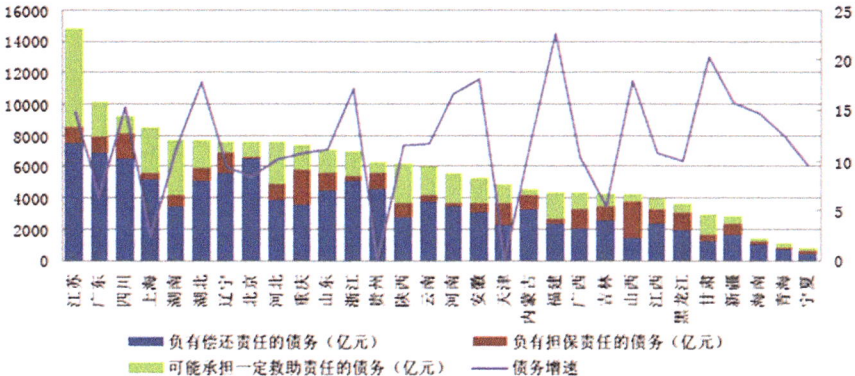

Fig. 7.1 *Local liability and debt growth rate. Source* Credit rating for Guangdong Provincial (in Chinese). 2014年广东省政府债务信用评级报告. *Note* a. Chinse translation of x-axis (Name of Provinces): Jiangsu, Guangdong, Sichuan, Shanghai, Hunan, Hubei, Liaoning, Beijing, Hebei, Chongqin, Shandong, Zhejiang, Guizhou, Shaanxi, Yunnan, Anhui, Tianjin, Neimenggu, Fujian, Guangxi, Jilin, Jiangxi, Heilongjiang, Gansu, Xinjiang, Hainan, Qinghai, Ningxia. b. blue bar represents explicit liabilities, red bar guaranteed liabilities, green bar aiding responsibilities, blue line growth rate of debt

concentrated at the county level. **Two, the debt accumulation has a strong sector association, especially in transportation and highway projects**. For example, railroad and highway projects amounts to around 150 billion RMB of debt. The average timing and magnitude of cash flow generated in each sector would impose diverse adjustment costs to local governments. **Three, mismanagement and appropriation of government managed fund were found in some localities and departments**. These projects mostly involve local government financing vehicles and inappropriate design of public-private partnership projects. Lack of supervision and reliable information would also breed corruptive behaviors in public officials.

Pronounced variations in the impact of indebtedness were observed across localities down to the lowest rung of local government at the village level. The Rural Affairs Committee (RAC) at Guangdong provincial level conducted a comprehensive survey into village debt in 2012 (RAC 2014).[6] This was a rare glimpse into the liability situation at a grass root level. To calculate fiscal risk at the village level, the RAC analysis presented four measures:

1. Debt dependency, defined as the ratio of current village debt over current revenue
2. Repayment rate, defined as the ratio of principal and interest paid at given year over current revenue
3. Burden rate, defined as the ratio of remaining debt over village GDP
4. Debt guarantee rate, defined as the ratio of cash balance over remaining debts.

---

[6]This section is based on the RAC survey and data presented in Guangdong Finance Yearbook (2013).

Table 7.1 *Local Liability at Village Level across Municipalities in Guangdong Province with Year 2011 Data*

Municipality	Debt dependency	Repayment rate	Burden rate	Debt guarantee rate
Huizhou	33.084	0.412	36.394	5.284
Zhuhai	11.321	0.332	4.855	1.162
Zhaoqing	10.722	0.859	8.21	1.28
Dongguan	1.802	0.526	0.843	0.461
Zhongshan	1.642	0.467	1.131	0.519
Qingyuan	1.557	0.323	1.42	1.742
Yangjiang	1.341	0.605	1.208	0.441
Shanwei	1.042	0.012	0.198	0.136
Foshan	0.488	0.2	0.257	0.645
Meizhou	0.4	0.133	0.257	1.09
Maoming	0.363	0.005	0.32	0.675
Chaozhou	0.362	0.206	0.332	1.312
Shantou	0.351	0.218	0.346	0.959
Heyuan	0.298	0.345	0.28	0.243
Jieyang	0.278	0.178	0.267	2.33
Shaoguan	0.183	0.167	0.138	1.092
Yunfu	0.146	0.231	0.132	2.126
Guangzhou	0.14	0.639	0.871	1.491
Jiangmen	0.065	0.473	0.063	1.289
Zhanjiang	0.0004	0.186	0.00007	2.077

Source RAC report, Guangdong Finance Yearbook, (2013)
Note Definition of key variables from the text: (a) debt dependency, defined as the ratio of current village debt over current revenue; (b) repayment rate, defined as the ratio of principal and interest paid at given year over current revenue; (c) burden rate, defined as the ratio of remaining debt over village GDP and (d) debt guarantee rate, defined as the ratio of cash balance over remaining debts. The unit of analysis is at village level. The measures in the tables are averages of all villages within jurisdiction

Using these four measures, the survey summarized fiscal risk measures for village level government across 20 municipalities in Guangdong (excluding Shenzhen). The result for the above four indicators is showed in Table 7.1. Taking debt dependency ratio as a benchmark, we find staggering divergence among villages across municipalities in Guangdong province. Although most of the villages had debt dependency around 20 to 40%, three outliners—Huizhou, Zhuhai, and Zhaoqing—had exorbitant debt and would have to save almost everything for at least the next 10 years in order to clear all the existing debts. This was quite appalling for future cleanups.

This heterogeneity was also reflected in the ratio for repayment rate. Debt-burdened villages in Zhaoqing, for example, had principal and interest payments reaching 85% of current revenue in 2011. Four out of twenty municipalities (20%) have village level debt beyond half of their revenue. The same fiscal picture can be captured by the measure of debt stocks to local GDP as well. The three municipalities with highest debt dependency coincide with those with highest debt GDP ratios. Huizhou seemed to have the most troublesome villages among all, reaching a stunning level of 36 times of the remaining debt over village GDP.

The ratio of debt guarantee rate captured the ability of villages to repay debts with their cash balances. We might be able to justify the high leverage taken by Huizhou by its high cash balance but the cash balance in Zhuhai and Zhaoqing did not seem to provide a strong case for such high debt leverage. Overall, these fiscal measures provide an overview of debt burdens at the village level, the lowest layer of Chinese bureaucracy characterized usually by autonomous governing bodies supervised by the county party committee. At village level of government, we can clearly identify variations of debt leverage and fiscal risks, complementing the observations reflected in National Audit Office report and Guangdong Audit Office report on the seriousness of fiscal risks at lower tier governments.

In short, the NAO report, the GAO and the RAC reports provide a multi-dimensional view of Chinese local government liability at different levels. We have documented substantial variations across provinces, between municipalities within provinces, and among villages at the lowest administrative body in the Chinese bureaucracy.

7.3   Central-Local Relationship: The 1994 Fiscal Reform, Revenue-Expenditure Mismatch, and Dependency Ratios

As argued in the introduction, the explosive growth in local liability has partially been a result of the preserve incentive structure with deep institutional roots. In this section, we discuss a critical amplifier behind the accumulation of subnational debts. The need for subnational entities to rely heavily on debt financing has been induced by and large by the mismatch between revenue sharing and expenditure assignment system for central and local governments, as a consequence of the 1994 fiscal reform.

The struggle over distribution of fiscal revenues between central and subnational governments runs through the core of every fiscal reform in China. Worried about declining total tax revenue and share of central revenue, the central government had four main goals to achieve in the 1994 fiscal reform, including (a) simplifying the tax system to improve production incentives, (b) raise the revenue to GDP ratio, (c) raise the ratio of central government to total revenue, and (d) make the fiscal federalism more stable by shifting from ad hoc, negotiated transfers to rule-based transfers (Wong 2000). These objectives were achieved with varied amount of success within a decade (Ahmad et al. 2002).

Table 7.2 Changing subnational share in spending, 2000–2012

Year	2012 (%)	2009 (%)	2000 (%)
Total	85	80	69
Transportation	89	77	66
Education	95	95	89
Health care	99	98	90
Social security	95	94	99

Source This table follows from Ahmad (2011) and updated with new data. *Source* Finance Yearbook of China, 2013 Edition

The impact of 1994 fiscal reform was immediate and significant in recentralizing revenue, as the central government increased its (pretransfer) share of revenue from 22% points at 1993 level to 55.7% points in 1994. Since 1994, the central government has been able to stabilize its share of revenue at around 50% of the total revenue. While the 1994 fiscal reform succeed at recentralizing revenue, the reform on spending assignments has been somewhat slower. The proportion of spending responsibility for local governments, **increased** steadily from 67.4% points at 1990 level to about 85% points in 2012 despite losing major share of revenue after the reform. The gaps were filled by equalization transfers, revenue returned to the provinces that generated it (to facilitate investment and growth) and special purpose transfers. These did not often percolate down to the lowest levels. Increasingly, deficits occurred—and some liabilities were disguised in one way or another.

At the end of 2012, subnational governments accounted for 85.1% of the spending responsibilities with steady increase over the past 20 years. Table 7.2 presents various components of spending responsibility for subnational governments. Every item, except social security, witnessed a substantial increase since 2000. Even in the case of social security, the share of local governments exceeded 90%.

The fiscal reality as a consequence of the 1994 fiscal reform enhances the bargaining power of the central government vis-à-vis subnational governments. Local officials in all regions, lacking own-source revenues rely heavily on central transfers to finance their spending responsibilities.

To understand the level of reliance on central transfers across provinces, we construct a dependency ratio, defined as the ratio of transfers from the center over total revenue including both transfers from the center and total tax and non-tax revenues at provincial level. As a caveat of this type of analysis, the construction of this ratio might not be consistent with the Government Finance Statistic Framework given data registration and compilation standards. The accounting framework for Statistical Yearbook in China should be viewed as an evolving response to the transition dynamics of Chinese economy (Holz 2004).

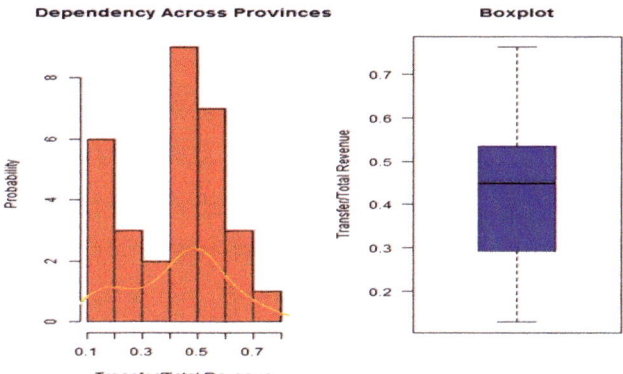

Fig. 7.2 *Heterogeneity of dependency across provinces. Data Source National Financial Yearbook, 2012*

7.3.1 Revenue: Dependency Ratio Variations

Figure 7.2 shows the heterogeneity of the dependency ratio, defined as the amount of transfers over total revenue in a province for 2012 final accounts.[7] More than half of provincial level governments (17 out of 35) have a revenue dependency ratio above 40%. The most dependent province is Tibet (about 77%) and the least reliant subnational governments are Beijing (12.83%), Shanghai (13.14%), and Guangdong (14.59%). The average dependency ratio is 42.33%. Our estimates of dependency ratio should be taken as an upper bound, given the assumption that transfers to the central government is negligible. For example, the amount of transfers to central government is about 1% of the amount received from central transfer on average. If we calculate the net central government transfer, then the disparity of dependency will increase further, as rich provinces rely less on transfers and poor provinces more. The large disparity in dependency ratio is partially a consequence of the incompleteness of the 1994 fiscal reform. Strategic policy designs would need to consider an appropriate match between revenue capacity and spending assignments between central and subnational governments and strike a balance between an adequate value of dependency ratio and central control over subnational governments. This requires careful design of fiscal instruments, implementing frameworks, and appropriate incentive structures.

---

[7]The measurement of dependency ratio might only be interpreted as a crude measure of central reliance. Another useful concept applicable here is own-source revenue. If we decompose provincial revenue into three types of revenue: (1) Collected by State Administration of Taxation (SAT); (2) Collected locally without control of rate; (3) Collected by SAT with some control over rate. Then the level of dependency could change drastically in favor of central government. **A finer characterization of dependency would need to consider not only the level of transfer required by the central government but also the tax setting ability of subnational governments. Also this definition in future work should consider the relevant accounting frameworks.**

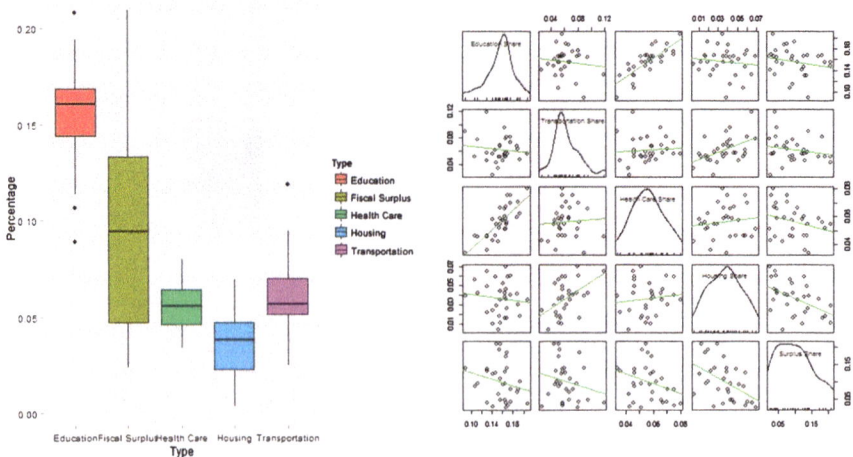

Fig. 7.3 *Spending patterns across provinces. Data Source National Financial Yearbook, 2012*

7.3.2 Expenditure: Heterogeneous Spending Patterns

The spending patterns across provinces are depicted in Fig. 7.3. Panel A presents a boxplot of the distribution for fiscal surplus, health care, housing, transportation, and education shares (percentage of total spending in a given province). Housing spending and health care spending vary little across provinces around 7% and 5% respectively. Transportation spending is a minor part of total spending below 5%. Education shares on average accounts for more than fifteen percentage points. The most variable part of the spending relates to fiscal surplus after own source revenue and central transfer. Some provinces (Zhejiang, Hubei, and Guangdong) have fiscal surplus around 20% while Anhui, Shanghai and Xinjiang only around 2%. Panel B shows a scatterplot matrix across these spending measures. The diagonal squares have distributional representation of each spending shares. It seems that the share of fiscal surplus is negatively associated with other spending measures.

Education spending shares, on the other hand, is negatively related to transportation and housing spending shares, indicating some delicate tradeoffs.

7.3.3 Linking Revenue and Expenditure at Provincial Level: Preliminary Analysis

The literature on fiscal decentralization stresses the potential efficiency gains from decentralization for various reasons (proximity, information aggregation, political selection effects, and so on). We perform two preliminary analyses to identify some correlations. First, we consider the question of whether the level of dependence is related to the provincial level revenues. Second, we ask whether there is a straightforward correlation between dependency ratio and spending patterns. Since correlation plots do not imply causality, these plots should be treated with caution given potential missing variables.

The results shown in Fig. 7.4 provide some curious insights. The first graph on the left confirms our intuition that lower dependency ratio is associated with higher local revenue in absolute terms. However, we should be cautious about the outliners as data points for many provinces do not fit into the confidence interval in the region for medium dependency ratios.

The relationship between dependency ratio and spending measures is much messier. Several observations can be made by scanning through the charts. There does not seem to have a simple and monotonic relationship between this definition of dependency ratio and spending assignments. There also seems to be no relationship between fiscal surplus and dependency ratio. However, we should be cautious in not pushing these results too hard because these patterns might reflect the impact of missing variables—notably the level of investment and economic development in a province—highly correlated with the dependency ratio.

7.3.4 Land Sales and Extrabudgetary Accounts

Shortages of local revenues and high dependency on central transfers are accompanied by political economy incentives of the local official to boost economic development. Alongside increased spending responsibilities, subnational governments were the main driver behind rapid urbanization over the past two decades, mainly through fixed capital investments in the form of infrastructure and public works. Interior provinces such as Hunan, Jiangxi, and others, saw more than a ten percent increase in urbanization rate. An average province in China has witnessed about more than 1% growth in urbanization rate each year.

Given the close links between administrative progression and economic performance for bureaucrats in charge of local governments, the political economy incentives induce two forms of financing in light of the mismatch: debt financing and reliance on land sales, both of which fall into the extra-budgetary arena. According to *Finance Yearbook of China* (2013, edition), extra-budgetary revenues include (a) revenue of administrative units and institutions, (b) revenue of government funds, (c) self-raised funds by township government, (d) revenue of state-owned enterprises and their administrative departments, and (e) other revenues. Post 1994 fiscal reform, there is an increasing use of government-managed funds (e.g., extrabudgetary source of revenue) to finance subnational expenditures (Hussain and Stern 2008). This incentive to finance outside the budgetary system is further strengthened given the limited tax setting abilities for subnational governments. Furthermore, the lack of sustainable, predicable, and reliable own-source revenues induces local governments to rely on land sales under the government

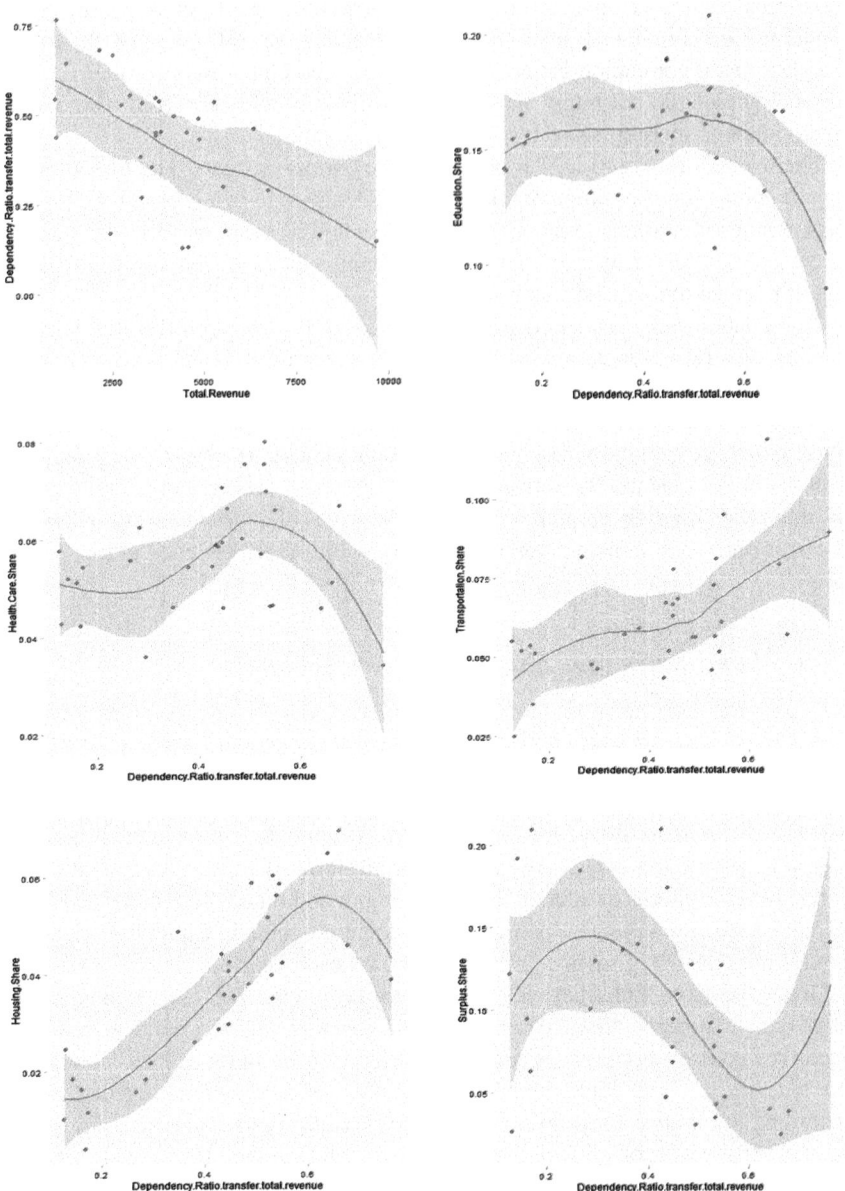

Fig. 7.4 *Linking revenue and spending: dependency ratio. Data Source National Financial Yearbook, 2012*

Table 7.3 Revenue from selling land usage right for local government managed funds

Year	Budgets	Final accounts	Final to budget as percentage points	Percentage of total revenue in final accounts
2013	25597.93	39072.99	152.6	0.79
2012	25304.52	26652.4	105.3	0.75
2011	18260.64	31140.42	170.5	0.79
2010	12447	28197.7	226.5	0.82

Source Ministry of Finance Website

managed funds and increasing use of Urban Development Investment Corporations (UDICs) and Local Government Financing Vehicles (LGFVs) that bypass the legal constraints on local governments to borrow.[8] We have covered debt financing in Sect. 7.2 and here we briefly sketch an overall picture for financing through land sales (see also Wang et al., this volume).

Revenue from selling land usage rights, a key item for local government managed funds, increased from 129.6 billion RMB in 2001 to 2,711.1 billion in 2010. In relative terms, the land selling ratio (defined as the percentage of land selling revenue to local government revenue) rose from 16.61% points in 2001 to about 80% in 2010 (Southern Weekends 2011). This trend of using land sales as a way to cover local government fiscal deficits has continued over the past 4 years. According to the Final Account Statements posted on the website of Ministry of Finance (see Table 7.3), revenue from land selling increased 40% from 2,711 billion RMB to 3,907 billion in 2013. In the past 4 years, revenue of this type accounted for about 80% of the total government managed funds.

Given the importance of land sales for local governments, the National Audit Office launched a national audit on this type of revenue for the first time ever. The land sale funds have become the incubators of corruption, and the People's Daily argued that "misappropriation, misuse, and embezzlement of land ssale funds are not exceptions" (China Daily 2014).[9]

In short, reliance on rampant land sale activities and reckless debt financing became a natural response for subnational governments in need of financing to cover their expenditures. The nature of extrabudgetary activities also afforded

---

[8]Latest amendments in the Budget Law provided legal permission for provincial governments to use debt financing as an option for infrastructure investments. See http://economy.caixin.com/2014-08-31/100723388.html. The actual amount of the debt will have to be authorized by the central government. Overall, this is an important legal step towards a transparent municipal bond market, as in the United States.

[9]Media have exposed some kickback and insider deals between real estate and developers where the land will be sold at a high price on the open market to the designated developer. Once the money passes through the local government account, there is guaranteed kickback payment to the developer returning the excessive bid they made during the open auction. This gray area of management of land selling revenue has become the seedbed of corruption. See http://finance.sina.com.cn/china/20140830/013420165823.shtml.

flexibility in spending, and minimized central supervision. These two forms of financing thus create fertile room for corruption and moral hazard.

7.4 A Case Study of Guangdong Province: Fiscal Heterogeneity, Land Sales, and Reform Experimentations

Heterogeneity of fiscal capacity manifest itself within as well as across provinces. In this section, we take Guangdong province as an example, highlighting fiscal heterogeneity and inequality within the province. The emphasis on fiscal inequality and heterogeneity should be interpreted along with previous studies on unbalanced development within the province (World Bank 2011).

7.4.1 Stylized Facts: Stunning Fiscal Inequality and Insufficient Sustainable Own-Source Revenue

The fiscal picture for Guangdong's municipalities, as with many municipalities in other provinces, are best characterized by two stylized facts. **One, there has been huge fiscal inequality across municipalities in terms of the budgetary gap between revenue and expenditure.** One immediate implication of this is that a significant portion of municipalities depend heavily on provincial transfers and debt financing through urban developmental corporations and/or local governmental financing vehicles, most of which have been using revenues from future land sales as collateral. **Second, no single municipality (even the richest of them, say Shenzhen or Guangzhou) has had a budgetary fiscal surplus over the past 5 years.**[10] The issue of long-term fiscal sustainability and fiscal autonomy even in "rich" municipal governments could be seriously in question in coming years, should major asset price corrections and change in expectations occur affecting their ability to borrow at reasonable rates.

Figure 7.5 presents a fiscal analysis of budgetary information across 21 municipalities in Guangdong province from 2008 to 2012. We calculated the average budgetary deficit for each municipality as a percentage of its revenue. To understand the volatility of budgetary deficits—the gap between budgetary revenue and budgetary spending—we consider sample standard deviation. The first panel depicts a boxplot of the average deficits. The distribution ranges from about 5% to

---

[10]One reader of the previous version of the draft commented that this should not be a problem depending on what surplus mean. But what we wish to highlight is the fiscal balancing condition within the budgetary framework. This is also consistent with the direction of the reform aiming at incorporating every aspect of government fiscal activity into the budgetary framework.

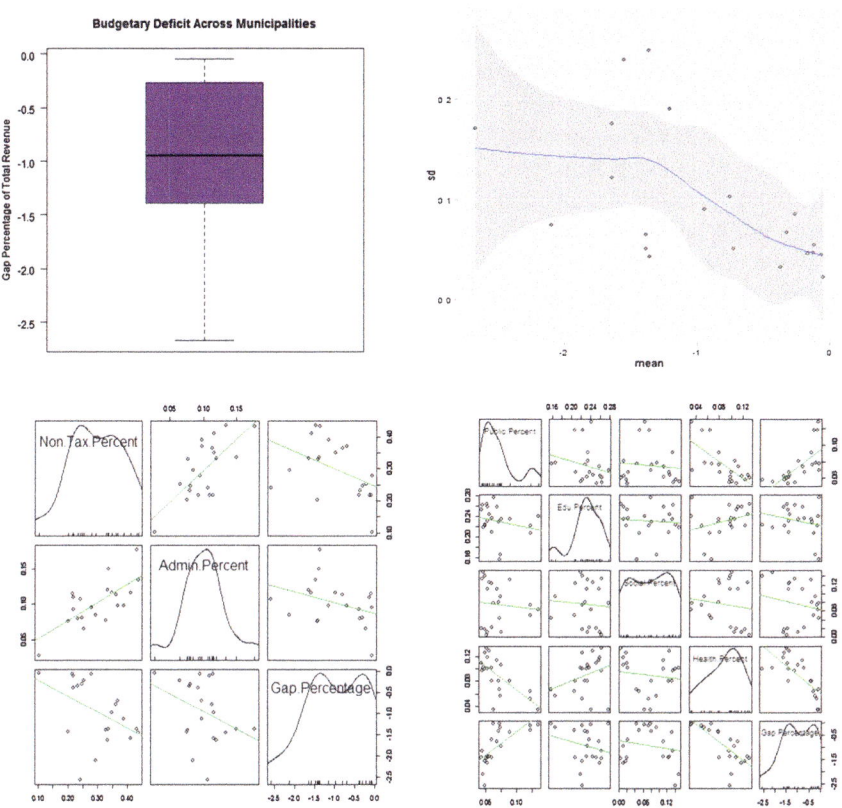

Fig. 7.5 *Budgetary heterogeneity across municipalities within Guangdong province.* Source *Guangdong Finance Yearbook. Calculated by the author*

more than 250%. The median gap hovers around 90%. About half (10 out of 21) municipalities have budgetary deficits over 100% of budgetary revenue. This is a rather crude measure given the unavailability of accurate measures of own-source revenue for each municipality. However, this fiscal picture highlights the severity of mismatch between revenue and expense at municipality level.

The following panel considers the relationship between fiscal gap and volatility. Despite the nature of correlation, the local linear approximation curve provides some evidence that higher budgetary gap might be associated with higher fiscal volatility. Any systemic assessment of fiscal vulnerability and risks would have to take into account the level as well as volatility of fiscal deficit.

The following panel shows pairwise scatterplots between percent of non-tax revenue in total revenue, percent of administrative fees in total revenue, and fiscal gap. These pairwise scatterplots are meant to test the anecdotal evidence that financially challenged governments might have perverse incentives to increase revenues in the short run through administrative charges and fees. This intuition is partially confirmed by the correlation plots that larger budgetary deficits are associated with increased share of administrative fees and non-tax revenue. However, we should be cautious in pushing this line of argument further as these correlations could also be affected by missing variables.

The last panel relates spending patterns with fiscal gaps. We cannot document substantial relationship between expenditure behavior and fiscal gaps. One huge confounding variable in interpreting these results can be the measure of fiscal activity in off-budget accounts.

As the best budgetary data available is in the Guangdong Finance Yearbooks, the analysis presented here should only be seen as preliminary. The critical missing fiscal information for these municipalities lies in off-budgetary fiscal activities. Ideally, we wish to know how these budgetary gaps across municipalities are financed. The information on government managed funds has not yet been integrated with the Guangdong Finance Yearbook and linked with municipality fiscal information. Without this information, we cannot provide a meaningful analysis on important fiscal questions such as the following: to what extent these gaps are financed by transfers from the province or the center and to what extent debt financing is dominant; the portion of land sale revenue in government managed funds in each year and volatility of this source of revenue. Some information is available on an ad hoc basis from each municipality finance bureau website, but the lack of standardized fiscal information makes comparable analysis rather difficult. In a few municipalities in Guangdong, the internal review for the People's Congress has been leaked to the press through which we have a glimpse of off budgetary activities. Even that information is quite unsystematic and items of expense are rather vague. We have discussed Guangdong's local debt financing situation in the first section and now we turn to land sales.

7.4.2 Land Sales Revenue

For 2011 and 2012, land sales were 182.9 billion and 175.4 billion RMB for Guangdong province, accounting for 56.36 and 53.06% of the government managed revenues. There has been a little surplus for government managed funds in the past 3 years, totaling around 4.74% of provincial GDP. The volatility of revenue streams in government managed funds is associated with developments in the real estate sector (Table 7.4).

One of the biggest risks of reliance on land sales is the volatile and unsustainable nature of this source of revenue. For example, Guangzhou city experienced big swings in land sale revenue over the past 4 years. In 2010, the land sale revenue was 45.5 billion RMB, but fell to only 30.6 billion RMB in 2011. The exact figure

Table 7.4 2011–2013 Guangdong province government managed fund and real estate development

	2011		2012		2013	
	Amount (100 million)	Growth rate	Amount (100 million)	Growth rate	Amount (100 million)	Growth rate
Revenue	2307.38		2265.02	−1.84	3673.72	62.19
Expense	2254.89		2172.55	−3.65	3370.01	55.12
GDP	53210.28	10.00	57067.92	8.20	62163.97	8.5
Residential sales	5852.54	6.78	6407.81	9.49	8941.05	39.53

Source Guangdong Government Credit Rating Report. Guangdong Department of Finance

for 2012 cannot be founded in the annual report in the 42.1 billion RMB in total government revenue. The year for 2013 reached recorded levels of 83.7 billion RMB of land sales revenue and the figure for 2014 is expected to be around 80 billion RMB as well.[11] A detailed analysis would require getting land sales information for each municipality for the previous years, which are unavailable in a systematic manner.

The reliance on land sales is not a sustainable and viable strategy in the long run given the saturation of housing demands and asset pricing risks. In addition to a finite and diminishing area of available land, any major corrections on the property market would inject volatility of the potential income stream that can be generated through land sales and jeopardize the efficacy and viability of this financing channel for subnational governments. Without full information, it is quite difficult to build macro level general equilibrium models to monitor and assess various risks through different plausible mechanisms.

7.4.3 Complementary Fiscal Reform Experiments: VAT Reforms and Competitive Transfer Mechanisms

In this section, we discuss two fiscal reform experiments in Guangdong province. One relates to transition from business tax to value-added tax (VAT).[12] The other reform introduces competitive transfer mechanisms for the allocation of public funds. Although these reform programs are important in achieve their policy objectives, we raise the concern that the short fiscal effect could be detrimental to local fiscal condition. Designing smoothing periods and countervailing policy might be considered to avoid exacerbation of the subnational balance sheets in the short run.

---

[11]Guangzhou City Municipality Final and Budgetary Report, various years.

[12]The official guideline for pushing VAT reform can be read in English in http://www.gd-n-tax.gov.cn/pub/gdgsww/ssxc/sxzt/yysgzzzs/zczypolicies_guideline/201212/t20121210_210566.html.

The VAT for business tax reform in 2015 was designed to reduce the cost of doing business, but had the effect of adding to the fiscal pressures on local government at least in the short run. Even with a higher share of the VAT for the services component, and central government transfers to compensate for the loss in **the short run, however, this could translate into higher dependency ratio at municipality level.**

Across municipalities in Guangdong province, the pace of VAT reform is unsurprisingly uneven. Using the ratio of VAT to business tax as a crude measure of the share of VAT in tax revenue for municipality governments across Guangdong province, we find an unequal share of VAT in taxable revenue. Using the ratio of VAT revenue to business tax revenue as a benchmark, we found that this ratio for Shenzhen[13] approximates about 45% while the ratio for Jieyang City, Maoming City, and Shantou City exceeded 150% in 2012 figure. **The unbalanced share of business tax to VAT within Guangdong province requires close provincial monitoring of the fiscal impact of the reforms.**

In addition, the distribution of gains for VAT reform has a strong sector association. Some companies in particular sectors could experience increased tax burdens after the reform in contrast with the policy objective of tax reduction. To smooth this VAT reform and alleviate positive tax shock to some affected companies, Guangdong provincial level government set up special purpose funds to subsidize companies experiencing increased tax burdens after the reform (Guangdong Finance Department 2014). In one analysis looking at VAT experiments in Foshan City, the author found that although the overall fiscal effect has been tax reduction transportation sector in fact experienced short term spikes in tax after transition to VAT regime (Guangdong Finance Yearbook 2014).[14] The biggest gainers in VAT reform is the service sector, especially related to property and capital leasing. Concluding the analysis of the case study, we can draw three conclusions: First, the VAT for business tax reform would change the revenue structure at the local level. Second, the reform would create an immediate and negative revenue shock to municipality revenue, in the absence of accurately calibrated transfers to finance deficits. Third, the transition period would require fiscal support and transfer from provincial level government to smooth the VAT transition. The second and third items however open up the possibility of game-play by the local governments, as they might seek to **increase deficits in order to generate higher transfers.**

The latest analysis (July, 2016) of VAT reform in Guangdong focused exclusively on reducing the tax burden for firms. Fiscal midyear review for Guangdong

---

[13]One commentator of the previous draft argued that Shenzhen is an outliner by nature of its status. So issue of comparability is a concern. My response is that this is also a level of heterogeneity we should document.

[14]Foshan Finance Bureau, Guangdong Finance 2013 Yearbook (Guangdong Finance Yearbook 2014).

in 2015 reported increased in general government revenue by 17.4%.[15] Detailed analysis on sectoral basis is yet to be reported. The uneven distributional impact on different municipalities deserve detailed public policy analysis comparing before and after effects of the VAT reform.

In addition to VAT reform, another complementary fiscal reform seeks to introduce competition mechanisms into the allocation of public projects for subnational governments. To increase efficient use of public resources and induce regional competition, the Guangdong provincial government invites municipal governments in underdeveloped regions in the province to propose public projects in a bid for the use of provincial special purpose funds. After receiving proposals from undeveloped regions, Guangdong Finance department organizes a panel of experts to evaluate the bids in an open competition under media scrutiny and public disclosure. **This is an ingenious innovation to facilitate regional competition through effective allocation of special purpose funds—a form of provincial transfer in essence.** The policy objective of competitive transfer mechanism is to avoid backroom dealings and potential corruption in the allocation of special purpose funds. However, the overall fiscal effect of this innovation might not be as clear cut as intended by the policy objective. One potential problem with this competitive transfer scheme could be further exacerbation of regional inequality as underdeveloped municipalities which might not have the expertise to propose attractive projects could be left further behind. In addition, the competition allocative schemes is by no means a substitute for ex-post fiscal supervision and monitoring. To ensure equalization of services across a hugely unbalanced province, the provincial level governments would have to examine transfer of human capital and expertise in addition to financial assistance.[16]

7.4.4 Information, Accountability and Supervision

When former Guangdong Party Secretary Wang Yang (subsequently vice Premier) visited Guangdong Finance Department in 2012, he recommended a book named *Big Data* to the staff. In a widely circulated remarks, the former secretary stressed the importance of applying big data thinking and techniques to fiscal affairs and reportedly urged for a modern data collection, compilation, and publication of fiscal data as a way to improve the operation of government fiscal activity.[17]

---

[15]Mid fiscal year report on 2016. http://news.southcn.com/china/content/2016-07/21/content_151958962.htm.

[16]One commentator remarked that this competitive transfer scheme is regarded as too tedious for many localities. The actual effect of this mechanism and its linkage with political promotion evaluations should be a good topic for further research.

[17]This anecdote is retrieved from the following website, widely circulated in Guangdong Finance Department. http://www.bbtpress.com/asp/pressnew.asp?id=518.

Indeed, Guangdong province has been leading the country in publicizing budgetary information at the departmental level.[18] Our interview with an official at the provincial congress confirmed that this line of reform has been actively pushed within the provincial congress and media despite resistance from the executive branch. Despite the incompleteness and lack of details in public budgets, Guangdong municipalities lead the country in publishing their budgets regularly to allow some degree of supervision from the public and media platforms.

Laudable indeed as these reforms are, further initiatives would have to be done. Consistent with Mr. Wang Yang's vision, efforts should be directed towards eliminating off budget activities and incorporate every fiscal activity into a transparent framework, a direction consistent with the newly-revised budget law. At the central level, the implementation of Treasury Single Account (TSA), which requires all the expense and revenues pass through an integrated account, is surely going to increase the level of transparency and squeeze the space for off-budget activities (Yaker and Pattanayak 2012). A provincial version of TSA encompassing local governments could be considered as a next step reform aiming at integrating fiscal information across different layers of subnational government below provinces, and was considered in the original design of the nested TSAs (see Ahmad 2015). **The implementation of transparency reforms would have to be complemented by assigning own-source revenues at the subnational level. Otherwise, perverse incentives at local level would generate expected local resistance and derail the intention of policy objectives.**

Another important initiative could be subnational reporting consistent with IMF's Government Financial Statistics Framework (GFSM 2001/14) (International Monetary Fund 2001). Efforts have been made in this front by the central government and the data completeness are better for the central rather than the subnational governments in the GFS database (see Ahmad and Zhang, this volume). To complete the standardization of the fiscal reporting framework, reforms at transitions into GFSM standards have to be worked out at the provincial level and below. The availability of standardized fiscal variables would be instrumental in constructing a fiscal monitoring system (Ma 2001).

In the end, accountability pressure for further transparency in budgetary process has to be complemented by technical support in standardizing and streamlining the fiscal reporting process. This could be a valuable reform experiment and opportunity to set up an example for the rest of the country to follow, totally consistent with the capacity building efforts at the Guangdong provincial fiscal information bureau.

---

[18]The provincial level government website posts all the departmental budgets for the public.

7.5 Conclusions: Towards Future Reforms—Direction and Feasibility, National and Guangdong

The misalignment between revenue sources and spending responsibilities has long been recognized within policy circles. The important question is designing response strategies in a new fiscal context. We discuss two upcoming reforms—one at the national level and the other at Guangdong provincial level—in addressing the fiscal challenges ahead.

Amendments to Budget Law were announced in September, 2014 made effective in January 2015.[19] Several important amendments are direct responses to the risks and vulnerabilities identified in this paper. We briefly summarize several highlights in this new amendments along with the intended policy objectives. First, the new budget law requires the incorporation of all revenue and expense into the budgetary framework. This is to rectify rampant use of off-budgetary funds and clarify the use of debt financing for subnational governments. Second, institutionalization of budgetary framework has to be achieved. This means that governments have to stick to the budgetary items unless there is a budgetary revision through the congress. Institutionally, this creates administrative constraints on off budget spending. Third, the public has the right to know details of budget consistent with experiments in Guangdong province. Fourth, reforms on transfer mechanism will be considered so that the use of special purpose funds would have to be regulated. Fifth, performance consideration has to be included in designing budget proposals. Sixth, provincial governments are allowed to borrow under the quota set by the State Council. Seventh, strict regulation will have to be put forth on the use fiscal surplus and stabilization funds. **Overall, these reform measures are intended to put forward a modern fiscal system institutionalized by legal procedures.** However, it is premature to assess the real effect of the new budget law given principal-agent and adverse selection problems at stake. Detail assessments should consider the gap between an ideal of a policy and the realities on the grounds. Without sustainable own-revenue source at the subnational level, budgetary reform risks being implemented only on paper.

Consonant with the spirit of newly revised budget law, Guangdong provincial government announce "its systemic plan to establish a modern fiscal system".[20] According to media announcement, the core of the reform agenda is to create a local fiscal system sustainable for long run development.[21] Specially, the plan made clear that real estate tax will be implemented as an own source revenue for municipal and county level governments. **If this plan could generate a sufficient**

---

[19]The amendments can be seen from the official website of National People's Congress. http://big5.gov.cn/gate/big5/www.gov.cn/zhengce/2014-09/01/content_2743208.htm.

[20]We present an outline of reform objectives for Guangdong province from a tentative proposal in the appendix.

[21]Other reform measures are being considered. See the appendix for an outline of future fiscal reform agenda in Guangdong province.

and stable local revenue stream, then complete transition to VAT could largely be smoothed and reliance on transfers from higher level governments allevi-ated to a great extent. In the end, the question should be more than finding new source of taxes to finance debt and public services. The core issue resides in enhancing efficient uses of public resources and provision of quality services. To what extent this can be implemented in reality will shape the fiscal foundation of China's long run growth potential.

Last but not the least, experiments with Private-Public Partnerships (PPP), vigorously pushed by Ministry of Finance, have been regarded as an important vehicle for managing local liabilities. Useful as they are, the success of PPP critically hinges on the design of financial contract between stakeholders and minimization of information asymmetry and moral hazards (Ahmad et al. 2014). Further work should delve into understanding the proper scope of preconditions for successful implementation of PPP contracts in managing subnational liabilities.

In conclusion, we stress the importance of incentive structures in the managing subnational liabilities. **The rapid accumulation of local liabilities is by and large a result of existing political economy incentive structures in response to the recent financial crisis and local-central relationships. Rather measured in terms of any policy target variables, future reform packages would have to be evaluated against the structural impact on existing incentives between central and local governments.**

Appendix: Possible Items of Reform on the Agenda (Proposals from Guangdong Finance Department, Tentative)

The central theme of this proposal is to launch some key fiscal reforms in accor-dance with the spirit of the 18th Plenary Speech:

1. Reforms on Budget Management

   • Deepening reforms on budgeting system
   (a) Perfect existing budgeting system
   (b) Clarify the responsibility of involved parties in the budgeting process
   (c) Detail budgeting items
   (d) Standardize departmental budgets
   (e) Control general administrative expenses
   (f) Perfect notification system of fiscal transfer
   (g) Perfect annual budgeting management
   (h) Establish intertemporal budget balancing system
   (i) Speed up building database for earmarked projects
   (j) Regularize mandatory expense items

    (k) Perfect budget verification system

    (l) Perfect budget hearing and consultation system

- Deepening reforms on budget execution management

    (a) Perfect constraining system for budget execution

    (b) Establish expenditure updating system

    (c) Establish monitoring system for expenditure

    (d) Deepen reforms on management of expenditure

    (e) Standardize management of special purpose funds

    (f) Strengthen management of fiscal surplus

- Deepening reforms on fiscal supervision and evaluation

    (a) Strengthen fiscal supervision

    (b) Perfect performance-based budgeting system

    (c) Establish evaluation system for special purpose funds

- Deepening reforms on government debt management

    (a) Research into building government debt management system

    (b) Clarify government management responsibility of public debts

    (c) Establish mechanism for risk monitoring and control

    (d) Establish debt management system in connection with the budget system

- Deepening reforms on budget transparency

    (a) Perfect materials prepared for review by People's Congress

    (b) Make public detailed items of the budget and financial statements

    (c) Make public information on special purpose funds according to rules

    (d) Deepened transparency reforms on county and municipal level budget and financial statement information

2. Reforms on Matching Expenditure Responsibility with Source of Revenue

- Clarify expenditure responsibility for each tier of government

    (a) Enumerate expenditure items for each tier of the government

    (b) Clarify expenditure responsibility of each tier of government

    (c) Clarify expenditure responsibility of each tier of government with respect to each aspect of governance

    (d) Establish a checklist of expenditure item for municipal and county level government

- Establish a fiscal system such that revenue and expenditure responsibility can match

    (a) Perfect transfer payment system

    (b) Standardize special purpose projects

    (c) Regulate management of transfer payment

3. Tax Reforms

- Deepen Reforms on Public Resource Trading System

    (a) Involve competitive markets in areas of public resource management

    (b) Establish standardized trading platforms and management system

    (c) Establish monitoring system for trading of public resources

(d) Explore reputation tracking system for trading of public resources
- Deepen Reforms on Fiscal Distribution
  (a) Perfect special purpose fund distribution system with the purpose of supporting economic growth and productive industries
  (b) Further reforms on equity management of fiscal funds with operation purpose
  (c) Further reforms on government purchase of social services
- Standardize Preferential Tax Policy

References

Ahmad, E. (2011). Should China revisit the 1994 fiscal reform? (LSE Asia research centre working paper).

Ahmad, E. (2015). Institutions and governance. In E. Ahmad & G. Brosio (Eds.), *Handbook of multilevel finance*. Elgar Revised in 2014.

Ahmad, E., Bhattacharya, A., Vinella, A., & Xiao, K. (2014). Information asymmetries and investment financing options, (this volume) Paper for the G-24.

Ahmad, E., Keping, L., Richardson, T. J., & Singh, R. J. (2002). Recentralization in China? International Monetary Fund.

Barnett, S., & Zhang, Y. S. (2014). Fiscal Vulnerabilities and Risks from Local Government finance in China IMF working paper.

Cheung, S. N. S., & Coase, R. H. (2008). The economic system of China: With conference opening and closing remarks by Ronald Coase. Arcadia Press.

Daily. C. (2014). Misappropriation of funding from land usage transfer is not exception (in Chinese). Retrieved from http://news.sina.com.cn/pl/2014-08-29/062930762336.shtml.

Guangdong Audit Office (GAO). (2014). Announcement on local liability. Retrieved from http://news.southcn.com/g/2014-01/23/content_90965741.htm.

Guangdong Credit Report for 2014. Chinese original. (2014). 年广东省政府债券 信用评级报告 (上海新世纪资信评估投资服务有限公司).

Guangdong Finance Department. (2014). *Document on subsidizing VAT transition*. Retrieved from http://www.gdczt.gov.cn/topco/yysgzzzs/gzdt/201211/t20121130_41185.htm.

Guangdong Finance 2013 Yearbook. (2014). The Impact of VAT transition on economic development (pp. 470–478).

Holz, C. A. (2004). China's statistical system in transition: Challenges, data problems, and institutional innovations. *Review of Income and Wealth, 50*(3), 381–409.

Hussain, A., & Stern, N. (2008). Public finances, the role of the state, and economic transformation, 1978–2020. *Public finance in China, reform and growth for a harmonious society*, 13–38.

International Monetary Fund (2001). *Government finance statistics manual*. Available from https://www.imf.org/external/pubs/ft/gfs/manual/. Revised in 2014.

Li, H., & Zhou, L. -A. (2005). Political turnover and economic performance: The incentive role of personnel control in China. *Journal of public economics, 89*(9), 1743–1762.

Liu. L. (2010). Strengthening subnational debt financing and managing risks, World Bank, processed; Review of Economic Research, Ministry of Finance PRC, 49-F9, August 16.

Ma, J. (2001). Managing fiscal risk of subnational governments: selected country experiences. 2001 World Bank Papers.

National Audit Office (NAO). (2011). No.35 Report. Retrieved from http://www.audit.gov.cn/n1992130/n1992150/n1992500/2752208.html.

National Audit Office (NAO). (2013). *Announcement*. Retrieved from http://www.audit.gov.cn/n1992130/n1992150/n1992500/n3432077.files/n3432112.pdf.

Rural Affair Committee, Guangdong Province. (2014). A survey report on village level liability in Guangdong province. Retrieved from Guangdong Finance Yearbook 2014.

Southern Weekends. *Revenue from land usage rights transfer amounts to 76.6% of local revenue in 2010. (in chinese).* Retrieved from http://www.infzm.com/content/54644.

Wong, C. P. (2000). Central-local relations revisited the 1994 tax-sharing reform and public expenditure management in China. China Perspectives, 52–63.

World Bank. (2011). *Reducing inequality for shared growth in China: Strategy and policy options for Guangdong Province*. Retrieved from http://www.worldbank.org/en/news/feature/2011/05/31/reducing-inequality-for-shared-growth-guandong-china-worldwe.

Yaker, I. F., & Pattanayak, S. (2012). Treasury single account: an essential tool for government cash management. International Monetary Fund.

Chapter 8
Hub-Periphery Development Pattern and Inclusive Growth: Case Study of Guangdong Province

Xubei Luo and Nong Zhu

Abstract The hub-periphery development pattern of the Guangdong economy, to some extent, is a miniature of that of the Chinese economy. The Pearl River Delta, drawing from its first-nature comparative advantages in factor endowments and proximity to Hong Kong (SAR China) and Macau (SAR, China) and the second-nature advantages as first-movers in the reforms in attracting and retaining domestic and foreign resources, has developed into a regional economic center. This paper examines the pattern of inter- and intra- provincial migration and that of the concentration of production to explore the challenges and opportunities for the success of "double transfer". It suggests a four-prong approach—improve the business environment, support the realization of latent comparative advantages, increase the skill level of labor force to support the upgrade of production structure, and protect the vulnerable—to support the inclusive growth of the economy in Guangdong in a sustainable manner.

8.1 Introduction

Since the late 1970s, institutional and economic reforms have played a crucial role in the unprecedented development of the Chinese economy. The reforms have provided the basis for the transition to market economy and facilitated the integration of the

---

The findings, interpretations, and conclusions expressed in this paper are entirely those of the authors. They do not necessarily represent the views of the International Bank for Reconstruction and Development/World Bank and its affiliated organizations, or those of the Executive Directors of the World Bank or the governments they represent.

X. Luo (✉)
The World Bank, Washington, DC, USA
e-mail: xluo@worldbank.org

N. Zhu
INRS-UCS, University of Quebec, Montreal, Canada
e-mail: nong_zhu@ucs.inrs.ca

© Springer Nature Singapore Pte Ltd. 2018
E. Ahmad et al. (eds.), *Fiscal Underpinnings for Sustainable Development in China*,
https://doi.org/10.1007/978-981-10-6286-5_8

domestic market with the international market. The interdependence of institutional reforms and opening up policies strengthened each other. Through incrementally reforming the centrally planned system to improve incentives and increase the scope of the market in resource allocation, and through building new institutions to support a market system before old institutions were destroyed, China's transition has achieved a remarkable success (Boublil 1997; Démurger 1997; Qian 2003; Wilmots 1997). Thanks to the advantageous factor endowment and favorable policy inclination, the coastal region soon took off. Export-oriented and globalized industries are largely concentrated in the coastal region and low tech and resource based industries are mainly located in the inland region. Disparities within the province increased as the economy rapidly developed. The dynamics of the coastal provinces and the relative stagnation of the inland provinces configure a center-periphery regional growth structure (Lu 2008; Naughton 1999; Chen and Fleisher 1996).

Guangdong province, once an economic backwater, is a pioneer in the process of reforms and opening up (ElSayed et al. 2006).[1] The economy of Guangdong is export-oriented, and largely supported by inflow of foreign direct investment (FDI), of which a significant share from Hong Kong (SAR, China) and Macau (SAR, China) to the Pearl River Delta (PRD), and migrant labor. The province hosts three of the four Special Economic Zones established in the early 1980s (Shenzhen, Zhuhai, and Shantou, along with Xiamen in Fujian province). The special tax policies and financial incentives provided to the Special Economic Zones have stimulated the development of the foreign and domestic private companies and changed the structure of the economy. The development of economy of Guangdong (particularly PRD), started with "three-plus-one" trading mix (custom manufacturing with materials, designs or samples supplied and compensation trade) and developed to diverse ownership. The large inflow of FDI created strong demand for migrant labor.

The long-term development of the economy of Guangdong is conditioned by the sustainable upgrade of the industrial structure and that of job creation to attract and retain the needed skills as well as provide workers (including migrant workers) adequate access to social services of good quality. In the recent years, partly related to the global crisis, the slow-down of the GDP growth rate and the decline of net inflow of migrant workers, reflected as an emerging shortage of migrant workers (*MinGongHuang*), in some cities in Guangdong, led to the hot debate of whether the development pattern of Guangdong has reached a turning point (Liang and Wu 2003; Meng et al. 2007; Wang and Fan 2006; Zhu and Wang 2006).

The objectives of this paper are to present a comprehensive picture of the hub-periphery development pattern of the economy in Guangdong as a miniature of that of China and examine the opportunities and challenges for sustainable inclusive

---

[1]The open-door policy began with the establishment of the first special economic zones (SEZs) in 1980 in three cities (Shenzhen, Zhuhai and Shantou) in Guangdong province and one city (Xiamen) in Fujian province, then the preferential status of the SEZs soon rolled out to 14 other coastal cities in 1984, to the three deltas in 1985, to Hainan in 1988, to Pudong in Shanghai in 1990, and then gradually to 11 border cities and eventually to all capitals of the inland provinces and autonomous regions during the 1990s.

growth. It focuses on areas that merit particular policy consideration in supporting the continuous upgrade of the economic structure through "double transfer"—transfer industries from the PRD to the rest of the provinces; and transfer labor in the lagging regions from the primary sector to the secondary and tertiary sectors, including transfer high-skilled labor to the PRD. The paper is structured as follows: The next section focuses on the hub-periphery development pattern between the PRD and the rest of the economy. Section 8.3 highlights the large concentration of FDI using the statistics from the China Statistic Yearbooks. Section 8.4 examines the massive inflow of migrant workers in the province, with a focus on the unique composition of migrant labor force in different cities drawing from the 5th and the 6th national population census data. Section 8.5 examines the industrial specialization and spatial concentration of the capital-, labor-, and resource- intensive industries in the province. The last section discusses, in the context of "double transfer", the challenges and opportunities faces the economy and presents a four-prong approach to support inclusive growth in a sustainable manner.

8.2 Hub-Periphery Development Pattern

The development pattern of Guangdong, to a certain extent, is a miniature of that of China. Guangdong province has witnessed rapid development since the reforms. Its average growth rate has been higher than the "four Asian dragons" during the periods when they took off. Since 1989, Guangdong has topped the total GDP rankings among all provincial-level divisions. In 2013, the province's GDP reached 6.2 trillion RMB (or 1 trillion USD) and accounted for 11% of China's GDP. Guangdong is also the largest exporter and importer in China. Its foreign trade accounted for about 28% of the country and the actual use of foreign investment accounted for about 22% of the country's total, both rank first in all provinces. In addition, Guangdong's many major economic indicators, including total fixed assets investment, total retail sales, savings deposits of residents, per capita disposable income of urban and rural residents, and local revenues, and non-income welfare indicators, such as life expectancy, education, and health services, both rank high (see Annex 8.1 for additional statistics of Guangdong).

The Pearl River Delta, drawing from its first-nature comparative advantages in factor endowments and proximity to Hong Kong (SAR, China) and Macau (SAR, China) and the second-nature advantages as first-movers in the reforms in attracting and retaining domestic and foreign resources, has developed into a regional economic center and well-known world factory, with many highly specialized towns and cities (Tuan and Ng 2004).[2] Its regional GDP exceeded that of Singapore in 1998, Hong Kong in 2003, and Taiwan, China, in 2007 (National Development and Reform Commission 2008).

---

[2]The Pearl River Delta region, including Guangzhou, Shenzhen, Zhuhai, Foshan, Huizhou, Zhongshan, Jiangmen, Shunde, and Zhaoqing, has been the pioneer since the opening-up.

The economy is highly concentrated: the Pearl River Delta produces 80% of the regional GDP and over 95% of the exports and imports, attracts over 90% of the foreign direct investment, and hosts 90% of the migrant population. The development gaps within Guangdong widened between the Pearl River Delta and the rest (the Northern Mountainous Area and the East and West Wings), and within the PDR between economic hubs (Guangzhou, Shenzhen and Zhuhai) and the other seven cities. We illustrate this regional development gap in 2000–2013 in the following three figures: the Kernel distribution of the real GDP per capita (Fig. 8.1); Gini coefficient (Fig. 8.2), and growth incidence curve (Fig. 8.3).

Figure 8.1 shows that Shenzhen, Guangzhou, and (to a less extent) Zhuhai are more developed than the rest of the economy in a significant manner. Figure 8.2 shows, the Gini coefficient of the gross regional product per capita in the 21 prefecture-level cities rose from 0.35 in 2000 to almost 0.40 in 2005–2006 before steadily declined to 0.34 in the recent 3 years. Figure 8.3 shows, during the period of relatively slow-growth after the Asian financial crisis in 2000–2003, the richer cities grew faster and inequality increased; during the period of high growth performance in 2003–2009, still the richer cities grew faster and inequality continued to increase; while in the recent period of 2009–2013, when growth slowed down (partly related to the global economic crisis and the restructuring), the poorer cities grew faster than the richer ones and inequality started to decline.

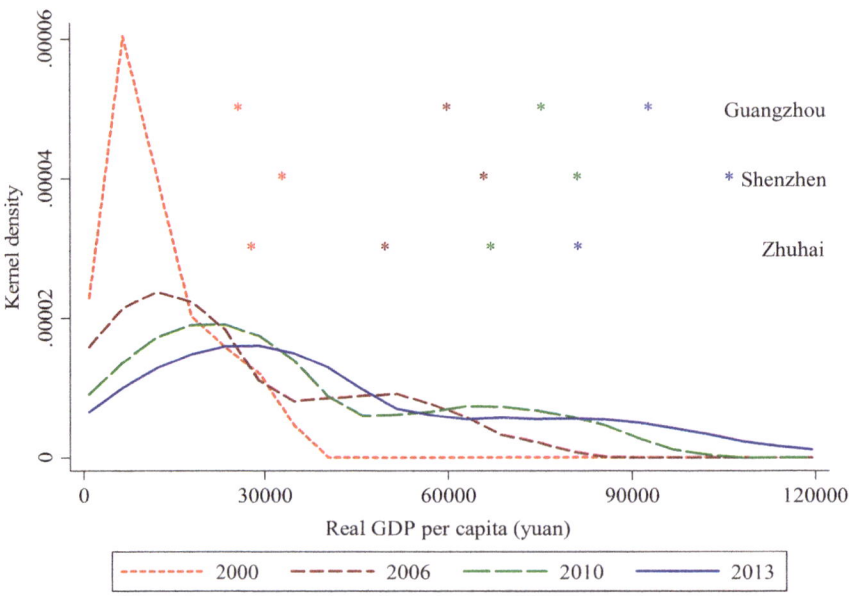

Fig. 8.1 Distribution of real GDP per capita of prefecture-level cities in Guangdong (2000–2013). *Data source* Guangdong Bureau of Statistics, Guangdong Statistical Yearbooks (several editions), China Statistical Publishing House, Beijing. *Note* The three rows of stars show the levels of real GDP per capita of Guangzhou, Shenzhen, and Zhuhai respectively, from top to bottom, with the color indicating the years of 2000 (red), 2006 (brown), 2010 (green) and 2013 (blue)

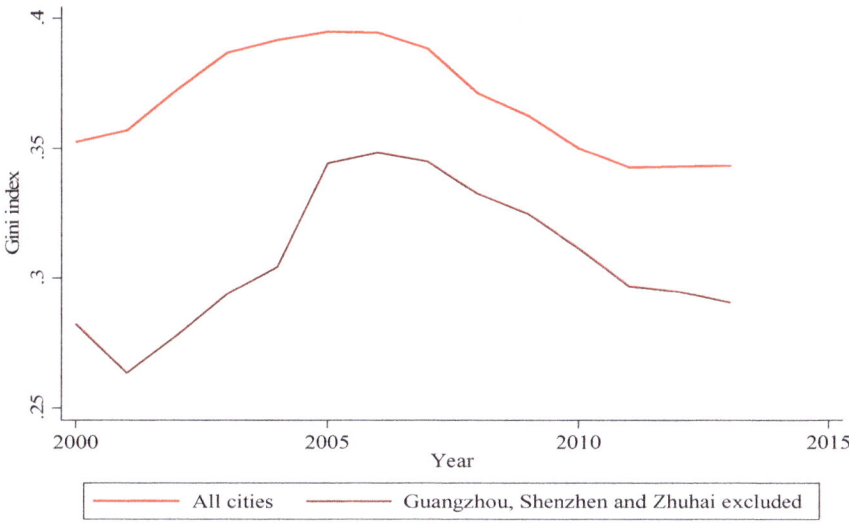

Fig. 8.2 Gini index of real GDP per capita of prefecture-level cities in Guangdong (2000–2013). *Data source* Guangdong Bureau of Statistics (2014)

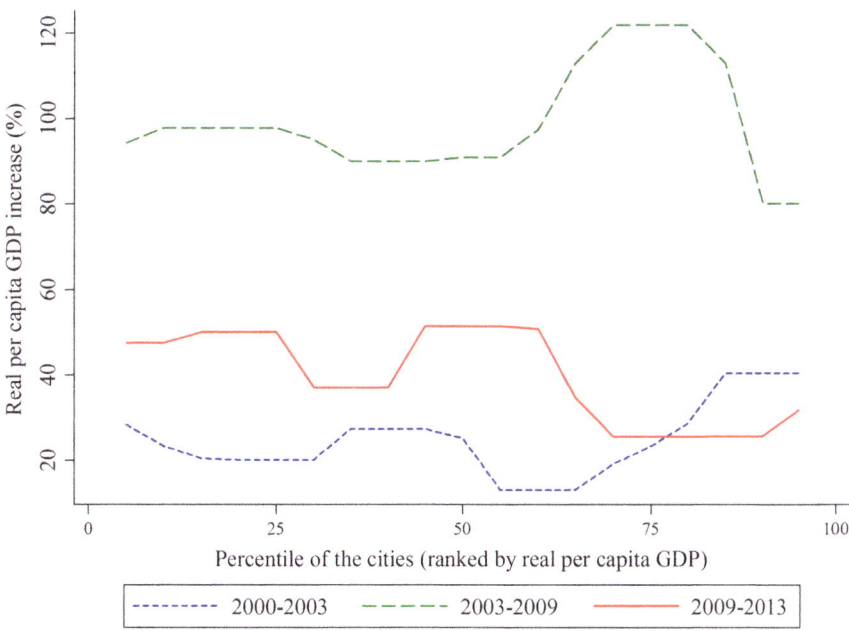

Fig. 8.3 Growth incidence curve. *Data source* Guangdong Bureau of Statistics (2014). *Note* The growth incidence curves are created with "smooth" function for readability

8.3   Intra- and Inter- Provincial Labor Migration

Worldwide, labor migration is a powerful tool to reduce distance to economic opportunity. Eight million Americans change states every year (World Bank 2008). In China, the gradual reform of the Household Registration System (*Hukou*) reduced the constraint on domestic labor mobility (Chan and Li 1999; Chen and Wu 2005; Fan 2005a, b; He and Pooler 2002; Li 2004; Liang 2001; Shen 1999; Zhang and Song 2003; Wu and Yao 2003; Zhao 2005). The significant inflow of capital and the development of an export-oriented economy in the coastal provinces created strong demand for labor (Li 1997; Wong et al. 2003; Zhu 2000). The large-scale migration from rural areas and inland regions to urban areas and coastal regions provided coastal and urban areas with a flexible labor supply at reasonable costs and contributed to the rapid development of their labor intensive industries (Luo and Zhu 2008). This in turn accelerated the formation and expansion of the small and medium size cities in the coastal provinces and increased the potential for the exploitation of economy of scale (Sit and Yang 1997; Li 1997).

A similar story applies for Guangdong, with PRD (especially Guangzhou, Shenzhen, and Zhuhai) as the hubs. The inflow of migrant workers largely contributed to the rapid development of Guangdong. Guangdong officially became the most populous province in 2005. Its total population hit 110 million then, with 79 million registered permanent residents and 31 million migrants who have lived in Guangdong for more than six months.[3] The PRD, the Yangtze River Delta, and Bohai Bay area, are the three largest regions with significant migrant concentrations in China (Trudel 2008).

The Chinese fifth census data shows, in 2005, out of the 93 million working age cross-county migrants, some two-thirds are urban labor and some one-third rural labor. Urban areas are the major destination of migration: roughly 67 million moved to urban areas and 26 million to rural areas. The scale of intra-provincial migration was higher than that of inter-provincial migration. At the national level, the average intra-provincial immigration rate is about 11.8%, and inter-provincial immigration rate 6.4%. In Guangdong, in 1978–2013, the average total migration rate is 2.8%, and the average net migration rate is 0.3%. The net migration rate is positive in most of the years. It gradually increased since 1978, peaked around 2006, and fluctuated downward in the recent years. The average gross inflow of migrants amounted to some 1.06 million per year. With an average outflow of migrants of some 0.84 million, this results in a net inflow of migrants of 0.22 million (see Fig. 8.4). This "demographic dividend" has played a significant role in contributing to the economic development in Guangdong.

The distribution of inter- and intra- provincial migration differs significantly between the PRD and the rest of the province. A closer look at the fifth population census data shows that nearly 90% of the migrant population concentrates in the Pearl River Delta, of which 50% in Shenzhen and Guangzhou. For the entire

---

[3]http://www.chinadaily.com.cn/english/doc/2005-01/29/content_413299.htm.

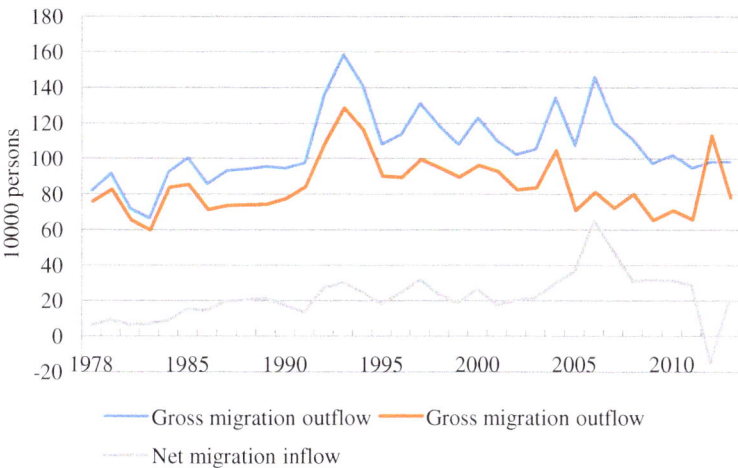

Fig. 8.4 Labor inflow and outflow in Guangdong (1978–2013). *Data source* Guangdong Bureau of Statistics (2014)

province, the intra-provincial migration and inter-provincial migration accounted for 40 and 60% of the total migration population, respectively. However, for the Pearl River Delta, the intra-provincial and inter-provincial migration ratios are 1/3 and 2/3, respectively; while in other cities in the province, intra-provincial migration and inter-provincial migration accounted for 3/4 and 1/4, respectively. In other words, most of the inter-provincial population is concentrated in the Pearl River Delta; while for other cities, the majority of the migrant workers are from within Guangdong. The net migration inflows in Guangdong are mainly the migrants to Pearl River Delta from other provinces.

The migration patterns also vary within PRD across cities (Table 8.1) with a sharp difference between Guangzhou and the other cities, and between PRD and the rest of the economy. In Guangzhou, an international metropolis and traditional economic center, about 50% of the inflow of total migrants (4.28 million) come from other parts of Guangdong Province, 50% come from other provinces. Shenzhen, followed by Dongguan, Foshan and Zhongshan, the dynamic export-oriented economy and emerging economic centers, the inflow of migrants are mostly from other provinces. For example, of the total inflow of migrants to Shenzhen (6.07 million) and that to Foshan (2.4 million), about one-third come from other parts of Guangdong, two-thirds from other provinces; for Dongguan and Zhongshan, respectively, out of the 5.01 million and 1.1 million total inflow of migrants, nearly 80% come from other provinces. While for the less developed cities, such as Zhaoqing, out of the 370,000 total inflow of migrants, some two-thirds come from other parts of the province. Non-PRD cities in Guangdong share the similar migration patterns as Zhaoqing. The ratios of intra- versus inter-provincial migration in most cities remained similar in 2000 and 2010.

Table 8.1 The distribution of migrant inflows in Guangdong

	2000					2010				
	Number of migrant inflow (10000 persons)			Percentage (Total migration = 100)		Number of migrant inflow (10000 persons)			Percentage (Total migration = 100)	
	Total	Intra-provincial migration	Inter-provincial migration	Intra-provincial migration	Inter-provincial migration	Total	Intra-provincial migration	Inter-provincial migration	Intra-provincial migration	Inter-provincial migration
Total	2530.4	1023.9	1506.5	40.5	59.5	3680.7	1530.9	2149.8	41.6	58.4
Pearl River Delta										
Sub-total	2170.4	753.0	1417.5	34.7	65.3	3136.3	1115.5	2020.8	35.6	64.4
Guangzhou	428.2	213.2	215.0	49.8	50.2	614.7	314.5	300.3	51.2	48.8
Shenzhen	607.1	201.5	405.6	33.2	66.8	851.5	271.9	579.6	31.9	68.1
Zhuhai	66.6	30.9	35.7	46.3	53.7	72.9	37.2	35.8	50.9	49.1
Foshan	240.3	86.2	154.1	35.9	64.1	387	136.8	250.3	35.3	64.7
Huizhou	111.8	46.6	65.2	41.7	58.3	205.8	88.6	117.2	43.1	56.9
Dongguan	500.9	87.3	413.7	17.4	82.6	658.3	125.1	533.3	19.0	81.0
Zhongshan	109.9	23.8	86.1	21.7	78.3	176.2	43.8	132.4	24.9	75.1
Jiangmen	68.3	36.1	32.2	52.9	47.1	111.1	59.5	51.6	53.6	46.4
Zhaoqing	37.4	27.4	10.0	73.3	26.7	58.8	38.2	20.6	65.0	35.0
Other cities	360.0	271.0	89.0	75.3	24.7	544.3	415.4	129.0	76.3	23.7

Data source China Bureau of Statistics (2005), Guangdong Bureau of Statistics (2012)

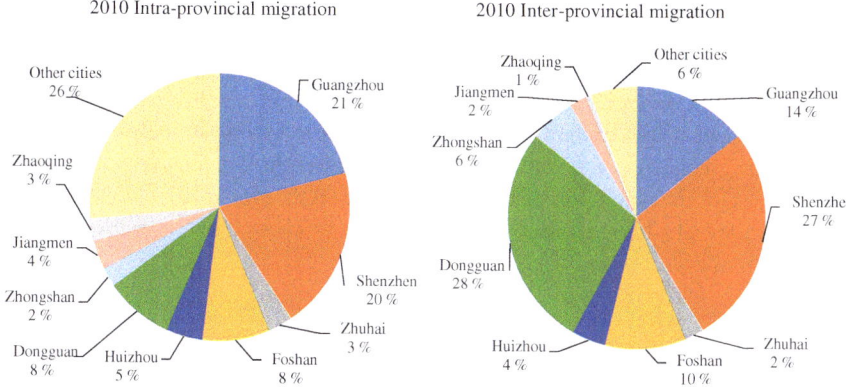

Fig. 8.5 Distribution of intra- and inter-provincial migration inflows in Guangdong (2010). *Data source* China Bureau of Statistics (2005), Guangdong Bureau of Statistics (2012)

The majority of the migrant workers from Guangdong chose to move to large cities, while those from other provinces largely concentrated in the PRD, particularly Shenzhen and Dongguan. As shown in Fig. 8.5, 75% of the intra-provincial migrant population concentrates in the PRD, of which 20% in Guangzhou and Shenzhen each, while 95% of the intra-provincial migrant population concentrated in the PRD, of which some 28% concentrates in Dongguan, 27% in Shenzhen, 14% in Guangzhou, and 10% in Foshan, and employed in the labor-intensive industries. The pattern is similar in 2010 as in 2000.[4]

8.4 Concentration of Resource, Labor and Capital Intensive Industries

As the economy developed, the production structure has gradually changed in Guangdong. The ratio of the primary, secondary and tertiary industries rose from 29.8:46.6:23.6 in 1978, to 5.5:51.6:42.9 in 2008, and to 4.9:47.3:47.8 in 2013. Nine major industries are particularly competitive in the domestic market and gaining shares in the global arena, including the three major traditional industries food and beverage, textile, building materials; the three major new pillar industries electronic communications, electrical machinery, petrochemicals; and the three emerging industries forestry and paper, pharmaceutical, automotive. The Pearl River Delta has become one of the world's major manufacturing base (for example, electronic information industry), attracting the investments from many multinational corporations, international consortia.

---

[4]Migration data in 2000 available upon request.

Compared with that in the Pearl River Delta, the production structure in the rest of the province, is less developed with a significantly higher share of the primary sector and lower levels of urbanization and export-orientation. To understand the different production structure at the industry level within the province,[5] we group the 43 industries listed in the Guangdong industrial economic statistical yearbooks into 3 large categories (called "sector" hereafter): resource intensive sector, labor intensive sector and capital intensive sector. We measure the relative concentration of sector i ($i = 1, 2, 3$) in region j in time t ($t = 2006, 2007, \ldots 2013$) by an indicator of specialization, noted as IS, as follows:

$$IS_{i,j,t} = \frac{va_{i,j,t}}{\sum_j va_{i,j,t}} \bigg/ \frac{\sum_i va_{i,j,t}}{\sum_i \sum_j va_{i,j,t}} \quad \text{with } va_{i,j,t} = \sum_{m_i} va_{m_{i,j,t}}$$

where m_i stands for the number of industries that belongs to sector i. In other words, $va_{i,j,t}$ is the sum of the value added of all industries in the sector i. In a relative sense, the more specialized a region j is in the sector i in time t, the higher is the value of this indicator.

We calculate the IS in two ways (or two levels). Table 8.2 presents the results of IS by region (grouping the 22 cities in 4 regions: Pearl River Delta, East Wing, West Wing, and Mountain area).[6] The results show a sharp difference in the patterns of concentration of industries: capital intensive industries largely clustered in Pearl River Delta, labor intensive industries mainly located in East Wing (followed by the Northern Mountainous area), and resource intensive industries highly concentrated in the West Wing and Northern Mountainous Area. The high specialization of the capital intensive and labor intensive industries in the PRD and East Wing, respectively, reveals their comparative advantages.

Further, to examine the extent to which the capital-, labor-, and resource-intensive industries concentrate in the four regions, we follow Wen (2004), Amiti and Wen (2001) to calculate the Gini coefficient as follows:

$$G_i = \frac{1}{2n \times n \times s_i} \sum_{k=1}^{n} \sum_{j=1}^{n} |S_{ij} - S_{ik}|$$

where s_{ij} stands for the ratio of the value-added of the sector i to the industrial value-added of province j; s_{ik} the ratio of the value-added of sector i to the industrial value-added of province k; n the number of regions ($n = 4$); s_i the average portion of the sector i in comparison of the entire 3 sectors. If the sector i is equally

---

[5]The empirical results of specialization at the industry and city levels are available upon request. For readability, we present in this paper the results of specialization of capital-, labor- and resource- intensive industries at the four regional level.

[6]In annex 8.3, we consider each of the ten cities in Pearl River Delta and consider all other cities as the rest of the province, and calculate the IS by these 12 entities.

Table 8.2 Specialization in resource, labor and capital intensive industries in Guangdong

	Resource intensive industries	Labor intensive industries	Capital intensive industries
2006			
Pearl River Delta	0.91	0.96	1.02
East	0.89	1.96	0.71
West	2.60	1.03	0.81
Mountain area	2.10	1.20	0.81
2007			
Pearl River Delta	0.91	0.95	1.03
East	0.92	1.89	0.70
West	2.70	1.05	0.80
Mountain area	2.37	1.15	0.80
2008			
Pearl River Delta	0.88	0.95	1.03
East	0.85	2.03	0.66
West	3.17	0.94	0.77
Mountain area	2.77	1.20	0.72
2009			
Pearl River Delta	0.86	0.94	1.03
East	1.11	2.05	0.62
West	3.47	0.97	0.80
Mountain area	3.34	1.35	0.68
2010			
Pearl River Delta	0.91	0.91	1.03
East	1.10	2.73	0.54
West	6.21	1.23	0.70
Mountain area	5.22	1.27	0.73
2011			
Pearl River Delta	0.86	0.91	1.04
East	1.13	2.12	0.57
West	3.09	1.09	0.78
Mountain area	4.07	1.21	0.64
2012			
Pearl River Delta	0.92	0.91	1.03
East	1.13	2.62	0.50
West	4.92	1.21	0.76
Mountain area	4.36	1.06	0.83
2013			
Pearl River Delta	0.83	0.88	1.07
East	1.58	1.77	0.61
West	1.63	1.08	0.91
Mountain area	4.00	1.01	0.74

Data Source Guangdong Bureau of Statistics (2014)

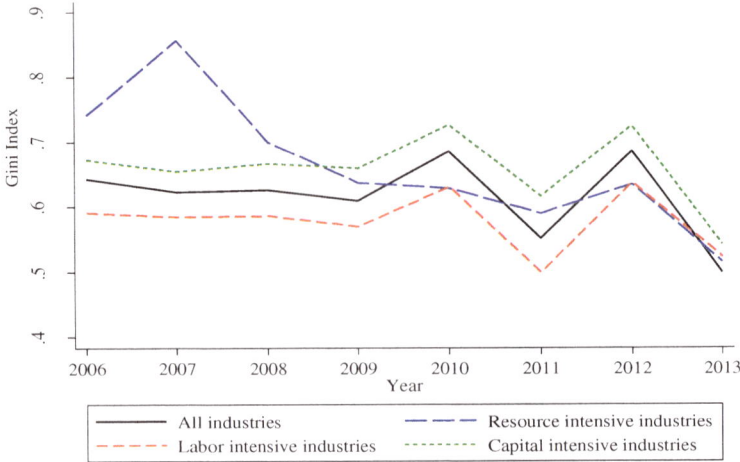

Fig. 8.6 Spatial concentration of resource, labor and capital intensive industries in Guangdong.
Data source Guangdong Bureau of Statistics (2014)

distributed among all regions, G_i is equal to zero; if the sector i is concentrated in
only one region or city, the value of G_i approaches 1. In other words, the higher the
value of G_i, the more concentrated the sector i.

Consistent with the results above on specialization, the capital intensive industries are slightly more concentrated spatially (mainly in PRD) than the labor
intensive industries. The declining concentration of resource intensive industries is
consistent with the emerging structural diversification in the West Wing and
Mountain Area.[7] As the resource intensive industries often locate close to the factor
endowments, it is natural to observe a higher spatial concentration than the other
two categories (Fig. 8.6).

8.5   Double Transfer and Policy Suggestions

Since the mid-2000s, possibly compounded by the 2008 global crisis, the GDP
growth in Guangdong slowed down from some 15% in the mid-2000s to some 8%
in the recent years. and the number of net migration inflow to Guangdong declined
(Fig. 8.4). While disparity (measured by Gini) within Guangdong declined

---

[7]The "M-shape" fluctuation of the Gini coefficient of the capital intensive and labor intensive
industries in 2009–2013 is of interest for further research. One possibility is related to the effects of
the effects of the fiscal stimulus on the industries.

(Fig. 8.2), heterogeneity of growth performance within the PRD as well as among the 21 prefecture-level cities emerged. For example, Zhaoqing (PRD), Jieyang (East Wing) and Yangjiang (West) more than doubled their GDP per capita in 2008–2013 compared with average annual growth of some 10% in the province. This begs for the questions of whether this showed sign of possible changes of the development pattern of the province, what policy interventions might have contributed to the changes, and what need to be put in place to support the inclusive development in a sustainable manner.

8.5.1 Double Transfers

Since the mid-2000s, to facilitate the upgrade of the production structure and support the sustainable long-term development, the government of Guangdong and the State Council have implemented several reform and development plans (Box 8.1). Industrial clustering and agglomeration have significantly contributed to the improvement of the productivity and competitiveness of the Chinese economy (Fan and Scott 2003; He and Zhu 2009). However, associated with the rising costs of land, labor, and environment, some studies suggest the negative congestion effects start to increase and could surpass the positive effects of specialization and agglomeration. Pollution and congestion have raised additional challenges for the continuous clustering in the PRD, particularly Guangzhou and Shenzhen. The relocation of industries from the more developed regions to the less developed regions is consistent with the economic theories and development experience. Filling the infrastructure gaps and providing basic local public services are essential for the emergence of the new hubs in the less developed areas; while developing own-source revenue basis is crucial for their sustainability.

The main objectives of the reform and development plans are featured in the "Double transfer"—transfer industries from the Pearl River Delta to the rest of the provinces; and transfer labor in the lagging regions from the primary sector to the secondary and tertiary sectors, including transfer high-skilled labor to the Pearl River Delta. More specifically, this means, first, strengthening the technological and innovation capacity of the PDR and phasing in the upgrading of its production structure with a focus on the advanced manufacturing sector and modern service sector to reach a GDP per capita level of 135,000 yuan by 2020 with at least 60% of value added from the service sector. Second, reducing the economic development gap between the PRD and the rest of the province and speeding up the intra-provincial relocation of industries to support the catching up of the lagging Northern mountainous areas, and the east and west wings. The latter might require the government to increase investment in the lagging regions, including investment in infrastructure and other public goods, to improve the business environment of the lagging regions and therefore their attractiveness to private capital, and to design and implement beneficial special policies to encourage the collaboration of the local governments of the PRD and the rest of the provinces to facilitate industry relocation.

> **Box 8.1: Regional development policies in Guangdong**
>
> In 2005, in order to promote the balanced growth of the regional economy, the Government of the Guangdong Province, developed special plans to stimulate the economic development of the East and West Wing areas. The plans focused on transport infrastructure, energy infrastructure, water infrastructure, industrialization and urbanization.
>
> In 2008, the government of the Guangdong province implemented the "double transfer decision" to encourage the transfer of industries from the PRD to the rest of the province and the transfer of labor in the northern mountainous areas and the east and west wings from the primary sector to the secondary and tertiary sectors, including the transfer of some high-skilled labor to the PRD.
>
> In 2009 the State Council approved the "Pearl River Delta Reform and Development Plan (2008–2020)". The PRD Reform and Development Plan indicated that the Pearl River Delta region should seize the strategic opportunity of the expansion of domestic demand to invest in infrastructure, promote economic restructuring and development pattern upgrading. The Plan positioned PDR as a pioneer of further reforms, gateway for international exchange, and national economic center.

There are signs that "double transfer" policies might have started bearing fruits. Many industrial transfer parks have been created in Guangdong and some labor intensive industries in the PRD have been transferred to the rest of the province. There also have been cases of industrial transfer from Guangdong to Jiangxi, Hunan, and Sichuan. Since the establishment of the first batch of Guangdong Industrial Transfer Park in 2005, there has been 35 provincial Industrial Transfer Parks at the end of June 2011. The establishment of the Industrial Transfer Parks contributed to the reallocation of rural labor force. The share of additional/new rural migrant workers from within Guangdong to the PRD declined from 43.2% in 2005 to 23.1% in 2010, and that to the rest of the province increased from 56.8 to 76.9%.[8] Some new towns and small cities have emerged along the establishment of the Industrial Transfer Parks, which, if designed and managed properly, can contribute to the acceleration of urbanization.

---

[8]"Double Transfer in Guangdong", NanFang Daily, 2011-09-14.

8.5.2 Policy Suggestions for Sustainable Inclusive Development

As demonstrated in the World Development Report 2009 *Reshaping Economic Geography* (World Bank 2008), economic concentration is a fact of life in modern economy. Growth is seldom balanced. Half the world's production fits onto less than 5% of its land. In China, industrial clustering and agglomeration has generated significant productivity effects (He and Wang 2012). A successful transfer of industries is not about spreading the economic activities equally across geographic areas, but about facilitating the allocation and reallocation of capital and labor to the areas where suit best the comparative advantages. Economic growth can be unbalanced, but development still can and needs be inclusive. The implementation of the double transfer strategy with a focus on the upgrading of the production structure and labor structure in both the economic center/Pearl River Delta and the lagging periphery is essential for the sustainable success of the economy.

For development to be sustainable and inclusive in Guangdong, we suggest a four-prong approach to improve the business environment, support the realization of latent comparative advantages, upgrade the skill level of labor force to support the upgrade of production structure, and protect the vulnerable (Box 8.2). Developing own-source revenues at the local level (including both own-source taxes and equalization transfers) and ensuring sustainable access to credit are key elements to support the emergence of the new hubs and their sustainability.

Box 8.2: Policy suggestions for inclusive development

First, provide an enabling business environment to support a level playing ground for all regions

- Realize the benefit of agglomeration economies through a higher density in traditional and emerging centers (develop Pearl River Delta as global economic center).
- Reduce the distance to improve regional transportation and communication infrastructure (link the lagging regions to the Pearl River Delta).
- Eliminate divisions to promote intra- and inter provincial market integration (support the economy of Guangdong to move up the global value chain).

Second, develop special regional policy to support the realization of latent comparative advantages

- Use the off-the-shelf technologies to build on the advantages of backwardness.
- Support "flying geese"/transfer of industries for the upgrade of structure.

Third, improve the skill level of the labor force to support the sustainable upgrade of production structure

- Improve education and match the market demand for skills.
- Provide on-the-job training to attract and retain high quality local and migrant workers.

Fourth, along with the national programs, strengthen inclusive social protection to improve equal access to social services and provide targeted support to vulnerable people.

- Support migrant workers integrate into host cities with an emphasis on the urbanization of people.
- Provide social services in an equitable manner, including formal and informal workers, unemployed, and their families.

Global experience and the economic geography literature suggest that most effective policies for promoting long-term growth are those that facilitate geographic concentration and economic integration, both within and across regions and countries. The path of development counts. To support the development of the economy with existing economic center and lagging areas, government initiatives should not focus on "reducing the gaps of the productive capacity" across cities, but "moderate differences in economic welfare" between them.

The business environment in Guangdong, in particular the major cities in the Pearl River Delta, is among the best in China. Further improvement can strengthen its attractiveness to investment and spurring innovation and fair competition. An enabling business environment can provide a level playing ground for all regions, hub or periphery, the needed institution and regulation to attract and retain private investment. The sustainable development of the economy in Guangdong depends on, how it can deal with the three "Ds"[9]: realizing the benefits of agglomeration economies through a higher *density* of economic activities in its major urban centers (particularly developing the PRD as global economic centers), overcoming the *distance* factor by making a concerted effort to improve regional transportation and communications infrastructure (linking the lagging Northern mountainous areas and the East and West Wings with the PRD) and eliminating internal and external

---

[9]Refer to the terminology developed in the World Development Report 2009 *Reshaping Economic Geography*.

divisions to promote intra- and inter provincial market integration and strengthen Guangdong's participation in the global economy moving up the value chain.[10]

Improved connectivity in a proper manner can increase efficiency and facilitate greater industrial specialization through agglomeration economies and reduce the geographic handicap to encourage the catching-up of the lagging regions. Reduced transport costs between northern mountainous area and the east and west wings to the PRD—and from there to overseas markets—can improve the attractiveness of the lagging regions and promote development of their firms in two ways: through lower costs of inputs delivered by these factories and through higher net revenue from sales to external markets. Greater access to both national and external markets can create more competition and reduce existing local monopolies. It can also facilitate the movement of labor, skilled and unskilled, to create greater economies of scale and rewards to innovation.

In line with the support to the establishment of Industrial Transfer Parks, facilitating the private sector actors to choose the right locations for investment with the right level of technology and capital/labor intensity can help. Special regional policy can be used in an appropriate manner to support the regions to move towards their latent comparative advantages. Improving market institutions can create and protect effective competition in the market. Measures can include addressing externality and coordination issues—such as provision of infrastructure, logistics, finance, skilled labor. The experience of the East Asian newly industrialized economies in using the off-the shelf technologies to build on the advantage of backwardness and upgrade their industrial structure in the past decades are successful examples (Lin 2012).

The government needs to promote economic integration, enhance the mobility of labor and capital, and provide targeted support to vulnerable population. This includes developing special regional policies to encouraging complementary regional development policies that recognize and build on the uniqueness of geographic and inherited economic comparative advantages. Facilitating the relocation of industries from PRD to the less developed regions in an appropriate manner can help accelerate the process and result in mutual benefits.

As the "double transfer" policies have started bearing fruits, the local governments can closely follow the comparative advantages of factor endowment of the economy to accelerate the proper upgrading of the production structures of the Pearl River Delta and the lagging regions and better match the demand and supply of

---

[10]See Huang and Luo (2009) for discussion at the national level.

labor while supporting the creation of more and better jobs in the secondary and tertiary industries. This is to include a careful consideration of the difference in the factor endowment between the Pearl River Delta and the lagging regions, and also the heterogeneity among each of the two groups. The different patterns of development in different cities discussed above illustrate the uniqueness of their advantages (or disadvantages) driven by their first or second natures.

As the economy of Guangdong, particularly the PRD, is undergoing the upgrading of structure from labor-intensive to capital-intensive or technology-intensive industries to maintain the competitiveness in the global market, the demand for skilled workers increases. Provision of on-the-job training and vocational skill training can play an important role in attracting labor and enhancing their quality, which is not only important for the sustainable economic development of the province but also the inclusiveness and harmoniousness of the society.

Building the skill level of the labor force, including the local labor force and the migrant labor force, can play an increasingly crucial role in the sustainability and inclusiveness of development. Compared with the older generation of migrant workers, the younger generation of migrant workers often place higher value in the provision of training opportunities and the potential of promotion when choosing jobs. The results of a survey conducted in 2006[11] showed that in the Pearl River Delta, vocational training helps to improve wages of migrant workers. To support the development in a sustainable manner, the government needs to improve the skill level of the labor force to support the sustainable upgrade of production structure.

It is worth noting that, despite the deepening of reforms and improvement of labor market regulations, *Hukou* still plays a role in conditioning opportunities to jobs and beyond. With or without an urban household registration means significant difference in the access to social services, including healthcare, education, and old-age pension. Recent studies have shown that in the urban labor market, there is discrimination against low-skilled migrant workers. Migrant workers are sometimes considered as "lower classes" in cities (Batisse and Sélim 2008; Solinger 2004). Several studies confirm the existence of significant wage gaps between urban citizens and migrant workers with similar skills (Knight et al. 1999; Meng and Zhang 2001; Meng et al. 2007). A survey showed that the average income of migrant workers is only one-third of the average income of urban residents (Ministry of Labor and Social Security Research Group 2004; Shao 2006). Some studies suggest, after taking into account inflation, real wages of migrant workers actually declined (He 2006). As cost of living increased in urban areas and the living

---

[11]See http://www.syntao.com/E_Page_Show.asp?Page_ID=6075.

standards improved in rural areas, the low level of wages hinders the willingness to migrate. The institutional fragmentation of the labor market goes beyond wage income (Hu 2008; Lu and Song 2006; Nielsen et al. 2007; Wu and Zhou 1997). In fact, many unskilled migrant workers can only find jobs in the informal sector, which are often characterized by low and unstable wage along with less decent working environment (Liang 1999; Liang and Ma 2004; Liang and White 1996; Day and Ma 1994; Fan 1999, 2002; Wang and Zuo 1999; Guo and Iredale 2004). Some studies (Gong 2009; Jiang et al. 2008) suggest that related to the lack of stability of employment, migrant workers cannot stay in one place for a long time and have to move periodically or frequently.

Measures to strengthen an inclusive social protection system requires improving the equal access to social services such as health care and education (and the quality of such services) and providing targeted support to the vulnerable, including migrant workers and their families. Appropriate design and implementation of the local policies, for example, provision of water and sanitation as well as healthcare clinics, in complement to the national policies are crucial. In an economy where the informal sector is non-negligible (the share of migrant workers who work in the informal sector is even larger), it can be a question for policy debate whether and how to use general revenue and user fees to fund such services. The potential sources of financing can include income taxes, property taxes, and value-added taxes.

Annex 8.1: Statistics of the Economy of Guangdong

The gaps between the PRD and some lagging regions seemed to tapper down in the second half of the 2000s—in 2013, but per capita GDP of the Pearl River Delta (93,114 yuan) remained significantly higher than the provincial average. In 2000, per capita GDP in the Pearl River Delta (20278 yuan) was about 3.8 times of that of the Northern Mountainous Area (5344 yuan), the 2.9 times that of the West Wing of the region (7099 yuan), and 2.8 times of that of the East Wing of the region (7294 yuan). In 2013, the regional GDP of PRD was about 3.6 times, 2.8 times and 3.4 times, respectively, that of the Northern Mountainous Area (25513 yuan), West Wing area (33,712 yuan) and the east wing area (27002 yuan) (Tables 8.3 and 8.4).

Table 8.3 Economic development indicators of the different regions in Guangdong in 2008 and 2013

	Pearl River Delta		East Wing		West Wing		Northern Mountainous Area	
	2008	2013	2008	2013	2008	2013	2008	2013
Population (10000 persons)	5138.5	5715.2	1644.9	1717.2	1521.1	1565.9	1589.1	1645.7
as % of total population (%)	51.9	52.9	16.6	16.4	15.4	15.0	16.1	15.7
Urban population (%)	80.2	84.0	56.6	59.4	39.3	40.5	43.3	46.0
Regional GDP (100 million yuan)	29745.5	53060.4	2492.8	4623.4	2750.3	5260.0	2484.4	4185.8
Regional GDP composition (regional total = 100)								
Primary sector	2.4	2.0	9.7	8.7	21.2	18.8	17.0	16.3
Secondary sector	50.3	45.3	54.1	55.9	43.4	42.2	50.4	41.7
Tertiary sector	47.3	52.7	36.1	35.4	35.4	39.0	32.6	42.0
Regional GDP per capita (yuan)	62644.0	93114.0	15396.0	27002.0	17973.0	33712.0	15539.0	25513.0
Fixed asset investment (100 million yuan)	7829.0	16030.8	861.7	2326.0	612.8	2054.8	1445.4	2417.1
Total export(100 million US dollar)	3872.1	6070.9	92.4	157.2	32.5	55.2	44.9	80.3
Total import(100 million US dollar)	2697.6	4403.4	37.1	63.0	20.6	36.0	37.7	52.2
Actual use foreign investment (100 million US dollar)	169.2	230.6	6.3	6.2	3.8	4.1	12.2	8.6

Data source Guangdong Bureau of Statistics (2014). *Note* Pearl River Delta includes Guangzhou, Shenzhen, Zhuhai, Foshan, Huizhou, Zhongshan, Jiangmen, Shunde, and Zhaoqing; East Wing includes Shantou, Chaozhou, Jieyang, and Shanwei; West Wing includes Zhanjiang, Maoming, and Yangjiang; and Northern Mountainous Area include Meizhou, Heyuan, Qingyuan, Yunfu, and Chaoguan

Table 8.4 The shares of regional GDP, export and import of different regions of Guangdong

	Regional GDP			Total Export			Total Import		
	2000	2008	2013	2000	2008	2013	2000	2008	2013
Pearl River Delta	75.2	79.4	79.0	92.2	95.8	95.4	95.0	96.6	96.7
East Wing	9.5	6.7	6.9	4.6	2.3	2.5	2.8	1.3	1.4
West Wing	8.5	7.3	7.8	2.1	0.8	0.9	1.4	0.7	0.8
Northern Mountainous Area	6.8	6.6	6.2	1.1	1.1	1.3	0.7	1.4	1.1
Guangdong	100.0	100.0	100.0	100.0	100.0	100.0	100.0	100.0	100.0

Data source Guangdong Statistics Bureau (2014)

Annex 8.2: Specialization of Labor, Capital and Resource Intensive Industries in Cities of the PRD and the Rest of the Economy in Guangdong (2006–2013)

	Resource intensive industries	Labor intensive industries	Capital intensive industries
2006			
Guangzhou	0.22	1.03	1.08
Shenzhen	1.79	0.48	1.07
Zhuhai	0.12	0.64	1.22
Foshan	1.15	1.12	0.94
Shunde			
Huizhou	0.19	0.71	1.19
Dongguan	0.17	1.36	0.98
Zhongshan	0.24	1.55	0.91
Jiangmen	0.53	1.35	0.94
Zhaoqing	1.32	1.25	0.88
Other cities	1.84	1.34	0.79
2007			
Guangzhou	0.18	0.99	1.10
Shenzhen	1.69	0.53	1.08
Zhuhai	0.12	0.56	1.26
Foshan	1.19	1.03	0.97
Shunde			
Huizhou	0.27	0.61	1.22
Dongguan	0.26	1.50	0.91
Zhongshan	0.26	1.43	0.94
Jiangmen	0.57	1.20	0.98
Zhaoqing	1.27	1.20	0.90
Other cities	1.91	1.32	0.78

(continued)

(continued)

	Resource intensive industries	Labor intensive industries	Capital intensive industries
2008			
Guangzhou	0.14	0.99	1.12
Shenzhen	1.55	0.50	1.11
Zhuhai	0.10	0.52	1.29
Foshan	1.11	1.00	0.98
Shunde			
Huizhou	0.31	0.65	1.21
Dongguan	0.29	1.61	0.87
Zhongshan	0.27	1.43	0.94
Jiangmen	0.54	1.25	0.97
Zhaoqing	1.45	1.10	0.91
Other cities	2.11	1.35	0.73
2009			
Guangzhou	0.17	0.93	1.11
Shenzhen	1.21	0.48	1.17
Zhuhai	0.13	0.49	1.27
Foshan	1.14	1.06	0.97
Shunde			
Huizhou	0.32	0.62	1.21
Dongguan	0.33	1.53	0.88
Zhongshan	0.34	1.39	0.92
Jiangmen	0.68	1.27	0.93
Zhaoqing	2.09	1.09	0.86
Other cities	2.32	1.43	0.71
2010			
Guangzhou	0.27	0.97	1.05
Shenzhen	0.68	0.50	1.15
Zhuhai	0.22	0.52	1.17
Foshan	1.65	1.25	0.90
Shunde	0.27	0.87	1.07
Huizhou	0.51	0.70	1.11
Dongguan	0.53	1.93	0.77
Zhongshan	0.58	1.63	0.85
Jiangmen	1.15	1.60	0.83
Zhaoqing	3.58	1.25	0.79
Other cities	3.05	1.87	0.65
2011			
Guangzhou	0.15	0.93	1.12
Shenzhen	1.34	0.48	1.16

(continued)

(continued)

	Resource intensive industries	Labor intensive industries	Capital intensive industries
Zhuhai	0.16	0.48	1.29
Foshan	1.11	1.10	0.95
Shunde	0.15	0.91	1.12
Huizhou	0.40	0.58	1.22
Dongguan	0.28	1.46	0.90
Zhongshan	0.34	1.33	0.94
Jiangmen	0.79	1.31	0.90
Zhaoqing	2.59	0.98	0.84
Other cities	2.31	1.49	0.67
2012			
Guangzhou	0.25	0.95	1.05
Shenzhen	0.78	0.68	1.11
Zhuhai	0.24	0.50	1.19
Foshan	1.76	1.23	0.89
Shunde	0.22	0.88	1.08
Huizhou	0.51	0.54	1.17
Dongguan	0.38	1.68	0.83
Zhongshan	0.52	1.51	0.87
Jiangmen	1.25	1.56	0.82
Zhaoqing	4.52	1.21	0.75
Other cities	2.60	1.81	0.67
2013			
Guangzhou	0.17	0.89	1.13
Shenzhen	1.13	0.41	1.25
Zhuhai	0.15	0.43	1.34
Foshan	1.12	0.99	0.99
Shunde	0.12	0.66	1.24
Huizhou	0.51	0.53	1.26
Dongguan	0.20	1.05	1.06
Zhongshan	0.32	1.01	1.07
Jiangmen	0.97	1.12	0.95
Zhaoqing	2.76	0.94	0.85
Other cities	1.81	1.33	0.77

Data source Guangdong Statistics Bureau (2014)

Annex 8.3: Spatial Concentration (Gini Coefficient) of Labor, Capital and Resource Intensive Industries in Cities of the PRD and the Rest of the Economy in Guangdong (2006–2013)

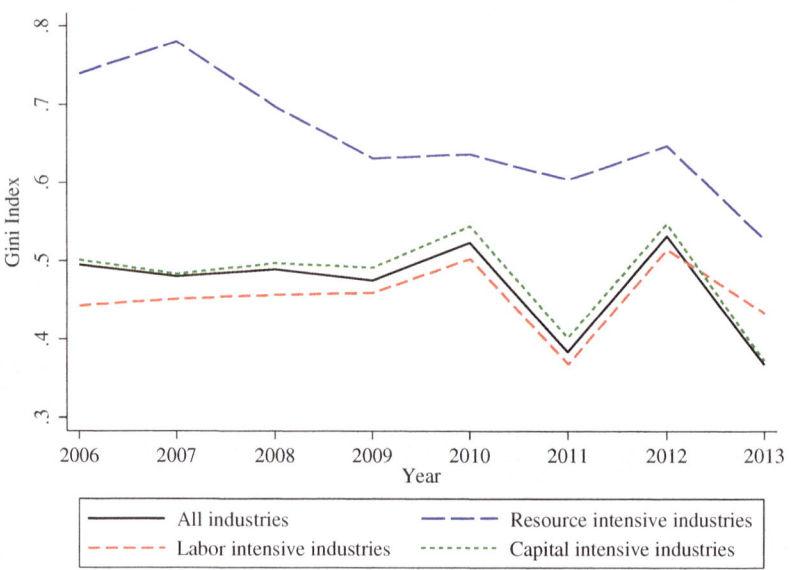

Data source Guangdong Statistics Bureau (2014)

References

Amiti, M., & Wen, M. (2001). Spatial distribution of manufacturing in China. In P. Lloyd & X. Zhang (Eds.), *Modeling the Chinese Economy* (pp. 135–148). London: Edward Elgar.

Batisse, C., & M. Sélim. (2008). Du socialisme (de marché) au post-communisme – Singularités et unicité dans la globalisation du capitalisme, Autrepart, N° 48.

Boublil, A. (1997). *Le Siècle des chinois*. Monaco: Rocher.

Chan, K. W., & Li, Z. (1999). The Hukou system and rural-urban migration in China: Processes and changes. *The China Quarterly, 160*, 819–855.

Chen, J., & Fleisher, B. M. (1996). Regional income inequality and economic growth in China. *Journal of Comparative Economics, 22*(2), 141–164.

Chen, C.-H., & Wu, H.-L. (2005). Determinants of regional growth disparity in China's transitional economy. *Journal of Economic Studies, 32*(5), 406–419.

China Bureau of Statistics. (2005). *China population census 2000.* Beijing: China Statistical Publishing House.

Day, L. D., & Ma, X. (1994). *Migration and urbanization in China*. New York/London: M.E. Sharpe.

Démurger, S. (1997). Ouverture et croissance: le cas de la République Populaire en Chine. Thèse de doctorat, Université de Paris I, Paris, Septembre 1997.

ElSayed, A. A., Kulich, R., Lake, L., & Megahed, S. (2006). *The Chinese apparel cluster in Guangdong* (Working paper). Harvard Business School May 5th.

Fan, C. C. (1999). Migration in a socialist transitional economy: Heterogeneity, socioeconomic and spatial characteristics of migrants in China and Guangdong. *International Migration Review, 33*(4), 954–987.

Fan, C. C. (2002). The Elite, the natives, and the outsiders: Migration and labor market segmentation in urban China. *Annals of the Association of American Geographers, 92*(1), 103–124.

Fan, C. C. (2005a). Interprovincial migration, population redistribution, and regional development in China: 1990 and 2000 census comparisons. *The Professional Geographer, 57*(2), 295–311.

Fan, C. C. (2005b). Modeling interprovincial migration in China, 1985–2000. *Eurasian Geography and Economics, 46*(3), 165–184.

Fan, C., & Scott, A. (2003). Industrial agglomeration and development: A survey of spatial economic issues in East Asia and a statistical analysis of Chinese regions. *Economic Geography, 79*(3), 456–469.

Gong, S. (2009). Those uppity peasant workers: The end of the era of cheap Chinese labor. *The International Economy, 23*(1), 10–11.

Guangdong Bureau of Statistics. (2012). *Guangdong population census 2010*. Beijing: China Statistical Publishing House.

Guangdong Bureau of Statistics. (2014). *Guangdong statistical yearbook 2014*. Beijing: China Statistical Publishing House.

Guo, F., & Iredale, R. (2004). The impact of Hukou status on migrants' employment—Findings from the 1997 Beijing migrant census. *International Migration Review, 38*(2), 709–731.

He, G. (2006). The shortage of peasant workers in the Pearl River Delta region: An explanation based on Todaro migration model. *Asian Social Science, 2*(12), 41–52.

He, J., & Pooler, J. (2002). The regional concentration of China's interprovincial migration flows, 1982–90. *Population and Environment, 24*(2), 149–182.

He, C., & Wang, J. (2012). Regional and sectoral differences in the spatial restructuring of Chinese manufacturing industries during the post-WTO period. *GeoJournal, 77*(3), 361–381.

He, C., & Zhu, S. (2009). Industrial agglomeration and labor productivity in China: An empirical study of Chinese manufacturing industries. *Post Communist Economies, 21*(1), 103–115.

Hu, B. (2008). People's mobility and Guanxi networks: A case study. *China & World Economy, 16*(5), 103–117.

Huang, Y., & Luo, X. (2009). Reshaping economic geography in China. In Y. Huang & A. M. Bocchi (Eds.), *Reshaping Economic Geography*. The World Bank.

Jiang, S., Lu, M., & Sato, H. (2008). *Happiness in the dual society of urban China: Hukou identity, horizontal inequality and heterogeneous reference* (LICOS Discussion Paper Series 227/2008). Katholieke Universiteit Leuven.

Knight, J., Song, L., & Jia, H. (1999). Chinese rural migrants in urban enterprises: Three perspectives. In S. Cook & M. Maurer-Fazio (Eds.), *The workers' state meets the market: Labor in China's transition*. London: Frank Cass.

Li, S. (1997). Population migration, regional economic growth and income determination: A comparative study of Dongguan and Meizhou, China. *Urban Studies, 34*(7), 999–1026.

Li, S. (2004). Population migration and urbanization in China: A comparative analysis of the 1990 population census and the 1995 national one percent sample population survey. *International Migration Review, 38*(2), 655–685.

Liang, Z. (1999). Foreign investment, economic growth, and temporary migration: The case of Shenzhen special economic zone, China. *Development and Society, 28*(1), 115–137.

Liang, Z. (2001). The age of migration in China. *Population and Development Review, 27*(3), 499–524.

Liang, Z., & Ma, Z. (2004). China's floating population: New evidence from the 2000 census. *Population and Development Review, 30*(3), 467–488.

Liang, Z., & White, M. J. (1996). Internal migration in China, 1950–1988. *Demography, 33*(3), 375–384.

Liang, Z., & Wu, Y. (2003). *Return migration in China: New methods and findings*. Paper presented at the Annual Meeting of the Population Association of American, Minneapolis, MN.

Lin, J. Y. (2012). *New structural economics: A framework for rethinking development and policy*. Washington, DC: World Bank.

Lu, D. (2008). China's regional income disparity: An alternative way to think of the sources and causes. *Economics of Transition, 16*(1), 31–58.

Lu, Z., & Song, S. (2006). Rural-urban migration and wage determination: The case of Tianjin, China. *China Economy Review, 17*(3), 337–345.

Luo, X., & Zhu, N. (2008). *Rising income inequality in China: A race to the top* (Policy Research Working Paper 4700). Washington, DC: The World Bank.

Meng, X., & Zhang, J. (2001). Two-tier labor markets in urban China: Occupational segregation and wage differentials between urban residents and rural migrants in Shanghai. *Journal of Comparative Economics, 29*(3), 485–504.

Meng, X., Lu, M., & Chen, Z. (2007, July 25). The time of labor shortage has not arrived. *Liberation Daily*. http://www.dooland.com/newspaper/217039.

Ministry of Labor and Social Security Research Group. (2004, September). *Survey report on the shortage of migrant workers*. http://news3.xinhuanet.com/zhengfu/2004-09/14/content_1979817.htm.

National Development and Reform Commission. (2008). *Pearl River Delta reform and development plan (2008–2020)*. http://politics.people.com.cn/GB/1026/8644751.html.

Naughton, B. (1999). Causes et conséquences des disparités dans la croissance économique des provinces chinoises. *Revue d'Economie du Développement, 7*(1–2), 33–70.

Nielsen, I., Nyland, C., Smyth, R., & Zhang, M. (2007). Migration and the right to social security: Perceptions of off-farm migrants' rights to social insurance in China's Jiangsu Province. *China & World Economy, 15*(2), 29–43.

Qian, Y. (2003). How reform worked in China? In D. Rodrik (Ed.), *In search of prosperity: Analytic narratives on economic growth* (pp. 297–333). Princeton University Press.

Shao, S. (2006). The end of cheap labour in China?—Implications for foreign invested firms of a new breed of 'economic man'. *Monash Business Review, 2*(1). http://www.gsb.monash.edu.au/industry/mbr/index.html.

Shen, J. (1999). Modeling regional migration in China. Estimation and decomposition. *Environment and Planning A, 31*(7), 1223–1238.

Sit, V. F. S., & Yang, C. (1997). Foreign-investment-induced exo-urbanization in the Pearl River Delta, China. *Urban Studies, 34*(4), 647–677.

Solinger, D. (2004). The Creation of a New Underclass in China and its Implications. Rapport préparé pour le forum intitulé "POSRI International Forum on China's Development: Key Challenges for China's Sustained Growth", Séoul, Corée, 10–11 novembre 2004.

Trudel, M. (2008). Les déterminants de la croissance de la population urbaine en Chine. Mémoire de maîtrise, INRS-UCS, Université du Québec.

Tuan, C., & Ng, L. (2004). FDI and industrial restructuring in post-WRO greater PRD: Implications on regional growth in China. *The World Economy, 27*(10), 1609–1630.

Wang, W., & Fan, C. (2006). Success or failure: Selectivity and reasons of return migration in Sichuan and Anhui, China. *Environment and Planning A, 38*(5), 939–958.

Wang, F., & Zuo, X. (1999). Inside China's cities: Institutional barriers and opportunities for urban Migrants. *The American Economic Review, 89*(2), 276–280.

Wen, M. (2004). Relocation and agglomeration of Chinese industry. *Journal of Development Economics, 73*(1), 329–347.

Wilmots, A. (1997). La Chine économique en l'an 2000, L'Harmattan, Paris.

Wong, K., Shen, J., Feng, Z., & Gu, C. (2003). An analysis of dual-track urbanisation in the Pearl River Delta since 1980. *Tijdschrift Voor Economische en Sociale Geografie, 94*(2), 205–218.

World Bank. (2008). *World development report 2009: Reshaping economic geography.* Washington, DC: The World Bank.

Wu, Z., & Yao, S. (2003). Intermigration and intramigration in China: A theoretical and empirical analysis. *China Economic Review, 14*(4), 371–385.

Wu, H. X., & Zhou, L. (1997). Rural-to-urban migration in China. *Asian-Pacific Economic Literature, 10*(2), 54–67.

Zhang, K. H., & Song, S. (2003). Rural–urban migration and urbanization in China: Evidence from time-series and cross-section analyses. *China Economic Review, 14*(4), 386–400.

Zhao, Z. (2005). Migration, labor market flexibility, and wage determination in China: A review. *Developing Economies, 43*(2), 285–312.

Zhu, Y. (2000). In situ urbanisation in rural China: Case studies from Fujian Province. *Development and Change, 31*(2), 413–434.

Zhu, Z., & Wang, H. (2006). To Foresee the demands and supplies of rural labor forces in the coming years by looking at the phenomena of "shortage of farmer-turned workers". *Statistical Research, 2*, 17–20.

Chapter 9
BRTs and Investment Fads: Civic Engagement and Fiscal Discipline

Xinghou Yuan

Abstract In countries without electoral competition, maintaining fiscal discipline and sustainable development represents a challenge. The paper shows that public participation and civic engagement might exert external pressure on the behavior of local governments in countries without formal institutional accountability. The effectiveness of public engagement in fiscal supervision depends crucially on several factors: (a) sustainability of public attention, (b) collaboration from motivated and dedicated public servants, and (c) decreased costs of information flows and transparency of bureaucratic apparatus. The case study of the Guangdong BRT project exemplifies the potential of public engagement as an idiosyncratic and yet powerful channel for local governmental fiscal discipline.

9.1 Introduction

It is sometimes argued that investment decisions in open market economies, especially with fiscal constraints, are made strictly keeping in mind alternative uses of public funds and opportunity costs. Besides, public satisfaction is perceived to be a benefit in such cases, and the electoral process punishes poor decisions. Such benefits, it is argued, do not apply in centrally planned systems, and consequently the danger of making inadequate investment decisions is high. However, we argue in this paper that the opposite may in fact be the case. In many market economies, including in the EU, there have been lots of investment projects of dubious benefit. However they are undertaken because liabilities are typically not fully recognized on the public balance sheets, especially with Public-Private Partnerships (PPPs),

This article was originally written in Chinese by Mr. Xinghou Yuan, Guangzhou Auditing Bureau Performance Auditing Division. It was finalized with the collaboration of Kezhou Xiao at London School of Economics and Political Science.

X. Yuan (✉)
Performance auditing division, Guangzhou Auditing bureau, Guangzhou, China
e-mail: 68xh@sina.com

217

and may not appear for a decade or so after the politician has retired, while all the politician cares about is perhaps just "cutting yet another ribbon" or laying another foundation stone (see the discussion of Madeira in Ahmad et al. 2016). And they require subsidies to operate—raising questions about the appropriate use of scarce public funds. Such projects have contributed greatly to the macroeconomic crisis in Portugal, and EU in general, and could do the same in emerging market countries.

In this paper, we show that honest and dedicated officials, and an openness to evaluate public responses in centrally planned countries, may lead to cancelling a "popular" project, the Guangzhou BRT that had been emulated elsewhere, including especially in Pakistan. This is of relevance, e.g., in the context of the China-Pakistan Corridor, and some of the lessons from China that might carry over to neighboring countries.

Maintaining fiscal discipline and supporting sustainable development are challenging tasks with the rise of public debt across the globe. The public debt in OECD countries has skyrocketed since the financial crisis in 2008 (Azzimonti et al. 2014). The tendency to overspend in democratic countries is well known in the literature (Alesina and Tabellini 1990). The conditions for fiscal discipline may not be met with poor information flows even in the Eurozone countries (Ahmad et al. 2016), and the criteria are unlikely to be met with weak fiscal institutions in emerging market countries like Pakistan. Despite the presence of nominal electoral competition, there may not be a proper structure of checks and balances—e.g., because the costs and liabilities are not known to the current electorates.

In the Chinese case, the central government has been presiding over strong economic growth in the past three decades by reforming its central-local fiscal relationships to accommodate market economy with "socialist characteristics" and encourage local competitions across within and across provinces (Zhou 2007). The question of balancing the two contrasting motives between spurring economic developments and controlling fiscal overspending impetus becomes critical in the study of local governmental behavior.

To some extent, investment projects that provide quick political benefits become very popular with elected officials and international agencies, whose officials are typically rewarded for getting projects out of the door rather than seeing them through to completion. Bus Rapid Transport (BRT) projects often fall in this category. The popularity is due to the adoption of BRTs in Brazil (Curitiba), the US and indeed Guangzhou itself (see Table 9.1). The latest example of a BRT is the Rawalpindi-Islamabad that operates in the Rawalpindi-Islamabad metropolitan area in Pakistan and has length of 24 kmh and 24 stations. The buses run on segregated lanes in Islamabad, the capital and on an elevated track in Rawalpindi, the fourth most populous city of Pakistan. The daily ridership exceeds 150,000 people—largely civil servants commuting to the more expensive city of Islamabad. The project is justified in terms of low capital and operating costs, but does not incorporate social costs or the opportunity costs of the alternative use of public funds in a cash-strapped and indebted economy—e.g., in creating productive hubs to benefit from the connectivity of the China-Pakistan economic corridor. The seven

Table 9.1 Some examples of BRTs

Location	System	Peak passengers per hour per direction	Passengers per day	Length (km)
Ahmedabad	Janmarg		1,32,000	89
Bogotá	TransMilenio	35,000–40,000	2,154,961	106
Guangzhou	Guangzhou Bus Rapid Transit	26,900	1,000,000	22
Curitiba, Brazil	Rede Integrada de Transporte	13,900–24,100	508,000 (2,260,000 inc. feeder lines)	81
Mexico City, Mexico	Mexico City Metrobus	18,500	850,000	115
Belo Horizonte, São Paulo		15,800–20,300		24
Istanbul	Metrobus (Istanbul)	7,300–19,500	800,000	52
Lahore	Metrobus (Lahore)	10,000	180,000	28
Tehran	Tehran Bus Rapid transit		2,000,000	150
Jakarta	TransJakarta		320,000	210.31
New Jersey	Lincoln Tunnel XBL	15,500	62,000 (4 h morning peak only)	
Brisbane	South-East Busway	15,000		23

Source Wikipedia, Bus rapid transport.

BRTs that are awarded the international "gold standard" include the Guangzhou BRT (see Table 9.2).

The story of this paper using the BRT project in Guangzhou is to present a novel mechanism through which public engagement may nudge the equilibrium policy to the direction of socially optimal by pressuring the local authority to re-assess the performance of public projects against alternative public needs. The effectiveness of public engagement in fiscal supervision depends crucially on several factors: (a) sustainability of public attention, (b) collaboration from motivated and dedicated public servants, and (c) decreased costs of information flows and transparency of budget processes. Sustained public attention translates into external pressure to which local authorities are forced to respond, even without electoral competition from an opposing political party.

In the Guangzhou BRT case, residents in Guangzhou careful monitored auditing reports from the municipality and demanded a detailed analysis of budgetary sources and uses of funds. The level of public engagement and civic-mindedness

Table 9.2 Seven gold-medal BRTs

City	BRT system (Corridor name)
Guangzhou, China	GBRT (*Zhongshan Avenue*)
Bogotá, Colombia	Transmilenio (*Americas, Calle 80, Calle 26, Norte-Quito-Sur, Suba, and El Dorado*)
Curitiba, Brazil	Curitiba BRT (Linha Verde)
Rio de Janeiro, Brazil	BRT (TransOeste, TransCarioca, TransOlimpica)
Lima, Peru	El Metropolitano
Guadalajara, Mexico	Macrobús
Medellin, Colombia	Metroplús
Dar es Salaam, Tanzania	DART (Kimara-Kivukoni, Kimara-Morocco, Kimara-Kariakoo)

Source Institute for Transportation and Development Policy

are critical for sustained attention and coordination to make public pressure effective. Collaboration from motivated agents (Besley and Ghatak 2005) within an honest bureaucracy (e.g., Guangzhou auditing bureau) facilitates the information flow and analysis of public projects. Finally, decreased costs of information transmission makes coordination and public engagement easier with a greater likelihood of success of effective public engagements.

Performance audits on Guangzhou Zhongshan Avenue BRT pilot line construction and operations (hereinafter referred to as the GBRT) were conducted jointly by the Audit Bureau of Guangzhou and Sun Yat-sen University Chinese Public Management Research Center in 2012. Audit findings showed that the BRT project achieved with positive effects many desired public objectives, thus making the BRT a new success story for Guangzhou city. However, the auditing survey also found that the overall economic and social benefits of GBRT were less than that of the bus lane; and the free transit schemes for GBRT projects were a wasteful use of public resources. The sustained public interest in GBRT projects after the announcement of the report resulted in the abandoning of Guangzhou Avenue BRT fast line projects on efficiency grounds. The decision process over BRT projects exemplified the interactive impact of public opinion, the media and the public advisory and the oversight committee (hereinafter referred to as the Committee) on the Guangzhou government's fiscal decisions. The central message of this case shows that public participation has the potential to serve as a fiscal constraint for the local government expenditures and a potential guarantor for the sustainable development.

9.2   Performance Auditing of Guangzhou BRT (GBRT) Projects—General Information

9.2.1   GBRT Project Information

GBRT (bus rapid transit) is a large capacity and rapid public transport classified between subway and the conventional public transportation. The GBRT project in Guangzhou spans from Tianhe Sports Center to the Huangpu summer garden, a total length of 22.9 km. There is a rapid bus transit lane and 26 central side type platforms in the middle of the road, with the pedestrian bridge (tunnel) and sidewalk connections. GBRT project includes test line sub-projects (hereinafter referred to as the test line sub-projects) and pedestrian system improvement project (hereinafter referred to as the pedestrian crossing project), the main building of GBRT lane, station and footbridge (tunnel), green matching, control center, scheduling system, bicycle parking and others. At the GBRT project location, during the construction of the GBRT project, the construction of the "large and medium renovation" project is one of the main municipal road renovation projects in Guangzhou. In the red line, in addition to the GBRT project, and the rest of the road repair, lighting facilities and other renovation projects fall into the category of "large and medium renovation" projects.

9.2.2   Goal for Construction

In September 2008, commissioned by the city government, City Urban Construction Committee (hereinafter referred to as the City Project Construction Committee) proposed the Zhongshan Avenue BRT line test scheme, in which the committee elaborated the BRT project outline whose construction goals are the following:

- **Systemic Model**: BRT with high standards with a flexible line "system model, in essence, it is "the development of high standards of bus lane", the goal is "to achieve intensive conventional bus, rapid, scientific, rational allocation of resources for the road, road to improve the efficiency of resource use, good road traffic order, and improve the service level of the existing conventional public transit."
- **Size of the Project**: The design of the test line has a length of 22.9 km, width of 60 m, with 26 stations. Project estimates an investment of 724 million yuan of which the construction investment costs 479 million yuan, mechanical and electrical equipment investment 99 million yuan, other expenses and preparation 146 million yuan, respectively.

9.2.3   Completion Information

The GBRT project groundbreaking ceremony took place in November 2008. In January 2009 the project officially started, and opened trial operation in February 2010. On February 10, 2010 the BRT construction project was officially put into operation. As of December 31, 2011, among 40 individual BRT projects, there are 38 project completions, with two to be completed. Out of these forty individual projects one project has passed evaluation of the Guangzhou city finance investment review. The remaining 39 projects have not yet completed the final clearance.

Large and medium renovation projects started in January 2009 and were completed in November 2010. Until December 31, 2011, 10 individual projects have been completed and received acceptance, but did not complete the final settlement work.

9.2.4   Budget Information

9.2.4.1   Investment Information

GBRT projects together with the large and medium renovation project budget were estimated at 2.1 billion yuan, of which the total amount of the GBRT project budget was 1.84 billion yuan. Among GBRT project budget, Guangzhou Urban Construction Investment Supervision and Management Center (hereinafter referred to as the Investment Supervision Center) approved 737 million yuan in January 2010 for land acquisition, demolition and relocation of the pipeline. In March 2010, the City Construction Committee approved the test line project budget of 66 million yuan, and the pedestrian crossing project budget amount of 45 million yuan (excluding fees for land acquisition, demolition and relocation of the pipeline).

9.2.4.2   Source, Use and Repayment of Capital

City Investment Group is responsible for raising funds for GBRT projects and large and medium renovation projects. Funding for these projects includes the city's public funds and bank loans from the city investment group. As of December 31, 2011, the GBRT project has funds totaled at 1.4 billion yuan on the books with the total expenditure of 1.4046 billion yuan. Large and medium renovation project has available funds of 204.71 million yuan with total expenditure of 204.718 million yuan. Given the fact that partial bank loans from city investment group used the model of non-operating project financing with limited information for each individual project and repayment amounts, it is difficult to delve into each project loan and repayment amount in detail. Because of the nature of the project, the repayment of these loans came from city funds, land transfer income, and other bank loans. Also given the existing budget law, the local government has little power to raise taxes as a financing vehicle to cover repayments.

9.3   Public Engagement and Fiscal Discipline: Performance Auditing for BRT Project

9.3.1   Reasons for Performance Auditing

The reasons for performance auditing of the project fall in the following four dimensions: importance, timeliness, feasibility and value added.

9.3.1.1   Importance

The importance aspect is the impact which the auditing unit or the project might exert on the social and economic dimensions. Specifically, it includes the nature and the capital size of the project. In general, the higher the value and larger the size of capital and, the greater the financial significance, the higher the probability for the project to be subjected to performance auditing. GBRT project funding is estimated at a total of 1.8 billion yuan. Currently, the daily passenger flow averages around 800 thousand passengers with the peak flows reaching 960 thousand daily, becoming the biggest one-way traffic BRT system in Asia. At times the GBRT traffic is even higher than that of the Guangzhou subway line traffic. Therefore, the GBRT construction, operation performance requires an objective and impartial analysis, conducive to BRT economic efficiency. Given the internationally high profile of the GBRT project, the performance audit work aroused widespread interest.

9.3.1.2   Timeliness

Timeliness means that the performance auditing must be undertaken after an appropriate period of time. Because of time-lags, the auditing bureau usually requires the project to be in operation for more than 2 years before performing the audit. The real performance can then be appropriately reflected for an objective and impartial evaluation of whether the GBRT project can achieve improvement of traffic congestion in Tianhe Road, Zhongshan Avenue, and Huangpu Road. In addition, the analysis seeks to understand whether the GBRT project achieved the investment objectives and in providing high quality transit services to the general public.

9.3.1.3   Feasibility

The feasibility of performance audit is to determine whether the subjective and objective conditions are met. (1) From 4 January 2011 to March 15, the audit bureau at Guangzhou city conducted their GBRT auditing for the construction and management until December 2010. In June 2011 the bureau issued its audit reports on the basis of preliminary results. Although there were two previous internal reports, the emphasis was placed on new discoveries and performance benchmarks; (2) On March 16, 2012 the audit group reported its information to the Commission of pre-trial investigation, City Traffic Commission, GBRT management company and other organizations and requested performance auditing; (3) The audit staff of the project team and the participants of the Chinese Public Management Research Center at Sun Yat-sen University have a wealth of experience in audit, budget management and performance evaluation. Finally (4) During the course of the audit, care was taken in coordination across auditing units and completion of designated plans.

9.3.1.4 Valued-Added

Value added in this case refers to the process of identifying fundamentals through details. The goal of the performance audit of the GBRT is to put forward valuable opinions and suggestions for related project management, system mechanism and other aspects. Pretrial investigation found that citizens reacted to the noise of the GBRT construction in Guangzhou, city leaders had been instructed to choose feasible roads to engage in GBRT; as the main management expectations for proper GBRT operations were that the social benefits were positive. But other data showed a different public reaction to the GBRT at the time of the project, construction, and operation.

Public reactions to GBRT include added congestion and increased traffic accidents. The public perception was that the station's design was unsatisfactory. The "GBRT" was dubbed the "do not pass" project. This shows that the project itself has room for improvement.

The more objective audit analyzed the GBRT project performance. It pointed out the inadequacies of the GBRT project, including in construction, and urged the relevant departments to intensify the improvement of supporting facilities, and also provided a reference for the future of the construction of other projects. The proposed suggestions to improve GBRT operations should provide a more complete traffic system.

9.3.1.5 Process of Performance Auditing: Engaging the Public

The audit investigation of Guangzhou Municipal Audit Bureau is based on the *Audit Law of the People's Republic of China* and the *National Auditing Standards* of the People's Republic of China. This audit investigation is on the basis of report produced by the audit bureau of Guangzhou City, from January to March 2011 on GBRT project and medium-sized renovation projects. The goal for GBRT and medium and large size renovation projects is to have performance auditing on operation of these projects before the end of 2011.

Subjective performance evaluation was carried out based on questionnaires and telephone surveys for analysis, evaluation, and a questionnaire survey was conducted in early 2012 June to late July. In the end, 900 questionnaires were collected by random choice, including 500 GBRT passenger questionnaires, 100 copies of GBRT bus driver questionnaires, 100 car driver questionnaires, 100 taxi driver questionnaires, 100 shops provided the owners' questionnaires. Telephone surveys by a quota sampling approach collected 1019 residents' questionnaires.

The objective performance evaluation is to analyze and evaluate the data provided by the survey unit. This audit investigation examined the city investment group in 2011. GBRT project and medium and large renovation project construction spending totaled 23.85 million yuan, accounting for 80% of total annual expenditure. The auditing team also checked operating expenses, that totaled 41.12 million yuan in 2011, accounting for 78% of annual spending. At the same time, an index of the feasibility study report was validated and the data collection process was conducted with and assisted by the Guangzhou Municipal Environmental Protection Bureau, Guangzhou City Public Security Bureau, Traffic Police Detachment, Guangzhou traffic command center, Guangzhou municipal engineering design and Research Institute (hereinafter referred to as Municipal Design Institute), Guangzhou Transport Planning Research Institute, Guangzhou City, the second bus company, Guangzhou third bus company, Guangzhou treasure Bus Co., Ltd., new bridge company.

The investigation of performance audit index system is divided into two parts: (1) **the construction aspect**, mainly from project management and financial management analysis and evaluation of its performance, analysis and evaluation of its performance goals from the system model and the degree of realization; (2) **the operation aspect**, mainly from the speed, passenger capacity, coverage, facilities platform, environment and service situation analysis and evaluation of the social benefits. The economic benefits were derived from the evaluation of resource development and business analysis, return and external economies, management system, GBRT electricity company use estimates, and the actual implementation and compliance with the financial regulations analysis, and assessment of the financial management from the internal control department. This audit investigation indicators and data collection were coordinated between the audit bureau of Guangzhou City and Sun Yat-sen University Chinese Public Management Research Center in which both parties work together to develop performance metrics for data analysis, questionnaire survey and telephone survey.

9.4 Evaluation of GBRT Performance Auditing: From Public Opinion to Public Decision

9.4.1 BRT Performance Auditing

Systemic Model:
This model evaluated the GBRT line setting, the platform dock design and examined whether the pedestrian overpass brought convenience to the public.

Survey results show that 54% and 62% of BRT bus drivers thought that line setting and the platform dock design are reasonable. 73% and 53% of passengers thought that transfer and middle platform are convenient. 86% and 54% of pedestrian were satisfied with GBRT convenience and overpass respectively. As on-site audit end date, GBRT stations connected with Shipaiqiao subway station hall only, failed to meet the expectation of connecting to the Shipai bridge, St. Augustine, and Jubei three subway station halls.

Size of the Project:
Project final expenses exceeded the planned investment size. In 2010 audited GBRT project budget amount was a total of 1.8479 billion yuan; exceeding the 2008 project estimate of 724 million yuan by more than 1.12 billion yuan, or 1.55 times the budgeted cost. The City Project Construction Committee report focussed on incompleteness of the construction and investment projections. As the GBRT project has not yet completed the settlement and final accounts, the actual investment projects could not be finalized at this stage.

BRT Operating Performance:
Since GBRT went into operation in February 2010, the City Traffic Commission and GBRT management companies have been continuing to improve and optimize the GBRT system operation management and site equipment and facilities, express station, originating shunt, 2 + 1 tailgating, borrow and innovative scheduling measures to strengthen security operation. The GBRT project generated improvements in speed, passenger traffic volume, coverage, facilities, the station environment and social aspects.

The GBRT project has become a "prize" project for Guangzhou with international recognition—hence very difficult to challenge. In 2011, with 41 business visits from domestic and foreign organizations, it won the "2011 Sustainable Transport Award" issued by Transportation Research Committee in the United States, low carbon inventory certification BSI ISO14064-1 certificate by the Technology Group chairman from the International Standard Organization, the green traffic transport transportation enterprises and 14 other Awards. During the audit review stage, GBRT project was named the United Nations 2012 climate change lighthouse project.

Speeds:
After the opening of the GBRT channel, the GBRT bus average operating speed increased noticeably. Early, late peak and non-working day average operating speed reached respectively 23.91 km/h, 23.65 km/h and 24.76 km/h, more than 20 km/h the minimum expected speed. Telephone surveys show that 74% of the respondents believed that the GBRT line bus speeds increased steadily. Compared with other cities, the average operating speed of the GBRT line in Guangzhou is in the middle. (See Fig. 9.1).

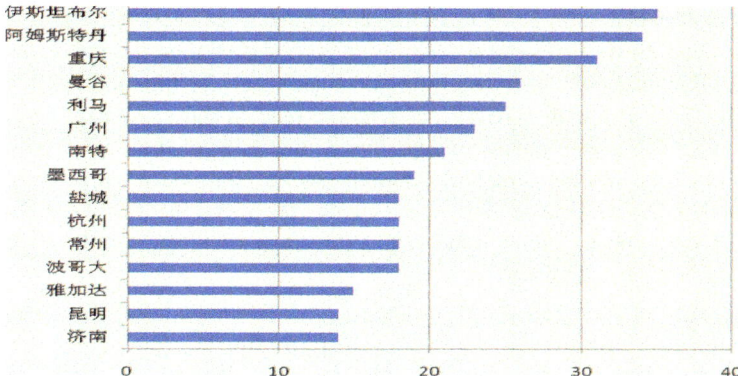

Fig. 9.1 BRT average speed (km/h), Guangzhou ranks the sixth. Translation from Chinese from top to bottom: Istanbul, Amsterdam, Chongqing, Bangkok, Lima, Guangzhou, Nantes, Mexico City, Salt Lake City, Hangzhou, Changzhou, Bogota, Jakarta, Kunming, Jinan

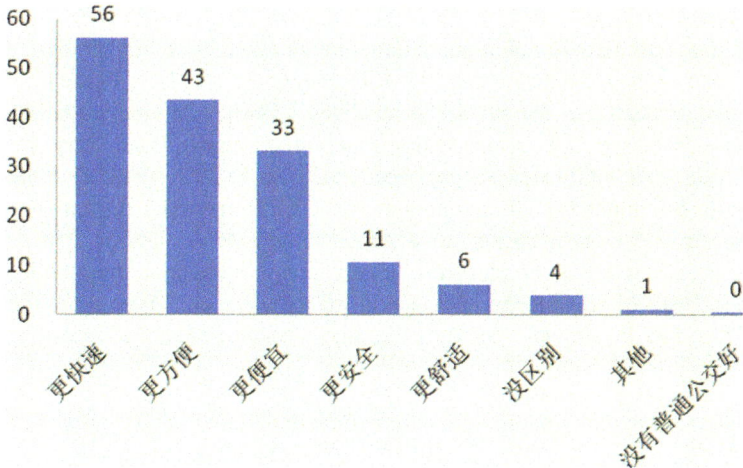

Fig. 9.2 Comparison of GBRT and other bus lanes. GBRT average speed is much faster. Translation from Chinese from left to right: Faster, More Convenient, Cheaper, Safer, More Comfortable, No Difference, Others, Worse than Normal Bus

Compared with the ordinary bus, the GBRT line bus has higher average operating speeds. The GBRT line during early, late peak and non-working days exceed normal bus lanes by 40%, 54% and 31%, respectively. The questionnaire survey shows that 56% of the passengers believe that the GBRT line is more rapid than the ordinary bus (Fig. 9.2).

The questionnaire showed that 79% of GBRT bus drivers reported that early and evening peak average speed were faster after operation of GBRT. 78% of passengers believe that GBRT channel improved traffic congestion. 50% of the public think GBRT routes are smoother after GBRT operation.

The smooth operation of the GBRT channel guarantees the timeliness of first and last rides and drastically reduces waiting timeline. Looking at the index data from the GBRT management company, the punctuality rate for first and last train was 100% for GBRT and the GBRT bus average time in the station time was only 38 seconds. The questionnaire survey showed that 64% of the GBRT passengers reported that the waiting time was generally within 10 minutes.

Although the average vehicle speed along the tracks has increased from the initial 13 km/h speed, Tianhe Road vehicles average travel speed did not reach the 31–38 km/h expected target.

Capacity:

In 2011, the average daily passenger volume for GBRT line reached 79.39 million passengers, exceeding the expected flow of 659 thousand people by 20%. System peak hour traffic volume was 2.74 million passengers/one-way hour (maximum section appears in Zhongshan Tianfu Avenue intersection section), exceeding the expected flow of 23 thousand people/one-way hour by 19%.

Coverage:

GBRT line coverage is not high, but it provides a certain convenience for the eastern part of the Guangzhou city. As of December 31, 2011, 31 of the GBRT line accounted for 4.28% of the city's 724 bus lines, 750 sites accounted for 14.75% of the city's 5084 center city bus station (excluding subway, taxi, ferry site). The annual ride 2.84 million passengers accounted for 12.39% of 22.93 billion passengers in bus industry. The opening of the GBRT, reducing the travel costs of residents in the eastern region, to a certain extent solves public transportation service problems and is conducive to public goods provision. The public survey shows that 4% of respondents use GBRT for daily travel, following the ordinary bus (42%) and the subway (28%) as the third ranking public transport (Fig. 9.3).

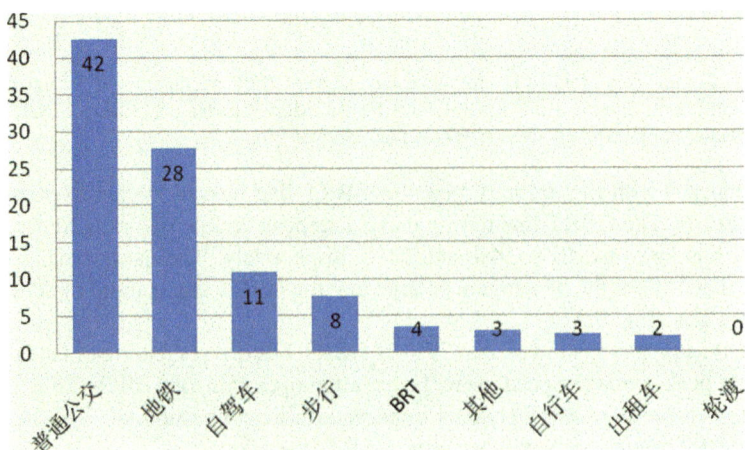

Fig. 9.3 Choice of public transport. BRT accounts for 4%. Translation from Chinese from left to right: Normal Bus, Metro, Self-Driving, Walking, BRT, Others, Cycling, Taxi, Ferry

9.4.1.1   Facility and Platform Environment

Passengers were generally satisfied with the GBRT facilities and platform environment.

In the setting of facilities, the survey shows that 69% of passengers think the sign information within and outside the platforms in GBRT stations is practical and accurate. Also 57% of the passengers think that the LED displays accurate messages and another 65% of passengers believe that the platform safety signs are clear. About 49% of the passengers feel that facilities for the disabled populations are designed in a humane way. The percentage of passengers who believe that inside the station fire safety measures were reasonably good was 59%. Satisfaction over platform benches, garbage cans and a fan set reached 71%, 71% and 62% of the users respectively.

In the platform environment, the questionnaire survey showed that the satisfaction of the passengers with the platform, the public order and the waiting environment were 74%, 63% and 52% respectively (see Appendix).

9.4.1.2   Quality of Service

Passenger satisfaction with the GBRT service is quite high. Investigation of bus drivers before and after operation of GBRT projects shows that although all drivers said after the opening of the GBRT their income has not increased, 79% reported greater work intensity, and only 37% of expressed satisfaction. Overall the bus drivers still expressed a good service attitude coming from GBRT. The questionnaire survey showed that passengers expressed their satisfaction over the service attitude of GBRT bus drivers, the guide service and the overall service satisfaction were 51%, 61% and 79% of the total respondents respectively.

Compared with other means of transport, the public experienced higher satisfaction with the GBRT system. Telephone survey shows (removing respondents with no GBRT experience), public satisfaction with the GBRT system overall is 43%, higher than 37% for the regular bus, 35% for taxi, 39% for bicycles and 18% for self-driving, but lower than the subway and ferry which are 53% and 64% respectively.

9.4.1.3   Resource Development and Economic Externality

Given the fact that the GBRT project is not-for-profit, the economic benefit is mainly reflected in the development of its associated additional activities and the external economy. The GBRT platform is equipped with 370 large and 1116 small light boxes, including 251 large light boxes for the release of advertising. GBRT platform advertising light boxes in the 2010–2011 years generated operating management fee income at 3.8 million yuan.

Questionnaire surveys of shop owners before operation of GBRT shows that 86% of the respondents said rents would increase after GBRT operation. But only 39% of these respondents report better business than before and 41% of the respondents reported no change in the business climate. Only 28% of the respondents thought there were better business opportunities after GBRT operations. The other 46% of respondents wished to open their shops in other places. Among people who would consider to open shop elsewhere, 43% of respondents believe that the rent is too expensive and other 35% of respondents report a bad business climate. We can conclude that BRT operation increased the rents along the route but with limited positive impact on business opportunities (see Appendix 9.2).

In the report prepared by Municipal Design Institute on GBRT feasibility, the staff calculated transportation cost saving benefits, passenger average saving time, improvement in the efficiency of traffic safety, reduction in noise pollution and improvement in air quality etc. benefit index, and other expected effect for GBRT projects. Given limited capability to measure and evaluate the aforementioned key indices, the auditing survey submitted to municipal government by the municipality construction commission, Guangzhou Zhongshan Avenue bus rapid transit (GBRT) pilot project evaluation report, reported the failure to verify critical information and difficulty to conduct a comprehensive evaluation. Furthermore, given the fact that relevant data was not available before GBRT operations, the municipality government failed to generate information from carbon emission trading rights, or related reduction in noise pollution and improvement in air quality.

9.4.1.4 Impact of BRT on Other Means of Transport

1. Average Vehicle Speed has not reached the expected target

After the opening of the GBRT, the average speed for vehicles during early and late peak as well as non-working day are: Tianhe Road 26.8, 16.22 and 24.89 km/h; Zhongshan Avenue 26.49, 26.71 and 31.59 km/h. Although vehicles experienced average speeds beyond 13 km/h, the average speed before GBRT openings, Tianhe Road vehicles experience an average travel speed lower than the expected target of 31–38 km/h.

This problem was also manifested in the questionnaire survey for drivers. About 64% of car drivers and 45% of taxi drivers reported more traffic jams after the GBRT lane opening. About 38% of the car drivers and 43% of taxi drivers believed that the average speed along the BRT route decreased after the opening of the GBRT. About 70% of the car drivers and 72% of taxi drivers would choose to avoid GBRT routes during peak hours. About 31% of taxi drivers will reduce the number of passing through GBRT routes because people choose to take GBRT rather than taxis in those lanes.

2. Parallel Roads become more crowded

Due to the lack of objective data for average vehicle speed in parallel sections before the opening of the GBRT, we cannot evaluate the impact of building GBRT on average speed and cannot eliminate impact of increasing volume of cars on the road. Hence, this section relies on a questionnaire survey for drivers in the parallel road sections, e.g. Huangpu Avenue, Tianhe North Road, Kwong Yuen Road before and after the opening of GBRT. Surveys showed that the drivers felt noticeable congestion in the Whampoa Avenue and Tianhe North road. Surveys also show that about 52% of the car drivers and 68% of taxi drivers feel that the traffic in Huangpu Avenue became more crowded after the opening of the GBRT. About 60% of car drivers and 56% of taxi drivers reported more crowded traffic in Tianhe North Road after the opening of the BRT. About 38% of the car drivers and 55% of taxi drivers responded that GBRT Guangyuan Road became more crowded after the opening of the GBRT projects (Fig. 9.4).

3. Fairness of Subsidized/Free Transit for GBRT Service

Generally speaking, bus transfers require extra charge. Although in order to encourage the use of public transport, some cities (e.g., Chicago) apply the policy of decreasing charges, in the GBRT project, transfers within the station are free.

Audit investigation showed financial subsidies to GBRT lines reached 114.35 million yuan each year to the benefit of mostly travelers with free transfers and those who paid originally 3–6 yuan (now only 2 yuan is needed for the same trip). In 2011, the GBRT serviced 284 million passengers, accounting for 12.39% of the total number of passengers in the bus industry. The city traffic Commission (hereinafter referred to as the Municipal Commission) GBRT system free transfer coefficient analysis showed that GBRT system free transfer passengers accounted for about 27% of total trips and pricing changes from between 3 and 6 yuan to a unified for 2 yuan per trip totaled 17 routes accounting for 28% of the total 61 routes. Comprehensive estimates reported that per bus passenger financial subsidies in Guangzhou city reached 1.30 yuan per trip. In the new free transfer pricing scheme and reduced fare system the financial subsidies per bus passenger recorded an additional 0.73 yuan. Due to limited number of beneficiaries in the free transfer scheme and highly subsidized price, the extent and fairness of financial subsidies should be examined given the principle of fees for service. At the same time,

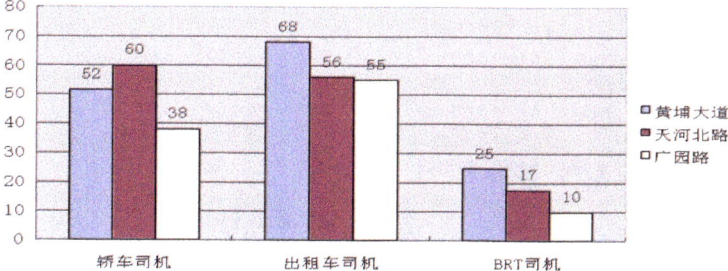

Fig. 9.4 Reasons for making parallel roads crowded (*Unit* Percent). Translation of horizontal labels from Chinese from left to right: Car Driver, Taxi Driver, BRT Driver. Translation of vertical labels from Chinese from top to bottom: Huangpu Road, Tianhe North Road, Guangyuan Road

another survey shows that only 12% of respondents would take price factors as main determinant in choosing public transport. Therefore, an appropriate increase in fares will not significantly reduce the willingness of the public to take GBRT. Of course, the process of public policy making has some rigidity and once implemented it is quite difficult to make a change (Fig. 9.5).

4. Audit Results

The choice of a bus system in a city has to take into account a diverse set of interacting factors, each of which has its own foundations and is difficult to ignore. Taking the advantages, disadvantages, adaptability and other factors into account, we reach some preliminary comparisons and evaluations.

The attractiveness of BRT is based on its rapid speed. Its success relies on an enormous investment of construction funds, sustained operating and maintenance costs, policies and measures to support including subsidies, and congestion in parallel roads. These policy measures include expropriation of land to broaden the road, the remediation of sidewalk, traffic control of left and right turns, passengers paying on the platform and free transfer, and others.

The speed of dedicated bus lanes is similar to that of GBRT but has far lower construction costs. **The average cost of GBRT project was about 80.7 million yuan/km**. But the average cost for **construction of bus lanes in 2011 was about 0.92 million yuan/km in 2011, or only 1.14% of the BRT project** (including signs marking, supporting harbor station renovation, electronic police monitoring device three parts).

In this case, it is necessary to appropriately expand the bus lanes or consider GBRT projects only during the planning of new roads. In addition, considerations would need to balance the fairness of financial subsidies and improve the efficiencies of resource usage.

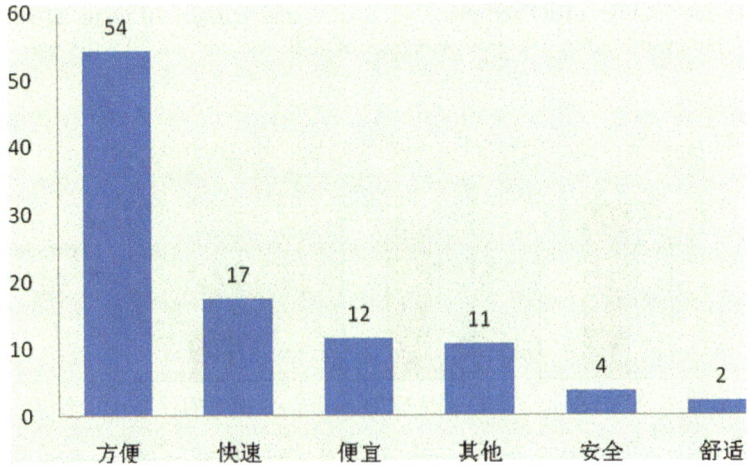

Fig. 9.5 Main determinants for choice of public transport (*Unit* Percent). Translation from Chinese from left to right: Convenience, Speed, Price, Other, Safety, Comfort

9.5 Implications of Performance Auditing

In November 2013, the Third Plenary Session of the party passed the **CPC Central Committee's decision on a number of issues of deepening reform, making clear the role played by the auditing bureau in performing statutory duties of supervision and accelerating reform measures.** The GBRT project performance audit result garnered attention from the city leadership and was recommended for departmental review. On 22 January 2014. The city party 19th document [2014] requested the City Commission and other departments to conduct a scientific evaluation of GBRT projects on the basis of past experience and rectify potential pitfalls according to procures. GBRT project performance audit reflected how the audit department fulfilled its roles and facilitated the reform process.

9.5.1 Orders from Municipal Leadership

On January 18, 2013, the Audit bureau of Guangzhou City reported issues related to "higher comprehensive benefits for bus lane," financial subsidies, and other performance auditing questions to the city government. Some responses from the city government:

Mayor Chen Jianhua instructed on January 25th,

"Please hand over to the Public Transport Bureau and Fiscal Bureau for review. Please refer to Mr. Gui." Mr. Chen Rugui, executive vice mayor on the January 28th instructed, "Please hand over to Public Transport Bureau and Fiscal Bureau for review. Request the Research Division for Fiscal Bureau to deal with justification of fiscal subsidy."

9.5.2 Recommendations for Adjustment and Restructuring

1. In March 2013, the city traffic Commission reported in Systematic improvement and Policy Package for City Center Restructuring in Guangzhou city to put forward the idea of continuing GBRT construction and speed up bus lanes.
2. In view of the proposal on "strengthening financial management and strict budget review" GBRT management companies made clear to establish their financial budget management system and the comprehensive budget management system.
3. Aiming at the recommendation of "strengthening project management and accelerating the unfinished work," City Project Construction Committee made clear to take the joint supervision in optimizing engineering and procedures.
4. For the recommendation of "strengthening of financial management and tightening strict budget review", the city investment group made clear to the subordinate investment company to cut spending on advertising light boxes.

5. On the basis of the proposal of "carefully examining the loss and waste, as well as defining the responsibility of the relevant units", on April 3, 2013, the city investment group requested careful financial auditing of GBRT project and analysis of waste as a step towards outlining responsibilities.

9.5.3 New BRT Project Cancelled, September, 2014

Southern Metropolis Daily, September 3, 2014 A08 version published an article titled Guangzhou Avenue first phase project will not use GBRT. The project for another BRT to be built was dropped. There are several possible reasons, but one of the main reasons—according to media quote from Mr. Fan, deputy director of the City Project Construction Committee and the Public Consultative Committee, since the bus lane is so much cheaper than BRT it is better to use the most cost efficient means. While BRT speeds were satisfactory, there was secondary congestion, and the overall environmental impact was not fully established.

9.5.4 Text Message from a Deputy in Municipal People's Congress

A deputy in Guangzhou Municipal People's Congress forwarded the text message sent to leaders in auditing bureau:

> Congratulations to the Guangzhou audit bureau. The audit report of the Zhongshan Road GBRT dared to tell the truth. As a member of the thirteen National People's Congress and the Municipal Construction Committee, I witnessed the questions raised to the GBRT project at that time in the Municipal Economic Commission and the municipal construction commission. We often praised the GBRT project without solid reasons. As an ordinary resident in Zhongshan Avenue, I often doubt the role of GBRT in solving the traffic problems around Tianhe and often looking at the dark GBRT stations in lonely nights asking whether these stations are justified. Even though I am a NPC deputy I am not a professional, nor do I have the ability to delve into numbers and prove with data that GBRT might be a failure. So thanks for the audit of GBRT. Also to mention, GBRT construction period placed huge burden on the residents along the route, I am not sure how to evaluate these costs.

9.6 Conclusions: Public Engagement and Fiscal Discipline

Despite the international hype, the GBRT project performance audit results have suggested concerns, approved by the city leadership, with the aim to improve future public decisions on transport. The issue of whether to build another BRT did not stop after the completion of the audit project. The public and the media continued to pay attention until early September 2014 when the Guangzhou municipal government executive meeting decided that the next phase of the Guangzhou Avenue project would abandon the use of BRT. This process presented the constraining ability by the public, the media and the public consultative committee on the abandoning of costly and inefficient BRT project for the welfare of residents in Guangzhou. Most importantly the report relied on the professional advice from the public, the media and the public advisory committee.

In countries with electoral competition (OECD and emerging markets like Pakistan) the electoral process could exacerbate problems of overspending and drive a wedge between the political choices and socially optimal outcomes. Tighter accountability through performance monitoring in China could generate better results.

This paper presents a novel mechanism through which the well-informed public could interact with public-minded officials to produce socially beneficial outcomes. The reliability and effectiveness of this channel might vary across context and localities. However, the case study shows a promising potential in the context without electoral competition where public engagement could serve as a powerful constraint to the inefficient local government pet projects and have the potential to improve the social allocation of resources.

Appendix 10.1

Satisfaction of consumers over facilities and platform

Item	Very satisfied	Basically satisfied	Neutral	Basically dissatisfied	Very dissatisfied	No opinion
Info in platform	15	54	26	4	1	0
Info outside Platform	16	52	22	6	0	4
LED info	11	46	32	11	0	0
Safety sign	18	47	40	4	1	0
Facility for needy	8	41	39	10	2	0
Fire facility	10	49	33	3	0	5
Long chair	27	44	25	3	1	0
Trash can	23	48	25	4	0	0
Fan	23	39	30	7	1	0
Public health	24	50	21	5	0	0
Security	13	50	32	4	1	0
Waiting room	6	46	38	8	2	0

Unit %

Rent changes before and after BRT operations

Change in Rent	Choice	A lot more expensive	A little more expensive	No change	A little cheaper	A lot cheaper
	Percent	26	60	12	0	2
Change in business	Choice	A lot better	A little better	No change	A little worse	A lot worse
	Percent	5	34	41	15	5
Reasons for opening up business	Choice	More opportunity	Others			
	Percent	28	72			
Consider moving to other places	Choice	Yes	No			
	Percent	46	54			
Reason why move to other places (Multiple choice)	Choice	Rents are high	Bad business	Others		
	Percent	43	35	22		

Unit %

Appendix 10.2: Media Reports on GBRT

iMedia Reports

The BRT audit project aroused sustained attention from media. The author here only outlined titles from some media reports as a way of showing how the public participated in the BRT discussion and decision making of building another BRT (with Chinese included).

1. Reports of Official Interviews in Auditing Bureau on BRT issues

- Southern Municipality Daily, 2013 May 24 GA08, *Guangzhou city audit bureau chief Zhang Jie pointed out that the BRT project audit concludes that the fast track bus lane is a better pick than BRT in terms of efficiency* (《南方都市报》2013年5月24日GA08版,题为《广州市审计局局长张杰明指出BRT项目审计的主要结论是公交快速道性价比比BRT高》的报道)
- New Express, June 3, 2013, *the ongoing construction of tram might be the next inefficient BRT.* (《新快报》2013年6月3日,题为《有轨电车会否重蹈BRT"性价比不高"覆辙》的报道)

Municipality Auditing Report to Congress

On September 24, 2013, the audit bureau of Guangzhou city in the twenty-first session of the fourteenth session of the NPC Standing Committee submitted the report, *the execution of government budget at the corresponding level and other financial revenue and expenditure situation,* in which problems have been pointed out over the BRT project.

- Guangzhou daily, September 25, 2013 A3 version, *Loss of BRT Project Reached Millions* (《广州日报》2013年9月25日A3版,题为《BRT工程损失浪费过千万》的报道)
- Southern Metropolis Daily, September 25, 2013 A06, *The auditing report BRT waste reached 10.73 million yuan.* (《广州日报》2013年9月25日A3版,题为《BRT工程损失浪费过千万》的报道)
- Yangcheng Evening News, September 25, 2013, *Should Guangzhou build a second BRT?* (《羊城晚报》2013年9月25日,题为《广州要不要建第二条BRT?》的报道)
- Guangzhou daily, September 25, 2013, *Guangzhou BRT project cost millions and 20 government departments spend 30 million on conference fees.* (《广州日报》2013年9月25日,题为《广州BRT工程损失千万20部门问题会议费三千万》的报道)

2. Online Reports on BRT Performance Auditing

- Southern Daily, January 10, 2014, *Do Guangzhou need to build a second BRT?* (《南方日报》2014年1月10日,题为《广州是否需要建第二条BRT?》的报道)
- Guangdong Net, January 11, 2014, *Guangzhou will build eight BRT length of 100 km with cost over 8 billion yuan* (大粤网2014年1月11日,题为《广州将再建八条BRT总长100 km造价或超80亿》的报道)
- Southern Daily, January 13, 2014, *The public is questioning:Guangzhou BRT is not valued against its cost, why build another one?* (《南方日报》2014年1月13日,题为《市民质疑:广州BRT性价比不高 为何还要建》的报道)
- Nandu network, January 10, 2014, *Guangzhou Avenue, the proposed second BRT Avenue,* (《新快报》2014年1月11日,题为《广州第二条BRT规划讨论延期》的报道)
- New Express, January 11, 2014, *Guangzhou plans to build another BRT project on Guangzhou Avenue* (数字报南都网2014年1月10日,题为《穗拟建第二条BRT广州大道列入备选》的报道)
- Guangdong Construction News, January 14, 2014, *Guangzhou will build another BRT* (《广东建设报》2014年1月14日,题为《广州或将再建BRT》的报道)

Special Issue for Province Party Secretary Office

Guangdong Provincial Audit Department published a brief on performance auditing 2014 version in which the report by audit bureau of Guangzhou City was titled *BRT performance audit: items and its effects.* (广州市审计局的《BRT绩效审计项目及其影响》)

Whether to Build Another BRT, July, 2014

- Southern Metropolis Daily, July 16, 2014, *BRT and the bus lane, who against whom?* (《南方都市报》2014年7月16日,题为《BRT和公交专用道,谁都不服谁》的报道)
- Southern Metropolis Daily, 17 July 2014, *Technical consultant for BRT Said BRT is safer than other Public Transport.* (《南方都市报》2014年7月17日,题为《技术顾问单位再发报道力推BRT称 BRT安全性强于普通公交》的报道)
- Yangcheng Evening News, July 17, 2014, *BRT statistical data good, Disadvantage cannot be ignored.* (《羊城晚报》2014年7月17日,题为《BRT统计数据靓,短板不能忽视》的评论)
- Southern Metropolis Daily, July 18, 2014, *Safer BRT? Not a good reason.* (《南方都市报》2014年7月18日,题为《BRT更安全?这个理由太牵强》的评论)

References

Ahmad, E., Bordignon, M., & Brosio, G. (Eds.). (2016). *Multilevel finance and the Eurocrisis.* Edward Elgar.

Alesina, A., & Tabellini, G. (1990). A positive theory of fiscal deficits and government debt. *The Review of Economic Studies, 57*(3), 403–414.

Azzimonti, M., De Francisco, E., & Quadrini, V. (2014). Financial globalization, inequality, and the rising public debt. *The American Economic Review, 104*(8), 2267–2302.

Besley, T., & Ghatak, M. (2005). Competition and incentives with motivated agents. *The American Economic Review, 95*(3), 616–636.

Zhou, L. (2007). 中国地方官员的晋升锦标赛模式研究 Governing China's Local Officials: An Analysis of Promotion Tournament Model. 经济研究, 7, 36–50.

Chapter 10
Risk Management of PPPs in China: A Case Study of Guangzhou

Meili Niu

Abstract Over the past decade, Public Private Partnerships (PPPs) have become more prevalent in public infrastructure construction projects worldwide. China is not an exception. Due to the slowdown of its national economy, China faces daunting challenges in matching its fiscal capacity with the fast-growing demand for public services. PPPs create a fiscal space for China to mitigate its debt risks and maintain local sustainability. This study uses the *Datianshan* Project in the city of Guangzhou as a case to examine the local experience of PPPs. However, in this case, the PPP did not reduce environmental or fiscal risks. And it certainly did not lead to a relaxation of the city's revenue constraints. What the *Datianshan* project did show was the need for local tax reform that would allow PPPs to move on to the next level of usefulness.

10.1 Introduction

Investment in infrastructure has been the Chinese government's favoured means of promoting full employment and economic development (Mikesell et al. 2011; Ansar 2016). As mentioned in earlier chapters in this volume (see e.g., Xiao 2018) there has been an increasing devolution of spending responsibilities along with a centralization of revenue bases. Chinese local governments have typically used land revenue to support economic growth (Wang et al. this volume) but this is a limited and decreasing source of finance. One of the most challenging issues of fiscal sustainability at present is to ensure that risks associated with local borrowing and debt are effectively managed.

This paper focuses on the role played by Public–Private Partnerships (PPPs) in recent decades—in the context illustrated in Ahmad et al. (this volume). As they point out, the main advantages of a PPP are the efficient management skills of, and

M. Niu (✉)
School of Government, Center for Chinese Public Administration Research,
Sun Yat-sen University, Guangzhou, China
e-mail: niumeili@mail.sysu.edu.cn

© Springer Nature Singapore Pte Ltd. 2018   239
E. Ahmad et al. (eds.), *Fiscal Underpinnings for Sustainable Development in China*,
https://doi.org/10.1007/978-981-10-6286-5_10

the risk sharing with, the private sector. Although there may well be an easing of short-term budget constraints for investment, PPPs do not reduce intertemporal resource constraints; public liabilities that are generated still have to be addressed in the medium-term.

There is a tendency, however, to think that partnering with private business is now an alternative to government financing for infrastructure projects. This non-recognition of liabilities "kicks the can" down the road, and has proved to be problematic in OECD and emerging market countries alike. There may also be a tendency for local governments to resort to PPPs with the expectation that the higher levels will take care of the liabilities (see Ahmad et al. this volume).

PPPs are not new to China (ADB 2014), however. Since the 1980s, Build-Operate-Transfer (BOT) contracts have been popular in China in transportation, water conservancy, municipal utilities, etc. PPPs surged in the 1990s but then faded. The resurgence of PPPs in China since 2010 is primarily a response to the fiscal constraints resulting from the global financial crisis (ADB 2013). But, there is a significant difference between the recent PPP experiments and the previous practice in China.

Risk-sharing between a government and a private company is the key for developing a PPP (Budina et al. 2007; OECD 2008; Ter-Minassian 2016). This requires complicated contracts to improve project efficiency and mitigate risks (Ahmad et al. 2015). However, this was not the practice in China until recently. In the past, efficiency and risk-sharing were not major concerns in China's infrastructure financing. Because most infrastructure development projects were also priority programs, the financing was guaranteed. Especially true for local governments, land financing was the major strategy for municipal infrastructure construction due to the centralized revenue autonomy (Wang and Ye 2015; and Wang Wu and Ye, this volume). However, the 2008 global economic crisis changed that; China now faces the same challenges as other countries when it comes to shrinking financial resources (ADB 2013 and this volume).

China's new approach to PPPs was introduced in 2014 when both the National Development and Reform Commission (NDRC) and the Ministry of Finance (MOF) issued several administrative orders to promote PPPs. After more than two decades of practice in collaborating with private companies, the PPP, as a specific policy instrument, had finally been officially introduced.

Unlike earlier PPPs, risk-management is now the core of China's new PPP policy. But the role of government is still unclear. Allocating risk between the government and private bidders has become an extremely challenging issue. So much so, the institutional mechanism to ensure this allocation of risk is still under development. As discussed in other papers in this volume, it is still unclear which government bears the resulting liabilities and the own-source revenues required to underpin the liabilities.

The new PPP reform is expected to have multiple goals. It must not only improve infrastructure financing but also policy making, project planning, and budget management. More transparent and accountable budgeting systems are needed to effectively manage PPPs. The key to achieving this multiplicity of policy goals is to effectively control risks (see Liu and Li, this volume). This study aims to explain the risk mitigation mechanisms of China's new PPP system and how these measures affect local budgeting systems.

This case study uses the city of Guangzhou to examine the new PPP experiment in Guangdong province. It may not be a representative case for China's PPP reform, however. Guangzhou is the capital city of Guangdong province and its GDP was RMB 1810 billion in 2015, making it the third highest in China after Shanghai and Beijing. Compared with most Chinese cities, Guangzhou's market economy is more developed, which gives Guangzhou advantages when partnering with private enterprises. However, Guangzhou is not necessarily any better than any other city at operating a PPP under the new policy scheme.

Actually, Guangzhou was reluctant to develop PPP projects for two reasons. First, Guangzhou has limited room to start new PPP projects under the MOF's new standards.[1] As the pioneer of China's economic reforms, Guangzhou has been partnering with the private sector for many years. Most infrastructure projects in need of a private partnership were actually operated under the traditional BOT system. Because those projects usually have long term contracts, Guangzhou does not need to develop a large number of new basic construction projects, especially projects that generate economic profits.

Second, in order to control risks, the MOF has developed more complicated rules to regulate PPPs, such as value for money evaluation, contracting, procurement, etc., which increase the uncertainty of project planning and operations. This is especially true now because the MOF has yet to publish detailed implementation instructions. Understandably, Guangzhou has been very careful when selecting experimental projects.

For the *Datianshan* project, the city adopted a bottom-up selection process. Unlike the previous selection of infrastructure projects, it started by having the relevant line agency—Urban Management Commission (GUMC)—prepare a project plan. The plan was then reviewed and approved by both the Development and Reform Commission and the Finance.

Guangzhou selected the *Datianshan* project for various reasons. For one, improving urban life by making the city cleaner was a priority for Guangzhou's PPP experiment. For another, the city had to follow the MOF's guidelines; private enterprises rather than state-owned enterprises were the target group for potential partners. In this, GUMC was seen as agency most likely to have a successful PPP experiment. Urban maintenance and innovation is a very promising area in terms of the potential for private enterprises to make a profit.

Given the explanation above, the most obvious questions would be: How did the Guangzhou Local Government deal with risk for this new type of PPP in the *Datianshan* project? Did the *Datianshan* project lower the pressure on government to reduce debt or did it just generate even more fiscal risks?

In order to address these questions, officials from Guangzhou's Finance Department, the Reform and Development Commission, the City Urban Planning

---

[1]interview FDW623.

Commission, the Project Company, residents of *Datianshan* and its committee's members were interviewed. Documents from the PPP's initiation and experiments were also examined in order to understand the policy context and evaluate the risk involved.

The rest of this paper is arranged as follows. The evolution of China's PPPs is described first. The mechanism of risk management through policy documentation evaluation is then introduced. Next, the *Datianshan* Project is examined in order to understand the risk related to the recent initiation of PPP projects. Finally, this paper discusses the risk mitigation approaches associated with PPPs in China's local finances.

10.2   The Evolution of PPPs in China

The emergence of PPPs in China began with the market economy reform of the late 1970s. For foreign investors, PPPs were used as a new model of collaboration between Chinese local governments,SOEs and foreign businesses. Guangdong province, as the pioneer of China's economic reform, was the first local government to use PPPs and did so for two reasons. First, the provincial government was encouraged to apply the market economy rule to attract foreign investment. Second, at the start of the economic reform, the largest investments in China came from Hong Kong and Taiwan, because of familial relationships in south China. Guangdong province became the most popular place for overseas investors.

The first PPP project in China was the White Swan Hotel project (with total investment of 180 million US dollars) in 1981 in Guangzhou. The second project was the Shajiao B Power Plant project (with total investment of 540 million US dollars) in 1984 in Shenzhen, which was also the first city to initiate economic reform in China. Both cities are located in Guangdong province and both projects were a collaboration with Hong Kong companies.

The contracts for these two projects were simple compared with conventional PPP contracts. At that time, managing risk was not a big concern for the foreign investors; the major purpose of the investment was to establish collaborative relations with China's governments at different levels (Jin 2014).

The debate on market reform was far from over in the early 1980's so PPPs did not become a predominant mode of infrastructure financing until the early 1990s. At the end of 1992, China's 14th National Congress Meeting of the Chinese Communist Party elaborated its strategic goal of establishing the market economy system in China. This provided an opportunity for infrastructure financing reform.

Leading the reform, the NDRC selected 5 projects as the experimental BOTs at the end of 1994. These projects covered water, power, bridge, and highway services. In 1995, the State Planning Commission, the Ministry of Power and Industry, and the Ministry of Transportation, promulgated *The Notice on Approving and Managing Franchise Pilot Projects for Foreign Investors*. At the same time, the Ministry of Foreign Trade and Economic Collaboration (now called the Ministry of

Commerce) promulgated *The Notice on Accepting Foreign Investment through BOT*. Because most BOT projects provided public services, such as power, water, sewage, gas, etc., the Ministry of Construction published the *Suggestion on Accelerating Marketization of Public Utilities* in 2002 and *Regulations on Franchises of Municipal Public Utilities* in 2004.

After that, PPPs, and especially BOTs, became the dominant approach to financing local infrastructure in China. Contractors included state-owned enterprises (SOEs), private enterprises and foreign companies. Among these three types of contractors, the SOEs are the most important in terms of the number of the projects contracted out.

Local governments favoured SOEs for two main reasons. First, a local government could easily negotiate with an SOE due to their close relationship. In addition, most public utility projects are government priority investments and are therefore important from both a political and an economic perspective. All in all, local governments feel more comfortable contracting with SOEs and see this as a way to reduce project risk. Second, SOEs have a big share of the market for infrastructure development. Their market access and preferences give them greater advantages than most other types of companies in China.

Even so, China's golden era of PPPs only began rather recently. Because of the global financial crisis, China's economic development has dramatically slowed. The central government promised a RMB 4 trillion stimulus package, but local governments were responsible for a large share of the financing. As a result, local governments faced daunting challenges to finance new infrastructure projects with their limited own-tax resources, while still subject to balanced budget rules.

The growth of local debt, especially contingent and hidden debt, has become the most challenging issue for budgetary reform in China (Ma et al. 2015). In recognition of the seriousness of the debt issue, the new budget law was amended in 2014. Though the new law clearly states that the central government will no longer bail out local debt, the problem remains. How can China's local governments finance infrastructure to maintain services and promote the economy? PPPs appear to be the central government's answer. However, PPPs are unlikely to significantly ease resource constraints without significant local tax reform.

Unlike China's earlier BOT approach, post-2014 PPPs emphasize collaboration. The public and private sectors are meant to work together throughout the process, including designing, building, and operating the project, as well as sharing the project's profits, risks, and social responsibilities.

In 2014, this new direction was not made very clear. The State Council issued *The Suggestions on Enhancing Local Government Debt Management* (the so called 43rd Document) to encourage PPP projects. This was regarded as a signal that the golden era of Chinese PPPs had arrived. But the golden glow dimmed a bit as the bureaucratic turf war over PPPs started up. Right after the 43rd Document, the NDRC and MOF simultaneously promulgated orders to promote PPPs, each taking a different stand on the issue.

The NDRC's stated goal was to promote more basic construction projects in order to promote the national economy and growth potential. In contrast, MOF saw

PPPs as the best way to control local debt and to maintain fiscal sustainability without sacrificing growth. These duelling approaches were viewed as competition for leadership of the PPP reform between the two most powerful ministries in infrastructure construction. While doing nothing to clarify the issues, the competition did succeed in confusing local governments regarding the definition and implementation of PPPs.

For example, in the NDRC's version, private investors included SOEs. However, including them would be a clear violation of MOF's concept. MOF envisioned excluding as potential bidders/partners, those enterprises under the Local Financing Platform (LFP) or state-controlled enterprises, although this rule was not enforced in practice later.

So far, MOF seems to have won the competition. The State Council empowered MOF to put forward the experiments and MOF published 16 documents in 2014 and 2015 to set up the rules for PPP projects, covering pilot project implementation, PPP operational guidelines, PPP contracting, government procurement related to PPPs, guidelines for evaluating fiscal capacity, and value-for-money analysis, etc. In order to better manage all pilot projects and make PPPs more transparent, MOF also created a center, called China Public Private Partnerships Center (CPPPC).

However, in reality, the NDRC still plays a very important role in China's PPP reform. The planning of infrastructure construction for public services must be approved by the NDRC, and local development and reform commissions. And, due to the difficulty of attracting non SOE partners, MOF had to give up its rules against SOE involvement in PPPs. According to China Public Private Partnerships Center's quarterly report, of the 105 projects that signed official contracts as of June 30, 2016, 55% (65) are contracted out with SOEs.

MOF even created a special fund to subsidize PPP projects with RMB 3 million for projects under RMB 300 million investment, RMB 5 million for investment between RMB 300 million to RMB 1 billion, and RMB 8 million for projects with over RMB 1 billion investment. The subsidy could be used for expenses during project planning and operation stages. Moreover, MOF also provides a 2% award for any debt under Local Financing Platforms (LFPs) that are successfully transferred to PPP projects (which was intended to replace government debt with private partner debt—although PPPs imply an element of public debt that should be recognized on the balance sheet of the respective level of government—see IPSAS rule 32 on PPPs).

By the end of the June 2016, 9285 PPPs projects (with a total RMB 10.6 trillion investment) were approved, and 619 projects (with a total of RMB 1 trillion) were under operation. Among them, 232 were MOF's pilot projects with a total RMB 892.5 billion investment.[2] Figure 10.1 shows the number of PPP projects by sector as of July 2016. Municipal engineering and transportation are the largest, accounting for 57% of PPP investment.

However, the growth of projects attracting private investment may also increase the risk. In theory, more developed areas have more advantages in operating PPPs.

---

[2]Data is from China Public Private Partnerships Center. http://www.cpppc.org/.

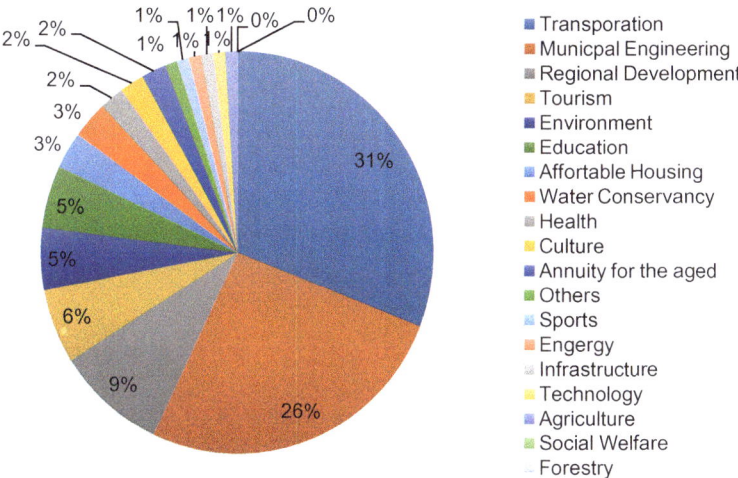

Fig. 10.1 Distribution of PPPs Investment by Sector *Source* http://www.cpppc.org:8082/ efmisweb/ppp/projectLivrary/toPPPMap.do

The more PPP projects are operated by less developed areas, the more risk the PPP projects may take on, as they typically have fewer resources to repay liabilities.

Surprisingly, Fig. 10.2 shows that the PPP investments of 18 provinces (60% of the provincial governments) as of the end of June 2016, were even larger than their government general revenues in 2014.[3] This means less developed areas with weaker fiscal capacity and more contingent debt are more interested in PPPs, perhaps as a means of relieving their budget constraints. In reality, this only postpones the reckoning that is only now being avoided because there are incomplete balance sheets at the local level (Ahmad and Zhang 2016, this volume). Therefore, this observation demonstrates an even a stronger concern for fiscal risk coming along with the resurgence of PPPs in China.

Ansar et al. (2016) argue that the poor implementation of infrastructure investment was one of the major reasons for China's fiscal problems over the past three decades. Although the key element of the new PPP design is to define and share risks between a government and its private partners, a PPP does not actually reduce liabilities. Furthermore, improper accounting of these liabilities may actually introduce elements of game-play between the local and central governments that has been quite damaging in the Eurozone context. There is still a tendency to see PPPs as a means of easing local budget constraints (IMF 2004, 2006; Ter-Minassian 2016).

The recent PPP program is an attempt to kill two birds with one stone: finance more infrastructure and manage local risks more effectively. The daunting result

---

[3]Besides, Hong Kong, Macau, and Taiwan, there are 31 provincial governments in China. Figure 10.2 presents 30 because Tibet is regarded as an outlier for financial analysis.

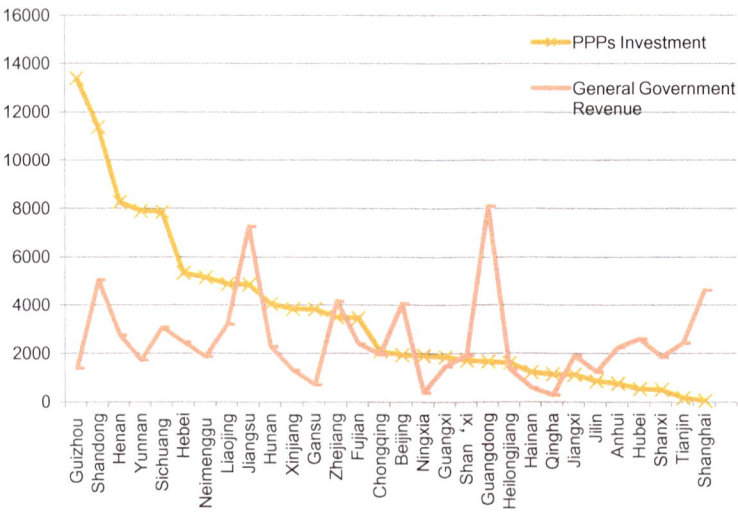

Fig. 10.2 PPPs Investment and Fiscal Capacity (unit: RMB 100 million)

demonstrated in Fig. 10.2 raises the concern, how does China develop strategies to share the risks? This is the core question we address in this paper.

The following analysis uses the city of Guangzhou's *Datianshan* project as a case to examine the mechanism of risk management at the local level in China.

10.3 PPP Risk Analysis in the City of Guangzhou

10.3.1 Risks Involved in a PPP

Despite the obvious advantages for the government, such as cost savings and improved efficiency, a PPP also involves a range of risks. These risks are highly associated with a country's political, economic, social and technological status, as well as the liabilities associated with the project and its implementation. Risk analysis for a PPP project is therefore context-based. The existing literature presents rich discussion on defining risks in PPPs based on experiences in a variety of countries Government of Victoria (2001), Ahmad et al. (2015), IMF (2006), Li et al. (2001), Office of the Auditor-General (2011) and Hwang et al. (2013).

Due to the complexities of risk structures, the mechanism to control risk varies in different countries. Nevertheless, several risk control strategies are common: develop advanced instruments (such as value for money analysis), improve organizational strength (such as contracting skills), enhance the credit of the government, and cultivate the market in order to increase the level of competition. But the literature is clear that contracts entered into by a local government should be covered by their own-source revenues, whether or not there are earmarked-fees for services rendered. Without own-source revenues, local governments will have an incentive to pass these liabilities on to higher levels.

China is not an exception to this trend. However, before analyzing Guangzhou's risks in its first post-2014 PPP, a brief description of the *Datianshan* project is in order.

10.3.2 Da Tian Shan Project at a Glance

As discussed above, GUMC was given the authority to select PPPs to experiment with in the City of Guangzhou. Due to the dramatic growth of its urban population, the treatment of kitchen waste became the concern of both the city government and residents. Besides enhancing the traditional approach, GUMC also looked for applying new technology to deal with this issue. The private partner, Beijing Goldenway Bio-Tech Co., Ltd. (BGB), was selected as the single private partner mainly because BGB was revealed to have the most advanced technology in China through the open bidding process.[4]

Da Tian Shan Project (DTSP) is officially called The Pilot Project for Food Waste Recycle Processing in Guangzhou. Launched August 1, 2011, the processing site is 15,943 square meters and construction was completed on March 1, 2015. The total investment was RMB 112.96 million. Based on the contract, the city government invested RMB 37.75 million for civil engineering and supporting facilities, such as roads, water and power. BGB invested RMB 75.21 in technology and equipment. The concession was for 15 years including one year of construction. It is expected to process up to 200 tons of food waste per day collected from the cafeterias of public offices, SOEs, schools, state-owned catering enterprises, and some 4-star hotels.

10.3.3 The Strategies to Control Risks

Although it is still a very challenging issue for Guangzhou to identify and manage risks in PPPs, the previous experience of collaborating with private partners provided valuable insights for GUMC and the city's Finance department to control the risk in DTSP. The strategies used to control risks include:

---

[4]BGB is a pioneer of fermentation technology in China. The technology transforms food waste into biological, humic fertilizer. The technology won the 15th WIPO-SIPO Award for Chinese Outstanding Patented Invention & Industrial Design. It created a breakthrough in organic waste recycle technology. Its investors include Goldman Sachs, East Sun, Continental Grain Company and some domestic partners. Bio-waste processing machines and the organic fertilizer from the food waste are BGB's two major products.

10.3.3.1 Careful Selection of the Partner in the Presence of Information Asymmetry

Competition among bidders is crucial to enabling the government to negotiate the best value at lowest cost, and can also ameliorate principal–agent problems (Posner et al. 2009). In China, one of the major challenges in using PPPs is the incomplete competition that is rooted in a less open market structure, which raises the concern of information asymmetry.

In 2008, during the Beijing Olympic games, BGB was the food waste processing contractor for the Olympic Village. This became BGB's best marketing point for extending their business later. Due to its reputation in the food waste processing industry, BGB became a very competitive bidder for DTSP. In order to reduce the risk related to limited bidders. GUMC conducted two field investigations before the contract was signed. First, the mayor of Guangzhou visited BGB's Beijing office to investigate its technology and the company's operations. Later, GUMC also organized a group to visit BGB's operation site in Sichuan province to confirm the operation plan would work for Guangzhou as well.

10.3.3.2 Avoiding Political Risk Through Open Deliberation

Due to negative externalities, environmental projects, especially waste processing projects, are very sensitive to public opinion. Recently, it has become very common that waste treatment projects fail due to the citizen opposition. In order to gain support from local citizens, GUMC invited the *Datianshan* Village Committee members and citizens to a few planning meetings. In order to convince them of the safety of BGB's fermentation technology, GUMC also brought the committee members to visit the ongoing BGB projects in Beijing and Sichuan. Moreover, BGB also promised to hire one citizen representative to monitor the daily recycling process.

10.3.3.3 Enhance Inter-Organizational Collaboration to Control Demand Risk

Traditional food waste processing is a very competitive industry due to its low cost and simple technology. BGB was selected because of its fermentation technology. But that technical advantage was not necessarily transformed into a comparative advantage. Most schools, cafeteria and hotels have contracted with other companies for waste treatment. The distance of delivery was also one of the cost concerns.

In order to reduce the demand risk, GUMC invited several departments, such as the Environmental Protection Department, the Food and Drug Supervision Department, Urban Management Authorities from the city's Districts, Community Offices, the Police Department, the Industry and Commerce Department, the Health

Department, and the Education Department to several meetings. They discussed how these authorities could help communicate with the suppliers of food waste.

10.3.3.4   Enhance Supervision to Reduce Operating Risk

Despite the advanced technology, food waste processing still must be supervised on a daily basis. The *Datianshan* project has two levels of supervision. First, GUMC established a real time electronic monitoring system directly connecting operation data with the agency's internal monitoring system. With this system, the GUMC staff could access the data on pollution and any other operation risk. Moreover, local officials also conduct on site supervision monthly.

10.3.4   Risks Beyond Controls

Compared with other projects, the *Datianshan* project partners signed a much more detailed contract in order to divide the risks between the government and the private partner. The strategies discussed above were written in the contract. However, in practice, the project still encountered daunting risks.

10.3.4.1   Planning Risk

In the original contract, the DTSP was well planned. However, because the selection of a construction site was a very sensitive to public opinion, the construction site was changed three times and the deadline to complete construction was extended several times as well.

Also, one of the key performance indicators was the proportion of liquid waste after processing. The original design was for food waste with 10% liquid waste, but the waste actually collected contained liquid waste up to 53%. GUMC complained during the trial operation, and BGB claimed to be working on improving the technology. But it was not very forthcoming during the improvement process. In the end, the liquid waste did not meet the agreed standard so that the trial period had to be further extended.

10.3.4.2   Demand Risk

In order for the project to be successful, BGB has to maintain a minimum demand. For DTSP, this is measured by the amount of food waste collected daily from the city. According to the contract, the government pays RMB 98 for each ton of food waste that the project processes. If the processing rate is lower than 150 tons, the government must still pay the fee as if 150 tons had been processed.

However, since the trial operation of the project in January 2016, the average daily processing was only 75 tons and the largest amount processed per day was only 145 tons. This means, if the demand does not grow, the government will subsidize the project with RMB 7350 every day, and up to RMB 220,000 every month and half of the subsidy has no service return.

This is not necessarily a planning issue. The city produces more than enough food waste every day. The problem is the government was not able to convince public and private organizations to deliver waste to *Datianshan*.

10.3.4.3 Environmental Risk

Since the trial operation, local residents have complained about pollution. Soil and air pollution were their major concerns in addition to an unpleasant odor. During interviews, respondents stated that the taste of the Wampee and Longan (two typical southern fruits) they planted have deteriorated. Although this requires professional testing, citizen concerns must be taken seriously.

10.3.4.4 Policy Risk Due to Leadership Change

Obviously, the risks discussed above require further negotiation between the government and BCB. However, after the previous Mayor resigned, waste management is no longer a priority for the city. BCB has complained that it has become very difficult to communicate with GUMC. Although the project continues to operate, the government is unwilling to pay the agreed service fees due to the low processing rate and the higher than agreed to liquid percentage.

10.4   Conclusion and Discussions

GUMC's self-evaluation of the *Datianshan* project was EXCELLENT (93 points). However, in view of the above, it is clear that the risks have not been properly accounted for. In particular, recognizing the public liabilities on the local government balance sheets, in accordance with IPSAS rules, is critical. Overall sustainability will then become a function of own-source revenues and ability to pay, as well as the transparent management of local liabilities.

Contracting is a key area where local governments will benefit from expert assistance. For example, BGB is still processing the food waste although the pollution associated with the project is obvious. How to deal with this is not written in the contract, that clearly has to better specify what needs to be done and at what cost.

The integrity of public contracts and dispute management mechanisms are also critical. If a new mayor can ignore previous commitments at will, there will not be much demand for PPP projects or for them to be efficiently managed. Thus, both transparency and accountability are important.

Technical assistance is also needed for handling PPPs. Although the MOF issued guidelines for VFM analysis, those rules emphasize a qualitative rather than a quantitative analysis. Depending on the types of projects, quantitative VFM analysis will clearly be needed in order to evaluate risk.

It is thus clear, at least from the Guangzhou example, that PPPs are in a very preliminary stage, and that they do not necessarily reduce either environmental or fiscal risks. They certainly do not lead to a relaxation of revenue constraints, and local tax reforms are clearly needed in order to move PPPs on to their next level of usefulness.

References

Ahmad, E., Bhattacharya, A., Vinella, A., & Xiao, K. (2015). *Infrastructure finance in the developing world: Involving the private sector and Public–Private Partnerships in financing investments: Public opportunities and challenges*. The global green growth institute and international group of twenty-four.

Asian Development Bank (ADB). (2013). *New directions for Public-Private Partnerships in the People's Republic of China*. Draft for discussion, 15 August 2013.

Asian Development Bank (ADB). (2014). Public–private partnerships in urbanization in the People's Republic China. Retrieved October 2, 2016, from https://www.adb.org/sites/default/files/publication/42860/public-private-partnerships-urbanization-prc.pdf.

Ansar, A., Flyvbjerg, B., Budzier, A., & Lunn, D. (2016). Does infrastructure investment lead to economic growth or economic fragility? Evidence from China. *Oxford Review of Economic Policy, 32*(3), 360–390.

Budina, N., Brixi, P. H., & Irwin, T. (2007). *Public-Private Partnerships in the new EU member states* (World Bank Working Paper No. 114).

Government of Victoria, Australia. (2001). Partnerships victoria guidance material: Risk allocation and contractual issues: A guide. SGoVA Department of Treasury and Finance (Hrsg.).

Hwang, B. G., Zhao, X., & Gay, M. J. S. (2013). Public private partnership projects in Singapore: Factors, critical risks and preferred risk allocation from the perspective of contractors. *International Journal of Project Management, 31*(3), 424–433.

IMF. (2004). *Public–Private Partnerships*. Washington, DC: IMF.

IMF. (2006). *Public–Private Partnerships, Government Guarantees and Fiscal Risk, IMF*. Washington, DC.

Jin, Y. (2014). See the future through the development of PPPs in China. *CAIXIN.COM*, August 1.

Li, B, Akintoye, A., & Hardcastle, C. (2001). Risk analysis and allocation in public private partnership projects. In A. Akintoye (Ed.), *17th Annual ARCOM Conference*, 5–7 September 2001, University of Salford. *Association of Researchers in Construction Management*, Vol. 1, 895–904.

Ma, J., Zhao, Z., & Niu, M. (2015). Budgeting for fiscal risk. *Journal of Asia Public Policy, 8*(3), 351–368.

Mikesell, J., Ma, J., Ho, A., & Niu, M. (2011). Financing Local Public Infrastructure: Guangdong Province. In Joyce Yanyun Man & Yu-Hung Hong (Eds.), *China's Local Public Finance in Transition, Lincoln Institute of Land Policy, Lincoln Institute of Land Policy*. Cambridge, MA: Lincoln Institute of Land Policy. 57–90.

OECD. (2008). *Public–Private Partnerships: In Pursuit of risk sharing and value for money*. OECD Publishing.

Office of the Auditor-General. (2011). *Managing the implications of Public–Private Partnerships*. http://oag.govt.nz/2011/public-private-partnerships/docs/public-private-partnerships.pdf.

Posner, P., Ryu, S. K., & Tkachenko. A. (2009). Public–Private Partnerships: The relevance of budgeting. *OECD Journal on Budgeting*, Volume 2009/1, 1–26.

Ter-Minassian, T. (2016). Fiscal and financial issues for 21st century cities: Background and overview. *Global economy and development*, Brookings.

Wang, W., & Ye, F. (2015). The political economy of land finance in China. *Public Budgeting & Finance, 36*(2), 91–110.

Xiao, K. (2018). Managing subnational liability for sustainable development: A case study of guangdong province. In E. Ahmad et al. (Eds.), *Fiscal Underpinnings for Sustainable Development in China* (pp. 163–187). Singapore: Springer. https://doi.org/10.1007/978-981-10-6286-5_7.

Printed by Books on Demand, Germany